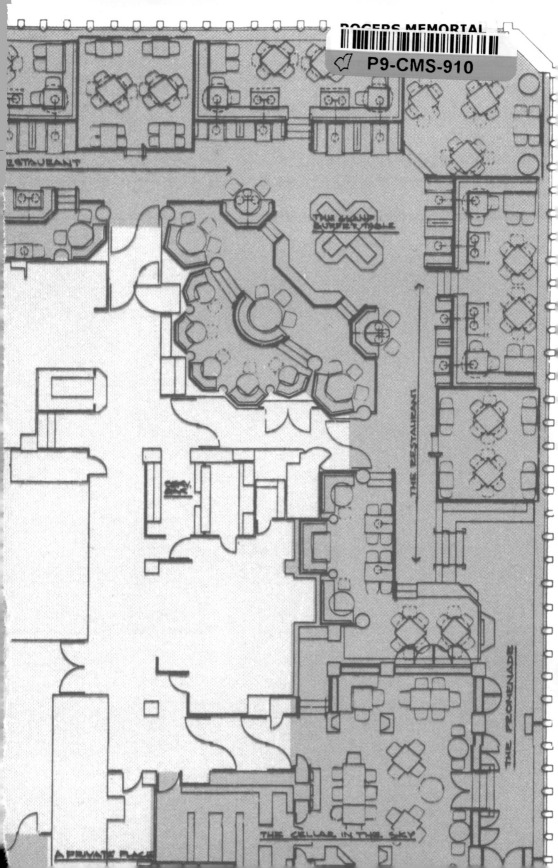

RESTAURANT

THE GRAND
BUFFET TABLE

THE RESTAURANT

THE PROMENADE

THE CELLAR IN THE SKY

A PRIVATE PLACE

The

MOST
SPECTACULAR
RESTAURANT
in the WORLD

ABRAMS The Art of Books
195 Broadway, New York, NY 10007
abramsbooks.com

The

MOST
SPECTACULAR
RESTAURANT
in the WORLD

THE TWIN TOWERS,

WINDOWS ON THE WORLD,

and the REBIRTH *of* NEW YORK

TOM ROSTON

ABRAMS PRESS, NEW YORK

CONTENTS

Prologue: The City on the 107th Floor 7

Chapter 1: Sin and Civility 15

Chapter 2: New York, C'est Moi 24

Chapter 3: The Three-Clawed Lobster 30

Chapter 4: Elevating the Act of Eating 37

Chapter 5: New York Audacity 47

Chapter 6: Blueprints in the Sky 56

Chapter 7: Chaos and Control 64

Chapter 8: Running on Fumes 77

Chapter 9: The City on a Wire 81

Chapter 10: Who the Fuck Are You? 92

Chapter 11: Seventies Splendor 98

Chapter 12: The Most Spectacular Restaurant in the World 102

Chapter 13: Success with Reservations 110

Chapter 14: The Meanest Man in New York 116

Chapter 15: Windows of Opportunity 126

Chapter 16: One Star 136

Chapter 17: To the Top, to the Bottom 140

Chapter 18: An Italian Wedding 154

Chapter 19: Glass Half Full 164

Chapter 20: Growing Up in the Eighties 172

Chapter 21: Chopping Block 184

Chapter 22: Looking for a Star 193

Chapter 23: February 26, 1993 201

Chapter 24: Danger and Opportunity 213

Chapter 25: King Lear's Kitchen 223

Chapter 26: Rebirth 236

Chapter 27: Rebirth Reboot 248

Chapter 28: The Show Goes On 256

To Hannelore and Bob,
an immigrant and an American
who made me a part of their New York story.

Chapter 29: The Highest-Grossing Restaurant in the World............................268

Chapter 30: The Last Meal 278

Chapter 31: The Morning of September 11 286

Chapter 32: That Terrible Day..292

Chapter 33: After..303

Chapter 34: Enduring Change 310

Epilogue: Ana's Story..317

Notes..321

Acknowledgments 334

Index..336

Photo Credits..352

PROLOGUE

THE CITY ON THE 107TH FLOOR

"America is a *gooood* country."

It was a joke, but not really. It's what the Windows on the World crew said to one another after a heavy night, after turning and burning a station of eight tables with more guests waiting at the door.

It's what the front waiters said to the back waiters, who said it to the busboys, managing the stress of six hundred covers or more through banter and a nod to something bigger.

It was one of the many running jokes for a staff that treated one another like family or fellow combatants. It was a sarcastic sign-off, as in, *This is what I signed up for? As in, I've got to be on my feet for six hours straight, in constant motion, doing a hundred things at once and always with a smile?*

But it also, in fact, meant: This is the answer to my prayers. As in, *I came to this country unsure I could survive the week, and now I make enough for my children to have a future I can be proud of.*

Most nights, it was said when tips were paid out, accompanied by handshakes and backslaps and competitive bravado about just how much one had made that night—two hundred dollars, three hundred dollars, five hundred dollars, the number always slightly inflated—and the recognition that, yes, everyone was happy to be there.

And it was followed by nights in fluorescent-lit restaurants where the Windows staff would go after their shifts were over, so that they could be together into the wee hours to laugh and drink and suck on black bean shrimp heads in Elmhurst, Queens, or wash down sushi with cheap sake near Tompkins Square Park.

Of its four hundred–plus employees, the Windows on the World staff included immigrants from more than two dozen countries: the Dominican Republic, Ecuador, Guyana, Ghana, Mexico, Bangladesh, Poland, Peru, China, Egypt, Ivory Coast, Nigeria, Pakistan, Cuba, and so on.

And here they all were, some undocumented, most living in the outer boroughs, working together, at the top of the greatest city in the world.

"I'm never going to leave this place," Paulo Villela, a captain and sommelier, would say to his friends on staff. Villela had studied agricultural engineering in his native Brazil but had moved to America in 1983 because his son, Bernardo, had a rare metabolic disease that required care he could find only in the United States. "Windows on the World gave us full benefits. I would have worked there just for the insurance," he says. "But the money was so good. There were busboys, straight out of Bangladesh, making sixty thousand dollars a year. People from all over the world. We got along great. It was the best place to work."

* * *

At two o'clock in the morning on September 11, 2001, Moises Rivas was still awake in his home in Queens, playing his guitar and singing to his wife, Elizabeth. A songwriter and musician, Rivas supported his family by working as a cook at Windows on the World. The alarm went off at 5:00 A.M., and Rivas turned it off. But by 6:30, the twenty-nine-year-old from Ecuador was up and rushing. He said he had to "fly," to get to work in the cafeteria serving breakfast on the 106th floor of the North Tower of the World Trade Center.

Luis Alfonso Chimbo, also from Ecuador and living in Queens, worked in the receiving department. When the thirty-nine-year-old got his first job at Windows on the World, he acted like a little boy getting a toy that he'd always wanted. He would walk in the market with his wife, Ana Soria, and their twelve-year-old son, Luis Eduardo, and show them how to smell a melon to gauge its freshness. He was up by five that morning and quietly left around five thirty. Normally, he would kiss his wife, still in bed, but not that morning. As he drove away from the house, Soria went to the window and said, "Goodbye, my love."

Executive pastry chef Heather Ho didn't want to be there. She'd given notice several weeks before, but she was staying on for a while— she was not the sort of person to leave someone high and dry—until executive chef Michael Lomonaco had a replacement. The daily grind of churning out hundreds of desserts wasn't the right speed for the Hawaii native. Ho was a tireless worker, but she wasn't about volume. She had a boutique sensibility.

The Gomez brothers—Jose and Enrique—from the Dominican Republic were doing prep work, as usual, cutting vegetables and cleaning seafood. Their other two brothers, Ramone and Miguel, weren't working that day. Lucille Francis, a grandmother from Barbados, arrived early to lay out the towels that she would be handing to patrons in the women's bathroom. Her son, Joseph, a Windows waiter, took the day off to oversee a construction project at home.

Most of the seventy-three Windows employees working that morning were in the banquet area on the 106th floor, one floor below the main restaurant. The morning was a cherished time, because it was relatively calm. It's when waiters might help themselves to a generous slice of yesterday's chocolate cake, if they could get to it. You could sneak five minutes, sitting at one of the east-facing tables, with your feet up and naval-style jacket falling open, watching the sunrise.

Windows had been annually serving hundreds of thousands of New Yorkers and visitors, putting on a massive and intricate high-wire act, for two and a half decades—with a three-year gap when the restaurant went dark after the 1993 bombing in the World Trade Center basement that killed six people, including one of its employees. Business was now at full throttle; Windows was the highest-grossing restaurant in the country and was preparing for its triumphant, twenty-fifth anniversary party in October.

The lion's share of the responsibility for the celebration would fall on the shoulders of Chef Lomonaco, a Brooklyn native who could remember, when he was a taxi driver in the 1970s, how Windows represented the ne plus ultra of great New York dining. He'd been running the kitchen since 1997 and was a primary force behind turning the restaurant's flagging fortunes around.

That morning, Lomonaco was on his way to work after voting in his Upper East Side neighborhood in the primary election for mayor—Mark

Green was in a tight race with Fernando Ferrer on the Democratic ticket, with billionaire media mogul Michael Bloomberg running as a Republican. Lomonaco had driven down FDR Drive and dropped off his wife at her office before parking in his lot near the World Trade Center. It was a little after 8:00 A.M., and he reconsidered his afternoon appointment to get his eyeglasses repaired at LensCrafters, which was in the vast mall underneath the World Trade Center plaza. *Why not just get it done now,* he thought.

In the store, the clerk said it wouldn't take long to get the glasses fixed and his eyes checked. Just twenty minutes, she said.

It took a little longer than that, and Lomonaco was settling the bill when he felt his chair shake. It was a heart-stopping rumble unlike anything he'd ever felt before.

He thought, *Is that the subway?* There was a station exit not far away. And then the lights flickered, and an alarm started wailing. Some seconds passed, and a woman appeared and said, "We have to leave." Lomonaco exited, forgetting his glasses on the counter, and joined a throng of people who moved through the concourse, not pushing, just streaming forward, toward the exits. When he walked through the glass doors to Liberty Street, he saw a massive, smoking, churning piece of metal surrounded by debris on the ground. It was the size of a car, but he didn't know what it was. And there was a strange shower of papers falling around him. Right across the street was a fire station, Engine and Ladder Company 10, and the firefighters were standing there, looking up toward the North Tower, which was blocked visually by the South Tower.

Lomonaco's cell phone wasn't working, but he wanted to call his wife to tell her he was OK. Ambulances, fire engines, and police were arriving with their sirens blaring. After he finally found a pay phone, he returned to the World Trade Center, remembering when the 1993 bombing occurred, and all those people streamed down the stairwells. He thought of who was working at the restaurant, and he wanted to be there when they got down to ground level. As he approached on Liberty Street, between Nassau and Broadway, he heard the drone of an airplane above, which made him reflexively look up at the South Tower. He saw a tremendous explosion: fireballs going in all directions. Someone grabbed him by the arm and pulled him away from the carnage.

* * *

New York City experienced an unfathomable tragedy on September 11, 2001. Windows on the World was one of the worst places to be that morning. None of the one thousand three hundred forty-four people who were above where the first plane crashed into the North Tower survived. The damage suffered that day is most aptly measured by the two thousand nine hundred ninety-six individuals who perished in all the attacks. So many family members and friends lost loved ones. More than three thousand children lost a parent on September 11. Of those killed were seventy-three Windows employees, six men working on a renovation job for the restaurant, and ninety-one guests at Windows on the World.

Also destroyed was the livelihood of the restaurant workers who survived. And there was the physical space: the two acres' worth of kitchen utensils, pots, pans, lighting fixtures, tables, forks, plates, and napkins, as well as the tens of thousands of bottles of wine that were mostly stored three levels belowground under the South Tower.

There were also less tangible losses, such as the destruction of a gathering place, an axis point for New York City's natives and its guests, a repository for their memories and dreams. It was the place where New Yorkers went to celebrate, the place they went when they wanted to show off their city. It had opened in 1976 at the top of a confounding, reviled building at a nadir in the city's history. But Windows on the World moved from being a controversial confection atop a billion-dollar fiasco to being a beloved icon on top of the world's most famous skyline.

The restaurant helped transform antipathy toward the World Trade Center into acceptance, making the complex an essential part of the city's identity. In the words of Guy Tozzoli, the director of the World Trade Center and its primary builder, it "turned the city of New York from looking at the Trade Center as some monster downtown to something that was theirs."

Looking down from a quarter of a mile up, the restaurant's audacity was integral to its makeup. At a time when New York City had become synonymous with fiscal mismanagement, poverty, rampant crime, drug abuse, burning buildings, and garbage on the streets, Tozzoli hired restaurateur Joe Baum to dream up a restaurant dubbed a "Versailles in the sky." With Windows on the World, Baum, a man with the chutzpah to never look down, gave the city a beacon.

Many New York restaurants hold a special place in the hearts of the people who cherish them. Windows on the World was one of them, but it was something more. Not only did it become the highest-grossing restaurant in the country during its twenty-five-year existence, it also became a landmark that embodied the city's greatness.

The restaurant's demise wasn't mere coincidence. Windows was at the center of a watershed moment in American history for a reason. It was a part of the splendor of the World Trade Center that made it a target to those affronted by American values and might.

And although what happened on 9/11 was extraordinary, the passage of time has allowed us to see the restaurant as part of the city's life cycle, which extends not only through the blood and grit of New Yorkers but also through all the concrete and the parks and the neighborhood storefronts. Every corner of the city is forever going through the process of birth, decay, death, and rebirth. Sometimes it's visible, as in the new bar that keeps the old bar's neon sign, but there are always invisible layers of the past coating anywhere you are in the city.

After the Twin Towers came down, a very real, ghostly white cloud of debris spread out over the city. It was everywhere. One particular stream of it was carried on a current of wind a half mile southeast across the East River over Brooklyn Heights and into a backyard where former *New York* magazine editor Kurt Andersen, one of the city's many champions, lived. For a time, Andersen ran the magazine that had once anointed Windows, an act that was partly credited for launching its success. And he had a strong personal connection to the restaurant: It was where he introduced his parents to the woman who would become his wife. How mind-boggling, then, that among the debris that landed behind Andersen's house, there was a letter addressed to Joe Baum, who had died three years before.

The paper was frayed and burned around the edges like a cartoonish pirate treasure map, but the words were quite legible; scrawled in blue pen, its sender wrote, "I felt as though I died and went to heaven, which I imagine is not too far from the 107th floor!"

* * *

There's a new building there now. You wouldn't know it, but since 2015 they have served food at the top, at One Dine, One Mix, and One Café, a tasteless trinity of names that immediately disappears from memory as if it never touched your tongue. Anyway, you can't eat there without waiting on a TSA-like line and paying the $37.37 per person observatory ticket, so what's the point?

There's nothing up there that commemorates what once occupied the nearby sky for twenty-five years, which is sad but perhaps reasonable. There are, after all, two enormous holes, the reflecting pools, in the ground, as well as a museum for anyone who wants to memorialize the past. The names of the Windows on the World staff who died on 9/11 have been grouped together on the north side of the north pool, closest to One World Trade Center.

If you do take the elevator up to the 101st floor, and you're willing to plunk down twenty-six dollars for a hamburger, and you start asking your waiter about 9/11, you may be surprised when he calls over Mohammad Quddus, a back waiter, originally from Bangladesh, who used to work the same job at Windows. He's the only one at One World Trade Center from before.

For five years, Quddus avoided Manhattan, because it was too painful. He remained in Queens, where he worked and helped raise his two young sons with his wife. But when One Dine began hiring, he returned. It was his way of moving on.

"Windows on the World was a dream," Quddus says. "We were a family from so many countries. I learned so much. I took care of my family. I sent money home. Everything I could do was because of Windows. When I lost Windows, I lost my dream."

Quddus sometimes forgets he's working in the new World Trade Center and he takes the wrong stairs to the locker room. Or, he intentionally tricks himself into thinking he's still working at Windows while carrying a tray from the kitchen to the restaurant floor. He often sits in the Memorial Plaza, not far from the Survivor Tree—a pear tree that was discovered in the charred rubble of Ground Zero and was restored and replanted—and he closes his eyes and sees the Twin Towers as they once were, and he imagines that the place is the same.

Clinging to memories is part of being human, but there's something particular to New Yorkers' attachment to the city we once knew, whether it's that slice of pizza you can no longer get, the basketball court where you had that fight, or the bodega where you met your husband, because those authentic, resonant experiences are what make New York City our own.

And 9/11 is something we—on a spectrum, of course—all share. It has had a significant impact on the city and where America is today. The destruction of the World Trade Center remains a wound that may never fully heal. And maybe it shouldn't.

The debris of the buildings has long since scattered in the wind, been removed to a landfill in Staten Island, or been placed in boxes like the one in Kurt Andersen's basement or in the National September 11 Memorial & Museum's large, off-site storage facilities.

So much was destroyed on 9/11, but the past still lives within us, in strange, powerful ways. You see it in the city's skyline, even as an absence. And the city perseveres, making it all the more magnificent. It is more diverse. Its culinary scene is outrageously vibrant. Downtown is thriving like never before. Its tallest buildings are now taller. The city keeps ascending.

CHAPTER 1

SIN AND CIVILITY

The fish were dead. Not all of them. But most. It was totally unacceptable.

Alan Lewis put the phone down in the cradle the only way he knew how: He slammed it. The *crash-ding* sound resonated in his office on the 106th floor of the North Tower, Building One, of the World Trade Center. Sitting in the room, which was laced with cigarette smoke, was his boss, Joe Baum. Lewis had to act. He picked up the phone again and dialed the line to the commissary in the B level, 107 floors below him.

"What do you want, Al?" asked Dennis Sweeney, the usually reliable director of operations who ran Central Services, the vast complex of kitchens, providers, and transport services that connected the twenty-two restaurants in nine different locations on various floors of the Twin Towers, from the central docking station in the garage all the way up to the top. Sweeney and Lewis got along well enough, but Lewis had a way of leaning on people. He was Baum's bulldog. Not that Baum needed one. For those who worked under Baum, it was hard not to do everything within one's power to satisfy him. Whether that was out of fear or respect or just self-preservation, it didn't really matter.

It was Lewis's role to carry out Joe Baum's wishes, no matter how impossible, bizarre, or indiscernible. Lewis, perhaps more than anyone, understood Baum. They had met at Cornell and risen together to the top of Restaurant Associates in its heyday, when Baum made his name as the greatest restaurateur in the country. What it took for Baum to get there probably showed more on Lewis's face than it did on Baum's. Lewis had weathered some personal bad luck and an ocean's worth of Baum storms, and you had to feel bad for the guy, except when he was tearing into someone himself.

Joe Baum's presence could electrify or freeze a room, depending on his mood. He carried himself like a king. He was a hefty five-foot-eight with a neatly thinning, cropped crown of receding hair, but he led with his chin and eyes, so sharp and challenging. His thick, solemn eyebrows arched with intelligence and reprobation.

He would crack wise whether he was charming or criticizing you, or sometimes both. And the smoking. He'd always have a menthol cigarette or cigar or pipe in hand, sometimes while another smoldered in an ashtray.

Sweeney worked for Baum as well, but because of the World Trade Center's byzantine food services hierarchy, Sweeney was in the role of representing Central Services, which was providing the fish to Baum's crown jewel, Windows on the World. And Lewis, as its director, was speaking on behalf of Windows, so he was in command.

"Dennis, I just heard from André. The trout are dead. What the fuck are you trying to pull?" Lewis's voice rose steadily with each word. "We need them alive. You know that. The dish can't be served if they come in dead. Cut this shit out. Get it right the next time."

The first time it happened, Sweeney was in his office. Of the forty or so rainbow trout, about half arrived in the kitchen dead. This time, he made sure to go down to the docking station when his provider, an upstate guy in a truck, arrived, having called him an hour earlier to tell him he was on his way. Unlike the rest of the restaurant's seafood, which came from the Fulton Fish Market just down the street, these trout were on special order.

Sweeney had counted the fish himself, not an easy task, considering they were still flipping and flopping around. As the numbers guy, the one counting costs and constantly trying to reel Baum in, it was a fun switch getting his hands wet.

One by one, he dropped three dozen trout into water in the large blue garbage can. It's what they used for fish. The green can was for the vegetables, and the red one was for the meat. The thirty-two-gallon plastic cans weren't pretty, but they didn't need to be.

The fish were alive when they entered the elevator—Sweeney knew that much. He saw them go in, the can pressed against the heavily padded walls, stuck among other containers that were destined for various food services locations spread throughout the World Trade Center—an area so large, it had its own zip code.

He'd packed them with ice this time. Could the provider have switched the fish? Or did someone kill them on the way up? In the restaurant business, anything could happen. That's why they locked the steaks for the ride up. And it's why they counted them a second time when they arrived. Wouldn't want those to disappear. But someone killing fish didn't make sense.

Still, everyone was on edge. The opening of Windows was just weeks away, and Joe Baum wanted his new restaurant to serve *Truite au bleu*, or blue trout.

The preparation of the dish is straightforward. What matters most is the freshness of the fish, because when the fish is alive, it is coated in slime that is integral to its preparation. You take the breathing fish, bludgeon it unconscious in the kitchen by slamming it on the counter, gut it, and then drop it into boiling court bouillon, a flavorful stock, with salt and vinegar, which turns the trout a luminous tinge of blue. Served with butter, salt, lemon, boiled potatoes, and ground pepper, it's hard to beat. The subtle, wet-earth taste of the fish is perfectly balanced by the butter, flavorful broth, salt, and the acid of the lemon.

That was why Baum needed the fish to be swimming in tanks in the kitchen. He was planning on serving blue trout at the opening. It had been printed in the advertising material. It had to happen.

Truite au bleu was pure theater, but it was also simple, fresh, good-tasting food with origins in continental Europe. It was perfect for Windows, because it was an extension of everything that was Joe Baum. He had made his name serving high-concept dishes that could capture people's imaginations at the same time that they satisfied their appetites.

Baum liked to think of customers in the same way a chef might cook rabbit stew. When it came to making the dish, the recipe was fairly simple. But first you had to catch the rabbit.

Truite au bleu had to be on the menu because Baum, although he may not have shown it, was petrified by how the restaurant was barreling forward like a runaway train. The opening had been delayed, and it was now just weeks away, and there were so many fires to put out, from the annoying—such as a delay in the plate delivery—to the catastrophic—such as the state liquor authority threatening to not issue a license. He needed to be able to play up his strengths, which would be hard to do if the fish were scared to death of heights.

* * *

Joe Baum was born into the hospitality business on August 17, 1920, in a refuge of health and hedonism just a few miles upstream from where those tender rainbow trout came from: the Hudson River valley, an abundant Eden of plants and animals that had fed the Mohican and Lenape people, who gathered nuts and berries, hunted deer and rabbit, harvested corn, beans, and squash, and fished more than two hundred types of fish.

The indigenous people also partook of the naturally carbonated mineral spring water, which flowed through faults in the bedrock, using it for bathing, rituals, and for healing. In 1771, Mohawks brought an ailing Sir William Johnson, the British superintendent of Indian affairs, to the springs. Word soon caught on, and settlers began to build hotels in 1803.

The water that bubbled up was rich in minerals and compounds that healed skin ailments and digestive disorders. More hotels sprouted up. Businessmen tubed the springs to make the waters more accessible, and Saratoga Springs quickly became a cosmopolitan, European-style spa where one could "take the cure."

The development of the Saratoga and Schenectady Railroad made access more convenient, and, in 1863, the Saratoga Race Course opened, making the region a prime recreation destination. The wealthy built grand homes there. Presidents and high society flocked to the town.

The expansion of the spa resorts depleted the springs until, in 1911, ordinances were instituted controlling overuse. But Saratoga Springs' reputation as a place free from restrictions was already set.

Illegal gambling houses cropped up around the horse racing. Nearby houses on Saratoga Lake became lavish sites for the elite to engage in fine-dining "Fish and Game Dinners," followed by games of chance. In the 1920s, the area became a bootlegging hub between Canada and Albany.

Brothels also cropped up; one of the most notorious madams of the Prohibition era—Pearl "Polly" Adler, known as the "Jewish Jezebel"—relocated her highbrow New York City operations there in an attempt to avoid conviction and to follow her clientele, which included the literati of the Algonquin Round Table, New York City mayor Jimmy Walker, and mobster Charles "Lucky" Luciano.

Baum's parents, Louis and Anna, ran Saratoga Springs' seasonal Gross and Baum Hotel, a formidable building with large white columns, more than one hundred fifty beds, and a kitchen permeated with the smell of cooked cabbage and pickled herring. Louis, a bakery truck driver when he met Anna, owned the establishment with Anna's father, Isaac Gross, who'd put up the money for the mammoth Victorian building on Broadway, the town's the main drag. Joe's father was an exuberant host who ran the front of the house while Anna ran a disciplined kosher kitchen. Open from May until the Jewish holidays in September, the hotel had many more rooms without baths than those that did. The effusive Louis, with a supple understanding of salesmanship, assured guests that they could adequately cleanse themselves in the nearby spas.

Although Joe lived the rest of the year in Lakewood, New Jersey, where the family owned another hotel and where he attended school, he credited Saratoga Springs for shaping him and introducing him to the world of hospitality.

In the kitchen, there was always something on the stove—soups and stews and stuffed cabbage—and the walk-in was a treasure trove lined with barrels full of pickles.

Young Joe observed the public personas of his parents as professional hosts in a town that valued gilt, glamour, excellence, and also value. They drove to faraway markets to find the best produce. His father believed in the dictum, "Find out what the customers want, then give it to them."

The kitchen's Hungarian cooks took Joe under their wing from a young age. He learned to wield a knife at the age of six. (Joe said that his mother was never more proud of him than when he sliced a tomato as well as she did.) They would tease him. He was once told to hang noodles on the clothesline to dry in the sun. The staff gathered to have a good laugh at the owners' son as he stood in front of the line and puzzled over his task. A voluptuous, blue-eyed cook wrapped her arms around him lovingly. Baum was hooked. He later said that it was then that he "fell in love with the human contact, the smells and the tastes. The sensuality" of a restaurant kitchen.

Joe's older son, Charlie, often heard stories of his father's childhood at the Gross and Baum. "He felt this enormous sense of family and community in that kitchen," he says. "It just touched him in ways that it clearly didn't affect his siblings." Baum's older brother became a cardiologist, and his older sister, Pearl "Pepper" Golden, was a prominent social worker. "He loved the people who worked there," Charlie says. "They were his extended family."

Early in life, Baum told an interviewer he learned "the pleasure of giving pleasure." He further said, "I had no sense whatsoever of being part of any service or servant class or self-consciousness because of the mixture of people who lived and played at Saratoga."

The warmth and civility of the hospitality business also had what Baum called "a wildly sinful" complement in the illicit leisure activities of Saratoga Springs. One bookie would wave his pearl-handled revolver in Louis's face and sometimes show up at three in the morning and demand a steak dinner; he was not a man you said no to. Baum was enamored with these "Damon Runyon types"—gangsters, con men, and hustlers on the make. In addition to working in his parents' pantry, he shuffled cards for the guests and ran errands, delivering packages on Broadway and selling racetrack scratch sheets on the steps of the United States Hotel. He played nickel roulette and developed a taste for gambling.

As the family legend goes—and, in keeping with Baum's love of a good story, this account will include some tall tales, within reason—the Gross and Baum once housed the illegal yet popular one-armed-bandit slot machines of the day in one of its parlors. When authorities came to investigate the premises, the family received a tip, and Uncle Simi, who was normally in the kitchen, made a mad dash to remove the machines, put them in the back of a truck, and drive them out to the woods to bury them. Later, Uncle Simi claimed to have forgotten where he hid them and rued his losses.

At around the age of thirteen, in what's passed down as the "Anticipation Story," a foundational tale that Baum repeatedly told to illustrate his approach to hospitality, he was brought by Uncle Simi to a bordello for his first sexual experience. As he was being led up the stairs by a prostitute, she turned to him and said, "This is the best part, sonny, so you'd better enjoy it." Whatever happened up there, one lesson was learned: The anticipation before an actual experience might be its greatest pleasure of all.

Baum also applied himself to more normative forms of education, attending high school in Saratoga and Lakewood, depending on the season. He was one of the few boys who took the home economics class at Lakewood High School, which he graduated from in 1937. Although his family was well off, he worked a variety of hotel jobs, washing dishes, waiting tables at his parents' place and tonier establishments such as the Greenbrier luxury resort in West Virginia and the Roney Plaza Hotel in Miami Beach, Florida.

Baum went to college at the Cornell University hotel school in Ithaca, New York, where he studied hotel administration and plied his gambling skills to earn money, primarily by playing bridge. When he fell into debt during the summer of 1941, Baum skipped town with his school pal, Curt Strand, to work at the Fort Benning Officers Club in Georgia. They joined a motley crew of a kitchen staff and waiters. Baum and Strand regularly broke up knife fights among the cooks. Strand was aghast to see an order of "eggs over" being delivered right side up, but as the offending waiter approached the table, he simply flipped them over with his hand.

After Strand returned to school, Baum took a managerial role at the club and engineered a change at the restaurant so that waiters could earn tips, an idea that allowed him to hire local women, who, as it turned out, began to provide a variety of services for the officers, making the club "the best whorehouse in all of Fort Benning." He was dismissed soon after.

During the school year, Baum went on a field trip with his class to New York City to the lush, fine-dining supper club that had opened the decade before atop 30 Rockefeller Plaza. The class was studying kitchen management, but Baum made his way to the front of the house to marvel at the Art Deco grandeur of the Rainbow Room. "I saw this wonderful room," he later said. "I saw all the people of consequence being served in this great, glorious room. I knew that was what New York was meant to be."

When not in class, Baum worked hotel jobs, including headwaiter at his parents' hotel, until he graduated in 1943. In Miami, he had met a pretty blonde named Ruth Courtman. The two married before Baum went to war and was stationed as a supply officer on the USS *Lindsey*, a destroyer-minelayer in the Pacific that engaged in battle at Iwo Jima and Okinawa. Baum oversaw the ship's financial affairs as well as the food services for the crew.

On April 12, 1945, the USS *Lindsey* was en route to assist a destroyer under heavy attack by the Japanese. Six miles from Aguni, a small island off Okinawa, the *Lindsey* was intercepted by a squadron of kamikaze pilots. Although the minelayer's gunners shot down many of the attacking planes, two managed to evade them and crash into the bow of the vessel, setting it on fire and killing fifty-seven sailors.

Most of the men, including Baum, went overboard. Before he did so, though, one of his duties was to recover the cash—seventy thousand dollars—from the *Lindsey*'s safe. After abandoning ship, Baum and his surviving shipmates were rescued, and their vessel was towed back to Guam.

In the aftermath of the war, the whole world was radically altered, as were individual lives. A new paradigm of American exceptionalism dominated a devastated planet. And mammoth, bold initiatives—from the G.I. Bill to the Marshall Plan—were put in place to foster a new, prosperous world order. For many Americans, opportunities abounded. Ambitions ran high.

"We had won the war, and everyone felt on top of the world," says Baum's friend Curt Strand, who had been stationed in Europe. Both men set their sights on New York City as the best beachhead for their young careers.

CHAPTER 2
NEW YORK, C'EST MOI

"It is quite likely that the fabulous mid-Forties will take their place alongside the elegant Eighties of the industrial barons, the gay Nineties of society, the turn of the century elegance of the Waldorf and Delmonico's, and the flaming youth years of prohibition," announced the *New York Times* in a wry, February 24, 1946, article entitled, "To Eat, Drink and Be Mentioned," about the city's booming nightlife scene.

Fueled by a successful postwar economy, there was money to burn—"we are in an amazing period of exaggeration and mass spending," the *Times* gasped, and restaurant nightlife was being chronicled regularly in the plentiful dailies, most stirringly by Walter Winchell, who sat at table 50 in the Stork Club, and Lucius Beebe, who wrote for the *New York Herald Tribune, Gourmet,* and *Playboy.*

Postwar New York City was thriving, with more than eighteen thousand restaurants serving a wide range of diners. An exploding population of office workers would elbow their way to the many counters of the various Schrafft's dinettes, Automats, and Horn & Hardarts chain cafeterias. The emerging middle class favored the more stylish, Art Deco–designed Longchamps restaurants. And, for the higher reaches of society and those who aspired to it, emerged an elite alternative: former social clubs and speakeasies, such as the Stork Club, El Morocco, the Colony, and "21."

Club owners no longer knew their own patrons, putting a strain on the credit system traditionally extended to regulars. But who cared, as long as people were flocking to be seen and to see the celebrities appearing in the papers and in photographs with signature restaurant markings, such as the zebra-print banquettes of El Morocco or the black-and-white ashtrays of Sardi's?

Food may not have been the primary attraction for this new nightlife, but it wasn't irrelevant. In 1938, the Rainbow Room proudly served a salmon dinner that, for the first time, had been caught that same morning in Canada and shipped to its kitchen. Lüchow's was famous for its Wiener schnitzel, sausages, and sauerbraten. The Stork Club and "21" Club menus were stocked with solid American fare, such as lamb chops and steaks.

Still, the gourmands of New York—and Beebe was one of them—went to just one kind of restaurant when they wanted to experience the definition of fine dining: French.

The root of the French word "restaurant" is "to restore or refresh" and can be traced to eighteenth-century Paris, when broths were served as a restorative to ailing urban dwellers. These new establishments caused some upheaval when they transcended their purely consommé-peddling status by adding such ingredients as sheep's feet for "pieds de mouton à la sauce poulette." Up to the time of the French Revolution, strict rules had defined the acceptable tasks of different tradesmen, such as butchers, bakers, and others. Restaurants serving actual meals disrupted that order.

But with an emerging urban culture and impending cultural and democratic shifts, Paris's restaurants began to flourish, and what's widely considered the first fine-dining establishment, the Grande Taverne de Londres, opened in 1782.

In America, taverns, such as Fraunces Tavern, began to appear in New York City in the late eighteenth century, serving food in a communal, "come and get it" fashion at set times. Soon, the most common New York City restaurants were called "sixpenny houses," because dish prices were low—six pence—matching the habits of the clientele. New York diners developed a notoriety for quickly, impolitely devouring their mundane meals of meat and vegetables.

Fine dining in New York City was another matter. The wealthiest families hosted exquisite dinner parties catered by private kitchen staffs. And, in 1827, a recently immigrated French-speaking Swiss family with an Italian name, Delmonico, opened a pastry shop in 1827 on William Street. In 1830, brothers Peter, né Pietro, and John, né Giovanni, moved next door to create the city's first upscale restaurant, Delmonico's, serving à la carte—a novelty then—French dishes. Crisply dressed waiters served turtle soup, artichokes à la Barigoule, and filets de bouef à la Victoria in an ornate room with chandeliers and white tablecloths. Napoleon III, Abraham Lincoln, Oscar Wilde, Mark Twain, and all of the city's upper class dined on signature dishes such as lobster Newburg and Baked Alaska at Delmonico's during its dominant reign through most of the nineteenth century.

New York City's French restaurants have a storied tradition—the father of haute cuisine, Auguste Escoffier, had had a hand in the kitchens of the Ritz-Carlton and Hotel Pierre in the early twentieth century. The standard for French restaurants was the exact execution of Escoffier's dishes, but many of the best establishments had been drained dry by Prohibition. A new generation of restaurant—Le Café Chambord, Baroque, Chateaubriand, and the Lafayette—were drawing the Francophile following. But no restaurant compared to the allure and refinement of Le Pavillon, opened by Henri Soulé, who had come to the city in 1939 as part of France's celebrated contribution to that year's World's Fair, Le Restaurant Français in the French pavilion. The dining hall was a sensation, serving reasonably priced, topflight wines, coq au vin, and crêpes suzette to eighteen thousand guests the first month and twenty-six thousand the second. Soulé, who was the assistant maître d' at the Café de Paris back in the French capital, oversaw the dining room.

With the threat of war, Soulé and many of his colleagues returned to their homeland to fight. But Soulé's service as a chef was deemed more valuable to France, and he was sent back to the States for the summer of 1940. By the time the fair ended, in October, the Nazis were in Paris, and Soulé and his cooking compatriots were stranded stateside.

Soulé made the most of it, tapping the connections he'd made—Joseph Kennedy is rumored to have helped finance him—and opening Le Pavillon on East Fifty-Fifth Street in Manhattan in 1941. Soulé, an exacting despot, dictated that Escoffier's dishes be enacted religiously in an elegant, luxurious setting of brilliant white tablecloths, endless roses, and Baccarat crystal and silver that had an exclusive staff dedicated to its immaculate presentation, including the constant shining of all surfaces. He served Dom Perignon, foie gras, tripe à la mode de Caen, and beef Bourguignon to a deliberately elite set—there were only seventy-five dinner servings each night.

Le Pavillon was Soulé's tribute to French culture and civilization with a Français-only menu. It achieved greatness. When *Life* magazine asked a Michelin inspector to eat there, he allowed that it could warrant three stars if the reference guide deigned to rate U.S. restaurants, at a time when there were only eleven such three-star establishments in all of France. Soulé had an uncompromising dedication to the restaurant. It was a mark of pride when he said, "Le Pavillon, c'est moi," but that came at a cost. He would brush waiters aside and take on their duties, providing table-side service if he thought something was lacking. He was the epitome of the snooty French caricature spoofed in American popular culture. Soulé's prickly career was marked by battles with unions, which led to staff departures and the creation of several rival French restaurants, including La Caravelle.

In 1945, waiters picketed outside Le Pavillon because they resented Soulé's demand that they remain at a particular station, his reasoning being, at least partly, so that they would become accustomed to the tastes of regular guests. The staff preferred to be in rotation, so that the higher tippers could be shared in a more democratic fashion.

The status and conditions for workers in the city, including within the restaurant industry, were undergoing dramatic changes. At the end of the war, the working class and unions dominated much of the city. Less than a month after the war ended, the elevator operators and related commercial-building workers went on strike, bringing business as usual to a near stop as fellow sympathetic union workers refused to cross picket lines. Bakers, Teamsters, port workers, and many other unions went on strikes to resolve their grievances, making shutdowns an everyday part of life in New York. Of the 3.3 million people employed in the city in 1946, a vast majority were working class, and nearly a quarter of a million of them went on strike that year.

And yet, drastic shifts in the economy meant that the city's working class was diminishing. Manufacturing was moving out of the city, and

Lower Manhattan's port industry was being replaced by New Jersey's as the hub of trade.

Still, the new prosperity prompted a building boom in midtown Manhattan. Between 1947 and 1956, 15.1 million square feet of office space was constructed—that alone was more than all the office space in the country's second-largest business district, the Loop in Chicago. From the first census in 1790 until 1950, the city had always grown, with the population doubling in the previous fifty years, and new neighborhoods—residential and commercial—growing outward or up. New York had risen to a status without equal. Paris, London, Tokyo, and Berlin were devastated by war. New York was the obvious choice for the new United Nations headquarters, built between 1947 and 1952 on a plot of land on the East Side of Manhattan, provided in a deal among three of the city's dominant urban planners: real estate developer William Zeckendorf, the city's "construction coordinator"; Robert Moses, who had been implementing roadway and park projects throughout the city for decades; and wealthy banker David Rockefeller. The men saw opportunity in hosting the international association to secure the city's position as the world's capital.

It was one of many such projects. City government and business leaders were led by grand visions, sometimes at odds with communities and the organic rhythms of the city, to make it, as they saw it, more livable and productive. They redrew the city map in the name of progress and development, building major works such as the Triborough Bridge, the Bronx–Whitestone Bridge, and the huge WPA swimming pools, under the stewardship of President Franklin Delano Roosevelt, elected to four terms, and three-term mayor Fiorello La Guardia.

When Bill O'Dwyer was elected mayor in 1946, Robert Moses gained even more freedom to carve up the city with housing initiatives in addition to his beloved roadways and parks. He created low-income housing projects such as the Patterson Houses in the Bronx, masterminded a second World's Fair, and broke ground in 1948 for what's considered to be his most controversial, costly, and invasive project, the Cross Bronx Expressway.

Moses had a reason for his top-down approach to redrawing the city: It was a mess. The growing population, the age of the automobile, the decay of shoddily constructed buildings, and an increase in poverty needed to be addressed. And those efforts needed direction. Moses and others in government and business who emulated him believed they could come up with master plans to plow away the blight and preserve the city.

While urban leaders rolled up their sleeves and debated plans to transform the city, for many young, postwar New Yorkers, it was simply the greatest place to be. The restaurants and nightclubs were full. As the *New York Times* reported, New Yorkers were "people in frenzied, almost desperate search for gaiety and entertainment. Yes, the fabulous mid-Forties are here."

CHAPTER 3
THE THREE-CLAWED LOBSTER

Joe Baum and his wife, Ruth, moved to New York City in 1946. The couple lived in a small brownstone on West Twelfth Street, not far from Joe's friend Curt Strand. "It was a great time to be in the city," Strand says. "It was exhilarating."

Baum landed a job at Harris, Kerr, Forster, a hotel accounting and consulting company, where he made fifty dollars a week writing up food-and-beverage reports that quickly vaulted him to a supervisory position, working with the likes of industrial-design pioneer Norman Bel Geddes, whose projects included hotels and restaurants. And Baum's consulting work so impressed developer William Zeckendorf that he hired Baum in 1947 to manage one of his restaurants, the theatrical restaurant-nightclub Monte Carlo, where Howard Hughes was known to spend a thousand dollars a week—and drop 30 percent tips— when he was in town.

Baum revered the balding, bushy-eyebrowed, and gregarious Zeckendorf, a larger-than-life personality with an intense attention to detail who could make grapefruits out of lemons, or so he claimed. He had an ability "to concentrate on a dozen things and go from discipline to discipline," Baum later told food critic Craig Claiborne. "[It] was a dazzling experience."

The Schine hotel chain brought Baum on board in 1950 and sent him to Florida to be director of its restaurant operations, where he made big enough waves to get noticed by the newly emerging Restaurant Associates food services company. RA owner Abraham Wechsler had consolidated two coffee shop and cafeteria chains to form a small unit of about a dozen outlets, which were presided over by his twenty-five-year-old son-in-law, Jerome Brody, who had vaulted to his position when a series of top executives passed away in succession.

RA ran a snack bar in the Newark airport for the Port Authority, which, curiously, wanted the airport to house a luxury restaurant. The agency asked a skeptical Wechsler, who didn't have the manpower—his cafeterias and coffee shops didn't even employ waiters—to run it.

Looking for outside help, Brody hired the thirty-two-year-old Joe Baum in 1953, just a month before opening the restaurant, which was called the Newarker. Baum made his own hires, taking on an unknown Swiss chef named Albert Stockli, who had once impressed Baum with his Swiss barley soup. He also poached a woman who had been working at a local chain, Huyler's, to be the hostess so that patrons would recognize a familiar face.

Its first year, the Newarker lost twenty-five thousand dollars. "People thought we were nuts," Baum later said, "for creating a restaurant in the swamps of Secaucus."

But Baum and Stockli dug in their heels and went bigger, hoping to turn the restaurant into a destination by developing an outrageous menu that would entertain and satisfy guests. First, Baum had to get their attention, so he released a live turkey in the concourse to draw air travelers to his Thanksgiving offerings. He used fire—so much that the air-conditioning system needed to be upgraded—for a variety of dishes, including shish kebabs or a parfait decorated with sparklers. "The customers like to see things on fire, or accompanied by fiery props, and it doesn't hurt the food that much," he liked to say.

Baum added an extra half lobster to create the "three-claw lobster" and threw in an extra oyster (on an extra plate) to an order of a dozen oysters. Within two years, the Newarker was serving a thousand covers (the industry term used for individual diners served) a day, and by 1956, it was grossing three million dollars and making a profit. The restaurant became the talk of the tristate region, a nightlife magnet with a majority of its customers coming just for dinner, without a plane to catch.

RA was also hired to improve the Hawaiian Room restaurant in Manhattan's Hotel Lexington, which was capitalizing on a Polynesian fad then sweeping the nation. Baum traveled to Hawaii and California to do research and served up that flaming appetizer delight, the pupu platter. With Stockli in place in the kitchen, Baum concocted Pacific-inspired dishes, including spare ribs with pineapple and kumquats. And Baum added buzz when he got Arthur Godfrey, the popular, ukulele-playing television entertainer, to host his variety show from the restaurant.

The midtown real estate boom was remaking Manhattan, and RA and Baum were developing a winning reputation along with it. In 1955, Baum was named the head of RA's specialty restaurant division; his first big job was to be a restaurant in the new Seagram Building, designed by Mies van der Rohe and Philip Johnson, on Park Avenue between Fifty-Second and Fifty-Third Streets. But while that was in development, he opened the Forum of the Twelve Caesars in tony Rockefeller Center.

RA's concept for a restaurant in a moribund space—"a dumb truck bay," Jerry Brody called it—of the ground floor of Rockefeller Center was partly spawned by the happenstance that one of Baum's interior designers, William Pahlmann, had come into possession of a set of life-size portraits of twelve Caesars. That, as well as the promise of a clientele made up of media titans working in the grand building complex owned by the Rockefellers, inspired Baum to conjure up an early milestone in theme restaurants.

With waiters dressed in purple velvet and bartenders in leather, and the walls covered with mosaics of gladiators, Roman baths, and aqueducts, the Forum of the Twelve Caesars was an immersive experience served triumphantly with tongue in cheek. To get it right, Baum traveled with staff to Rome and Pompeii, and he studied the classics, including the writing of Apicius, a Roman chronicler of the empire's culinary tastes.

The menu was specifically Roman, not Italian. It, ostensibly, covered the reaches of the empire, including crayfish that could have come from Egypt, oysters from England, and wine from France (or, rather, Gaul). It was presented with a sense of humor. There was "sirloin in red wine, marrow, and onions—a Gallic recipe Julius Collected While There on Business." Wine buckets were upturned centurion helmets. The large oysters were "Oysters of Hercules, which you with sword shall carve." Potatoes were served in ashes, and pheasant arrived on a shield.

Before the opening, Baum sent the copper plates back to the manufacturer multiple times because he wanted Bacchus to smile rather than leer. His idiosyncrasies suggested innovation—or delusion. He put the forks, which were larger than normal, on the right side to emphasize "heartiness." He made the tables an inch lower than customary because he thought it would make guests more comfortable.

Alan Lewis, a Cornell classmate of Baum's, and Lee Harty, both thick-necked tough guys, managed the restaurant in sharp, dark, Brioni suits like the ones their boss, Joe Baum, began wearing after he discovered the designer during a trip to Rome. The restaurant was supposed to have a "lusty elegance," according to Baum.

"Joe Baum is an intellectually emancipated person," RA founder Abraham Wechsler would later say. "I believe the Forum swung the center of gravity of the culinary arts in our direction." Indeed, it was perfect timing.

Still aglow with his Newarker and Forum successes, Baum was given the canvas, resources, and enlightened mandate to create a masterpiece. The lobby of the ultramodern Seagram Building rising on Park Avenue was intended to be an exhibition space. But Phyllis Lambert, the daughter of Seagram head Samuel Bronfman, was determined to make the building a crowning cultural achievement. RA president Jerry Brody wooed Lambert, an aesthetically inclined scion living in Paris, by entertaining her at the Newarker. She helped convince her father to turn the floor over to RA, which would eventually burn $4.5 million (close to $40 million in today's dollars; said to be, at the time, the most expensive restaurant constructed) creating what many consider to be the first truly American fine-dining restaurant.

Baum came up with the name for the restaurant, the Four Seasons, after having recently visited the Vier Jahreszeiten (literal translation: "Four Seasons") hotels in Germany, although legend says he developed the concept from a haiku. The restaurant represented a radical departure from the notion that the best restaurants had to have red-velvet banquettes and ornate crystal chandeliers. Most of all, it didn't have to be French. When the Michelin inspector was brought there by *Life* magazine, he said, "This does not look like a restaurant to me. . . . I think it was designed by your Cecil B. DeMille" (although he grudgingly approved of the food). With Stockli again in the kitchen, Baum devised the concept of the restaurant—including the food and the decor—that would change with the seasons. And the food and decor would have a philosophy: *shibui,* the Japanese concept of simple beauty.

When it opened in 1959, the Four Seasons' walls were adorned with a Pablo Picasso tapestry and artwork by Joan Miró. Chairs costing four hundred ninety-five dollars apiece were designed by van der Rohe, Johnson, and Charles Eames. Garth and Ada Louise Huxtable designed the stemware. Two impossibly high windows were adorned with shimmering gold anodized aluminum drapes that rippled like waterfalls. The annual budget for flora, which included seventeen-foot ficus trees gracing the corners of the white marble pool of water that centered the dining room, was fifty thousand dollars.

"We feel we have a restaurant that is a style in itself, as well as being a mirror of New York," Baum said. "We decided it was really somewhat French, somewhat Italian, and very much American."

For the food, Baum instilled a near-religious reverence for fresh, seasonal ingredients, a novel concept at the time. James Beard, who had been on the payroll as a consultant for RA since 1954, was on the team that would build a menu—written in English, not French—including unheard-of items such as edible nasturtium flowers, fiddleheads, and ramps. Baum sent Beard to Turkey to acquire an authentic vertical broiler to make the proper doner kebab, and he haggled over the price of wild mushrooms with composer John Cage, who moonlighted as a mycologist.

The *New York Times'* Craig Claiborne praised the restaurant soon after its opening as "perhaps the most exciting restaurant to open in New York within the last two decades." He waxed on about Stockli's use of freshly picked herbs such as rosemary, sage, and chervil and mushrooms heretofore only known in Europe. Flaming dishes, such as a beef Stroganoff, were prepared table-side, which was "unconventional but thoroughly tempting." Claiborne, a proud Francophile, noted through clenched teeth that "the cuisine is not exquisite in the sense that la grande cuisine française at its superlative best is exquisite," but the point was made: Baum had taken fine dining in New York to a new level.

Baum delighted guests by upending expectations; amid all the sleek grandeur, a popular appetizer was a solitary yet exquisitely in-season beefsteak tomato, carved table-side as if it were the last one on earth. And the desserts! Baum knew that it was imperative to end on a high note. And Swiss-born pastry chef Albert Kumin, whom Baum hired away from the Ritz-Carlton in Montreal, created the definitive chocolate velvet cake, with a mousse-like filling, among other instant classics. *Holiday* magazine dubbed the food at the Four Seasons "the New American Cuisine."

The same year RA opened the Four Seasons, it also bought Mamma Leone's, a popular Italian restaurant with big portions and a "traveling antipasto" cart that could be brought to your table. It cost $2.5 million, but it was a moneymaker. And, in 1960, it opened the more innovative La Fonda del Sol, an authentic Latin American restaurant in the Time & Life Building. The doorman wore a sombrero and poncho. Elena Zelayeta, the blind—she taught herself to divine a pan's temperature by smell—Mexican cooking savant, was advising chef Albert Stockli in the kitchen. Baum had traveled with his wife, Ruth, through South and Central America, where they collected dolls, puppets, hats, and other artifacts to adorn the walls of the new restaurant.

At La Fonda del Sol, there was a large rotisserie with spits of lamb, chicken, and beef turning over the coals, drinks such as Pisco sours and sangria, and Torta de Chocolaterias for dessert. Designed by Alexander Girard, better known as Sandro, the restaurant was festooned with sun motifs on ceramic tiles and cheerfully drawn words such as *poblano, palmitos, seviche,* and *escabeche* on the walls. It was garish and fun and, in the words of *New York* magazine writer Gael Greene, "fiercely, perhaps fatally, authentic."

RA's restaurants and chains soon blanketed the city with strategic placement in its most stylish, and busy, office buildings. La Fonda del Sol, the Tower Suite, and Forum of the Twelve Caesars were all in Rockefeller Center. Most had a particular theme, often rooted in an ethnic tradition. In the Pan Am Building, which was connected to the commuter traffic of Grand Central station, there was Zum Zum, a popular chain of German sausage-and-beer eateries; Trattoria, a mid-price Italian restaurant (with a self-described, "casual Dolce Vita look"); and Charlie Brown's Ale & Chop House (a pub and country kitchen).

Baum analyzed the spaces, the demographics of the local populations, and the flow of passersby to optimize profit volume. Among the many restaurants that RA opened, there was the Brasserie (a French bistro on the floor below the Four Seasons), Paul Revere's Tavern and Chop House (where the menu replaced *s*'s with Old English *f*'s), and the Fountain Café (sangria and guacamole served under tiger-striped awnings in Central Park).

RA's success and its signature distinctive, thematic restaurants were widely attributed to Joe Baum, the creative force, akin to the lead designer at a fashion house. Before Baum, there had been ethnic restaurants and chains and even theme restaurants, but never had anyone so systematically implemented the theme—or because that term has developed a plasticky, Hard Rock connotation, perhaps the better word is "concept"—into the DNA of a restaurant, including its design, food, and marketing.

He remained under Jerome Brody until 1963, when the young president became perhaps too personally involved in a project at a resort and casino complex of hotels in Divonne-les-Bains in France. Brody had an affair with an overseas RA secretary. He approached his father-in-law, Abraham Wechsler, who still controlled the company, with the news that he wanted to divorce Wechsler's daughter but that he would continue to work for RA. Wechsler wasn't sympathetic to the notion. He immediately dumped Brody and appointed Baum president.

CHAPTER 4
ELEVATING THE ACT OF EATING

"A restaurant takes a basic drive—the simple act of eating," Joe Baum said in a speech at the Restaurant Show in Chicago in 1965, "and transforms it into a civilized ritual, a ritual involving hospitality and imagination and satisfaction and graciousness and warmth. A restaurant elevates a human need to a subtle and sophisticated pleasure."

As the president of RA, Baum animated each of his restaurants with that belief. He wasn't the first restaurateur to feel this way. But, previously, the dining experience had been the result of, say, an owner-chef's personal taste or the calculation of an entrepreneur looking to capitalize on a culinary craze. For Baum's RA restaurants, it was a result of his idiosyncratic creative process being applied to a number of eateries in a big-business manner.

By the 1960s, increased wealth, leisure time, and improvements in such technology as food transportation and refrigeration were opening the way to realize Baum's belief that the dining experience could be heightened for an expanding upper middle class. As both the business and creative head of RA, Baum fashioned a brand of restaurants based on his oft-repeated principle, "People don't come to eat at my restaurants because they're hungry." They came for an experience. They came for culture. RA was bringing more than merely good food to Manhattan. Baum's teams of forward-thinking creatives were delivering design and attitude, a new standard of living, to New Yorkers, who were sitting on mid-century modern chairs by Charles Eames and being inundated by irreverent advertising by Julian Koenig, George Lois, and Ron Holland.

And Baum established a successful business model by working with well-financed partners and patrons such as the Bronfman and Rockefeller families, in heavily trafficked locations like the Pan Am Building and the Time & Life Building, where rents could be kept artificially low by self-interested landlords who wanted to see the restaurants thrive. Michelangelo may have had the popes, it has been said, but Baum had the Rockefellers.

Baum also applied his personal brand by developing his own intensely exacting management style. "He scared the living shit out of everybody," George Lois says. "But in a sweet way. He had this wonderful grouchiness. And everything had to be perfection."

He was obsessive about details and would demand countless corrections until he was satisfied. He was never satisfied. He liked to have a phalanx of managers and assistant managers to whom he would dictate his ideas. And yet, he was hard to follow. Baum spoke in circumlocutions, peppered with malapropisms such as "don't push a dead horse," "someone threw a monkey into the works," and "there's a flaw in the ointment." Sitting in on a meeting with Baum was a jabberwocky of misdirection and myopia. And he could speak for hours. After a meeting, the managers would compare notes to figure out what they were supposed to do.

"If you lacked self-confidence, you had a hard time with Joe. He terrorized people in his quest for perfection," says Tony Zazula, a close confidant who worked for Baum in his later years. "Not just for the sake of perfection. Or for control. But for the whole picture. It was all part of the artist's creative process where no detail was too small to make it an integral part of the total composition. He believed someone would notice and would appreciate the level of detail and authenticity."

Al Ferraro, a fellow Cornell graduate who ran the Hawaiian Room and later the Trattoria, agrees that Joe Baum could be intimidating. But Ferraro says that he inspired respect more than fear. Baum wouldn't yell at him but would instead quietly correct him, such as the time at the Trattoria when Baum noticed a salt shaker was out of place. "One thing like this, it ruins the whole operation," he said quietly. It was Baum's version of the restaurant industry maxim that you have to check the light bulbs. If one is out, then everything seems wrong.

Baum tended to reserve his wrath for lieutenants, but anyone could be targeted, including vendors. Cascade Linen and Uniform Service provided most of the RA tablecloths, napkins, and uniforms for Baum, beginning at the Newarker. Its president, William Troy, claimed he never got a compliment from Baum. Still, he considered him a friend, despite the high drama the relationship sometimes entailed. In one incident recalled by Troy, a wrinkle in a waiter's coat prompted Baum to call an all-hands-on-deck meeting with his staff and the Cascade brass in attendance. Nobody spoke except Baum, who ceremoniously lifted the waiter's wrinkled jacket and tore it in half, "to demonstrate his contempt," according to Troy.

"It may sound like I am bitter," Troy said. "It's just the opposite. The demands that Joe made probably were the major reasons why our company became the premier supplier to the better restaurants in New York City." And Troy would push back. When Baum made a request to supply the Forum of the Twelve Caesars with impossibly thick linens, Troy instead puckishly had a suit made for Baum of the same material.

Baum liked to "bust balls," making the rounds of his restaurants, checking up on four or five in a night. Once he was on the prowl, the "RA tom-toms" would sound, and managers would call one another. "He's on his way, and he's loaded for bear," they'd say.

One time, he caused a commotion in the kitchen when he entered the Forum—or it could have been the Four Seasons; the story has been told so many times—and hollered, "What's wrong with the consommé?" The chef went into contortions to correct the offense. How did Baum know without even tasting it? Because, according to Baum, there was always something wrong with the consommé.

This devilish browbeating had a ripple effect within the RA hierarchy. Restaurant Associates ran the food at a resort in Divonne-les-Bains, France, where Alan Lewis emulated his boss by demanding to hear why the chef didn't include blood in the coq au vin, even though he knew that was an outdated practice. "I wanted him to know he wasn't dealing with just a fat Jew from New York," he said.

Busting balls was both recreation and management for Baum (and, perhaps, if Lewis was any indication, also a psychological shield), who found a worthy foil in Ron Holland, one of his on-again, off-again ad men—he fired him seven times over the years—who could turn a phrase and tell a joke that would send the room into stitches.

The first time they met, Holland was new to the advertising business, having recently given up work as an ice cream truck driver. Holland recalls arriving early to a meeting and Baum drilling him, asking, "What do you know about advertising?" "Nothing," Holland said. "What do you know about the restaurant business?" "Nothing." "What do you have to show me?" "Nothing."

"I've had more rewarding conversations with a vending machine," Baum muttered.

The two men had what Baum's wife later called a "forty-year fist-fight." In one heated meeting, Holland told Baum, "I hope you die. . . ." But, to soften the blow, fellow ad man George Lois interjected, ". . . a rich man."

Lois also recalls being tested by Baum early, during a meeting at the Four Seasons, in another story that's been repeated in various iterations. Baum brought Lois to the bar, where the bartender asked, "What will you be having, Mr. Baum?" "Make me a Bloody Mary, Jack," Baum responded, casting a sideways look at Lois. The bartender placed the drink on the bar. Baum looked at him, hard, and said, "Jack, could you taste it?" "Of course, Mr. Baum," the bartender replied, and he took a sip. "What do you think?" asked Baum. "Terrific, Mr. Baum," he said. "Could you make an even better one for me?" Baum asked. As the bartender complied, Baum rapped his fingers on the bar and sang to himself, "Hum-dee, hum-dee, hum." He gave Lois another glance, with an arched eyebrow. When the bartender placed the new drink on the bar, Baum jutted out his chin and asked him to taste it again. "Is it better?" Baum asked. "Why, yes, Mr. Baum," the bartender said, to which Baum retorted, "You schmuck, then why the fuck didn't you make it that way the first time?"

What impression this made on the bartender is unclear, but Lois says he was invigorated by this lesson "to do the best work I can."

RA engaged the city in a brassy, ballsy sort of public repartee through a steady stream of ad copy by the firm Papert, Koenig, Lois. In meetings, Baum would reply to their copy with a catchphrase: "Run the shit." They came up with material such as, "Will the lady who lost her composure during fiesta at La Fonda del Sol please come back every Sunday?" Or, "The Newarker must be a great restaurant—look at all those planes parked outside!"

Advertising, a PR team, and Joe Baum's ability to engage and entertain the city's cultural, business, and political elite put RA in the center of New York nightlife. President John F. Kennedy's forty-fifth birthday dinner at the Four Seasons was the same night Marilyn Monroe serenaded him with her coquettish rendition of "Happy Birthday." The Four Seasons was the common ground for the city's top tiers, whether it was Senator Jacob Javits, Truman Capote, Philippe de Rothschild, Richard Burton, or Andy Warhol.

Lois, whose offices were in the Seagram Building, would get a call from Baum in the morning, asking him to go on his restaurant rounds. When Baum got together with his ad men, there was bound to be eating and drinking, laughter, and plays on words, such as Lois telling Baum of his idea for Zum Zum, using a sausage in the place of one of the u's: "You never sausage a good logo!" Baum would order half the menu for the table, comp it, and then rib them for costing him a fortune.

Baum would also take his wife and guests out to dinner several times a week or, at home, make friends pot-au-feu, the French beef stew dinner. By the time he was appointed president, he and Ruth, who now lived in a ten-room duplex penthouse on Park Avenue, had three children: Hilary and Charles, both at Fieldston High School, and Edward, still in elementary, at Ethical Culture. The decorations of their grand apartment with a circular staircase reflected Baum's international passions, including pre-Columbian figurines, thanks to reconnaissance trips to South America, and Roman busts facing Peruvian dolls. On one wall he hung a pair of burlesque tin tassel pasties that he claimed Ann Corio, the legendary striptease artist, once wore. On another, a Picasso print mischievously shared space with an abstract work by Baum's youngest child.

The children didn't see much of their hardworking father—"It seemed like there was a restaurant opening every month," Charles says—and when Joe was home, he was consumed in a cloud of sales reports and architectural plans that he would roll out on a table alongside restaurant models that he'd study for hours. His version of telling fairy tales to his children was to sometimes regale them with his visions of an upcoming restaurant. Ruth and he would host cocktail parties—both were adept at mixing drinks and cooking—and then head to one of their restaurants, the theater, or a jazz club.

New York City in the early 1960s fostered an expanding, cultured, white-collar class spurred on by rapid growth in the entertainment, legal, media, tourism, and finance industries. City business leaders and planners, including the Rockefellers and Robert Moses, sought to serve this affluent or aspiring class of New Yorker. The grand Lincoln Center project had broken ground in 1959, opened its Philharmonic Hall in 1962, and promised more highbrow artistry to come.

And yet, stock market gains, New Deal–era government spending, and a bloated municipal payroll were veiling immense strains on the city. President Johnson had declared a war on poverty, which was disproportionately affecting rural America, so it was hard to see its presence in the city, on the fringes, away from the midtown lights. Forty-one percent of nonwhite America was in poverty, and African-Americans looking for a better life were crowding Harlem and the outer boroughs, which lacked the infrastructure to support them. Their movement helped advance white New Yorkers' flight to the suburbs, which was already happening due to the continued decrease in jobs.

Sidestepping this underlying tension and decay, the 1964–65 World's Fair, held on the same site as 1939–40's, in Flushing, Queens, was a dazzling display of New York prominence and optimism. The fair was not an official, government-sanctioned, or certified World's Fair but a private business affair dreamed up by the city's business and municipal leaders to initiate development, draw capital, and energize the economy. The official World's Fair oversight committee discouraged foreign nations from attending. Although many nations represented themselves, the fair was largely populated by such companies as General Motors, AT&T, Ford, Disney, Coca-Cola, and Kodak. In name, the fair's theme was "Peace through Understanding," yet, in reality, it was a celebration of American commercial prowess.

Joe Baum and RA were in the thick of it, running the Top of the Fair, the official restaurant, dramatically housed one hundred twenty feet up on giant, tapered columns inside the Port Authority Heliport building, where diners could feel the vibrations of landing helicopters. With views of the entire fairgrounds as well as of the Manhattan skyline, RA's Top of the Fair aligned itself with excitement, refinement, and the city's powers-that-be.

But neither Baum's food nor the hopeful technologies and futuristic displays could materialize crowds. Organizers had estimated that seventy million people would attend over the two years, but only fifty-two million showed up. The fair's rosy profit projections turned into losses for the city.

As the fair's first season closed in October 1964, Baum and RA were focused on a momentous occasion of their own: being the subjects of an extensive profile by Geoffrey Hellman in *The New Yorker*. Baum had wined and dined Hellman at several of his restaurants. He had also coached his staff on how to talk and act in front of Hellman, even running them through rehearsals of seemingly authentic interactions with the writer.

Although Hellman was droll and haughtily bemused, the October 17 *New Yorker* article burnished Baum's reputation as brilliant, excessive, opaque, and a delicious new presence on the cultural landscape, an entrepreneur of food, design, and taste. The ten thousand-plus word story didn't once refer to him, as we would now, as a restaurateur, because the word hadn't yet been applied to this hybrid of businessman, aesthete, and gourmand. There had been other distinctive proprietors of popular restaurants in Paris and, in New York, owners such as the Delmonicos and Henri Soulé. But Baum was a businessman who developed multiple restaurants with a sophistication and style that could only be attributed to him. Even though he didn't own his restaurants, he created the modern-day iteration of the restaurateur. Baum was a hired gun, but his signature seemed to be everywhere.

Baum's influence was so novel and pervasive that he would sometimes get credit for innovations that he might or might not have come up with. At RA's Tower Suite, at the top of the Time & Life Building, where dinner guests had, in addition to a waitstaff, their own butler and footman, it was said that Baum introduced the now-ubiquitous greeting, "Hello, my name is so-and-so, and I'll be your waiter tonight." At the Forum, ashtrays were removed by "cupping" for the first time: covering the dirty one with a clean one. Another reputedly unprecedented event occurred at the Four Seasons: When a guest left the table, his or her napkin was refolded by attentive waitstaff.

* * *

By 1965, Baum was running a company with 130 restaurants and food services operations in its stable. But, like the city it had come to dominate, it was peaking. In *The New Yorker*, Hellman floated some uncertainty about the underlying financials of the business. Baum was notoriously profligate, a charming trait on the surface but unsustainable for those watching the bottom line. The company had gone public in 1961, selling two hundred forty-five thousand shares at a price of eleven dollars each. RA would soon be grossing more than one hundred million dollars and with a stock high of forty-seven dollars in 1968, but losses quickly snowballed. Overexpansion and high costs were compounded by a weakening economy. The stock plummeted to just four dollars. The excitement of a hot new company led by a daring visionary wasn't earning dividends—either the literal or figurative kind. Bullish profit predictions for 1969 didn't pan out.

What was once new was feeling very old. RA's once-stylish European themes at Kennedy airport needed to be replaced by something more modern—and American. La Fonda del Sol, never a moneymaker, was temporarily shut down for a reboot. The peripatetic Baum could never sit still for long, but as the dawn of a new decade approached, the wolves were at the door. Instead of dreaming big and coming up with fantastic new plans, he was putting out fires, such as RA's giant retail candy franchise being crippled by a crisis in the cocoa market. Or its new food services operation at Baltimore's Friendship airport running into trouble because of an airport strike. RA began selling Zum Zums to raise cash.

As the headaches accumulated, Baum began feeling a pain in his stomach that he tried to ignore. As the summer of 1970 came to a close, the RA board organized a meeting. Baum knew his time was up; he had to meet his executioners. But first, Ruth finally convinced her husband to go to the doctor to assess his condition. When he arrived in the office, he fell on the floor. The doctor stabilized his patient and diagnosed him with peritonitis—a stress-induced, burst appendix that could prove fatal—and told him to go to a hospital.

But he had business to attend to. A big meeting. "You can ignore my advice, and you could die," the doctor said.

There was a history of similar ailments in the family that had proved fatal, so Baum checked himself in. Bedridden in the hospital, he was miserable, unable to keep up with the constant flurry of work. Nonetheless, he sat propped up in his bed with the phone cradled under his neck like a second IV. Baum knew the board was preparing to fire him. As he flicked ash from his cigar, he said, "Oh, well. Easy come, easy go." The signs had been clear for weeks. Restaurant Associates' board kicked him out. It relieved him of his role as president and removed him from the company entirely, minus his stock options.

In a *New York* magazine article, published November 2, 1970, entitled "Twilight of the Gods," food writer Gael Greene chronicled Baum's fall as epic, Shakespearean tragedy. The great artist brought low by the suits. "[They're] killing him and stamping on his grave," Abraham Wechsler's daughter, Grace, cried. "They're not food men."

Greene ate eel in green sauce and Baum had baked bass in spiked Dijonaise at Quo Vadis, an aging, haute cuisine standard. He looked tired. Fragile. Near tears. A broken man.

"We were furious," George Lois says of RA's firing Baum. Accompanying the feature article, *New York* magazine included Greene's reviews of the RA restaurants, which Lois casts as revenge for the termination. "Gael went nuts, basically slamming everything," he says. The Forum of the Twelve Caesars was "cursed," she wrote. The Tower Suite: "Doom at the Top." Zum Zum: "Absolute wurst." And, at the Four Seasons, "the penny-pinching already shows." The carpets were dirty, she wrote.

The next week, the Four Seasons was plagued by lunch cancellations, according to Lois, who says Baum felt Greene had gone too far. But as dire as things seemed to be, Baum provided Greene with a positive twist. She was happy to close the article with the news that an old friend of his had offered him a new job, which could literally put him back on top.

CHAPTER 5
NEW YORK AUDACITY

Guy Tozzoli, the director of the World Trade Department of the Port Authority, had a taste for the good things in life. He frequented Joe Baum's restaurants, especially Charlie Brown's and his stylish French bistro, Le Madrigal, where he drank wine and traded stories with the restaurateur. Tozzoli had grown close to Baum when they both worked on the 1964 World's Fair. The two were proud, impeccably dressed men with a belief in the power of appearances and a zealous drive to succeed. Like Baum, Tozzoli, affectionately known as "Mr. T," was intense and always deep in thought and didn't believe in the word "no." He also treated his work projects as his babies, and now he had the biggest baby of them all.

Tozzoli, like Baum, was part of the wave of GIs who had started their careers in New York City in 1946. He went to work for the Port Authority, the dual-state—New York and New Jersey—agency that oversaw all roadways, trains, and transportation hubs between the neighbors. He made his mark as an effective manager of construction projects. And after the agency lent him to Robert Moses, for whom he helped develop the World's Fair, Tozzoli was appointed by Port Authority executive director Austin Tobin to oversee the construction of the World Trade Center, the most complex, massive urban-development project in New York City history, bigger than Lincoln Center or Rockefeller Center.

The World Trade Center was a seven-building, thirteen-block section of Lower Manhattan that would amount to more than thirteen million square feet of office space, including two enormous skyscrapers, one of which would be the tallest in the world. It was a mammoth undertaking, financially, logistically, and politically—the Port Authority's move into real estate development was considered by many to be an egregious case of government overreach. And it might have been a relatively minor part of the puzzle, but with the prospect of tens of thousands of people working at and visiting the Trade Center each day,

Tozzoli would have many mouths to feed. He had dabbled with the idea of hiring Restaurant Associates for the job of consulting him on how to ramp up food services at the World Trade Center, but he and the Port Authority had seen Joe Baum work magic on their own turf, first at the Newarker and then at Kennedy airport and the World's Fair. Baum had done the impossible when he turned the Newark airport into a dining destination. Maybe he could do the same with downtown Manhattan. Sure, he didn't have a company with the resources, but he was still the king of the restaurant consultants.

In September 1970, Tozzoli hired Baum, for a one hundred twenty-five thousand dollar annual consulting fee, to advise him on food services for his billion-dollar project.

* * *

The World Trade Center first came into being in 1939, not far from Le Restaurant Français where Henri Soulé was delighting Americans with buttery, flaming crêpes suzette at the World's Fair. The International Chamber of Commerce and other trade groups wanted to create an entity that could represent their interests in expanding exchange among nations. They called it the World Trade Center and set up in an exhibition hall across the Lagoon of Nations in the Hall of Nations, in a space originally intended for China, which decided not to show up. They created an optimistic banner that read, WORLD PEACE THROUGH WORLD TRADE.

Tucked away from the larger spectacles of the "the world of tomorrow," the World Trade Center hosted ho-hum trade and travel exhibits from Finland and South Africa and other countries. One of the World Trade Center's organizing committee members was Winthrop W. Aldrich, the president of Chase National Bank. Aldrich had become John D. Rockefeller Jr.'s brother-in-law when the financier married Winthrop's sister Abby in 1901. An avid boatman and navy sailor, Aldrich had been to ports in Latin America, Europe, and Asia as the powerful and wealthy head of the largest bank in the world. In the 1930s, Aldrich was one of the first of America's powerful bankers to recognize the profit potential in creating a financial hub for international trade. His ideas about the potential of a global capitalist empire based in New York City were shelved, however, at the advent of World War II.

In 1946, politician and real estate businessman David Scholtz picked up the torch when he envisioned a commercial development financed by public money in downtown Manhattan. He wanted to tap the port economy to create a vital new center of trade for the emerging global economy, where international products and services could be promoted and purchased in one physical space.

New York governor Thomas Dewey reviewed the idea with Port Authority chairman Howard Cullman, who dismissed the proposal as "primarily an extensive real estate operation." Nevertheless, Dewey and the New York state legislature initiated a World Trade Center Corporation to look into creating a World Trade Center to promote and facilitate international trade for New York businesses that wanted to reach new markets around the world. Dewey tapped Aldrich to be on the board for a World Trade Corporation in the spirit that, as Dewey said, "expanding international trade, conducted on a basis of mutual confidence and for mutual profit, looms as one of the great hopes for permanent peace."

The initiative eventually floundered in the halls of the state capitol in Albany, but the seeds of an ambitious plan were planted at the Port Authority, particularly with its recently appointed executive director Austin Tobin, who was at the beginning of a three-decade tenure. He asked for an internal review within the PA for a potential World Trade Center.

Like Aldrich, Tobin was expansive in his aspirations. And he was the head of a very powerful, unusual municipal agency. The Port Authority had been formed in the wake of World War I, when there was a need to coordinate the comings and goings at the massive port region that encompassed New Jersey and New York. The two states had been at odds and, at times, overwhelmed by the boat shipments to Manhattan and the system of trains that ran through New Jersey, where they loaded and unloaded a constant stream of goods that were transported to and from the city by barges.

In 1921, with consent from Congress, the Port Authority was created "to promote and protect the commerce of the bistate port and to undertake port and regional improvements not likely to be financed by private enterprise or to be attempted by either state alone." Commissioners of the PA, who were appointed by the governors, would oversee its budget. It could raise funds by issuing bonds based on its ability to collect income through tolls, fees, and rents on its roadways, bridges, and tunnels that covered a vast area in both states, with the New York Harbor at its center. It served an important role in the evolution of New York City, overseeing the construction of bridges, including the George Washington Bridge, as well as the Lincoln Tunnel. After World War II, the area's airports were also taken over by the Port Authority.

Another powerful force, and potential Port Authority ally, with an interest in the city's infrastructure, was David Rockefeller, Winthrop W. Aldrich's nephew, who began working at Chase in 1946 when his uncle was its chairman. Rockefeller had worked his way up at Chase to executive vice president for planning and development. At a time when the business district had shifted to midtown, closer to Grand Central Terminal, the Empire State Building, and the Chrysler Building, Rockefeller made a move to consolidate nine buildings that the bank owned near Wall Street to create a new base downtown. With the assistance of Robert Moses, he made a deal stewarded by Baum's former boss, real estate magnate William Zeckendorf, to establish the new Chase headquarters a block north from Wall Street. The bank began construction of One Chase Manhattan Plaza, a sixty-story skyscraper, in 1957.

David's father, John D. Rockefeller Jr., had created Rockefeller Center uptown, a monument to the family name, and this was the younger Rockefeller's opportunity to build something monumental. In 1956, Moses, who was intent on creating a Lower Manhattan Expressway, advised Rockefeller to support his Chase building by creating the Downtown–Lower Manhattan Association to corral powerful business interests—members came from Morgan Stanley, American Express, and the New York Stock Exchange—intent on revitalizing the area.

As One Chase Plaza went up, the DLMA made plans to remake the neighborhood, issuing its first report, in 1958, calling for the removal of the "obsolescence" of decaying ports, dilapidated buildings, and the long-deteriorating Washington Market, to be replaced by office buildings, banks, and parks. That year, the stars began to align: Nelson Rockefeller, David's brother, was elected governor of New York.

The Rockefeller brothers found the perfect tool in the Port Authority, an ambitiously led, quasi-public agency with the potential to get hundreds of millions of dollars in financing and an interest in updating the downtown area once dominated by its ports.

In January 1960, the DLMA asked that the Port Authority "be requested to make detailed studies" for a World Trade Center. And in the spring of 1961, Nelson and David Rockefeller met with the Port Authority's Austin Tobin, New Jersey governor Robert Meyner, and various other officials to survey the proposal for a World Trade Center that would cover more than thirteen acres on the East Side of Manhattan, near the Fulton Fish Market. Spread out for them, rendered in a giant model, was a series of new buildings, including one with a World Trade Club on top. It had a one thousand five hundred-car parking lot. They said it would cost two hundred fifty million dollars.

Unfortunately, Governor Meyner deflated the booster atmosphere in the room when he reportedly blurted out, "What's in it for me?"

He had a point. As a Port Authority project, it would have to satisfy the needs of both states. But the plan failed to do much for New Jersey. The PA went back to the drawing board and made a leap from the East Side to the West Side of the city, so that, by December of that year, the World Trade Center would be integrated into an even larger deal to have the PA take over the money-losing Hudson and Manhattan Railroad. Part of the agreement was the approval for the PA to develop the new center for international trade. The PA formed the PATH (Port Authority Trans-Hudson), which was tasked with funneling commuters back and forth between New Jersey and Manhattan, with hubs between Newark and Hoboken and under a future World Trade Center.

On February 12, 1962, Austin Tobin assigned Guy Tozzoli, a tough but smooth operator who had surpassed expectations working temporarily under Robert Moses, to oversee the construction of the World Trade Center. "I'm going to create the largest department the Port Authority has ever had, the World Trade Department," Tobin told him. "And I'm going to put you in charge of it."

A few months later, Tozzoli was on a reconnaissance mission for Moses at the Seattle World's Fair, where he stopped in his tracks in the Federal Science Pavilion, about seven acres of buildings surrounding a courtyard with reflective pools. In contrast to the busy life that permeated the rest of the fair, it exuded a deep serenity.

Tozzoli wanted the Seattle-born, Japanese-American architect Minoru Yamasaki, who had designed the pavilion, to design the World Trade Center. Yamasaki, who had designed the Pruitt-Igoe housing complex (a model of poorly planned public housing) in St. Louis, Missouri, and more successful apartment buildings elsewhere, didn't initially believe he should be considered for the project, but, teamed with New York architectural firm Emery Roth & Sons, which could help him handle the immensity of it, he accepted the assignment.

As the project made headway, gale forces approached. Despite Tobin's claim that there was "overwhelming public support" for the World Trade Center plan, there was a very public community that wasn't: the people who would be displaced by it.

* * *

Despite the downtown area's being relatively barren, dead at night, and generally inhospitable to the moneyed class that the Rockefeller family hoped to draw to the area, within the footprint of the planned World Trade Center was an abundance of flower and plant stores, hardware stores, book stalls, even restaurants, and, most notable of all, some four hundred shops that sold radio and television equipment, which gave the area its name, Radio Row. In the spring of 1962, Oscar Nadel, who had owned Oscar's Radio there since 1920, was at the forefront of the Downtown West Businessmen's Association, which promised to fight the World Trade Center. Promises of relocation compensation, as much as three thousand dollars for his radio shop, wouldn't be enough, he said. "This is not some foreign country where the government can come in and just take a man's business," Nadel told the *New York Times*.

When, in June of that year, Austin Tobin, Guy Tozzoli, and others sat down with Nadel in their 111 Eighth Avenue offices, Nadel said he wanted to protect his and his neighbors' livelihoods. Tobin offered him a storefront in the newly constructed World Trade Center. But Nadel declined.

A series of lawsuits, hearings, and street protests ensued. Nadel had powerful allies, especially Lawrence Wien, an owner of the Empire State Building, which he had bought with Harry Helmsley in 1961. Wien had a self-interest in opposing the construction of a taller skyscraper than his, which was at that point the tallest in the world. But Wien surrounded himself with a dozen other real estate titans who controlled approximately one-fifth of the city's office space. Calling themselves the Committee for a Reasonable World Trade Center, the group entered the fray to stop construction, fearful that all the new office space would depress their assets.

But the Port Authority kept moving forward. It announced Yamasaki as the chief architect on September 20, 1962. And its last major legal hurdle was cleared when its case made its way to the U.S. Supreme Court. In November 1963, the high court refused to take up an earlier decision about whether or not the construction was permissible if private property was being seized for nonpublic use, because it wasn't "a substantial Federal question," according to the court.

Still, the contentious PR war waged on. On January 18, 1964, at the New York Hilton Hotel, Tobin and Yamasaki unveiled the model of the design of the World Trade Center with its enormous twin towers. Outside, picketers called for a halt to the project. The next month, Wien announced that the World Trade Center was a huge risk, considering its height and proximity to air traffic. He published an ad with an image of an airplane crashing into the proposed towers. After all, his Empire State Building had suffered just such an accident when, in 1945, a B-25 bomber pilot lost his way in the fog and crashed the plane into the seventy-ninth and eightieth floors, killing fourteen people. A year after that, another thick fog contributed to a U.S. Air Force plane crashing into downtown's 40 Wall Street, killing five people. Wien warned that Yamasaki's proposed building materials—an innovative network of multiple lightweight columns and steel trusses—weren't as stable as the heavy concrete columns of the Empire State Building.

But Tobin defended his Twin Towers—sometimes derided by opponents who called them "Nelson" and "David"—by presenting an analysis by an outside firm, Worthington, Skilling, Helle & Jackson, that had investigated the unlikely prospect of a plane crash and found that even if a Boeing 707, much larger than a B-25, flying at six hundred miles per hour, were to hit the building, the towers would remain structurally sound, and "only local damage" would occur.

The new city mayor, John Lindsay, was another obstacle for the World Trade Center proponents to overcome. Lindsay's predecessor, Mayor Robert F. Wagner Jr., had handed over the thirteen city blocks for a measly annual fee of $1.7 million, a far cry from the estimated $25 million in taxes that a private landlord would be expected to pay. Lindsay was ready to block the project, which he could do with his power over permits to break up the city streets to create the Trade Center's superblocks. But Tobin convinced Lindsay: The Port Authority agreed to sweeten the deal for the city, adding more than $250 million in waterfront investments and a number of short- and long-term concessions.

As the World Trade Center's projected costs rose from $280 million to $575 million, construction began in March 1966, with the demolition of a building at 78 Dey Street. But, even then, clouds lingered. The architecture and design community was appalled by Minoru Yamasaki's proposed towers. Respected writer and urban authority Lewis Mumford called them "filing cabinets" in 1967 and later would describe them as acts of "purposeless gigantism." The Pulitzer Prize–winning architecture critic Ada Louise Huxtable, who had worked with Joe Baum on the Four Seasons, was more diplomatic but acknowledged the wide concern that they were "barbaric, oversized wreckers of scale and sunlight." And while she wrote that the WTC's "potential is greater than its threat," Huxtable added, "The Trade Center towers could be the start of a new skyscraper age or the biggest tombstones in the world."

One particularly persistent foe was Ted Kheel, a renowned lawyer and mediator who had been in the thick of many of the city's frequent labor disputes. Kheel was on a "personal crusade," according to a 1969 story in the *New York Times*, in which he described the Center as "socialism at its worst," pointing out that the Port Authority's ability to borrow money in the bond market, tax-free, competing with private interests at a time when the city was in financial trouble, was untenable.

But by then the buildings were going up at a rapid pace—the use of prefabricated sections of the exterior and a new "kangaroo crane" system developed in Australia sped up the process—and the war over the towers had moved from a question of whether or not they could exist to how the city could live with them.

CHAPTER 6
BLUEPRINTS IN THE SKY

Standing a quarter of a mile in the sky with a God's-eye view of the curvature of the earth can have a strange, mind-altering effect. For most, there's an instinctive reaction to recoil, a self-preservation impulse that pits the body against the brain. The primal self says, *I should not be here. The earth is too far below.*

The light is different, higher contrast. Real-life chiaroscuro. And sound is muted, still, almost absent. Except when the wind is kicking up a tremendous, otherworldly howl. And the city looks so small, innocent, like a child's train set, the Statue of Liberty a tchotchke in a tourist shop. Sixty-mile views that reach the Hudson Highlands up north, the Atlantic Ocean to the east and south, and, much closer, planes landing and taking off at three major airports.

These bracing impressions were coursing through the minds of Joe Baum's ad men—George Lois, Ron Holland, and James Callaway—as they ran on the 107th floor of the World Trade Center, their collective, giddy excitement propelling them, like schoolboys, forward through the raw construction space toward the far windows to get a closer look at the views. Most of the windows were coated with construction dust, workers' fingerprint smudges, and grease pencil markings, but there was one, off in the distance, that was clear.

When they reached it, Callaway nearly fell through, because, in fact, there was no window yet in place. It was just open space. Lois grabbed him by the arm, and Holland took hold of his belt, and all three men tumbled backward in a heap on the concrete floor.

Lying in construction dust, in a state of breathless exhilaration, they looked back toward the footsteps approaching them.

"What the fuck are you guys doing?" asked Baum with a rascally grin. "Stick with the dirty windows, Jim, if you want to be around for the opening."

The trip up the rickety construction elevator—just plywood nailed together, really—to a top floor of the North Tower of the World Trade Center, followed by a perilous ascent up a concrete staircase without railings, past the gaping holes where the building's elevators would go, was Baum showboating. But it was also his way to galvanize his team to envision the wonder of the restaurant that would be there. Baum would lay his blueprints out on the ground and envision the kitchen, the bar, and the restaurant's various spaces.

When the North Tower topped out on December 23, 1970, tenants began moving in, but the highest floors remained raw, open space for years to come. In the South Tower, which would host the observation deck on its roof, occupancy would begin in January 1972. And the official ribbon-cutting for both buildings wouldn't be until April 4, 1973.

Baum's mind-boggling task was to figure out how to feed a projected fifty thousand employees working in the building, in addition to their eighty thousand guests. Every day. But before he could spawn his big ideas, he needed two things: more information and a team.

Baum's modus operandi at Restaurant Associates, all of his success, was marked by a process in which he gathered the best and brightest; harangued them with ideas and directives and, alternatively, charm and abuse; and then micromanaged them to tears as they put his plans into effect.

"Joe needed good people to make tangible what he could just barely verbalize. And he had a belief that if he surrounded himself with the right kind of people, they wouldn't know what couldn't be done," Michael Whiteman says. "So they'd go ahead and do it." Whiteman was an out-of-work editor from the *Nation's Restaurant News* when Baum asked him to join his new consulting company, Joseph Baum Associates, Inc., which was then composed of only Harold Simpson, a crusty old former sailor and chef who had overseen purchasing at RA and had been looking forward to retirement before being hired by Baum. "Joe's brain trust was primarily people who were not necessarily fit for the job but tangentially so," Whiteman says.

Baum hired John Cini, a food services consultant based in Maryland, to work on the development of the World Trade Center kitchens, among other duties. Cini sent one of his number crunchers, Dennis Sweeney, to New York to work under Baum, joining Simpson, Whiteman, a secretary, and a Port Authority man who was in the office as a liaison.

The PA had given Baum a small, drab set of offices on the third floor in its headquarters at 111 Eighth Avenue, a squat monster of a building that was only eighteen floors tall but contained more square footage than the Empire State Building because it spanned the entire block. Baum's space was adorned with a blackboard and diagrams, sketches, and plans precariously pinned to the walls.

As the monolithic World Trade Center buildings rose in the sky, daily headlines covered different aspects of the project, whether it was a tugboat strike that slowed down delivery of parts or other construction snafus. Plus, a lot of press was given to how the complex might change the city, such as the expansion of Manhattan thanks to Guy Tozzoli's decision, which struck him one morning while shaving, to use 1.2 million cubic yards of excavated earth, rock, and other materials to create Battery Park City along the Hudson River.

There was also great interest in what Joe Baum was dreaming up. In 1970, he told the *New York Times* he was planning twenty restaurants in the WTC, mostly housed in the concourse, which was beneath its open plaza, as well as private cafeterias for the Port Authority, the United States Customs House, and New York State employees. He also said that the restaurants included a "luncheon club" on top of the North Tower, with exclusive access for its one thousand members during the day. At night, the restaurant would be open to the public, which could use the World Trade Center's two-thousand-car underground garage for free.

"This will not be a tourist trap," Baum said, perhaps a defensive impulse that the *Times* reporter ran with when he highlighted the irony that the creator of the Four Seasons was now setting up snack bars— which he very much was: about sixty of them and other small-food operations throughout the complex.

But Baum positioned his task as just as impressive as any of his previous grandiose projects. He emphasized the international flavor of the restaurant, which people would want to go to, he suggested, before heading uptown to the theater. As for feeding the masses, he was thinking big, conjuring carefully planned eating aeries that would form "vertical neighborhoods . . . little cities, each with a life of its own."

It was flowery language for a series of restaurants and food courts that had little culinary context. This was before food courts such as the Faneuil Hall Marketplace in Boston, which would open in 1976, existed. The closest comparisons were smaller eateries Baum had set up with Restaurant Associates in Montreal building complexes Place Bonaventure and Place Ville Marie, both of which had restaurants and shops.

What went unsaid in the *Times* was the name of the main restaurant, a subject that had become an obsession for Baum. He asked everyone he spoke with to weigh in. Hundreds of names were considered. Tozzoli even set up a contest within the Port Authority to come up with a winning name. Baum thought he had a good one. It was evocative, patriotic, American, and grand. "For Spacious Skies" was his front-runner. In honor of it, he began signing his letters with *For Gracious skies*.

In 1971, Baum commissioned Harris, Kerr, Forster, the accounting firm where he first got his start in New York City, to produce an analysis of the most efficient and cost-effective way to run food services at the WTC. It issued a report that championed a centralized system to take advantage of the economies of scale and mass production. It used terms, "major profit centers at key points of demand," "convertibility of selling space," "volume purchasing," and "bulk preparation," that provided the foundation for one of Baum's big ideas: that food services should be run by a single operator. He brought the concept to Guy Tozzoli, who liked the idea. A single company operating all of the WTC's food systems meant competing businesses wouldn't overwhelm the loading bays, elevators, and garbage disposal. Baum wanted to construct a central commissary for food delivery, processing, and storage in the basement.

Baum would have liked to be the one running this system, but, according to Whiteman, "Enough people at the Port Authority said,

'Number one, he doesn't have an organization. He's got three people. Two, he doesn't have financial backing. Three, he has no history running large projects. So you're going to have to put this out for an RFP (Request for Proposal).' Joe was in the difficult position of considering potential operators for a project that he wanted to run."

Of the innumerable challenges facing Joe Baum and his team, one of the most troubling was the size of the windows themselves. World Trade Center architect Minoru Yamasaki had developed an unprecedented design for the pair of 110-floor buildings that were to be the tallest in the world. Yamasaki created an inside-out structure: a framed tube made of relatively thin steel columns on the perimeter anchored by a central core that housed the elevators, stairwells, and forty-seven tapered steel columns.

Yamasaki designed the perimeter columns to be 18 3/4" wide, interspaced by windows that were 20" wide. From the outside, the windows virtually disappeared, giving the buildings a nearly seamless, silver appearance. From the inside, the narrow windows were less than ideal, blocking views and creating a shutter effect or the appearance of a large venetian blind. Yamasaki's windows were at least partly inspired by his own fear of heights. Near the roof, at the 108th and 109th floors, where the building's mechanical equipment was, Yamasaki had designed the columns to be wider, as a subtle flourish to top things off, but on 107, where the restaurant would be, the shutter was in full effect.

It wouldn't do. "We were building a view restaurant with a limited view," Tozzoli told *New York* magazine's Gael Greene. Tozzoli argued for widening the windows on the 107th floor, but Yamasaki wouldn't budge. The integrity of his design was at stake.

There is some gray area as to when Tozzoli had a final confrontation with Yamasaki, but the story goes that Baum played a part, telling the architect, "Look, Yama, all I'm asking for is a few inches. Who will ever see it 107 floors up in the air?" "I'll see it," the architect replied. "What do you mean," Baum asked, "you'll see it?" "When I die and go to heaven, I'll pass by and see those windows," Yamasaki said. Baum cracked, "What makes you think you're going in that direction, Yama?"

But Yamasaki wasn't joking when he threatened to quit over the prospect of disrupting his uniform design for better restaurant views. Tozzoli didn't believe he would, telling Austin Tobin, "There's no way the son of a bitch is going to quit."

The PA refused to back down. It was paying for the building, and it needed the restaurant to be a success. So Tozzoli ordered his architect to change the windows. And, to maintain symmetry, he'd have to do the same with the South Tower. Yamasaki conceded. He agreed to increase the width of the windows on the 107th floor. It was only by about half a foot, but it would make a world of difference to the human eye.

* * *

It was Guy Tozzoli's job to rein in Joe Baum to avoid accusations of Port Authority profligacy. In particular, criticism was building about how a private club was being constructed with public money. Politically, it didn't look good. To mitigate the bad impression, Baum needed good marketing. Instead of an amorphous, nameless eatery, Tozzoli and Baum needed an exciting restaurant with a name that would attract New Yorkers, deflect opponents, win over the media, and draw potential tenants. After Tozzoli's naming contest produced some two thousand possibilities, there were no sure winners. And "For Spacious Skies" had waned for Baum. But a jewel surfaced. It had come from the quarries in Puerto Rico, where Tozzoli and his team had been acquiring building materials. The stone guy who was showing Tozzoli the granite and marble took him to a restaurant where Caterina Valente was singing. The Italian entertainer did a melancholy version of "Windows of the World," first sung by Dionne Warwick and written by Burt Bacharach and Hal David. The quarry guy turned to Tozzoli and said, "*That* should be the name of the restaurant."

After changing "of" to "on," it was perfect. It was grand. It was inviting. Especially to tourists. And it was a literal description of the restaurant's greatest attraction. Windows on the World would function as an umbrella name for the group of eateries and bars on the 107th floor, most of which, other than the main restaurant, had unique names as well. There was the City Lights Bar, the Statue of Liberty Lounge, a smaller restaurant called Cellar in the Sky, a casual, small-plate restaurant—the Hors d'Oeuvrerie—and Hudson River Suites for private catering.

It was a great relief to Baum to have a name. It gave shape to his vision while he was mired in the details. For the main restaurant alone, he would need to hire dozens of companies to provide the different necessary elements. A partial list gives a sense of the exhausting enormity of the project:

Carpet, Brintons; Installation of carpet, Anchor Carpet & Linoleum; Special rug in West Parlor, Joy Wulke; Wood flooring, Bangkok Industries; Plastic laminate, walls and window mullions, Wilson Art; Gold ceramic tile in main dining room, Designers Tile International; Wall textiles, South Bay Design, Scalamandre, Jack Lenor Larsen, Central Shippee; Fabric on handrails, F. Schumacher; Upholstery fabrics, Jack Lenor Larsen, Scalamandre, Zographos, American Leather, Product Sales Associates, Gilford; Chairs, Stendig, Knoll, CI Design, Steelcase, Thonet; Tables, Chicago Hardware & Foundry, Vecta, ICF; Table tops, William Bloom and Sons; Millwork, Capitol Cabinet, William Bloom and Sons; Standard lighting fixtures, Solux, Lightolier, Halo; Special ornamental lighting fixtures, Louis Baldinger & Sons; Standard hardware, Corbin; Ornamental railings, J. W. Fiske Architectural Metals; Main buffet and wine racks, Craft Architectural Metals; Wine stands and coolers, Resco Hotel & Supply; Mirrors, Bell Glass & Mirror; Acoustical ceiling tile, U.S. Gypsum Acoustone; Installation of ceilings, Jacobson; Contractor for mirrored ceiling in bar, Metralite; Fabrication and installation of mirrored ceiling in bar, James Catalano & Sons; Gold leaf decoration on doors, Spanjer Metal Signs; Glassware, highball, juice, brandy, Cardinal International; Glassware, water, wine, Louie Glass; Glassware, champagne, Schott Zwiesel; Glassware, wine, Seneca; Crystal, Lenox Crystal; Silverware, Reed and Barton; Flatware, Sambonet; Linens, James G. Hardy; General contractor, Dember Construction; Kitchen Equipment, Heifetz Metal Crafts; Contract supplier for furniture, Desks, Inc.

While those elements were in their earliest stages of procurement or production, Baum was also overseeing the essential task of creating a kitchen 109 floors below, on the B2 level of the World Trade Center, to streamline food production through an efficient system that took advantage of economies of scale. There were to be twenty or more different food services operations. On the 107th floor were the five restaurants and bars, plus catering, that fell under the Windows on the World rubric. On the 44th floor would be a high-end cafeteria. In the concourse, there would be Market Square, which would include a full restaurant called Market Dining Rooms & Bar as well as a coffee shop called the Corner, and then the Big Kitchen, which itself contained a variety of stations; one of the nation's first food courts would house the Rotisserie, the Grill, the Seafood Market, Nature's Pantry, the Bakery, the Deli, the Fountain Café, and the Coffee Exchange. And there was also the Observation Deck Snack Bar in the South Tower.

Baum wanted all of these eateries to share a central commissary, called Central Services, on the B2 receiving dock off Barclay Street. Most restaurants have a porter who works an early shift and opens the door, receiving the sunrise deliveries. At the World Trade Center, Central Services would be a vast receiving and processing station for everything bought in bulk. There would be a cold kitchen where produce would get washed, peeled, and chopped and dressings mixed. Meats and fish would be cleaned and cut to size. There would also be a hot kitchen where, on one side, stocks, sauces, and stews were made, and, on the other, a bakery baked all the breads and most of the desserts.

Windows on the World would do a greater share of its preparation work in its own kitchen, but the rule for the restaurants and food stations below the 107th floor was to have Central Services, which covered twenty-seven thousand square feet, provide almost all the initial preparation of raw materials. For instance, cabbage would be sliced and slaw dressing mixed, and then the food services employees in the separate sites could mix the two together.

"The only difference between us and a high-school cafeteria is care," Baum said to a journalist of his future food Shangri-La.

CHAPTER 7
CHAOS AND CONTROL

In 1972, construction had progressed and equipment had been installed in Central Services, making it operational, in time for the opening of the World Trade Center's first food services operation, Eat & Drink. It wasn't part of the original plan, but Guy Tozzoli realized that he had a building with thousands of moving-in tenants—predominantly New York State and Port Authority workers—as well as construction workers still on site for the months, even years, of final construction.

Tozzoli told Baum he didn't want anything fancy. It would be a temporary establishment until Baum's twenty-plus eateries could be built. The location was in a vast section of the Grand Concourse below ground level. Baum's theme was a cafeteria-style eatery that embraced its construction-site surroundings with a wink and a nudge. He used construction scrap as the primary decorating theme; plywood, sheet metal, and drywall were already on site. The servers wore white aprons and hard hats. They called the bar the Loading Zone.

As lowbrow as it was, Baum still wanted everything to be just right. This was their first foot forward, and he wanted to impress the Port Authority. Three weeks before opening in September 1972, as signs were being painted and corned beef portions tested, Baum went to Dennis Sweeney with a special order for the opening party. "Get me some penguins for the refrigerator case," Baum said.

Along the wall were the air screen refrigerators, the shelved cooling cases from which customers could grab a yogurt, fruit cup, or drink and go. Baum wanted to put the live birds in them for the opening; a few of the flightless birds milling about in the refrigerated cases would be a nice touch, he thought. Sweeney, being the good Boy Scout that he was, went to the Bronx and Central Park zoos, but they weren't willing to loan out their penguins. He turned to his alma mater, Cornell University, and asked the veterinary school for help. No luck.

Sweeney just couldn't come up with the birds. He sheepishly approached Baum and tried to diminish his failure. "Joe, I don't think penguins are a good idea," he said. "Anyway, they will be the only ones there in black tie and tails." Baum settled for a painted penguin and snowman on the back wall of the refrigerated cases.

Eat & Drink was a success. Office workers swarmed there for lunch, sending Baum into fits when lines for the cashiers got too long. At night, the Loading Zone drew a mix of construction workers and janitorial and maintenance staff who would drink until fights broke out. "It was nice during the day," says Michael Whiteman. "And like *Star Wars* at night." He hired a man to quell the nighttime brouhahas, but the bouncer became a target for guests, so Whiteman—thin, reserved, and not unlike cerebral actor Christopher Walken—took the role of enforcer and ended up in the hospital with stitches for a busted lip.

Whiteman was spending considerable time at the World Trade Center while Baum was at 111 Eighth Avenue consolidating a team of intensely motivated, hardworking consultants and professionals from various walks of life that would later call itself "the Baum Squad." Many of them were Cornell grads or from Baum's Restaurant Associates years. Roger Martin, first his assistant and then his PR man through the 1960s, was back with Baum after having opened, and closed, his own restaurant. Milton Glaser, who had designed the psychedelic poster for the *Bob Dylan's Greatest Hits* record in 1966 and founded *New York* magazine with editor Clay Felker in 1968, was a Baum favorite. Glaser was working on a variety of Windows design elements, including the logo and a look for the Big Kitchen, which was going to be in the Grand Concourse, below ground level.

In Baum's constellation of consultants, few were more important than his culinary experts, who worked alongside or sometimes above his executive chefs to help him come up with the menus and food themes that provided the raison d'être for his restaurants. The most important of these advisors was James Beard, the author of *Complete*

Cookbook for Entertaining, James Beard's American Cookery, and *Beard on Bread,* among more than a dozen other cookbooks.

Baum didn't yet have a clear idea of what kind of food he wanted to serve at Windows on the World. Something European, maybe global cuisine, but what did that mean? He needed people like Beard to help him refine a concept.

* * *

By the 1970s, James Beard was an icon. His cooking classes, which he taught across the country, were the ultimate rite of passage for any self-styled gourmand.

A man of great girth—he was over six-foot-three and weighed close to three hundred pounds most of his adult life—Beard was also a social butterfly. Like Baum, he was raised in the hospitality industry. An only child born in 1903, Beard was a self-professed "mama's boy" who lived under the sway of his opinionated mother. She had a passion for entertaining and owned a hotel and catering business in Portland, Oregon, where she reigned over many social circles. Young Beard started out as a big boy, and he wielded his appetite as a skill set. His mother's business partner, a Chinese immigrant named Jue-Let, taught him to identify and recall particular tastes, an aptitude that he would use to great effect through decades of dining and writing about dining.

Beard was kicked out of Reed College for improper sexual liaisons—he was unusually open about being gay—and his doting mother sent him to Europe, where he feasted on French food. Beard wanted to be an actor or an opera singer but never found success on the stage. After moving to New York City, he spun his greatest passions—food, drink, and conviviality—into a solution for his inability to make ends meets: He bartered his cooking services for supper and invitations to the theater. He called himself "a gastronomic gigolo."

Beard was appalled by the uninspired hors d'oeuvres served at the parties he frequented. To him, the food was an essential, entertaining element of a gathering. He started a catering company and published his first book, *Hors d'Oeuvre and Canapés,* in 1940. He wrote for magazines, including *Gourmet* and *Bon Appétit.* In 1945, he was one of the first chefs to appear on nascent network television, in a segment called "I Love to Eat" on the show *Elsie Presents.*

He continued to write books, which weren't lucrative enough to sustain him. So, with a guy's-got-to-eat, irreverent panache, he began a lifelong career as an unabashed pitchman for a string of products, including Planters Peanuts, Ceresota unbleached flour, Corning kitchenware, Cuisinart, Camp maple syrup, Cannon Mills, Irish Mist Liqueur, Shasta sodas, and French's mustard. It wasn't a total leap for Beard to be peddling pop and peanut butter. He had always appreciated basic American cooking as well as the most sophisticated French dishes. He loved a simple sandwich made of mayonnaise, onion, salt, and parsley between two slices of white bread. He adored casseroles and hashes. He looked for the "homely quality" in foods from both sides of the Atlantic.

For Beard, good food started in the markets. He could recall the abundance afforded by Portland's grand marketplace, where his mother would pick out the best apples or seafood. He could wax rhapsodic for a razor clam. Given the right amount of fresh tarragon, he once quipped, he might consider cannibalism.

In 1954, Baum hired Beard, who was a fan of the Newarker, to consult for Restaurant Associates to develop rum- and wine-based drinks. But it wasn't until years later that they would achieve greatness together, in 1959, with the Four Seasons. Beard was a vital sounding board during the development of the menu. Beard also helped Baum with menus for Charley O's and Charlie Brown's and became a fixture at the Four Seasons, where he would simply sign the check without paying, knowing Baum would cover him.

Beard admitted to having tantrums, and he could be a "shit," according to Baum, if you asked him the wrong question. He simply wouldn't answer, or you'd get a couple of terse words. But if you pushed the right button, he would release an erudite, poetic stream of culinary consciousness.

And Baum was listening. So when Beard suggested in 1973 that Baum meet Barbara Kafka, a food writer who had helped him edit his kitchen appliance book, *The Cooks' Catalogue*, Baum did.

Kafka was a sharp straight talker. She was a native New Yorker, a gifted only child whose mother, a lawyer, wasn't very skilled in the culinary arts but hired a live-in maid who was a fabulous cook. The family went out to restaurants, mostly French, on Manhattan's Upper East Side and in Greenwich Village. Her father, who was a glass and china purchaser for the Gimbels department store, let her taste wine when she was ten. Going out to eat was a solace for Kafka, because her parents would often argue at home.

She pursued a career in publishing. But her refined palate, encyclopedic taste memory, and iron will helped her gain traction as a food writer for magazines, including as a restaurant reviewer for *Playbill*. In 1972, Kafka was brought by Burt Wolf, who was overseeing *The Cooks' Catalogue,* to meet Beard at his home on Twelfth Street. The two immediately clashed over pâté. Kafka insisted she could use kidney fat for pâté, but Beard was appalled. He said it would break apart. She said that deft use of wax paper would preserve its consistency. He shouted, "I can't work with this woman!" But he was impressed. Beard asked Kafka to teach classes with him in California.

When she left the *Cooks' Catalogue* project, Beard sent her over to Baum, who tapped her to consult on the purchasing of china, glassware, and silver—just what her father did when she was a child—for Windows on the World.

Kafka shared with Baum a wealth of food and wine knowledge. But where Baum could be vague and allusive when imparting his wisdom, Kafka was direct and concise, sometimes to a caustic fault. When a French sous chef saw her carrying a platter through the kitchen, he said, "*Ma chère,* let me carry that for you." She gave him a withering look and said, "Get the fuck out of my way. I can carry it myself."

When Baum and Kafka were together in a tasting session, she might appear to be the one in charge, because she'd directly ask for ingredient changes or a different preparation method, while Baum would drop hints or shake his head and push the dish away.

Baum's staff had to navigate his propensity for oblique comments, subtle teasing, and carelessness. He would often leave his coat, umbrella, or pipe at a restaurant, forcing Dennis Sweeney or someone else to return to retrieve it. Intentional or not, there was power at play. Michael Whiteman recalls a meeting when he was certain Baum knew he was leaving his glasses on a table. But Whiteman refused to remind him. Or go back to get them.

Meetings that would extend to lunch or dinner at restaurants near 111 Eighth Avenue—Coach House and Trattoria da Alfredo were favorites—were opportunities for more mischief. Baum sometimes tested waiters by ordering a steak. "I'll have the steak," he'd say, without looking at the waiter, who was forced to ask for clarification. Everyone at the table knew that there was a rib eye, a T-bone, and a strip on the menu. But Baum wanted to see how the waiter would handle himself.

Back in the office, with blueprints taped to the walls, mental games continued, and tempers flared. Early in his tenure with Baum, Sweeney said something during a meeting that rubbed Baum the wrong way. In the middle of writing on the blackboard, Baum turned to him, called him a "schmuck," and said, "That's a stupid idea." He then threw the chalk, which beaned Sweeney squarely in the head.

Stunned and embarrassed, Sweeney stood up, walked out of the room and went to his desk, grabbed his coat, and left the office. He didn't come to work the next day. Or the next. Baum called John Cini and asked, "Where's Dennis?"

"You hit him on the head with a piece of chalk," Cini said. "He thinks he's fired."

"What kind of schmuck is he?" Baum asked. Sweeney returned to work the next day. He was happy to be back.

But Sweeney was the exception. Baum would regularly fire people on the spot. He discarded them the way he flicked the ashes off a cigarette. For the ones who weathered the initial tumult, there was an exhilaration about working for him. The rancor he invoked was part of an intensity that fueled the team. "It was good-natured friction," Whiteman says. "And, you know, sparks come from friction."

Baum's passions ran hot and cold. "Joe had these important sides to him. The Apollonian and Dionysian," says his younger son, Edward, recalling raucous food fights that his father would instigate. Baum would sometimes randomly toss hard-boiled eggs around the Market Dining Rooms & Bar. One of Baum's favorite weapons was Albert Stockli's celebrated Black Forest cake, which he'd sometimes toss at family members and friends. Baum's kids looked forward to the "fabulous insanity," according to older son Charles.

"This was a guy who wore starched shirts and French cuff links," Edward says. "There was this chaos as well as this belief in a rigid, beautiful form. He enjoyed the unscripted spontaneity of using food, this object that we all appreciated as part of fine dining, but it also could be used for riotous family fun."

Baum could also be unsparingly generous. You could see in his smile and the glint in his eye the pleasure he felt at giving other people pleasure. If a staffer mentioned a particularly loved dish, Baum might surprise him or her by having it specially prepared for the staffer's birthday. He'd pay for meals or defray costs for a wedding. Baum's commitment to hospitality wasn't a nine-to-five endeavor; it was how he lived. He would host all-day work sessions at his weekend house in North Salem, Westchester, about an hour north of the city. He and his staff would sit in the backyard, where Baum's wife, Ruth, would serve Bloody Marys and even bloodier steaks.

* * *

As occupants set up their offices on the lower floors of the North Tower of the World Trade Center, Baum was hiring more specialists to consult for his team, which was entering a routine of planning meetings at 111 Eighth Avenue. They also made frequent visits, donning hard hats, to the WTC site. Dennis Sweeney would drag the enormous, heavy cable reels—the sort that look like oversized sewing-thread spools—around the 107th floor. Baum and his associates took turns standing on the reels to gauge sight lines for the restaurant, something he'd been thinking about since taking a helicopter to the same airspace to assess the views soon after getting the job. They decided, at a certain height, if you moved farther away from the windows, you were actually able to have a better, unobstructed view. It encouraged the restaurant's architect, Warren Platner, to design a multitiered restaurant in which, they hoped, there wouldn't be a bad seat in the house.

The layout was emerging. Banquet rooms would go on the west side of the building, because the views were less important; the restaurant would face uptown, toward the north and east, and the bar would look south, toward the Statue of Liberty.

The entire floor was dedicated to the restaurant, a vast acre of space, more than forty thousand square feet, with minimal columns or major structures, other than the elevator banks, hindering the flow. The initial, basic design concepts were focused on taking advantage of the views. The first priority was to put dining areas along the perimeter. Service areas (kitchens, storage, bathrooms) would be toward the interior, as were private club amenities, such as a reading library and a small spa. The second was to terrace the seating areas in the main restaurant, so that the farther you were away from the windows, the higher up you'd be. The third was to position the largest dining areas in the corners so that diners would have two views.

Platner had been working on the plan since 1968, thanks, at least partly, to Joe Baum. A decade earlier, Baum had been so impressed by Platner's work on RA's Le Monde restaurant at Kennedy airport that he had recommended him to Guy Tozzoli before he himself had been hired as a consultant. Minoru Yamasaki also knew Platner: The two men were friends since working together at architecture firm Raymond Loewy Associates after the war.

Tozzoli had hired Platner, giving him only one specific directive for the design of the restaurant: that it include a fireplace, an indication of the warmth, comfort, and opulence that the PA was hoping for.

(Although it was included in early designs, the fireplace was eventually dropped.)

Baum and Sweeney made weekly Friday trips to Platner's offices in New Haven, Connecticut, riding in Baum's BMW, which he drove so fast that Sweeney joked he should have additional life insurance. (When arms dealer and billionaire Adnan Khashoggi found out Baum also owned a German car, he said, "I thought Jews didn't like German cars," to which Baum quickly replied, "I treat it very badly.") With Platner, they would discuss the minutiae of the design. The architect had created a massive model of the restaurant at one-eighth scale so that Baum could literally walk through a theme-park version of what he was envisioning.

In addition to the model, Platner used even more tactile visual guides. One afternoon, the team was discussing a small-dish, tapas-style serving area inspired by Spanish restaurants. Baum couldn't quite understand Platner's design concept for a multilevel serving station manned by chefs. So, in the middle of the meeting, Platner told everyone to put on their coats. They complied, and Platner marched them out of his office, across a field, and into a nearby forest. "We all thought Warren had lost it," recalls Sweeney. When they reached a tree, Platner pointed out the polypores, or bracket fungi, growing on a trunk, nature's manifestation of multiple levels—and the origination of his design. "How the hell am I going to create an efficient working open kitchen based on a shelf fungus?" one of Baum's team groused.

On Mondays and Wednesdays, Baum would weave between phone calls and meetings at 111 Eighth Avenue, hosting John Cini and one of his team, Bill Eaton, who flew up from Maryland each week. Cini and Eaton would present their ideas and designs with different engineers, architects, designers, and contractors. The meetings would begin around 10:30 A.M. and last four or five hours, thanks to Baum's propensity to talk endlessly, streaming from one thought to the next. Eight or ten men would crowd into Baum's office, and he'd fill the room with ideas, questions, and a constant flow of smoke.

Michael Whiteman was Baum's rudder. He would try to keep Baum focused. They could spend two months deciding where to put the fryer in relation to the grill or the precise dimensions of a long-stemmed cocktail glass. Sweeney wrote everything down while Baum circled the room and drew his chicken scratch on the blackboard on the wall. With Cini suggesting certain types of machinery, refrigeration, and stoves, Baum would make snap decisions, so Sweeney's minutes were invaluable.

Then Cini and Eaton would fly back to the Dulles airport on the Eastern Airlines shuttle on Mo. 1ay night, combing over the minutes and discussing what Baum had said, and the next day they would draw sketches and plans, as instructed. And then they would return on Wednesday to present what they thought he wanted, to be subjected to more fine-tuning and direction. The routine went on for four years.

The enormity of the project was a good fit for an obsessive like Baum, who asked that those who worked with him be willing to work similar hours, whether it was attending a meeting that went into the morning hours or over weekends. "It took 100 percent of your brain," Whiteman recalls. "You never turned off."

Cini was indebted to Baum from the beginning, because he had suggested a lump-sum consulting fee of one hundred thousand dollars or so—what he considered to be an adequate, if sizable, fee for four years' work. But Baum told him, "You'd better do this on an hourly basis, I have a feeling it's going to consume a lot of hours." Baum was right: Cini's company ultimately made $1.2 million over the four years.

It wasn't Baum's money, after all. The Port Authority was paying his and Cini's contracts. Baum's role was to consult for the Port Authority on how to approach food services in the World Trade Center and to help the agency hire an outside company to finance and operate that plan. And although Tozzoli and Baum were working well together, the single-operator concept was facing a major obstacle: potential companies were not willing to pony up the costs. Baum and Sweeney met with about a half dozen outfits, including the restaurant operating chain Ancorp National Services and Stouffer's Restaurant and Inn Corporation, which ran more than a dozen "Tops" restaurants, including Top of the Hub (Boston), Top of the Sixes (New York), Top of the Rock (Chicago), Top of the Rockies (Denver), and so on. Sweeney went to each meeting toting a suitcase that would open, fold out, and reveal a miniature model of the World Trade Center. It provided the visuals while Baum sold his vision. But no company was willing to jump. The costs were too prohibitive.

Tozzoli had no choice but to have the Port Authority fund most if not all of the food services operation and hire a company to execute its plan. "I hadn't planned to spend a dime building the club," Tozzoli told *New York* magazine. But the PA was forced to budget more than twenty million dollars to create food services in the WTC, with seven million dollars dedicated to the main restaurant at the top of the North Tower.

Even though it was spending its own money, the PA still needed an operator. Baum turned to his old Cornell friend Curt Strand, who had recently been appointed president of Hilton International, a separate entity from domestic Hilton. Company founder Conrad Hilton had sold all of the hotel chain's overseas properties to Trans World Airlines, which was prohibited from functioning using the Hilton name in the United States.

"Joe said to me, out of the blue, 'You should operate this,'" Strand recalls. "I thought he was kidding me. I said, 'Joe, you know we don't operate in the U.S. We don't have anyone here to do that.'" Strand turned him down.

But Baum called him again. And again, until Baum finally got Strand to meet with Guy Tozzoli, who said to a puzzled Strand, "Let's work out a deal."

In March 1972, Baum received another report from Harris, Kerr, Forster, this one a detailed study about restaurant costs and contract terms, which he delivered to the Port Authority. He also gave Strand the report and asked him to look it over. Such a high-profile development was tempting, as was the prospect of working with his old pal Joe Baum, whom he admired. They agreed to make it happen and that Baum would fox-trot from being the Port Authority's consultant to the president of Strand's operating company.

But not everyone at the Port Authority was as comfortable as Tozzoli was with this cozy relationship. At least one of the PA's board commissioners—the board members were appointed by the New York and New Jersey governors—insisted that the Harris, Kerr, Forster report be presented to other potential bidders, which it was. Nonetheless, in January 1973, the Port Authority commissioning body voted to accept the bid from the newly formed company Inhilco, run by Strand.

The PA was on the hook for about $24 million to build all the food services in the World Trade Center, with approximately a third of that earmarked for the 107th floor. The total came to $26 million, with $7.5 million dollars budgeted on Windows.

The Port Authority would pay ninety-three percent, and Inhilco would pay seven percent. All expenditures would be split in that manner for the three-year "pre-operating" period. And then profits were to be split 85 percent for the Port Authority and 15 percent for Inhilco. And if there were losses during the first three years, Inhilco would be off the hook.

These were, in the words of later state investigators, "unusually generous terms" on the part of the Port Authority, to the benefit of Inhilco and Baum, who would retain his one hundred twenty-five thousand dollar contract as well as a 20 percent share of Inhilco's operating profit. By comparison, Austin Tobin, who had recently retired as the executive director of the Port Authority in 1972, was said to have been the second-highest-paid public official in the country, after the president of the United States, with a salary of seventy thousand dollars.

" 'Windows is the most important thing in this complex. I don't care if the place is burning down. If Windows has a problem, you fix it first,' " Bob DiChiara, then the top electrical operations supervisor for the building, recalls Tozzoli saying. "That was Guy's mantra. Windows had to be successful. If it failed, he failed."

So the terms were fine by Tozzoli, who wanted a man he could trust and a marquee name, no less, for what he hoped would be a major city attraction. The food services, and most notably, the top-floor restaurant, were essential amenities in a building complex with more than ten million square feet of office space to fill. Next to offering the thrill of the new and the big and a seventy-foot-high cathedral-like lobby, the restaurant was Tozzoli's favorite way to pitch his towers to potential residents.

Unfortunately, Tozzoli was struggling to get businesses interested, despite offering deeply discounted rents. He was partly handicapped by the restriction that tenants had to be involved in foreign trade due to the World Trade Center's stated purpose that it had been constructed for global commercial exchange. That's why he rejected accounting firm Lybrand, Ross Bros. & Montgomery's offer to rent three hundred thousand square feet. But that doesn't entirely explain why he was having such a hard time. The World Trade Center, a highly criticized, unproven swath of real estate, was simply not attractive to most private companies.

Aware of this potentiality, before the Port Authority had even broken ground, Nelson Rockefeller had committed to consolidate New York State government offices in the World Trade Center so that they could take up 2.3 million square feet in the South Tower. And the Port Authority and U.S. Customs Service took up another 2.2 million square feet. But other tenants were so scarce that the buildings were struggling to get past 50 percent capacity by the official opening in 1973.

Without occupants, the World Trade Center would be a sham. When a private real estate developer builds a building that doesn't attract tenants, the developer and investors take the hit. But if the Port Authority were to commit a similar blunder, it would be the public's loss and suggest an unprecedented misuse of government authority and resources.

CHAPTER 8
RUNNING ON FUMES

From the first day of construction of the World Trade Center in 1968 through its opening in 1973, the city around it had been reeling. Its dysfunction was piling up on the sidewalks. In 1968, teachers' strikes had left more than a million children at home for thirty-six days. That same year, a sanitation strike dumped a hundred thousand tons of trash on the streets of the city, creating walls of filth that prompted the Department of Health to proclaim the city's first public health emergency since the polio epidemic of 1931.

In 1973, the West Side Highway collapsed under the weight of a dump truck—on its way to repair other broken roads—near Greenwich Village. The murder rate had doubled in a decade, and in the 1974 school year, there were 6,817 reported acts of crime or violence in schools, a 64 percent rise from the previous year; they included hundreds of incidents in which teachers were assaulted by students. It was estimated that, each day, two hundred thousand pounds of dog feces were deposited on the streets, parks, and playgrounds of the city. The once-proud Bronx was being compared to Dresden after the World War II bombings, because it was riddled with rubble, abandoned lots, and fires set by miscreants or by landlords looking for an insurance payout.

The threat of getting mugged was a part of daily life. Kids were sent out with "mugging money," enough to appease his or her daily assailants. The poor souls forced to take the subway would pass the time scouting for pickpockets and gold-chain grabbers. In 1974, excess subway cars were closed off at night so that passengers would huddle together, making them less easy prey. Even John F. Kennedy Jr. was mugged in Central Park that year, robbed of his bicycle and tennis racket.

Just one of the countless tales of New Yorkers surviving their city: Charles Baum, then a student at NYU film school, went out one night and left his friend Ira, whom he used to tease because he lived on such a seedy, dangerous block, near the Astor Place subway station after midnight. A guy came up on Baum with his hands in his pockets, suggesting he had a gun. The guy told Baum, "I want everything in your pockets." Baum gave him the twenty or thirty bucks he had and ran to his apartment on Waverly, where he called to tell Ira, who just laughed and laughed. Dark humor was a common response to the city's situation.

Grim sights abounded, from winos to the skeletons of abandoned cars. In 1970, the city had towed 72,961 vehicles in various stages of neglect. Tires gone, glass shattered, the battery, stereo, and engine were usually excised first. Then came the wiring and lights. At least there was a side benefit: Kids without functioning playgrounds could play on the car carcasses on their street.

By 1974, New Yorkers were accustomed to the daily deluge of bad news befalling the city. One week, the cops would be in a shoot-out with a nut who'd hijacked a helicopter to the top of the Pan Am Building; another, the same cops would be dragged through the muck during the Knapp Commission's investigation into New York Police Department corruption. So, for many, it was just another headline when a twenty-four-floor office building near the United Nations exploded on the morning of April 22, raining glass, bricks, and mortar on Forty-Fifth Street.

It was a "miracle," according to Fire Commissioner John O'Hagan, that no one was killed, although dozens were injured, some critically. After the cleanup, what concerned most of the city—and, in particular, the Port Authority—was the report that a gas leak was the source of the explosion. A water-pressure system in the basement was the likely cause of the gas pipe rupturing, and then an electrical switch ignited the explosion.

PA engineers were ordered to reexamine the dangers of the gas pipe system running more than a thousand feet up to light the stoves and ovens in the kitchens on the 107th floor. It's wasn't as if the potential danger hadn't been considered before, but the Forty-Fifth Street explosion spooked the PA.

The agency broached the subject of using electric instead of gas for cooking with Baum, who laughed it off. Just two days after the explosion, on April 24, the Port Authority and Inhilco had finally signed the contract for the operation of all food services in the World Trade Center. It was a fifteen-year contract with a ten-year optional extension. And Baum was given the title of president of Inhilco, with a three-year deal to manage Windows on the World. He was catapulting ahead, but now the PA was suggesting hamstringing his kitchen with all-electric appliances.

Professional kitchens didn't run on electric. It was unheard of. Gas flames are versatile and immediate. So much of cooking is the relationship between heat and timing, and gas provides direct and subtle control. Electric doesn't respond quickly, and a few seconds of too much heat can be the difference between medium and medium-well-done. There's also a particular char on a steak or pepper that only flames can achieve.

But a sense of dread was infecting the caution-prone PA. And the truth was, "Electric does work. It's an engineering principle," says Bill Eaton, who was working with John Cini supplying the kitchen equipment for Baum. "You can cook on electric."

Tozzoli pushed Baum to review his alternatives. Baum suggested using propane gas in tanks that could be kept in closets upstairs. No, the PA replied—it was still too dangerous.

Everyone knew that running a gas line a quarter of a mile into the sky was unprecedented and that you had to consider how much the building moved back and forth. By design, the building had to have elasticity, just enough to absorb the wind but not too much to disturb people on the higher floors. But, boy, did the towers sway: four to eight feet. There was no real-world precedent to how an extremely long gas pipe would respond. "It could have been a disaster if there was gas," Michael Whiteman concedes. "The building deflected so much more on windy days. We couldn't run the express elevators on windy days because it sounded like the number 2 train coming into Cortland Street, screeching on the rails."

A compromise was suggested: How about adding a charcoal pit? That, the PA would consider. If the stoves and ovens ran on electric, a finishing char and other flame-necessary dishes, such as steaks, chops, and some fish, could be cooked on a giant charcoal grill, which would vent out of the roof.

It was a logical resolution. Baum was planning to do a share of his signature, flaming, table-side service in the front of the house anyway. But it took more than just that to convince the normally intractable Baum, who could generally gnaw problems into submission. It just so happened that despite the nearly uniform use of gas in the restaurant industry, James Beard had a history of working with electric appliances because he'd been selling their wares for years. *I can honestly say that the Corning Gourmet Range not only meets my demands, it surpasses them,* read the copy of one 1973 advertisement, with an aproned Beard standing proudly beside the electric stove top he used in his cooking school. If it was good enough for Beard, it surely could be good enough for Baum.

And, anyway, there's a code in the restaurant business: Just get it done. Professional kitchens are like war zones. Bursts of potentially fatal heat, intense, necessary acts of execution, barked orders, reliance on the guy next to you, and the overwhelming pressure to get the plate to the pass in time—it all feels like nothing less than a struggle to survive. And as much as there's a hierarchical necessity to appease the boss, there is also an ethos, a pride, in getting the work done. Do what you must, or you might as well pack your knives and go home.

Joe Baum took great pride in rolling up his sleeves and making things work. If that meant cooking on goddamn electric, then so be it. He agreed to make the switch, as long as he got to have a charcoal grill.

CHAPTER 9
THE CITY ON A WIRE

On August 7, 1974, the 107th-floor restaurants were under construction, when Joe Baum met his impish match, a man who shared his passion for showmanship and his infatuation with New York City: Philippe Petit. The twenty-four-year-old Frenchman, who had been planning his assault on the World Trade Center for years with a team of accomplices, snuck his way onto a freight elevator to the 110th floor. In the night, they used a bow and arrow to shoot a fishing line, which was connected to a steel cable, from one tower to the next. On the hazy, humid following morning, he walked back and forth eight times on the wire, as a crowd of onlookers gawked from far below. Petit sat on the wire a couple of times and playfully taunted the stunned, stammering cops for forty-five minutes.

Petit finally stepped off the wire on the South Tower, into the arms of the police, who asked him why he'd done it. Petit said, "There is no 'Why'!"

Baum saw it all. He had arrived with Ron Holland at the towers that morning, and upon seeing Petit's aerial ballet from the street, he rushed to the 107th floor to watch from the restaurant. He was dazzled, along with everyone else.

The Port Authority certainly wouldn't sanction the act, but Guy Tozzoli picked up on the sense of wonder that Petit's act had inspired in New Yorkers and people around the world. It was apparent when the delighted cops arrested him. The charges of trespassing were dropped when Petit agreed to do a free performance for children in Central Park. Tozzoli also gave Petit a permanent, complimentary pass to the yet-to-be-opened World Trade Center observation deck on top of the South Tower. Petit would also become a frequent guest at Windows on the World.

Petit's walk marked the beginning of a softening of hearts toward the towers. For what seemed like the first time, the foreboding buildings were a source of joy for a city in dire need of a lift. Everywhere else that New Yorkers looked, there was a rising tide of crime, filth, and poverty that the city's government seemed incapable of stemming. A spate of abandoned buildings and lots hosted a proliferation of rats, garbage, and spindly junkyard trees that became the common flora. Deteriorating housing conditions provided rationale for the city's urban planners to champion possibly less hazardous but institutional, inhospitable housing projects.

Sex shops crowded Times Square. Three-card monte games played out for suckers. Hustlers hung out on street corners. Prostitutes wearing too-short shorts stood in doorways under signs for girls, girls, girls. And it wasn't just on the seedy side of Forty-Second Street; unregulated sex shops dotted neighborhoods throughout the city. It was a city of smut.

The next year started with a terrorist bombing, on January 24, of Manhattan's historic Fraunces Tavern by the Puerto Rican nationalist group Armed Forces of Puerto Rican National Liberation. An explosive device was detonated in the entryway of an annex where club members were eating lunch. Four people were killed and dozens more injured.

The violent attack exemplified the city's troubles, which had reached a palpable nadir after three decades of shortsighted, postwar governance. The wealthiest, most promising city in the world had been maintaining itself on a diet of borrowing and leveraging itself to cover shortfalls. But the consistent loss of jobs in manufacturing meant that the stakes were increasing as its total tax roll decreased. The city's once-reliable foundation of union-organized labor and municipal services had become unsustainable. Short-term debt had grown from virtually zero in 1970 to about six billion dollars in 1975. Bank managers shut down the city's ability to raise money through issuing bonds, putting it on the precipice of bankruptcy. Mayor Abe Beame and Governor Hugh Carey traveled to Washington, D.C., hats in hand, to meet with President Gerald Ford in May 1975 to discuss the city's inability to pay its debts. But the president said the federal government couldn't help.

Mayor Beame, a former accountant and Democratic-machine veteran who won office in 1973 with the slogan "He knows the buck," had been slow to react to the city's fiscal turmoil, even though he had campaigned on being the right man to fix it. He appeared to be a turtle in its shell as Governor Carey intervened with the creation of the state-monitored Municipal Assistance Corporation (MAC), which would allow it to issue bonds backed by sales taxes, securing aid from state funds and setting up an Emergency Financial Control Board to manage the city's budget.

* * *

As Beame struggled to find a way out of the crisis, Joe Baum was getting what he needed most from his friend James Beard—a culinary vision for the 107th floor. As tyrannical as Baum could be, he was always solic-iting the advice of those in his inner circle. Beard, who most embodied Baum's belief in the symbiotic relationship between giving and enjoy-ing pleasure, came closest to being his muse.

"Beard was the biggest influence on Joe's life, in terms of his atti-tude toward food preparation and cooking," Michael Whiteman says.

Beard's specific advice on the food at the World Trade Center had been largely impressionistic until he and Baum talked on the phone on May 5, 1975, when Beard was living in San Francisco. After talking in the morning about the Grill that was next to the main restaurant on the 107th floor, and which became the Hors d'Oeuvrerie at night, Beard finally began to "click" on what he thought the food should be. That same day, he dictated a letter to his assistant. It is a gourmand's manifesto that might as well have been nailed to the doors of the World Trade Center. Baum not only used it to inform the food that he would serve, but he also internalized its sentiment and philosophy—phrases in the letter would later fall from his lips as if his own.

The letter is more than five thousand typed words of Beard's elo-quence, droll discrimination, vast knowledge, and purple passion. Throughout, there are notes, circles, and underlining, no doubt by Baum.

"If we're going to climb 107 floors, let's tickle the senses from top to bottom," Beard writes. "The whole thing must have an overall sensual quality that awakens the sensual feeling in the eyes, the nose, and the taste buds and which gives one almost an orgasmic delight in looking at the table and sheer sexual or sensual thrill, whichever you want, as to taste. This is something that has been missing in restaurants in this town much too long, and this is what we need. If we're going to have people enjoy, they've [got] to roll in it and love it, and this is true of every course that comes along."

Beard opens the letter by writing about a meal he recently had at the San Francisco home of Chuck Williams, the Williams-Sonoma founder. "The most perfect Irish stew I have ever eaten in my life. I could go on eating it for a thousand years. It was so simple, so pure, so good."

He unleashes an exhilarating avalanche of gastronomic passions that includes, "Croissants that float through the air"; "the most extraordinarily smoked chickens"; "Gorgeous Bacon Cheese Burgers"; hashes (fish, chicken, roast beef); "A great, bulging lobster roll"; "Lovely Suckling Pigs"; "Mushrooms!"; oysters (pan roasted, stewed, in an omelet): "Birds" (capons, squab, and game birds in season); "Wonderful headcheese"; "Old-fashioned jellied veal [an American version of veal and eggs in aspic]" but "not too many" aspic dishes; and "Fruits, fruits, fruits . . . If there were ever hard, unripe fruit on the buffet, I think they should be catapulted from the roof. They must be perfect!"

Beard could be charmingly imperious when describing "exquisitely good, and perfectly cooked, Grilled Trout. I mean, away with all this crap of heavy sauces and things like that on trout. Give them the honest thing with lemon and butter."

The letter suggests a cuisine that is Continental, global, and yet also proudly American—something for everyone. To a less enthusiastic audience, his suggestions might sound overblown, but Beard's vast appetite and disregard for limitations or budget found a willing listener in Baum and laid out a philosophy for the restaurant. He exhorts Baum to put the market fish on display on ice for diners to see upon entering. "This means so much," he says. "It's sheer, absolute theatrical performance in food that we've always talked about and loved."

He concludes, "There must be a constant and ever-changing panorama of food de grand lux and food of infinite flavor, exquisite presentation and brilliant execution. I cannot think of another opportunity as great as the one we're all looking forward [sic] and feel that it's impossible to imagine anyone having created as admirable and as wondrous a background for feeding people. All we need are those who are hungry."

There was still so much to be done, a cavalcade of obstacles before them, but by the spring of 1975, Windows was on its way, with less than a year to opening.

* * *

In the summer of 1975, Baum could realize some of Beard's vision with the debut of Skydive, a cafeteria on the 44th floor of the North Tower, intended for office workers, who could switch elevators on the floor where there was a bank, gift shop, and drugstore in a "sky lobby." The cafeteria's Milton Glaser–designed theme was cheerful and bright, with sky blue ceilings and staff uniforms covered with puffy clouds.

The name of the eatery came to Baum when it was nearing completion. On July 22, two men appearing to be construction workers had taken an elevator to the 80th floor and walked up to the 110th, where they convinced a security guard that they were there to repair the antenna. One of the men, Owen Quinn, was a Bronx-born misfit who'd found focus in life from the thrill of amateur skydiving. He'd worked as a merchant marine and joined the dockworkers' union, for which he helped lay the foundation for the World Trade Center, putting giant caissons into the bedrock where the Trade Center plaza would be. While on the job, Quinn had walked by a model of the completed skyscrapers and thought, *I could jump this.*

Over the years, after getting his master-jumper license and becoming an instructor, Quinn didn't let go of the idea. And on that July day on the roof, he removed the tools from the top of his green duffel bag to retrieve his parachute and helmet, put them on, and walked to the northwest corner of the building.

Quinn jumped while a friend and co-conspirator took a picture. After falling fifty stories, he pulled the cord and released the parachute, which brought him safely down after two minutes in the air to the central plaza, where he was arrested.

As with Petit's wire walk almost one year earlier, the city was enchanted by the daredevil's moxie. So was Baum, who, that same week, proposed to Guy Tozzoli that they call the new cafeteria Skydive. The PA pushed back, saying "he had a lot of balls" calling it that, according to Michael Whiteman, but it ultimately agreed. (After Quinn made several court appearances, the charges against him were dropped.)

The one hundred eighty-seat Skydive was run by Ruth Kraus, who was terrified of Joe Baum but didn't let on. Although she admired Baum, he could drive her up the wall, like the time he demanded a particular food basket to contain fried chicken with French fries. He didn't like the depth proportion of the baskets Kraus had acquired, so she scoured the city for a replacement. Baum called a meeting and had Kraus and other staff line up while he held up her chosen basket. "This is not the basket," he said, and he threw it on the floor, fries and all.

Baum's edict for Skydive was to do more than "funnel workers into fluorescent cafeterias." So its guiding culinary principle was that all the food would be made to order. Skydive served hamburgers, sandwiches, pasta, and even omelets individually. Spaghetti was cooked in the morning and then rinsed cold. When an order came in, the pasta would be dipped in a colander with boiling water, drained, and quickly placed on a plate.

There was the other level of prep that Skydive benefited from, happening belowground in Central Services. Green salads were already washed, fruit salads already chopped, and the stew base already made so that Kraus could add cooked lentils or freshly made noodles to create different soups.

The culinary consultant overseeing Central Services was chef Jacques Pépin, whom Baum had known since he was a saucier at Le

Pavillon in the early 1960s. Pépin, a dashing Frenchman who had been raised in a restaurant owned by his parents, had been trained in Paris, and had cut his teeth in America under Pierre Franey in Le Pavillon's kitchen, was particularly well equipped for running the Inhilco commissary. After he and Franey had a dispute with Henri Soulé in 1960 and walked out, they were both hired by Howard Johnson, a regular at Le Pavillon, to revamp the menu for his vast hotel and restaurant chain.

After heading the research and development department at Howard Johnson's for ten years, Pépin had opened a soup restaurant, La Potagerie, in the city. It closed in 1975, the same year that Baum and his wife drove up to Pépin's country house in the Catskills, where Pépin made them a simple roast chicken. As he tore into his meal, Baum told Pépin of his unprecedented World Trade Center food operation and how, at its core, there would need to be a central commissary and that no one would be better at running it than he.

Pépin, who had become a familiar face in New York's tight gourmet circles, had admired Baum since his Four Seasons years and was aware that others were "in awe and also in fear of him" but found him to be charming. It was just fun and games when Baum would, on occasion, imitate Pépin's strong accent. The Frenchman was also encouraged that Baum had hired his Four Seasons pastry chef, Albert Kumin, to run the bakery, which would be in Central Services. Pépin had worked with Kumin at Howard Johnson's, where the Swiss chef had also adapted his classical training for mass American production, overseeing a national production line that turned out ten tons of Danish pastries and thousands of pies each day.

Pépin signed on for a one-year consulting gig, but when he met Baum at Central Services, he was troubled. "Everything was wrong," says Pépin, who was particularly concerned by the low ceilings. If this was to be a central kitchen where thousands of gallons of soup and stock were to be produced daily, they'd need two-hundred-gallon kettles. The standard way of extracting hundreds of pounds of chicken bones from the stock is to remove them with a basket system that is rigged to a ceiling rail. But there wasn't any space for that. That and a host of other miscalculations could make Central Services an inefficient kitchen.

But Baum had had a hard enough time getting the Port Authority to sign off on the kitchen as it was. "We have to make it work," he said.

So Pépin devised a plan to remove the bones from the giant kettles by having two cooks climb a ladder and remove them with shovels. It was more manual labor than necessary, but it would get the job done. He also began writing a vast recipe book with recommendations for how each kitchen could use the different prepared ingredients. A couple dozen soups could be tweaked at the point of service with different garnishes and ingredients to diversify the product.

* * *

And yet, not everyone shared the excitement about the food services being developed by Baum et al. In October 1975, State Senator Franz S. Leichter, Democrat of Manhattan, and Assemblyman G. Oliver Koppell, Democrat of the Bronx, held a news conference in the World Trade Center, where they denounced Windows on the World to the gathered press, saying a fine-dining establishment was an "extravagance at a time when the mass-transit system of the metropolitan area is in desperate need of help."

To these elected officials, the one-operator food services setup was ripe for graft and overspending. They believed that there should instead have been multiple, competing restaurants in the Trade Center. They predicted that the restaurants would lose money. Tozzoli countered in the press by citing his own accounting, which he said indicated that the PA was looking forward to a food services profit of about a million dollars per year.

Such optimism was difficult to embrace for a city that was backed against a wall, with four hundred fifty-three million dollars in debts due in October but only thirty-four million dollars in its coffers. Banks were unwilling to lend any more money. So the city once again turned to its shaky dependence on borrowing against pension funds by asking the teachers' union to invest in its MAC bonds with one hundred fifty million dollars. Faced with an impossible choice—to put in its good money after the city's bad or else let the city declare bankruptcy and, therefore, imperil the jobs of the teachers—the union's head, Al Shanker, chose to back the city.

But it was a temporary solution. And so, two weeks later, President Ford sent a clear message to New York City in a speech he gave at the National Press Club. The president stated that he would veto any bailout of the city in a "quagmire" of its own making. He blamed the "insidious disease" that the city was suffering to be "spending more than we have, providing more benefits and services than we can pay for." It was a day of "reckoning" that the New York Daily News famously translated with the imposing, large-type headline, FORD TO CITY: DROP DEAD.

It would have been a grim epitaph for a once-great city. But municipal leaders found a way out. City leadership convinced union leaders to agree to wage freezes and a 20 percent reduction in the labor force. There were massive cuts to the municipal payroll—some sixty-five thousand were laid off, including police and firefighters. And the city implemented a transit fare increase, tuition—for the first time—for City University of New York students, and tax increases. This new commitment to austerity prompted new willingness from the banks, and the federal government, to back the city.

Despite—and, in fact, partly because of—these new measures, the city's downward spiral was even more apparent on the streets. Libraries had limited hours. Half-built schools lay in limbo. Garbage was being tossed about on sidewalks to protest cuts in sanitation, and laid-off firefighters occupied firehouses or blocked traffic on the Brooklyn Bridge.

Striking sanitation workers, who allowed forty-eight thousand tons of garbage to accumulate on the streets, protested in the streets, calling New York "Stink city." Teachers weren't far behind with their own strike, which they punctuated with placards that called it "Stupid city." But the most disturbing name-calling came from the police, some of whom dubbed it "Fear city."

Tourists arriving at the city's airports were welcomed with pamphlets with a cover line that read, *Welcome to Fear City.* The widely distributed survival guide featured a human skull and contained enough grains of truth to make it terrifying. Visitors were advised to never leave midtown nor to ever take a subway or walk the streets after 6:00 P.M. Hotels were portrayed as death traps, vulnerable to fire and theft. The pamphlets were the brainchild of the forty-thousand-member Patrolmen's Benevolent Association (PBA), the city's rank-and-file cops, who were putting pressure on Mayor Beame to stop laying off their own.

The New York Convention and Visitors Bureau launched a counter-propaganda campaign around the world in an attempt to retain the brave ten million–plus annual visitors who were predicted to be coming to the city.

But the perception that the city was on the brink was hard to shake when New York's sorry state of disorder was getting ribbed on prime-time cop shows such as *Kojak* and *Barney Miller.* For an even less forgiving self-portrait, audiences could go to the movies and be cinematically terrorized by the goons assaulting Charles Bronson's family in 1974's *Death Wish.*

Skeptical politicians continued to dog Baum through the unusually tepid holiday season, fueled by reports in the local papers that Windows spending was out of control, plunking three thousand five hundred dollars—each!—for four bespoke chairs that were to be used in a lounge area. In December, the Committee on Public Authorities held hearings questioning the validity of the Port Authority's involvement with Windows. Guy Tozzoli again dismissed the hand-wringing and, in fact, teased the committee by trumpeting how the hubbub was bringing even more attention to the impending opening. "We have booked over one-half million in parties since the publicity on our restaurant started prematurely," he said.

And yet, 1975 had been a dismal year that ended awfully when a bomb went off on December 29 in the baggage claim section of LaGuardia Airport, killing eleven people and injuring seventy-five. The unclaimed (and never solved) attack was the worst terrorist incident in the United States since Italian anarchists blew up a horse-drawn wagon on Wall Street, killing thirty-eight people, in 1920. It was a grim book-end to a terrible year. No one knew how low the city could go.

The state of affairs made the December ad campaign steered by Tozzoli, the Twin Towers' 24/7 pitchman, all the more lugubrious. The slogan was, "It's hard to be down when you're up." As New Yorkers trudged through another holiday season, he treated them to billboards touting the Trade Center's December opening of the South Tower's observation deck, plastered on public buses and kiosks. "It's hard to be down when you're up" was a twisted admission of the city's sorry condition. The TV ad showed the buildings shining in the golden sunlight, promising a better day. It was painfully incongruous for a city that seemed to be hopelessly sinking.

No wonder that the grand December opening of the South Tower's observation deck was a mockery. Mayor Beame, who compensated for his short stature by sometimes delivering speeches standing on an attaché case, stood before a phalanx of reporters and two hundred grade-school children to deliver a message that began, "You're going to be the first on top of . . ." But the microphone died. After it was fixed, Beame said, "I'm very happy that . . ." But, again, the mic malfunctioned. So the mayor, accustomed to such indignities, left his words unsaid and bounded toward the escalators, on which he led the gathering to the 110th floor. But the escalators also broke, jerking to a stop. Climbing the rest of the way on foot, he said, "Well, I can say I walked to the top."

CHAPTER 10
WHO THE FUCK ARE YOU?

The origins of *Truite au bleu* date back to the nineteenth century, in the Alsace region of France and the nearby mountain villages in Switzerland. In 1936, revered American food writer M. F. K. Fisher recalled in an essay that it was the best fish she had ever tasted. A decade earlier, Ernest Hemingway had mythologized blue trout when he wrote in the *Toronto Star Weekly* that you couldn't get it at a proper restaurant but had to "go back in the country to get fish cooked that way. It preserves the true trout flavor better than almost any way of cooking."

Customers and critics raved about the blue trout served by chef Albert Stockli at the Four Seasons and Forum of the Twelve Caesars. In a 1960 letter to his friend Helen Evans Brown, James Beard wrote of a "perfect" lunch he had had with Baum at the Four Seasons. "I had blue trout with a spoon of butter sauce on it, one little new potato, a piece of good cheese, and a double espresso. The trout had come that morning and was torn from the water when I ordered it." He called *Truite au bleu* "a piscatorial delight."

Dennis Sweeney had all this history and the impossible expectations of Joe Baum bearing down on him. He had to figure out how to keep the trout alive. As if he didn't have enough on his plate. He was chasing down porcelain Rosenthal ashtrays, importing Sambonet coffee thermoses from Italy, and getting the proper materials for a brass railing that would hold up a movable ladder used in the City Lights Bar. "Everything we do is marketing," Baum would say, meaning every item that a guest would see or touch or taste was another way to sell the restaurant.

The soft opening in March 1976—when friends, family, and associates of the restaurant were to be invited to dine—was quickly approaching. Six years after being called up by Guy Tozzoli, Baum was facing a wave of anticipation from different pockets of the city: the media, the fine-dining elite, downtown workers, the restaurant and nightlife industry, and his extended circle of fans and colleagues. And a large part of the local food services industry had something at stake. The World Trade Center was going to have a population equivalent to a small city, which meant a major new buyer for food providers, liquor salesmen, kitchen supply stores, delivery trucks, and the myriad other services that are a part of the restaurant business. On the 106th and 107th floors alone, more than four hundred people needed to be hired: cooks, stewards, bartenders, and legions of waiters and busboys.

In a wrecked city that was enduring an unemployment rate of more than 11 percent, the restaurant's help-wanted ads in local newspapers— START AT THE TOP, they read—drew long lines. No matter that the World Trade Center had endured years of bad press; here was a shining tower of opportunity with a new restaurant on top having an open call. Inhilco processed more than fifteen thousand applications and ended up hiring one thousand one hundred people.

Interviews were conducted downstairs in a nondescript room. A committee of men and women with pads and pens sat at a table facing the interviewees, one of whom was twenty-seven-year-old John Bernieri, a baby-faced son of a firefighter. He needed a waiting job that would pay for his method acting classes, because he was going to make it like Pacino or De Niro. Never mind that his restaurant experience was thin, thinner still if you didn't include working room service at the Playboy Club in Vernon, New Jersey.

But he didn't scare easily. As he faced an impeccably dressed, tan, blond maître d', Bernieri tried to bluff his way through, saying he'd worked in restaurants for years and had even been a maître d' himself. His inquisitor, Paul Egger, who had James Bond–like ruggedness and refinement, asked him in a strong Austrian accent, "What languages do you speak?"

"Italian," Bernieri replied. Egger then said something to him in fluent Italian. "What the hell are you saying?" Bernieri asked with his most endearing smile. "All I know is what my grandfather taught me."

"You should be ashamed of yourself," Egger said as he coldly looked Bernieri up and down. "But we'll hire you as a busboy," he said.

"I'll take it," Bernieri said happily.

Word spread that the good-looking guys, not necessarily pretty boys but guys with a certain *je ne sais quoi,* were finding favor with Windows' male management. There was also an international tendency; a number of Chinese and Thai men, many of whom barely spoke English, were hired to be busboys and back waiters. Another category of applicants being hired consisted of many waiters, managers, and cashiers who had worked with Joe Baum or the restaurant's director, Alan Lewis, during their RA days.

Of the women being hired, one stood out: Claudette Fournier, with long blond hair up in a bun and well over six feet tall in her heels. She carried herself with a refinement that captivated men, including her interrogator, another maître d', who asked if she'd be comfortable supervising men. "I have never had a problem telling men what to do," she said with a salty, no-nonsense, Boston accent that was in sharp contrast to her name.

Fournier had come hoping to get a job as a cocktail waitress at the City Lights Bar on the 107th floor, the same job she'd had for years at Dionysos, a Greek restaurant on the East Side that was big with shipping magnates. But the maître d' wanted her to be a captain, which was the top waiter at a table, with front and back waiters and a busboy reporting to her. Female captains were practically unheard of at fine-dining restaurants. At the time, a class action lawsuit against several of New York City's top restaurants, including "21," Lutèce, and the Four Seasons, was making its way through the courts demanding fair hiring treatment for women.

When Alan Lewis saw Fournier, he suggested she would be a good fit in the Smorgasbord, which was a lunchtime food station that served Scandinavian-inspired sandwiches such as liver pâté on dark bread. But the maître d' insisted on putting her in the main dining room.

* * *

Veteran restaurant staff tended to wait until a place had proven itself, but Lewis had a deep Restaurant Associates bench to draw from, so he was able to supplement the pool of green hires with former RA employees, including waiters from La Fonda del Sol and cooks from Brasserie and Charley O's.

Kevin Zraly, a liquor salesman with a finely trimmed, short, boxed beard, had no such advantages. What he had was a zeal for wine that was unusual for a twenty-five-year-old. He had grown up in upstate New York, where he first entered the restaurant business at age fifteen, working at his uncle's bar near the Kensico Dam. He had a wealth of wine knowledge, having traveled through France and California to develop his palate.

Still, he was just a kid salesman with four hundred fifty accounts and no connections at the Trade Center, where he wanted to sell his wares, like many other providers looking for a way in. Without an appointment, he made it to the eighth-floor reception area, where Baum and his team were in temporary offices while the final construction was being completed on the 106th floor. He asked for Barbara Kafka. The receptionist turned him away, but Zraly returned the next week. Both times, he was told Kafka wasn't available, and he was asked to leave.

On the third week, Zraly was again dutifully waiting for Kafka when he finally saw her walking toward him. He didn't have time to introduce himself before she barked, "What the fuck do you want?"

"I'm here to help you with your wine list," Zraly said.

"Who the fuck are you?" Kafka asked.

Zraly told his story: how, as a boy, he'd watch his uncle proudly prepare the best ground beef he could get for the hamburgers served at his place; how he'd paid his way through college at SUNY New Paltz by working at the nearby Depuy Canal House in High Falls, New York, which had remarkably received four stars by New York Times critic Craig Claiborne; and how, before the review, he and the other waiters would make guests' cocktails but after, they were so busy that he took on the role of bartender; how he'd developed his wine palette traveling in stages, first through the Hudson River valley, then New York's Finger Lakes and California, and finally, after graduating, through Europe. He was an amiable, articulate talker, young, energetic, and crazily, infectiously, in love with wine.

They spoke for two hours, and Kafka brought him in to meet Baum and Lewis. Zraly was quickly hired to be what Baum called "the cellar master"; he didn't want to use a snooty title like sommelier. This young American man with respect for the history and value of the grape was what Baum wanted to be the face of wine for his restaurant; Kevin Zraly was the opposite of the conventional, clichéd French sommelier. He told Zraly, "I want you to create the biggest and the best wine list New York has ever seen." Zraly asked how many people would be helping him in the wine department, to which Baum replied, "None. You're it."

* * *

Baum had chosen André René, an Alsace Frenchman who had run the Oak Room at the Plaza Hotel, to be his executive chef at Windows on the World. At the Plaza, René didn't smile often. He considered his job to be the most difficult in the house, requiring him to be both a paternal presence and the exacting boss to more than a hundred cooks of various ethnicities, but it was a diversity that he believed in. "You can't run a good kitchen with only one nationality," he said. "They each make a beautiful contribution."

Baum, Whiteman, Pépin, Kafka, and Beard made up quite a daunting tasting committee for René. But the chef was both respected and unflappable. René endured waves of tasting sessions. The waiters brought different permutations of each dish—the ragout of duck livers in a brioche with and without raisins; the quail eggs in aspic with more and less tarragon—to the assembled tasters, who jotted down notes.

What scored well was pelmeni, a Russian meat dumpling simmering in broth, served with sour cream and dill; cioppino, an Italian, tomato-based seafood stew; striped bass grilled over fennel; Greek lamb ragout with sorrel; and a paillard of grilled veal.

But one dish that was not going to be served was *Truite au bleu*. Those live trout were not going to be able to ascend to the 107th floor. As with the penguins, Dennis Sweeney had turned to Cornell to see if the "geniuses" at the school's College of Agriculture and Life Sciences could come up with why the fish were dying.

He reached a professor who had a convincing theory: the bends. The quick rise a quarter mile up was causing tiny bubbles of air to expand in the fish, resulting in the sickness commonly associated with scuba divers.

Baum's modus operandi was to ask for the impossible. He acted as if it would be the end of the world if a particular idea couldn't come to fruition. And then, just like that, he'd be over it. He was never satisfied, but he was also always moving on.

After considering a way to slow the elevators during their ascent to the restaurant, Baum let the live trout go. He couldn't dwell anymore on the physiology of fish. He reluctantly struck *truite au bleu* from the menu, undoubtedly to the relief of André René, who could use one fewer complicated dish to prepare.

CHAPTER 11
SEVENTIES SPLENDOR

Windows on the World's members-only club lunch service was set to open on April 12, 1976, but first there were private events and a pre-opening phase for friends and family. Those initial guests coming to eat at Windows basked in the frisson of being there before anyone else, always a goal in the hypercompetitive city. Whether they drove in from New Jersey, took a cab from uptown, or rode the subway from Brooklyn, they were dwarfed by the awesomely gigantic buildings. Walking up close, either through the five-acre plaza or along West Street, a visitor could arch his or her neck in order to grasp the entirety of the buildings or else just submit to their overbearing height.

Walking through the North Tower's revolving doors on ground level, the guests passed between Minoru Yamasaki's steel columns that extended all the way to the sky. Once inside the lobby, they encountered an air of churchlike solemnity and grandness, with modernist arches clad in Italian marble that supported seventy-foot-high ceilings. Walking on a vast sea of purple carpeting, guests found their way to the express elevator bank, the two elevators that would take them directly to the 107th floor, guarded by a page at a lectern. Dressed in a long white jacket uniform with epaulets and white gloves, the young host offered to check coats and hats at the ground floor coatroom. The page provided another essential duty: to confirm that guests were in proper dress code. Men had to wear jackets and ties. Jeans and sneakers were forbidden for men and women. If a man wasn't wearing proper attire, the page would offer a temporary jacket or tie that would be waiting for the guest when he arrived upstairs.

If everyone checked out, the page would lead the party into the elevator with the flair of a theme park usher. The page leaned in, pressed the 107th-floor button, and said, "Prepare for liftoff," or something similar, which elicited a round of laughter, often with a tinge of nervousness. Forty people could fit in the living-room-sized (by Manhattan standards) space, which propelled them upward at fourteen miles per hour. It was hard to resist counting the floors out loud as they ticked upward on the digital display above the doors.

Upon reaching the 107th floor, the giddy passengers would usually be in some state of excitement as they walked on the gold carpeting, to be greeted by two more young pages on either side of the opened doors. Facing a textured wall of gold leaf that was covered with geometrically aligned gold balls with lighting cast upward, lunchtime guests would approach a table that looked like a space captain's console, behind which a host would check in club members. The lush wall set a theme that appeared throughout the restaurant: textured, pointillist patterns that were repeated on walls, columns, carpets, and tufted seating.

The restaurant's architect, Warren Platner, had followed the vanguard of mid-century modern, having worked under I. M. Pei and produced furniture for Knoll. Platner had struck out on his own shortly before working on the World Trade Center. In 1974, he designed Kansas City's American Restaurant, which Baum worked on for the Hall family (of Hallmark fame) as a consultant on the project. Platner's Midwest creation was "a huge lace valentine" with red-lipstick cushions and enough shiny brass to build a yellow brick road to New York. It was a glimpse of the rich, bold vision he had for Windows, where he exercised a similar penchant for opulence, dubbed "sensuous modernism" by architecture critic Paul Goldberger.

Dinner guests could check their coats at a chest-high podium to their right, and if they had to wait, they could take a few steps to their left to catch the first spectacular view of the city: looking through the doorway over the Statue of Liberty Lounge southward over the harbor. The bar had descending tiers, allowing for an astounding range of vision. If they were eating at Windows' main restaurant, they would walk down a sixty-five-foot-long hallway that was both of and out of this world, with a gold carpet and floor-to-ceiling mirrors of multilayered reflective surfaces that actually covered the ceiling and the perimeter of the floor. There were also four giant geodes (invoking primal yet precious offerings from four different continents) strategically placed on polished brass-and-steel stands along the way, as well as photomural images of the city and other civilizations' greatest hits (the Eiffel Tower! Big Ben!) superimposed on the walls, all of which created a dizzying kaleidoscope.

Once through Platner's "fantasy" experience, guests would walk down some stairs to their first full city view along a bank of windows looking east over Brooklyn and beyond. (If the guests had turned right at the end of mirror-paneled "Gallery," they would have come to the Hors d'Oeuvrerie or, in the day when it was part of the Club, what was called the Grill room, which took up the southeast corner of the North Tower.)

As awesome as the views might be to the right while moving forward along this "window walk," to the left would be another stunning design element: the Cellar in the Sky, the intimate thirty-six-seat restaurant that was enclosed by glass and tall, geometric wine racks filled with wine.

Finally, the page would lead the guests to an area studded with two dozen large floral arrangements in gold pots at the bottom of a short set of stairs, where they would usually be greeted by the smiling, gracious maître d', Paul Egger or one of his proxies, who would then escort the guests to a table. The main restaurant was an L shape constituting the northeast corner of the building. Three hundred fifty seats take up a lot of space, but the area was designed by Warren Platner to not feel as big as it was. He built terraced levels that rose as you walked away from the windows, as well as enclosures and banquettes to create more intimate spaces, all the while making sure each table would get some view of the city below: Even guests who might have their backs to the windows would be facing mirrors.

Hidden from the guests was the fact that they had walked around the kitchen, which occupied the interior of the floor and was surrounded by what was essentially an enormous square hallway that doubled as the entrance and egress for guests as well as the waitstaff's access between the kitchen and all of the eateries.

The west side of the floor was dedicated to versatile private and banquet rooms that could contract or expand with partitions that could be added or removed. The rooms were decorated with welcoming motifs such as flowers or fruit, including bold paintings and photographs of tulips, autumn crocuses, and apples that either repeated in Warholian patterns or appeared oversized (à la "the Big Apple").

The entire floor had an over-the-top aesthetic that seemed commensurate with the expectations and showmanship of the occasion: being on top of the world. Columns were encased in gold ceramic three-dimensional tile, rose tapestries abounded, an intricate mirror ceiling loomed over the bar, and all that glass and reflective brass contributed to a luminous quality that might not have competed with the views but at least tried to earn its place next to them.

Even a trip to the bathroom was an extravagant experience. The women's powder room seemed grander thanks to mirror paneling that was broken up by sheets of silk embroidery. Exposed globe bulbs lit the marbled space with a celestial glow. And the men's restroom was even more regal—women would poke their heads in just to get a look at the fabric-domed, pink-marble-columned "temple" that seemed to envelop you.

The $7.5 million price tag for a restaurant was unheard of (that's more than $34 million today, adjusted for inflation), but Warren Platner believed he was restrained, citing unavoidable costs such as for the construction of the many tiers as well as Baum's being "a spendthrift" who "couldn't make up his mind expeditiously about anything," Platner wrote in a letter to Kevin Zraly. "This cost me and other[s] extravagant cost overruns. Yet look at what we achieved."

CHAPTER 12

THE MOST SPECTACULAR RESTAURANT
IN THE WORLD

During those initial weeks, a sense of chaos prevailed among the staff. Many didn't understand their roles. They would get conflicting commands from different managers. At the steely center of the storm, trying to maintain a semblance of order, was maître d' Paul Egger, an acre of a man standing more than six-foot-three with powerful shoulders that pressed against his finely tailored suits. His Austrian accent could be mellifluous despite its unavoidably Germanic edge.

Egger had worked as a captain under Alan Lewis at the Forum of the Twelve Caesars, but when the restaurant closed in 1975, he went to the storied "21" Club. There, within months, he rose from waiter to assistant maître d', serving guests who included Kennedys, the Duke and Duchess of Windsor, and former president Richard Nixon. The "21" owners, cousins Peter Kriendler and Jerry Berns, were livid when Egger told them he was taking the position at Windows. So he promised he would stay on for several more months to mitigate the loss.

But the delay meant that Egger arrived after the initial wave of hiring, and he was disappointed by the crop of captains, waiters, and busboys, only half of whom he thought were qualified for their positions. He tried to whip them into shape, giving them instructions on basic service, such as how to approach a seated guest from the left and remove plates from the right, the correct way to pour water, and simply how to walk across a room. Captains, waiters, and busboys also went through two-week trainings in which less experienced hires shadowed more seasoned staff.

The order of service was supposed to be that, after being introduced to the maître d', guests would be escorted by Egger to their table, where the captain would introduce himself or herself, present the menus, and ask for drink orders. Then the front waiters would bring out the drinks, and the captain would take the order. The back waiters would bring food from the pass—the gateway between the kitchen and the restaurant floor—and carry it to a station near the table, where the front waiters would serve the table.

The captains would remain present to attend to guests' needs, perhaps refill water glasses, and provide table-side service on gueridons—side tables on wheels with shelving and sometimes a heat source that would be rolled ceremoniously for the many dishes that required it, such as steak tartare or rack of lamb. When the meal was over, busboys would clear the tables, and the captain, finally, would present the check.

Each team of captain, front waiter, back waiter, and busboy would be assigned to one of the ten or more stations of six to eight tables. There were also stewards who would support each station by supplying and restocking glasses, flatware, napkins, and whatever else was needed on the floor. It was an intricate dance with many players that required reliable timing. And in those early days, in the heat of service, duties could become jumbled when a guest would ask a busboy to refill a water glass or a back waiter was waylaid at the pass, leaving the front waiter to fill his spot.

* * *

Just five days before the April 12 opening of the Club, Kevin Zraly was furiously stocking and curating a wine list that would satisfy Baum's command to be the best and largest. But disaster struck. After years of criticism in Albany and City Hall over using public money for a private club, a government power finally stepped forward to block the restaurant. The State Liquor Authority, which happened to have its offices in the North Tower along with other New York State agencies, deemed that the public had a right to "a substantial portion of the premises at all times" if it were to be granted a liquor license.

Baum met with the SLA to hash out a resolution, knowing there was no way that the Club could open on the twelfth without libations. Baum agreed to allow one hundred twenty nonmembers into the Club for lunch, as long as they paid ten dollars for the host and three dollars for each guest. But the liquor authority rejected Baum's proposal to put the nonmembers in a separate room. And because the resolution couldn't immediately take effect until the paperwork was cleared, the SLA issued temporary, day liquor licenses, which meant that every day, for at least one minute, all alcohol, including wine and beer, had to be removed from the restaurant. The booze could then be returned and a new, twelve-hour license would be in effect.

During the soft opening, there was an all-hands-on-deck urgency among the staff, who were asked to move pianos, tables, chairs, and other furniture on a daily basis. When they weren't doing heavy lifting, waiters were literally bumping into one another and spilling coffee in guests' laps. Fortunately, they managed to efficiently serve Guy Tozzoli, who came to eat a meal with his son and father, without a major fracas. But it must have been disappointing to chef André René when the threesome ordered hamburgers and French fries.

A special rush order of plain white plates had to be called in for the table settings because Baum had had such a hard time choosing the official ones that they weren't going to make it in time. Walls were still being painted, light fixtures still being installed, and wall art was still arriving. The waitstaff was originally expected to work lunch and dinner, but it was proving too overwhelming, so two shifts were implemented, and more applicants were sped through the training process.

Baum spent a considerable amount of time cooing over his private party guests, especially one, *New York* magazine food writer Gael Greene, who had documented Baum's implosion at Restaurant Associates six years earlier. Baum, Whiteman, and their PR man, Roger Martin, had come up with a primary press strategy, with an assist from their design consultant, Milton Glaser, who was also the design director at *New York* magazine. It was agreed that the magazine would do the first major story on the restaurant, and Greene would be the writer. She came to the restaurant several times that early spring to eat while scribbling notes onto a pad.

With two hundred or so items still remaining on a punch list that Dennis Sweeney dutifully carried with him, the Baum team met one night in April in his office on the 106th floor to hash out dinner menus. In a Spartan room with cookbooks strewn about the floor, while Greene looked on, Baum presided over Kafka, René, Lewis, and Roger Martin from behind a desk. On paper taped to the wall was written, *Country Pâté, Stuffed Baby Zucchini, Iced Cucumber Cream, Tomato Consommé with Thyme, Fresh Ham with Cream and Cider, Shrimp Creole, Contrefilet with Mushroom Purée.*

For a $13.50 prix fixe dinner, Baum wanted to make sure guests would think it was worth coming downtown. "Give me something you can sink your teeth into," he said. Baum wanted a "soup with guts."

"We have to have a fish dish," Lewis advised. Fatigue had descended over the room. Kafka had her coat on and wanted to go. Baum was worried about getting home before midnight, because there was a building maintenance workers' strike, and he'd have to man the elevator himself to get up to his apartment.

The night before the opening, Baum scrutinized every detail as he marched down the floor-to-ceiling, mirror-paneled gallery with his wife and a friend, Phyllis Feder. Standing on ladders, men frantically Windexed the hell out of the glass and mirrors while Baum pointed out smudges that only he could see with what Feder called "360-degree vision."

On opening day, a shortage of captains meant Dennis Sweeney had to step in and slice smoked salmon for five hours straight, going through fifty sides. "Openings are tough. We probably opened up too soon," Zraly says.

The restaurant started with two hundred covers a night. Kevin Zraly asked Baum, "Joe, what do you think we can do?" Baum said, "Three times as much." Zraly, who had been running himself ragged, discreetly removing the dozens of boxes of booze each night so that guests wouldn't see him and spending some nights sleeping in the wine cellar, said, "Holy shit."

Not being a Club member, the State Liquor Authority chairman Michael Roth was expected to pay the thirteen dollars fee to eat lunch when he came in with a guest the first Friday in May. Never mind that he and his agency had thrown a temporary wrench into the restaurant's opening plans; Baum made sure that Roth scored a window seat.

Another seemingly surprising guest was Ted Kheel, who had for years been on the front lines to prevent the building of the World Trade Center and, when it was up, tried to take it away from the jurisdiction of the Port Authority. A lawyer by trade, Kheel had been appointed to a number of arbitrating roles by different city mayors, as well as by President Lyndon Johnson, to negotiate settlements to stop walkouts and strikes in the sixties.

Kheel had filed a lawsuit against the Port Authority that alleged that by constructing the World Trade Center, it had forgone its mandate of overseeing mass transit, and so it was costing him twenty-five dollars a week in taxi fare, one thousand three hundred fifty dollars a year, that he'd be able to save if he could rely on adequate mass transit.

In addition to being a wily arbiter, Kheel was a savvy native New Yorker with a sense of flair. He also was a gourmand, a frequenter of the city's best restaurants, including the Four Seasons and other Baum achievements. He had invested in Le Pavillon. Baum had been entertaining Kheel for years. But this occasion was even more heightened, because Kheel was the guest of Gael Greene, who was working on her *New York* magazine feature.

According to Greene, her story was a "puff piece" that had come to be at least partly because Milton Glaser had persuaded editor Clay Felker, "and rightly so," she says, because it also deserved to be on the cover.

"Clay was very excited by the whole story of what was happening," says Glaser, who created the Windows logo design, color palette, and many of the restaurant's other design elements. "The city was not in great shape. And so Clay found an opportunity to once again state how great the city was. And to really exploit the affirmative message that you could still build the best restaurant in the world with money that was here to do it, and you could attract a constituency that you couldn't find anywhere else in the world. It was a big deal. We were all concerned about the city going bankrupt, dog shit on the street, all of that."

New York magazine's Felker was invested in the city's finding a path toward prosperity. He had been publishing the city's dynamic, dirty, glitzy, and glorious stories by such writers as Tom Wolfe and Jimmy Breslin. His magazine was a hardscrabble chronicle of the city, but it was also, increasingly, a celebration and guide. He needed the city to thrive as much as anyone did. And so he too was putting his best foot forward by anointing Windows. "You were afraid to go out at night on Sixty-Seventh Street," says Glaser of his affluent Upper West Side neighborhood. "Which is an example of how far the city had fallen in the minds of its inhabitants. You actually feared going out in the street. It was all across town. People were running from the darkness and wanted change. Many of us felt that we just had to do whatever we could to restore a sense of affirmation and confidence to change people's minds."

And, according to Gael Greene, it wasn't just an act of civic duty or wishful thinking. "It was actually incredibly exciting that something was being built in that incredibly depressed moment," she says.

The May 31 cover illustration of *New York* magazine depicted the 107th floor of the World Trade Center with its unmistakable, vertically slotted windows resting on faint, dotted lines, making it seem to be a floor floating on air. It hovers over the Manhattan skyline, standing directly above the Empire State Building. Above that striking image, the cover line reads, *The Most Spectacular Restaurant in the World*. And, in smaller text, *How a Brilliant Restaurateur Created a Masterpiece on the 107th Floor of the World Trade Center*.

The article opens with Greene's exuberant invocation of a once-mighty city that she unabashedly connects to the fate of Windows. "Suddenly I knew— absolutely *knew*—New York would survive," Greene writes. "As Joan of Arc knew she would save France, as St. Theresa knew, and Charles Colson . . . I knew. If money and power and ego and a passion for perfection could create this extraordinary pleasure . . . this instant landmark, Windows on the World . . . money and power and ego could rescue the city from its ashes. What a high. New York would prevail."

Greene breathlessly describes an oasis far from the deprived, desultory city below. She lauds Joe Baum as a genius and waxes on about the grand design, comparing the experience to that of being on "an extraordinary luxury liner sailing through blue skies," thanks to its shiny brass railings and plentiful, doting staff in white uniforms with epaulets. Layered into the gushing are Greene's less noticeable peppered barbs as well as an admission that, although Albert Kumin's desserts are "splendid," the food itself is "good. Perhaps someday it will be very good. Perhaps it will never be." Still, the eclecticism of the restaurant's Grand Buffet tickles her: bay scallops in seviche, herring in dilled mustard, bass in aspic, sesame Japanese noodles, a roast.

"I thought it was too early to write it as a review," Greene says, decades later. "I loved spending all the time there and watching them as they formed it. That was a wonderful way to do the story."

In the article, she writes, "The entire staff is an emancipator's dream—male and female, assorted colors, different ethnic backgrounds." A doting Baum presides—he appears "everywhere"—as she experiences "sweetly confused" waiters. Greene presents Baum as a tough taskmaster, an off-kilter king benignly berating Al Ferraro, director of food operations, for not producing the best dough for the morning Danishes. "Don't give them to me as right unless they're right. Tell me what's wrong," he says and then comically smashes a napkin. We see Pépin, Beard, Kafka, and Lewis all working to achieve greatness as Greene describes Platner overseeing "doodads on the wall." Platner tells her, "There are no compromises here," and we believe it.

"We were really going to do everything we could to reposition the city to its inhabitants," says Milton Glaser. "What had happened was that people began to feel that they no longer had a future here. The city was beginning to suggest it was no longer a city without boundaries—that you now were stopped by lack of services and dirt."

"The city was down," Greene says. "And so it was right to put on the cover. But it was also nice to have a spokesperson standing right next to Clay, the man who was in charge of creating the covers."

Greene and Baum shared history and an appreciation for the sensual nature of culinary life. (She once wrote that "the two greatest discoveries of the twentieth century were the Cuisinart and the clitoris.") She could also be similarly withering. Greene had gleefully filleted the venerable "21" Club in 1971 as "a dreary disappointment, a bore." So even when she wrote a "puff piece," Greene grounded her adulation by noting that Baum might have been a "sorcerer" whose greatest skill might have been showmanship.

On Greene's part, bringing along Kheel, the high-profile master arbitrator, was a provocative stunt. Kheel remained convinced that Austin Tobin "diverted a billion dollars of Port Authority funds that should have been spent on mass transportation," but he never saw Baum "in the same light."

Kheel considered Windows to be "a monumental event in food history." He nevertheless relished Baum's nervous looks in his direction as he ate sushi with Greene. But Baum didn't need to worry. In fact, Kheel gave Greene a doozy of a quote with which to seal Baum's triumph in the article.

"This place is fabulous," Kheel quipped. "This is New York. I said they should tear down the building. Now I say, tear it down, but leave the 107th floor."

CHAPTER 13
SUCCESS WITH RESERVATIONS

In the summer of 1976, *A Chorus Line* was finishing its first year on Broadway and had recently won nine Tony Awards, and the Yankees were back in dynasty-making form in a newly renovated Bronx stadium and on their way to the World Series. And the most talked about restaurant in the city was one thousand three hundred feet above it all.

"New Yorkers are star fuckers; they will chase the hottest restaurant and the hottest show," says Jules Roinnel, the Club director from 1979 to 2001, who, with many others at Windows on the World, credits Gael Greene's "spectacular" article for creating "this incredible buzz."

The impact of the article was ringing nonstop in the reservation department, which was overwhelmed by hundreds of calls a day. Alan Lewis asked the Port Authority to help him with the deluge by supplying him with operators from its bus telephone switchboard, increasing his staff of six to thirty. Managed by Bill Johnson, the reservation area resembled the chaotic bookie room in *The Sting*, with operators crammed into their 106th-floor office with a bank of telephones. They posted long sheets of kraft paper on all four walls, where reservationists scribbled bookings. "No one expected it," says Kevin Zraly, who swears that Johnson's black hair went gray overnight.

Weekend tables were impossible to get unless you booked months ahead. The Hors d'Oeuvrerie, the more informal Windows on the World restaurant, didn't take reservations, but you'd have to wait for more than an hour on a line that snaked around the concourse. The Hudson River Suites private rooms were being booked by companies such as American Airlines, Citibank, Honeywell, CBS, Yves St. Laurent, and Price Waterhouse. The wait-list for the Club had one thousand three hundred people on it. Or, at least, that's what Joe Baum was telling people, keenly aware that exclusivity was a way to create more fevered interest.

Baum had been telling his team that his goal was no less than to make Windows the best-known restaurant in the world within a year, but this rush was beyond his bullish expectations. Whatever Baum had accomplished to engineer a success—the food, the design, the staff, the public relations—and whatever was already built into the fundamentals—the real estate, the deep-pocketed investment of the Port Authority—he also had good luck. Two events that July helped put Windows into the heart of the zeitgeist in an era when a cultural moment could last weeks or even months. First, July 4 marked the two hundredth anniversary of the Declaration of Independence, a Bicentennial celebration that the entire country had been preparing for—refurbishing Revolutionary War sites and creating culturally relevant works—ever since President Richard Nixon appointed an American Revolution Bicentennial Commission in 1971. On the weekend of the Fourth, New York City was hosting tens of thousands of visitors from around the world, culminating with a Tall Ships procession just below the World Trade Center in the Hudson River along with an unprecedented fireworks display. And then, just a week later, Madison Square Garden was going to be the site of the Democratic National Convention, the first in the city in more than fifty years. The World Trade Center, being a product of American ingenuity, wealth, prowess, and political expediency, was a picture-perfect symbol for both occasions.

But before those events could draw splurging guests to Windows on the World, a sobering one took place on June 24, when the restaurant received its first major food write-up, in the *New York Times*, by new stringer Mimi Sheraton. The review was not quite a review—Sheraton, who had been a consultant for Baum when he opened the Four Seasons, would become the paper's food critic months later—so it was without the standard star rating, but it loudly proclaimed culinary judgment on the city's hottest new restaurant.

STYLISH MENU IS FULL OF PROMISE THAT ISN'T YET FULLY REALIZED, reads the headline. In the article, Sheraton applauds the restaurant's eclectic menu but sounds rueful when she writes that her six visits to the 107th floor "revealed many flaws." She lets Baum have a say: "I have the capability to produce excellent food, but what I need most is time," he tells her. The fundamental problem, she writes, is seasoning—there is either not enough salt or too much.

Sheraton gives the reader much to consider. In the Hors d'Oeuvrerie, she lauds the "impeccable" sushi and sashimi, the coconut fried shrimp (a novelty at the time), sesame baked clams, and a "mild but pleasant" guacamole. However, she writes that the satays, veal pâté, and taramasalata (a Greek fish roe dip) are "worth skipping." In the restaurant, she praises the "beautiful" pike and spinach pâté, served with a white wine and butter sauce; clams with a spring onion aspic, which "would have been lovely too had the aspic not melted"; and a "delicately steamed" cut of striped bass enveloped in lettuce leaves that sweetened the fish flavor. Disappointments included a brochette of sea scallops "that tasted as washed out as they looked" and an "eminently skippable" club sandwich that featured cold, half-fried bacon, overripe tomato, and limp lettuce. And she praises Kumin's desserts, especially the "ecstatically sinful" chocolate pastry cake and a frozen soufflé with bitter Italian macaroons amaretti that "were nothing less than extraordinary." She also gives mostly positive marks to the lunch buffet, with its "exceptional" herrings, pickled shrimp, and cold Japanese noodles, but the omelets, she writes, were "dry and saltless."

As middling as Sheraton's review may have been, it was just some mild shade in a season aglow with excitement. The city was in full-on hype mode to celebrate its status as host to both the Tall Ships celebrations and the Democratic convention. Newspapers, magazines, and local television stations were full of service-oriented, promotional guides providing advice to out-of-towners about what to do, what to see, and where to eat. Windows on the World, they said, was not to be missed.

On the weekend of July 4, two fleets entered New York waterways. Operation Sail '76 was an armada of two hundred twenty-five sailing ships from thirty different nations, the tallest being the one hundred ninety-four-foot-tall *Libertad* from Argentina, that had sailed down from Newport, Rhode Island. The International Naval Review was the other magnificent gathering, made up of fifty-two military ships—cruisers, destroyers, and frigates—from thirty-two countries, including the U.S. Navy's *Forrestal* aircraft carrier, on which President Ford landed in a helicopter and from which he observed the massive procession. He, Queen Elizabeth, and thousands of other international dignitaries watched the tremendous display of maritime engineering and progress, the gorgeous sailing ships breezing gracefully by contemporary warships while fireboats launched "water salute" plumes into the air and bands situated on piers played patriotic songs.

The pomp and circumstance extended for several days and down Broadway, where two thousand sailors marched in a ticker-tape parade. Hundreds of thousands of New Yorkers and out-of-towners attended different events, many to board the docked ships. On one day alone, one hundred fifty thousand people crowded Pier 8 to watch the water parade.

The networks covered the events from helicopters while the Goodyear blimp hovered benignly above. The Statue of Liberty, France's gift to the United States ninety years before, presided over it all. And higher up stood the World Trade Center, which was filled with revelers, tourists, and celebrities who had long before booked viewing parties in the North and South Towers. Never mind that some, like Mimi Sheraton, were frustrated being so far from the boats, where one couldn't appreciate their size, so she left to be down by the water. Windows catered more than five dozen office parties in both towers, using a fleet of its own—Cres Cors, the rolling metal catering racks with shelves filled with hors d'oeuvres and American classics such as pie and sandwiches. "How are we going to do it?" Barry Weisberg, head of receiving in Central Services, remembers asking Dennis Sweeney, who looked him dead in the eye and said, "Barry, just do it."

On Sunday night, as a fireworks display rained over the Hudson, private parties took over the entire 107th floor with every table decorated with arrangements of red carnations, blue cornflowers, and white daisies. Prince Rainier accompanied Princess Grace at a party hosted by the Port Authority.

Her Highness wore a navy blue Roman-striped, two-piece, long silk shirtwaist. She asked the coat checker, Melvin Freeman, who was given the task of attending her, to hold her hand, because the fireworks made her nervous.

Henry Kissinger attended with his wife. And historian Arthur Schlesinger, wearing a red shirt with a white collar and blue bow tie, mingled with the city's political and financial elite, including Governor Carey and members of the Kennedy family clan. They ate jellied shrimp madrilene, roast filet of beef with sauce Perigourdine, purée of broccoli, and endive and watercress salad. For dessert, they had frozen strawberry soufflé with strawberries and kirsch.

After working morning-to-night shifts all week, Skydive manager Ruth Kraus finally headed home, barely able to walk, the skin between her legs chafing, her feet hurting, her back aching. But the relief of a job well done kept her moving purposefully through the long underground passage toward the subway, where Baum happened to be rushing by. He called out to her, "What, Ruth, just a half day today?" She rolled her eyes, kept going, and raised a middle-finger salute over her head without seeing or caring what her boss might think.

And then they did it all over again one week later, when the city welcomed five thousand Democratic delegates and the tens of thousands of relatives and others who came with them to nominate the party's presidential favorite, Jimmy Carter, and to revel in a city desperately trying to improve its image with parties, bus tours, receptions at Lincoln Center, and restaurants open later than usual. The Convention and Visitors bureau predicted a boon of twenty million dollars in visitor spending.

A couple of days before the convention, to assist delegates with their dining choices, the *New York Times* published a guide by Mimi Sheraton of what to eat in the city. She acknowledged that elite-level, haute cuisine belonged to the likes of Lutèce and La Caravelle, "head and shoulders above their myriad competitors," with nods to Coach House and La Grenouille, but she also included a tip of the hat to Windows, "the most exciting and talked about eatery in town," in which she highlighted the restaurant's design and the best dishes she'd written about previously in the paper.

The restaurant was packed. Delegates and dignitaries lobbied for window seats. The line to get into the Hors d'Oeuvrerie went out the door of the building's lobby below. Maine senator Edmund Muskie, whom Carter was considering to be his vice president, was spotted at Windows. As was Colorado senator Gary Hart, who attended an evening cocktail party where he watched the sunset with Mayor Beame and solemnly whispered, "What a terrific town."

CHAPTER 14

THE MEANEST MAN IN NEW YORK

Amid the sparkling brass, delighted dignitaries, and eager Windows staff, a balding, broad-backed man in an expensive if slightly wrinkled suit prowled the floor, causing subtle ripples wherever he went. Perceptive guests might have noticed that waiters would quietly recede from view as he approached, while the ones who couldn't escape would appear suddenly busy, refolding napkins and offering water to guests even if their glasses were full.

Alan Lewis, the director of Windows, the terror of the World Trade Center, Joe's hit man, had been entrusted by Baum to oversee the day-to-day decisions about staffing, menu selections, and guests. No one had worked as long or as intimately with Baum. They shared a history that spanned four decades and a way to maintain the highest standards: Manage through intimidation. Or, as Lewis put it, Baum had taught him to wear a glove—velvet on one side, leather on the other.

A few inches taller than his boss, Lewis had a heavier brow than Baum. There was something unsettling about him even when he wasn't coming after you. "You didn't know if he was going to whack you or if he was about to buy you a rack of lamb," John Bernieri, the Windows busboy who rose to waiter and then captain, says.

On the floor, Lewis ruled with a glance or a whisper. He enlisted Kevin Zraly as his first lieutenant, sending him to "PX" tables, the code derived from "person extraordinaire" and used instead of the too easily recognizable "VIP" to make sure important guests were given special treatment. But before opening the doors at 5:00 or in his office, it was a different matter. If the kitchen was underperforming, he threw plates and screamed. He tore into a waiter for removing a glass that was not completely empty. He'd stand, nose to nose, with a steward who came to work unshaven and curse him out, turning bright red in the process, sending him back to his locker to shave or go home. "The running joke was that he was the meanest man in New York," his son, Seth, says.

Inhilco had placed Toni Aigner, a longtime German Hilton International employee, to oversee Lewis, but the buck stopped with Lewis. Aigner was from out of town. Lewis knew everyone in the city, from career politicians in City Hall to the best chefs in every kitchen. If a delivery from Macy's came in with less than what was expected, he'd get the president of Macy's on the line.

He was wired tight. But if you worked for him, he worked for your bottom line as well. And he commanded fealty through more than terror. Lewis was adept with the velvet side of the glove. In the right mood, he could be endearing and accessible. He told great stories of the ridiculous extents he'd gone to to make guests happy and confessed the mistakes he'd made. He was a gracious host to friends such as writer Art Buchwald, politician David Dinkins, and sports personality Phil Rizzuto. He could be down-to-earth. He would ask staff to give him their mothers' best recipes. They'd feel honored.

Paul Astbury, an associate director of the Club, wasn't alone in seeing a heart of gold beneath Lewis's thorny surface. Lewis helped people by getting them tickets to shows or assisting his employees to work out immigration problems.

Awal Ahmed, who immigrated from Bangladesh to work as a waiter, was once serving Lewis, who was asked by his dinner guest, "Why are there so many people from third-world countries working here?" Lewis replied, "I need these kind of people. They're honest and hardworking." Ahmed proudly relayed the story to his coworkers.

Bernieri had been begging Lewis for a promotion to captain but was repeatedly shut down. Lewis said he wasn't ready. Bernieri figured Lewis hated him. Lewis would snipe at him for his actorly wisps of hair. One day, the waiter decided he'd finally have it out with his boss when he saw Lewis storming over in his direction. Standing a foot away, with his face in Bernieri's, Lewis grunted, "When are you going to get a fucking haircut, captain?" Bernieri wasn't sure he'd heard him right. "Captain?" he asked. He had been promoted.

"You loved him and you hated him. But Windows wouldn't have worked without Alan," Zraly says. "He was a total maniac, but he knew both wine and food. And he was a very good taster. That doesn't sound like a big deal, but he knew what things should taste like."

Lewis also knew Baum. The two of them could talk about the texture of a bread roll with an implicit understanding, despite Baum's elliptical way of speaking. "They both appreciated the sensuousness of food and wine in a European way," says Seth Lewis, who recalls his father wearing satin ties because he loved how they felt against his skin. "He appreciated the richness of food and wine and fabrics. But without being a snob about it."

"My father saw Joe as someone who was incredibly talented and able to scale heights that he couldn't reach on his own," Seth adds.

The head of banquet catering, Gladys Mouton Di Stefano, who had moved from France, worked directly under Lewis. She was terrified of him. When he called her up to the 107th floor from her 106th-floor office, she'd shake with fear. "He was a monster," she says. "Joe Baum was a pussycat compared to Alan Lewis."

He would enter a rage if Mouton Di Stefano made a mistake, spewing profanities into the air. But he would also take the time to explain what she'd done wrong. After the first few weeks on the job, Mouton Di Stefano wanted to quit and return to Paris because he was so hard on her, but she stayed because she knew at Windows she could learn more in a month than she could in a year somewhere else.

Despite the abuse—no, in fact, because of it—she knew that Lewis was trying to teach her. He liked to say that when you worked in hospitality, you worked three jobs: the one you have, training the person who'd be replacing you, and learning the one you wanted to move up to.

Mouton Di Stefano would take notes in meetings and be alternately fascinated and horrified by her boss, inwardly wincing as Lewis bludgeoned Barbara Kafka over a particular idea. "If she came up with a recipe, he would fight her to the death and try to prove why his dishes were better," she says. "They were tough on each other. Everyone wanted to win."

It could be a harrowing environment. John Desanto, a young waiter from upstate New York, saw Baum yank the tablecloth from a fully but incorrectly set table, crashing everything to the floor. Whoever had set it learned a lesson, just as Desanto did when he handed a cold plate for a hot soufflé—a no-no—to his captain, who literally threw the dish right back at him.

"Next time I want to be embarrassed, I'll ask for you!" Lewis screamed at Desanto when he committed an infraction. "He would tell you what a miserable human being you were," says Desanto, who was aware he was being hazed. "And then he'd say, 'Tomorrow you're going to be serving Nelson Rockefeller. Don't fuck it up.'"

Edwin Heimer, another Hilton import, also suffered culture shock when he was brought in as the VP/treasurer to straighten out the books, which were in disarray. He was daunted by Lewis's profanity-laced diatribes. "He used the f-word so many times," says Heimer, who had come from the genteel Kahala Hilton in Hawaii. "I told a colleague I couldn't work with these people."

* * *

Alan Lewis was born in the Bronx in 1921, but most of his childhood was spent a half hour up the Hudson River in a working-class neighborhood in Nyack, New York. For years in the Lewis family, meat loaf passed for turkey for Thanksgiving dinners. Lewis's mother passed away when he was twelve, but he found stability working for his father, who opened a roadside diner, with a counter, a soda jerk, and burgers on the menu. The Bobin restaurant was an unfortunate name that reputedly came about as a result of a misunderstanding between the sign maker and the previous owner; it was supposed to be Bob's Inn. Lewis's father didn't have a knack for the business. Nor a passion, unlike his son, who was thrilled working behind the counter. He loved being in charge, slipping free ice cream sodas to girls he liked.

His interest didn't waver, propelling him to Cornell's hotel and hospitality school, where he met Joe Baum. After fighting in the war, he went to work for the Schine family in Florida. When Baum, who was also working in Florida, landed the Restaurant Associates gig, he brought Lewis with him, and he eventually asked Lewis to fill his shoes to be the manager of the Newarker. Lewis transferred to the Forum of the Twelve Caesars and the Lexington Hotel's Hawaiian Room, where he oversaw Baum's test kitchen, working his way through thirty-seven different kinds of soufflé, each one priced out to the penny, each one with marginally different amounts of egg yolk or butter.

Lewis had become one of Baum's most trusted managers—he ran the Four Seasons for several years—but by the late 1960s, he had left RA to become director of operations under Larry Ellman, a budding restaurateur who'd had great success with the Cattleman, an Old West–themed steak house in midtown where there were nightly sing-alongs. As the radio jingle went, the Cattleman was "Where you can get your steak rare and entertainment well done."

Ellman was also president of Longchamps, an Art Deco–designed chain of restaurants serving an emerging middle class that could dine in style on filet mignon or chicken chow mein ("prepared by native chefs"). He was making a move buying up fine-dining, "tablecloth" restaurants, such as Lüchow's, and he wanted Lewis's versatility and experience. Lewis took several RA associates with him.

"Sometimes, the band breaks up for a while," Seth Lewis says, explaining the parting between his father and Baum. "They say, 'We can't keep doing this at this pace.'"

Lewis was with Ellman until 1975. It was a tumultuous time for him. While Baum was transitioning from RA to the World Trade Center, Lewis was going through personal hell. His wife left him in 1970 for one of his wealthy friends, leaving him devastated. "He was never the same," says Al Ferraro, one of his managers. "He was a different man."

A jazz aficionado, Lewis absorbed himself in the nightclub scene, going all over town, from Sweet Basil to Michael's Pub to a number of joints in Harlem. He would go out all night with his skirt-chasing buddies.

In 1975, Baum asked him if he'd want to manage Windows, but Lewis declined. He wanted to be his own boss for once. He borrowed money from a friend of his ex-wife's husband and opened a small place in Westchester, a solid little restaurant in a Holiday Inn. Good-quality steaks and drinks. Not big-time, but it was his. He called it Alan's Place.

But it was a hell of a time to open a restaurant. The nation was in a recession. Gas prices were raising the cost of deliveries and keeping diners at home. One bad winter, and Lewis saw the money run out. He went back to Baum and accepted his offer.

"I think he was bitter about losing his restaurant and bitter about his wife," captain Claudette Fournier says. "He was a bitter man."

Lewis walked the 107th floor like an agitated shark, carrying an armory of tasting spoons, which he'd use to sample the food at the banquet table or in the kitchen. During service, he enforced the air of civility and conviviality that were the defining characteristics of the Windows experience.

But when something set him off, and guests weren't around, he would transform. He tasted a soup that chef André René had prepared and was so appalled by its seasoning that he threw the spoon at him and demanded that he "taste that fucking soup." René blew him off, which only enraged Lewis more. He grabbed the chef by his white smock and yelled at him, telling him to fix it. René sullenly obliged as Lewis stood six inches away, breathing down his neck until he was satisfied.

During one meeting, while Lewis was hurling invectives at a junior member of the staff, a senior manager left the room, unwilling to sit through the bloodbath. Lewis followed the manager into his office and began yelling at him, "What the fuck is the matter with you?"

"He was a madman," recalls the Port Authority's Bob DiChiara. "A total maniac."

"There were times I detested him for the way he treated his staff," Club director Jules Roinnel says. "But he got results."

Michael Skurnik was a young musician who was told that young artists made their money waiting tables, so he got a job at Windows. The job was all right, but he was not impressed by Baum or Lewis. "The Napoleonic style of intimidation was effective, but I didn't respect it," Skurnik says. "I didn't have a lot of respect for them."

Others did. Barry Weisberg, who worked in the receiving department, was one of the many World Trade Center food services employees who considered Baum a mentor. Weisberg believed his tirades were by design. "He was the king of icebreakers," Weisberg says. "His screaming was about breaking the tension." He recalls a meeting that was growing increasingly acrimonious, and Baum literally threw himself on the floor, rolling onto his back and kicking his feet in the air and screaming. "He got everyone laughing, " Weisberg says. "He instinctively knew how to motivate people."

Al Ferraro, the director of food operations who had worked under Alan Lewis during the Restaurant Associates days, called him his "rabbi" because he was such a helpful advisor.

Lewis lacked Baum's madcap charm, but he wasn't humorless. The staff felt comfortable enough to rib him on his birthday, which was on October 31, by putting on a pumpkin-carving contest to see who could create the most accurate rendition of the birthday boy.

The best, perhaps the only, way to defend oneself against Lewis's invective assaults was to push back. After Lewis, who was sitting with a guest at a table, openly censured Kevin Zraly for something, the young cellar master waited until the next day when the two of them were alone, and he said, "If you ever do that again, I'm going to punch you in the face right there."

Jules Roinnel, the Club director, had endured a series of Lewis's profanity-laden criticisms until he turned to the World Trade Center director, Guy Tozzoli, and told him about how Lewis was treating him. "You don't ever let that son of a bitch talk to you like that," Tozzoli said, "You don't work for him. You work for me."

A week later, Lewis was berating Roinnel on the phone, so Roinnel just hung up on him. Lewis called back and yelled, "What the fuck do you think you're doing, hanging up the phone on me?" And Roinnel hung up the phone again. Lewis's assistant called and asked, "Will you meet Alan up in the bar?" Roinnel and Lewis shared an affinity for Coca-Cola and Parliaments. When Roinnel approached Lewis, there was a pack of Parliaments and two Cokes on the bar, and Alan said, "So you went to see *The Wizard of Oz* and got some courage."

From then on, Lewis was more cordial with Roinnel, and the two men eventually became close friends. "That was Alan," Roinnel says. "A real New York character."

When Lewis leaned on his female staff, however, his brash approach could become especially unseemly. Lewis told Claudette Fournier, the captain he'd wanted for the Smorgasbord, that she reminded him of his ex-wife. When a large silver platter about seven feet long was being taken into the banquet department, Lewis stood behind her and said, "You see that tray? I'd love to see you lying on it with sauce Mousseline all over you." Fournier said, "Dream on," and walked away.

Fournier had been an immediate favorite of the guests. Many in the Club would ask to be seated in her section, number one, which happened to be closest to the door, where everyone could see her. Lewis would greet Fournier by puckishly saying, "Miss Claudette," and dipping slightly while pulling at his jacket as if curtsying. The dynamic had been set early, after an incident when Lewis told her he had a special reservation for table number 34, the prime one facing due north, at noon. But no one came. And at 1:30 another guest, a French businessman who had a particular liking for Fournier, arrived and asked if he could have table 34. She gave it to him.

At 1:45, Lewis stormed over to Fournier. "Who said you could give that fucking table away?" he screamed. "Your guest didn't show up, and Club members have a right to a table if it's empty," she replied. Lewis walked away in a huff.

Simmering with anger herself, Fournier waited until lunch service was over before marching into Lewis's office, where he was sitting with his feet up on his desk. "Don't ever do that to me again," she said. "If you have anything to say to me, you have me come to your office and say what you want. You understand, Mr. Lewis?" Betraying a hint of a smile, Lewis said, "Yes, Miss Claudette. I'm sorry." That's when the curtsying began.

Whatever it was possessing Lewis at work took a different form when he left the restaurant. "Alan would go off into the night," says manager Paul Astbury. "God knows what he was into." One of Kevin Zraly's first memories of Lewis was of him clutching his head after going out the previous night, saying, "I have a fucking headache. Who's got aspirin?"

Lewis's appetites were intense, diverse, and plentiful. He would go out with people a couple of decades younger than he. He was often seen with different women. "He was living the 1970s lifestyle," Seth Lewis says. "And I think he had a very robust constitution."

Different, attractive, usually African-American women, dressed to the nines, would visit the restaurant as his guests. They would sit alone, eat a meal, and leave. He liked to go to the Garage, an over-the-top disco also known as the "Gay-rage."

Lewis was known to have one of the best jazz record collections in the city and was well-read, visited museums often, went to the theater, and, of course, had been to every restaurant worth going to. He would go to Chinese restaurants without English menus and order randomly or arrive late so he could see what the cooks were eating. He picked Italian places that didn't accept credit cards, because they were more authentic.

Lewis clued his son into one motivation behind his higher-end proclivities. He told him that he went to the Metropolitan Opera so that Windows on the World guests would see him there. He didn't want them to think that he was "just a greasy maître d'."

Seth Lewis relays that the inherent tension and complexity of being in a managerial position in the service industry—"serving but not servile"—weighed on his father. He was hell-bent on beating forecasted revenues, taking great pride in achieving his goal, even if was by thirty cents. "He liked to operate with precision," Seth says. He would tell his son that he had hundreds of families depending on him and that his drive to execute was for everyone, from the guests to the porters who cleaned up at night.

What a grind. So much churning inside him night and day. He was at work by 10:00 A.M. and home at 10:00 P.M. or, often, later. Sometimes, when he arrived at his apartment on the East Side, he'd let his coat fall to the floor, an act suggesting imperiousness, perhaps, but being wound up so tightly all day, he also must have been exhausted.

CHAPTER 15

WINDOWS OF OPPORTUNITY

As the weeks flowed into months, the members of the Windows on the World team worked together to control the chaos, focusing on the details, keeping those water glasses full, plating the short ribs, and wiping the lips of the soup bowls before they left the pass. Routines set in.

At 4:45 P.M., before the doors opened for dinner service, maître d' Paul Egger and a manager and often Alan Lewis would inspect a lineup of the waitstaff near the buffet table. Captains, waiters, and busboys would stand at attention and get drilled by Lewis. "I want you in a line," he'd say. "You know what a line is?" He'd berate them for forgetting to charge for coffee or warn them not to rubberneck when Liza Minnelli or Danny Kaye came to dinner that evening. "Stay away from where you don't belong," he'd growl.

Egger set the standard. He had all the charm and imposing grace of the Old World. His nose was aristocratic, his sideburns formidable. His shoes sparkled, and his side-parted hair was never out of place. Egger would inform the staff of the "PXs" dining that night and discuss changes to the menu. And, at 5:00 P.M., two pages would ceremoniously open the door, indicating that dinner had begun.

Where guests sit—next to what they eat, drink, and end up paying—is one of the most valuable, and fluid, currencies at a restaurant. And at Windows on the World, where almost everyone wanted a window seat, the maître d' controlled the bank. It was up to Egger's discretion, unless Lewis had a special appointment for a PX, where to seat them. And although there were many great seats to choose from, a majority of the house was not by a window. Most on staff shared the belief that sitting farther back on one of the tiered landings afforded a better view of the city, because you could see more of it, but for first-timers or anyone looking to impress a date, anything less than a window seat was a disappointment.

Before service, Egger would review the reservations with Lewis and Zraly and sometimes Baum, when they would seat special guests. But a vast share were in Egger's hands. And no measure of whining or pleading by guests could get through to him. But there was a standard way to influence his decision making. Greasing the maître d's palm was a common practice in New York restaurants, but at Windows, like many things, it soared to new heights.

Egger was a master at reading a situation. Some guests, who would slip him a twenty, would be escorted to the back of the room, confused and deflated. For many, Egger would gracefully decline the offer with a noble smile and an air of moral rectitude. But for those who handed him fifty dollars or more, Egger would swiftly slip the money into his pocket and then stride toward the tables.

Waiter John Desanto was impressed when Egger would decline an offer from a guy with a hot date. He'd put him by the window anyway and pointedly say, "If you like your experience, come let me know after," knowing that, after the guest had had a great night and a bottle of wine and a few cocktails, he'd be dropping Egger a hundred.

On one particularly clear summer evening, when the guests felt that the skies were treating them, and only them, with a once-in-a-lifetime view, Lewis stopped Egger near the buffet table on his way back to his station overlooking the eastern side windows. Lewis grabbed at his hand. Egger didn't resist. He looked Lewis in the eye and stoically opened his palm, revealing a hundred-dollar bill. Lewis took the bill and tore it in half. And then he continued tearing it into more pieces, letting them fall to the floor. Guests gawked, and waiters watched impassively but with interest. Lewis then just walked away, and Egger returned to the podium, where he whispered something to one of his assistants, who briskly picked up the pieces from the floor. ("Don't worry," Desanto says. "Paul probably had three more hundreds in his pocket.")

It's not as if Lewis didn't know what was going on. Old-school maître d's don't seat guests—they sell real estate. But this time Egger may have given away a table that Lewis had been holding for one of his preferred guests. Anyway, what did one torn-up hundred-dollar bill matter when there was a stream of them flowing up the elevator shafts every night?

With a couple of straggler tables remaining, Egger would end his evening eating dinner with Zraly at 11:00 P.M. They'd eat almost anything they wanted, because the kitchen was eager to please Zraly, who would send them choice bottles of wine. Egger would count his evening take, which could add up to a thousand dollars.

Zraly, who would decline tips from lunchtime Club members but wanted to tap the revenue stream flowing during nighttime service, said to Egger, "I am not making anything on the floor. How do you do it?"

"Look at your shirt, your shoes," Egger said, indicating his own immaculate attire. "Look at me." Zraly began taking a more fastidious approach to his appearance, and he began reaping the rewards, sometimes making as much as five hundred dollars in one tip for a party of ten.

The amount of money being thrown around the 107th floor fostered an entrepreneurial spirit. It was all about tips; no one cared about the few bucks an hour that went to your paycheck at the end of the week. Most of those earnings went to the government or to union dues. "We all learned how to make money," says Desanto, who would go out of his way to soothe the ego of a guest spurned by Egger. "Don't worry, I'll take care of you," he'd say. And he would, and then get a nice tip for it.

Lunchtime Club waiters might make five hundred dollars a week in tips. But the nighttime, à la carte waiters were regularly pulling in eight hundred dollars and sometimes much more. You could make your rent in one night.

How the flow of money was distributed was a subject of constant manipulation, discussion, and debate. Maître d's would not seat certain prime tables—to the chagrin of the waiters—saving them for guests from whom they hoped to earn big tips. Some sections of the floor garnered better tips for everyone who worked there, so managers were supposed to constantly rotate the staff so that everyone got a chance to work the big-earner stations. Harder to manage was when maître d's would favor some waiters over others and give them the bigger parties and probable bigger spenders.

Most of the tips earned by the front staff were on the checks, distributed by a formula, which changed over the years. But, generally, tips were divided, with 35 percent going to the captain, 30 percent for the waiter, 15 percent for the busboys, 10 percent for the back waiter or runner (who worked more tables), and 10 percent for the pool of bartenders who supplied the drinks that the waiters brought to the tables. At the end of the evening, a cashier tallied up each of the staff's checks and then handed the share of cash to the employee.

There were always opportunities to make more money—on or off the books. Some waiters took on as many shifts as they could. Some, like waiter John Desanto, worked hard for a promotion. When he saw captains pocketing hundred-dollar bills, he wanted in on the action. He studied the job. The captain's featured role was during table-side service: filleting a fish or carving a rack of lamb or côte de boeuf. And the captain needed support. Desanto would dutifully roll out the gueridon, while the captain strolled to his or her position. The captain would place a silver platter on the gueridon flame as Desanto presented two plates. The captain would then carve the meat, and Desanto would assist with plating the vegetable sides. Eventually, Desanto was promoted to captain.

The job benefits weren't only pecuniary. The thrill of being part of the Joe Baum show had an appeal to many of the waiters, some of whom were in between callbacks and rehearsals for shows. And there was an extra kick when the guests were celebrities: Michael Jackson, Mick Jagger, Dolly Parton, and Richard Burton were part of the constant parade. The Hors d'Oeuvrerie was a favorite of high-profile guests, including Dick Clark, Jack Nicholson, Muhammad Ali, Tony Bennett, Andy Warhol, Diane Keaton, Elizabeth Taylor (with Senator John Warner), Jacqueline Kennedy Onassis, John Travolta, Paul McCartney, and so on.

Lucille Ball was particularly friendly and a good tipper. Dustin Hoffman didn't even get in—Alan Lewis kept him out because he wore sneakers. Some stars were unpleasant. Comedian David Brenner was particularly pissy when asked to check his fur coat. Cher would come with her on-again-off-again husband Gregg Allman. When starstruck guests gawked at her, she asked waiter Walter Szumski to tell them to stop. A classically trained singer himself, Szumski wasn't a fan of the headline-grabbing television star and replied, "You should do it your-self." Szumski was surprised and relieved when Egger sidled up to him and said, "I've been dying to tell her that."

When KISS band members had a three-hour lunch, ordering vari-ous dishes and drinks, one of the rockers began doodling with a pen on the tablecloth. Egger approached the table and seethed, "What are you doing to my tablecloth?"

The perpetrator looked up and smiled, shrugged, and said, "Don't worry, man. I'll buy it."

"I don't want you to buy the fucking tablecloth," Egger said. "I want you to leave."

Some young waiters, with ample cash in hand, hopped up after their shifts had ended, would go out together, to bars, clubs, and other restaurants to unwind. The Commuters Cafe bar downstairs, near the PATH entrance five levels below the concourse, was the lone survivor of the Port Authority's destruction of Radio Row and the neighborhood, the only business that had been granted a second life in the World Trade Center. It was the preferred watering hole for many waiters, who told stories of service foibles, favorite guests, and their latest callback over beers and rum and Cokes.

Amorous connections were also made. People who worked until 11:00 P.M. generally didn't have very wide social circles. Plus, New York's 1970s gay subculture was in full bloom at Windows, where gay wait-ers would razz heterosexual ones. Waiter Michael Skurnik was caught unawares when he was asked to lunch with a waiter who gave him a sym-bolic gift—a Greek coin that indicated the carnal bliss of the ancients.

When Skurnik's ragtag rock group wasn't jamming at a roach-infested studio, they'd gather at the Raccoon Lodge, a dive-bar oasis sur-rounded by warehouses and the random Canal Street prostitute, where they'd drink cheap beer and well drinks under an enormous moose head. Skurnik, one of the pioneer inhabitants of Tribeca, a neighborhood that just recently had been redistricted to allow residents, would roll into his loft apartment at 4:00 A.M. with his stoned and drunk fellow waiters, where they'd pass out and sleep on the floor until past noon.

Not everyone joined in on the fun. The long work hours were enough for much of the staff. Management mostly kept away from fraternizing with their charges. Alan Lewis ran with his own crowd. Claudette Fournier, the awe of many of the guys, was as discreet about her private life as her "tips," which were brought to her by club members' assistants in envelopes. She didn't go out with her fellow waiters. She had kids and a steady boyfriend.

* * *

The lofty views and lavish, giddy atmosphere at Windows on the World could have an infectious and deleterious effect on guests, some of whom would show their appreciation for Joe Baum's exacting attention to detail by taking ad hoc souvenirs. Forks, knives, silver salt and pepper dishes found their way into women's handbags and out the door. Waiters became accustomed to the soft, crushing sound of one wineglass too many being stuffed into a woman's purse. The porcelain Rosenthal ashtrays were disappearing so quickly that they had to be replaced with pedestrian glass. Even big items such as silver trays and the insulated Italian Sambonet coffeepots vanished.

Baum himself noticed a large man in an oversized suit whom he purposefully bumped into, causing a distinctive clanking sound. In another incident one afternoon, Claudette Fournier couldn't resist following a trail of shrimp that led from the buffet table to the women's room. When the culprit scurried out of the restroom with a large purse on her way to the exit, Fournier sidled up to her and said, "You can keep the shrimp, but can I have the linen napkin back?"

An accusation of theft is a double-edged knife in the restaurant trade. It's hard to prove that there hasn't been an honest mistake. And it's embarrassing for everyone. It also opens the possibility of a lawsuit for false accusation. That's why most absconders weren't pursued. But when storage room food was lifted by the crate or a guy tried to walk off with a case of crystal from the loading dock, the Port Authority police were called in to handle the situation.

Although Baum pressed Lewis to resolve the unplanned exodus, he was also flattered. Widespread thievery was recognition that his guests couldn't get enough of his restaurant. And a nicely placed Windows on the World ashtray at a party in someone's den was the sort of deft marketing that money couldn't buy. He was used to it. The Forum of the Twelve Caesars and La Fonda del Sol had also inspired acquisitiveness: Brass and copper service plates and silver salt dishes would regularly vanish. Even in the ladies' room, the Forum's gold-plated hot- and cold-water sink taps went missing.

An air of lavishness had been one of the intangibles of Joe Baum's best restaurants. Guests bathed in excess. But, of course, there was a literal cost. Baum's attentiveness to detail didn't extend to his restaurants' finances. Not that he wasn't aware of the finances—he would spend evenings reading spreadsheets like novels, according to his son Charlie—but he didn't always reconcile his visions with the needs of his financiers.

"Joe had no idea how to run the business side of the business," says his partner, Michael Whiteman. If he wanted to serve a particular bonbon at a banquet, it didn't matter to him that they came only in a box with other bonbons; he'd put the order through and discard the chocolates he didn't need.

He had always been adept at partnering with deep-pocketed investors who could absorb his profligacy. But Curt Strand saw that his old friend needed reining in, so he enlisted Edwin Heimer, the comptroller from the Kahala Hilton in Hawaii, to be Inhilco's vice president/treasurer.

"They got into trouble in the accounting department," Heimer says. The restaurant wasn't keeping up with its overwhelming volume. "Joe Baum was quite disorganized. He was a genius at food preparation but not at the accounting end of it."

Baum and Lewis would take cash out of the cash registers, sign it out on a slip as petty cash, and use the money for various exchanges. "They were running the operation like it was theirs," Heimer says. "There was a lack of procedures. I had to put controls on."

Baum had to present the food services financials to two boards of directors, for Inhilco and the Port Authority, on a regular basis. On the way to the Inhilco board meetings at the Waldorf Astoria, Heimer would sit between Baum and Lewis in the cab, and he'd review the numbers on a spreadsheet. "I'd run them up to make them look better just for the meeting," Heimer recalls. "We would have a good meeting and go out for a drink afterward. Listen, I had to live with those guys."

The true financials of Windows on the World are difficult to pin down. There were reports that Windows grossed more than two hundred thousand dollars a week, giving it a potential annual gross of more than ten million dollars and possibly making it the world's biggest moneymaking restaurant. The entire World Trade Center food services operation was expected to earn twenty million dollars. Although Whiteman and others close to the restaurant doubt that it was profitable during its first year, Heimer asserts that it might have broken even. Still, Baum was told to reduce his expansive payroll.

At least one part of the restaurant was doing stellar financial business in addition to drawing positive attention from both guests and the media: Kevin Zraly's wine cellar. When Spain's King Juan Carlos I and Queen Sofía dined at the restaurant in June, the *Wall Street Journal* lauded the restaurant's wine list and bold business model of defying the convention of overpricing wines by 200 percent or more and instead just marking up the cost of a bottle by 100 percent plus one dollar. So a bottle that cost the restaurant five dollars would be listed for eleven dollars. It was consistent with Baum's belief that guests should be treated as guests, rather than as opportunities to make a profit. "I'd rather sell two bottles at six dollars apiece than one at twelve dollars," Baum told the *Journal,* which referred to Zraly as a "25-year-old, bearded iconoclast."

Kevin Zraly was quite a departure from the sommelier cliché. He didn't wear a striped apron or don standard accessories like a tastevin.

Instead, he wore a white lab coat and a boyish enthusiasm for great-tasting wine. He served the Spanish royal couple two California wines—Chappellet Chenin Blanc ($4.50) and Schramsberg champagne ($13.50)—among the cheapest on the list. He darted around the floor like Peter Pan, from the main restaurant to the Hors d'Oeuvrerie to the recently opened Cellar in the Sky. He had the effusive, amiable manner of a game-show host and could give his guests what they wanted before they knew they wanted it.

Baum wanted to impress diners with an immense list, but Zraly had a different idea. If he was the only cellar master, then he told Baum, "I'm not going to send out waiters who know nothing about wine." So, instead of one list with seven hundred wines on it, he created two. There was the standard list handed to all guests, with one hundred or so wines on it and nothing costing more than a hundred dollars. At the bottom, it read, *If you would like to see our larger selection of wines, then ask the waiter.*

For the 5 or 10 percent of guests who asked for it, the waiter would bring Zraly to the table, where he would offer the extended list on twenty loose pages in a manila folder. There was an air of exclusivity and personal discovery about it. Older oenophiles would sometimes challenge Zraly, but more often than not, they would be impressed by his knowledge and come back for more. The affable Zraly would further endear skeptics with his willingness to acknowledge learning a thing or two from them.

Zraly was largely on his own, overseeing ten thousand bottles in the Cellar in the Sky and another ten thousand bottles in the basement, all of which grossed fifteen thousand dollars a week. He had scored a coup by adding an incredible selection of Bordeaux wines to his list, which was 90 percent French. A recent downturn in the market for the French region had made distributors desperate for cash. Zraly scooped up 1921 Château Lafite Rothschild for twenty bucks a bottle. He could cherry-pick the wines he wanted. "We had the funds to do it, and they were ready to sell it, especially the Bordeaux and Burgundies," Zraly says.

He was ordering thirty or forty cases of wine for banquets. Within weeks, he'd gone from being a hard-luck salesman knocking on doors to being the number one buyer in New York. He was hustling, running back and forth to the cellar, working more tables than seemed possible.

That a small-town kid from upstate could rise to such a central role at the restaurant was noticed by *Playboy* magazine, which tapped Zraly in a full-page ad as a quintessential *Playboy* reader: a man whose "lust is for life." The ad shows Zraly playing basketball, sitting comfortably on a rock with a lady friend, and pouring wine in a three-piece suit. In bold text, he is quoted saying, "How do you get to be a cellar master at Windows on the World at twenty-five? Well, you start by not knowing how to pronounce 'Nuits-Saint-Georges.'"

CHAPTER 16

ONE STAR

The first major review of Windows on the World appeared in the *New York Times* on January 28, 1977. Mimi Sheraton, the newly appointed food critic, opened the review by embracing the restaurant's cultural significance. "Few additions to the local scene have been so outright an affirmation of confidence in New York City's future as Windows on the World," she wrote. It was a bullish beginning, but it went downhill from there.

Having worked her early years as a consultant researching seasonal foods such as fiddlehead ferns for Joe Baum's Four Seasons, Sheraton was aware of the hair-raising hoops that his staff had to leap through to bring the food to her table. But Sheraton was as tough as she was professional, and she had to prove her mettle in her new, vaunted role. Her earlier, June assessment of the food had been before her appointment, so this time she had to give the restaurant an official reckoning. It appears the food was still not "fully realized."

Like most critics, Sheraton wanted the restaurant to succeed—who wants to eat bad food?—but she wrote that Windows was still plagued by "unevenness."

There were some high points. The talmouse of ham, a diced ham dish with cheese inside a pastry, a croustade of chicken livers, and the duck pâté were all "excellent." But the soups were "consistently poor," the game consommé was "flavorless," and the corn and crab soup was "starchy." Sheraton enjoyed the Salmon Coubliac, even though its insides had "disintegrated into an indistinguishable mass." And she liked the rack of lamb James Beard enough, but the Louisiana shrimp étouffée tasted like chili.

She gave better marks to the Hors d'Oeuvrerie; the "batting average here is high," she said, again lauding the kitchen's coconut shrimp, baked sesame clams, and sushi, the "very authentic" Greek tarama and the guacamole. A downside, however, was the price, with her check for four coming out to fifty dollars.

Sheraton also again favored Kumin's desserts but ultimately gave the restaurant one star, a "good" rating, and the Hors d'Oeuvrerie rated two stars, or "very good." For Baum, to be called anything less than great was infuriating. His bottom line wasn't financial but to receive adoring, universal praise and accolades from the people who mattered to him. Mimi Sheraton was one of those people.

Sheraton's ambivalence, however, didn't stem the flow of reservations; Saturday-night tables were booked four months ahead, and weekday evening reservations weren't available for two months. As with some blockbuster movies, certain restaurants, such as Tavern on the Green, the Central Park destination spot that had been reopened by Warner LeRoy the same year that Windows opened, are critic-proof, and Windows was riding its tremendous momentum since the beginning of the summer. Maybe the quality of the food wasn't on a par with the crème de la crème of French restaurants, such as La Caravelle, La Côte Basque, La Grenouille, or other A-listers, such as Lutèce, the Four Seasons, or even "21" (all of which received four stars in *Forbes* magazine). The food at Windows was more on par with the theatrical, Japanese teppanyaki grill, Benihana, the fading grande luxe continental legend Quo Vadis, or a popular steak house such as Christ Cella (all of which, like Windows, received three stars from *Forbes*).

Sheraton had closed her review with the most relevant question: "Would one go to Windows on the World for the food if it were set down on street level?" she asked. "The answer, with enormous regrets, has to be, not often, at least not yet."

Fortunately for Baum, most people looking for a spectacular dining experience didn't quibble about such existential distinctions. And, indeed, the restaurant was hit with cancellations on rainy nights. Waiters were constantly cheering up guests with gratis drinks or desserts when the weather was inclement. And, thankfully, sometimes a cloudy day could reveal a magical sight: a vast carpet of clouds as far as the eye could see, with just the Empire State Building's majestic top piercing through, punctuating an unforgettable view.

Still, Sheraton's question was pressing on Baum's mind for a different reason: He was in the process of opening a series of sub–street level eateries at a rapid clip between 1976 and 1977. And the food, he knew, did indeed need to shine on its own without endless views. Windows on the World might have been the top of the pyramid, but the other restaurants were supposed to provide the base of the food services income for the World Trade Center.

In the concourse, directly beneath the World Trade Center's open plaza, Minoru Yamasaki had created a vast arcade for business and shopping. Within it was a twenty-three thousand square-foot section dubbed Market Square for the public. Baum, who compared it to the Piazza San Marco in Venice, filled it with places to eat.

On one end, the Market Dining Rooms & Bar was a proper restaurant. There was also the Coffee Exchange, a sparkling kiosk that, in the morning, was a coffee shop that produced a thousand breakfasts and could be converted to sell soup in the afternoon and then retail coffee and tea for people heading home at night. The Corner, a slick diner with a big GOOD FOOD ON THE SQUARE sign, was where office workers could eat a six-ounce burger with fries for $1.95 at the counter. And in the Big Kitchen were eight thousand square feet dedicated to a several small food stations that mostly featured cooking in the open: the Rotisserie, with a wall of pork, lamb, and chicken spinning on rotisserie spits; the Grill; the Deli; the Seafood Market; Nature's Pantry; the Bakery; and the Fountain Café.

Market Square was whimsically designed by Milton Glaser, working with architect James Lamantia and interior designing firm Harper+George, who created a black-and-white motif centered by seven-and-a-half-foot, checkered letter sculptures that spelled out the words BIG KITCHEN. People could sit on the letters or use them as tables.

Baum visited the Big Kitchen area daily. He commanded all of his managers to eat lunch somewhere in the complex so that they could assess how things were going. The Market Dining Rooms & Bar was the flagship of the concourse. Baum had modeled the restaurant on the traditional food market in honor of Washington Market, which had been in decline when it was torn down for the World Trade Center. The Market menu featured its food sources. The "first-class purveyors from the city's wholesale markets" were listed front and center: Jos. Kenney & Co. (smoked salmon), Long Island Beef Co. (boiled short ribs), M. H. Greenbaum (strawberries, peach tarts), and B. Eisner (blueberries, raspberries).

Market's proud German-Swiss chef, Arnold Fanger, disliked the supply chain of ingredients that came out of Central Services. Beef in red wine sauce came up in big, frozen, gallon-sized milk containers. In his kitchen, Fanger would add chunky vegetables and sell it as beef stew. The same basic sauce would also be sent up to Windows, where it was finished off with mushrooms and put on the menu as beef Bourguignon.

Baum would show up in Fanger's kitchen for inspections and tastings, scowling in the tight space populated by Fanger, his sous chef, John Downey, a couple of prep cooks, an oyster shucker, and a dishwasher. "We all lived in fear of Joe Baum," Downey says. "Everyone cowered, waiting to see who would be on the receiving end of his whip."

Fanger tried to bypass Jacques Pépin's Central Services kitchen by sneaking in his own ingredients. "The commissary wasn't working," says Downey, who recalls freezing a rare bunch of cilantro so that it could be parceled out later. "We would get a little bunch of fresh basil and spread it thin for three hundred people."

When guests entered the Market restaurant, they would pass enormous displays of vegetables and eggs that were placed in market crates. They were given oversized napkins with buttonholes in the corner so that they could wear them as bibs, inviting gluttonous dining. Lunches were jammed with commodities exchange workers, many of whom would return to work loaded after several drinks.

CHAPTER 17
TO THE TOP, TO THE BOTTOM

By 1977, other than the Bicentennial, no event had cast the Twin Towers in as warm a public glow as Philippe Petit's walk, although Owen Quinn's skydive was a nice reminder of how exciting the World Trade Center could be. And, in December 1976, Dino De Laurentiis produced a remake of the *King Kong* classic, this time sending the big gorilla up one of the twin buildings with Jessica Lange in hand and Jeff Bridges giving chase. The movie was a hit, and even if it showed Kong falling to his death in the World Trade Center plaza, it gave the towers prominence and Hollywood cachet.

Baum was constantly drumming up new ways to turn the World Trade Center into an attraction. In the disco era, the Big Kitchen had its own dance floor for dance contests, street games, and parties. He had Billy Taylor's Jazzmobile come on Saturdays. And when celebrities visited Windows on the World, Baum would sometimes give them a tour of the Big Kitchen, which would draw a throng of onlookers. The morning before Muhammad Ali, for instance, visited, Baum had the idea to suspend a swarm of butterflies and bees above a makeshift boxing ring. He asked his secretary, Jane Dawkins, to come up with the decorations. Dawkins called a number of novelty and toy stores in the city and dispatched several of the staff to retrieve the props and get them in place just minutes before Ali's arrival.

And, on May 26, 1977, yet another daredevil helped open New Yorkers' hearts toward the towers. George Willig was a twenty-seven-year-old toy designer and amateur rock climber from Queens who, like Petit and Quinn, saw the enormous scale of the World Trade Center as a personal challenge. The thrill seeker and tinkerer constructed a rig with clamps that could lock into the grooves on the side of the building's exterior intended for window-washing equipment. At night, he climbed onto the bottom of the South Tower's facade several times and tested it out over the period of a year.

On the clear morning at the end of May, accompanied by his brother and some friends, he hoisted himself up at 6:30 A.M. and was well out of reach when Port Authority police arrived in the plaza and told him to come down. He declined and began his three-and-a-half-hour ascent. A considerably larger crowd than the one that had witnessed Petit gathered below and cheered Willig on. At the halfway point, he was met by a Port Authority cop who was lowered in a scaffolding platform. "We have to stop meeting like this," the cop said. Willig again declined the suggestion that he should stop climbing, and instead he signed an autograph for the officer.

After he made it to the top and was arrested, Willig was booked, and the Port Authority announced he would be fined two hundred fifty thousand dollars. But Guy Tozzoli and Joe Baum were aware of the positive vibe of the city (Willig was immediately hounded for autographs during his perp walk) and the media coverage (he would be dubbed "the human fly" by the *Daily News*), and so they invited Willig to a free dinner at Windows with his parents, lawyer, girlfriend, and none other than Philippe Petit, who was living in a downtown apartment and who had run to the building to witness the climb.

Willig and Petit made a toast "to the people looking up," which was the attitude that city leaders were hoping could spark New Yorkers to look beyond their current sad state. Mayor Beame, running for reelection, called Willig's climb a "courageous act," and his fine was reduced to $1.10, a penny per floor.

* * *

The New York Convention and Visitors Bureau was also trying to lift up spirits by putting on a happy face with a "Big Apple" campaign. The New York State Department of Commerce's Deputy Commissioner William S. Doyle enlisted Milton Glaser to create a design motif for another campaign with the slogan "I Love New York." In a cab on the way to a meeting, Glaser scrawled *I ♥ NY* on an envelope. He instantly knew that the form and content had an "inevitability" to it that every designer hopes for. He gave it, pro bono, to Doyle, who launched the design the same month as Willig's climb. It was a hit.

If only finding something to ♥ about New York City was as easy as its new logo. But the austerity measures that had been implemented during the fiscal crisis were only further gutting the life of the city. The abandoned lots that dominated the Bronx were creeping throughout the city, filling with rats, virulent sumac trees, and dumped garbage. Health officials determined that the Bronx River was as toxic and polluted as the Ganges.

Hundreds of felonies were being committed every week in a public transportation system that was riddled with graffiti. The lack of order was sprayed on every available surface. You couldn't walk the streets without considering escape routes. Paul Astbury, Windows' new Club manager, just in from England, kept his money in his sock as a precaution. Mostly, you had to push the fear away and rely on luck, faith, or superstition. Claudette Fournier had a notion that women who were about five-foot-six or five-foot-seven were most vulnerable, so, at more than six feet tall in heels, she had little to worry about. "Nobody would mug me," she said. "You'd need two people." Her son, however, was mugged, and she never wore her jewelry on certain streets. No point being stupid.

And in the winter of 1977, as it was becoming increasingly accepted that criminality was synonymous with New York, panic spread that a serial killer was on the loose. Dubbed the ".44 Caliber Killer" because of his choice of weapon, a man was shooting young women, sometimes in parked cars and sometimes with men, in Queens and the Bronx. By April, after the sixth shooting incident, with four people dead and more wounded, the media reached a fever pitch when a crazed letter from the assailant, calling himself the "Son of Sam," was found near the latest crime scene.

When the tabloid press wasn't featuring victims or exhorting mobs to hunt down the killer, there was an urgent, cantankerous mayoral election to cover, further reminding New Yorkers how dissatisfied they were.

"Put your anger to work. Make New York what it can be again" was New York Secretary of State Mario Cuomo's campaign slogan. It was a reactionary campaign that reflected the grim mood of the electorate.

Beame's failure to save the city from near ruin—much of the credit for the city's stopgap solutions went to Governor Carey—and inability to control crime left him vulnerable to a hodgepodge of Democratic rivals, which included leftist activist and former congresswoman Bella Abzug, shoot-from-the-hip congressman Ed Koch, and Cuomo, whom Carey championed.

Feminist firebrand Abzug was initially the assumed favorite, but the *New York Times* endorsed Cuomo, who had become the darling of the limousine liberal set. And then there was the little-known Koch, whose campaign asked, "After eight years of charisma and four years of the clubhouse, why not try competence?" Koch was growing in stature with his repeated attacks on Cuomo, but as a Jew taking on an Italian, he was having a harder time winning over the outer boroughs with his tough-on-crime message.

The city's power base and economy were crumbling, creating room for change. From 1970 to 1976, six hundred thousand jobs had left the city. The recent budgetary cutbacks and the declining manufacturing industry marked a shift from an economy held up by the working class and an expansive municipal payroll to a financial–real estate–media–tourist matrix. Men such as Lazard Frères investment banker Felix Rohatyn, picked by Governor Carey, led the advisory committee to help steer the city out of the crisis.

The city's power structure was undergoing change. Newcomer Australian conservative media tycoon Rupert Murdoch committed a hostile takeover of *New York* magazine in late 1976, and, the following year, he bought the *New York Post* and directed his readers' eyes to the world of gossip, fashion, and celebrity. Mayor Beame said that the new *Post* made "*Hustler* look like the *Harvard Review*."

"Something vaguely sickening is happening to that newspaper," the rival *Daily News*' Pete Hamill wrote. "And it is spreading through the city's psychic life like a stain."

Murdoch put the power of the *Post* behind Ed Koch, who got a call from the Australian in August, telling him that he was going to have the paper's endorsement. "Rupert, you've elected me," he replied.

Whatever one thought of Koch's politics, there was an authentic dynamism to the Bronx-born son of immigrants. Even though he was a congressman, he was perpetually the underdog, an unpretentious if brash man who wore ill-fitting suits and lived alone in the Village.

He talked tough about fighting unions and bureaucracy. When signs saying VOTE FOR CUOMO, NOT THE HOMO appeared on Queens Boulevard, the race for mayor took a particularly dirty turn, but Koch persevered. "It's none of your fucking business" is how he later characterized his response to speculation about his sexual orientation. Many found him grating, others amusing. But there was something about Koch that made New Yorkers believe he would endure. They hoped he would take them with him.

Like Koch's disheveled shirttails, 1977 New York was about letting it all hang out. Gay hookup spots extended from the shadows in Central Park's Ramble and the Greenwich Village piers to clubs such as the Anvil, Mineshaft, and the Vault. It was the year Larry Levenson opened Plato's Retreat, a drug-free, heterosexual swingers' club, in the basement of the Kenmore Hotel. And a new public access channel, "J" on New Yorkers' TV dials, started airing the city's libidinous id, with ads for "Chicks with dicks" and the craven Al Goldstein showing porn on his *Midnight Blue* show.

Fissures in the social order created cultural openings. In the Bronx, where Latino and African-American gangs such as the Savage Skulls, Savage Nomads, and Seven Immortals were drawing disaffected youth, a new sound, rap, was emerging at block parties and underground clubs. Former Black Spades gang member Afrika Bambaataa intentionally used hip-hop music to win kids' hearts and minds away from the violence and drug trade prevalent among the gangs.

Graffiti was another popular youth pastime; breaking into the rail yards and tagging subway cars with one's name was a rebellious personal expression and a literal assertion of identity. Plus, it was something to do. How else were kids supposed to have fun? Under-funded schools didn't have art, music, or sports programs. Recreation centers were few and far between. Subway surfing—riding on top of train cars—became a thing, as did riding skateboards while holding on to the backs of city buses.

On the Lower East Side of Manhattan, new sounds, punk and new wave, were emerging, led by such bands as the Ramones, Television, and Blondie at clubs like CBGB's and Max's Kansas City. At the same time, disco clubs dominated the weekend scenes in the outer boroughs. A new New York City was emerging. And the daily media coverage, especially the *New York Post*'s new "Page Six" column, which chronicled the all-night partying at Steve Rubell and Ian Schrager's recently opened Studio 54, magnified it.

Disturbingly, the illicit side of disco culture was heightened by the looming threat of the Son of Sam. Everyone knew that the killer was targeting young women with long, dark hair who were out at night, and one of his victims had been at a discotheque. Dark-haired women cut their hair short, wore wigs, and stopped going out to the clubs.

On May 30, 1977, *Daily News* columnist Jimmy Breslin, who'd been closely covering the killer, received a letter from him, invoking an orgy of anxiety and interest, which the paper milked with several teaser articles. It was sick, but the Son of Sam gave voice to what everyone saw around them. He wrote about the "gutters of N.Y.C., which are filled with dog manure, vomit, stale wine, urine, and blood." On June 26, he struck again, shooting and, fortunately, only wounding a young couple sitting in a car in Bayside, Queens.

But despite the grime, fear, and dysfunction, the life of the city went on. Children went to school, adults went to work, the trains were maddeningly slow, but they eventually got you where you needed to go. Whatever morass the city was in, it was still full of life. Food buffs were finding new, exciting restaurants in different corners of the city. Against reason and advice from city officials, Michael "Buzzy" O'Keeffe opened the River Café, where he wanted to serve truly fresh food, in an industrial wasteland below the Brooklyn Bridge. Other notable openings that year included Alan Stillman's Smith & Wollensky steak house in midtown Manhattan and the quaint Cornelia Street Café in Greenwich Village. Or the foodies were discovering something old but still incredibly exciting; the impossibly small Rao's—a Southern Italian, *alla casalinga,* "home style" restaurant that had been serving a loyal clientele since the turn of the century—became a sensation after a three-star rating by Mimi Sheraton.

Balducci's, a specialty foods store that had moved to Sixth Avenue in the Village in 1972, was successfully serving buffalo mozzarella and olive oil to sophisticated food lovers. It spawned imitators: A former publishing professional, Joel Dean, and a schoolteacher-turned-cheese seller, Giorgio DeLuca, started their own gourmet food market, Dean & DeLuca, in 1977, on a barren corner of Prince and Greene Streets, where the recent rezoning of SoHo was making the area north of the World Trade Center more livable. Dean & DeLuca introduced New Yorkers to such delightful delicacies as radicchio and balsamic vinegar.

New York was finding a way to persist in 1977, despite more than one in ten of its inhabitants being unemployed and 14 percent of them on welfare. Even the sky seemed to be falling on May 16, when a helicopter landing on the Pan Am Building helipad crashed, killing four people on the roof, and its rotor blade plummeted to the ground below, where it killed a pedestrian.

The thing about living in a city on a downward spiral is that normally you don't know when you've reached rock bottom. That year, however, New York found a pretty literal definition.

* * *

Wednesday, July 13, had been a sweltering hot, ninety-three-degree day, the beginning of the city's longest heat wave in its history. It was disgusting. You stayed indoors if you could. The humidity was so thick, walking on the un-air-conditioned subway platforms felt like passing through walls of urine. Aboveground, the pastiche of discarded sidewalk gum became maliciously soft. The smell of dog poop could be nause-ating. At least a chance of showers was forecast for later in the night.

The stock market was down a fraction but buoyed by a late run, a positive sign that things were finally heading in the right direction. Yankee fans were worrying about their injury-prone, two million dollar pitcher, Don Gullett—dubbed "Smokin' Don" because of his scorching fastball and tobacco habit—who had looked shaky in his last start. You could still catch Woody Allen's hit, *Annie Hall*, at the Gramercy The-ater on Twenty-Third Street. And the Ziegfeld was showing the recently released *New York, New York*, a musical tribute to the city's glory years by director Martin Scorsese, a misfire demonstrating that he was perhaps more adept at portraying its mean streets, as in his 1976 *Taxi Driver*.

It was another busy night at Windows, where guests and staff were relieved to be far from the oppressive stench below. At 9:30 P.M., waiter Michael Skurnik was working six tables, making his way across the floor, when he noticed something in his peripheral vision. A stir among the guests, a collective turning of their heads toward the northwest, made him look in the same direction through the wall of windows toward the sparkling Manhattan skyline extending northward. What was normally a blanket of twinkling lights now looked strangely like a grid. And if you imagine the island in four quadrants, there was one-fourth of Manhat-tan, north of Forty-Second Street and west of Fifth Avenue, in a blanket of darkness. All those people, all those buildings, just lopped off like a big piece of pie.

There was an initial hush, through which only the three-piece band could be heard, and then, suddenly, excited voices rose to a heightened din. Kevin Zraly was passing by the Cellar in the Sky when he looked toward Brooklyn and was confused by what he didn't see. The usually brightly lit borough was cloaked in darkness and now looked as if it wasn't there. Zraly then looked to his left at Queens. But it had also disappeared.

At about the same time, Skurnik watched as the other three quad-rants of the city succumbed to darkness. Zraly walked quickly toward the windows, looked down, and saw inky darkness surrounding the North Tower.

That's when the restaurant lights went out. They popped off with a palpable thwacking sound—it made you flinch—but the brain had to catch up with what was actually happening. Before you could utter, "What the—" the backup generators kicked in, and spotlight bulbs cast an eerie glow throughout the restaurant.

Paul Egger briskly walked the floor, passing tables and smiling confidently at guests, reassuring them with his effortless calm. Alan Lewis bolted from his office and found Kevin Zraly. "Champagne," he said. Zraly walked briskly to the storage room where the "cellar rats" readied the bottles for the night's service and told them to grab as many bottles of champagne as they could. Zraly used an old trick, mixing ice water with salt, and dropped the bottles of champagne in for a quick chill. And then the waiters arrived, grabbed the bottles, and streamed toward their tables and began pouring liberally.

The band played on. Someone said it was like being on the *Titanic*. People laughed. The bartenders made drinks and placed them on the bar. Waiters brought them to the tables. Or drank them themselves, something they'd never do if things were normal.

But this wasn't normal. Lewis heard a phone ringing and rushed to get it. It was Dennis Sweeney, who was downstairs in B2, where the phones were out of order, but he'd made his way to the police command station next to Central Services. "Thank God! It's good to hear your voice," Lewis said. "Everything is OK here. We have candles and flashlights."

"I am going to work with the cops and see when we can get an elevator up there," Sweeney said. "I'll meet them in the concourse."

Lewis said that he had a full restaurant but that no one was panicking. He didn't need to ask Sweeney if he knew what was going on. It was obvious. A blackout. It was a hot day. You could see a lightning storm off in the distance over Westchester County. You could put one and one together. Still.

Power outages were not unheard of in the World Trade Center. But not for long—five or ten minutes. Nothing like this. What had happened was that a particularly powerful electrical storm north of the city had struck a substation, which knocked out a couple of circuit breakers of a grid system that was already taxed by the hundreds of thousands of people who had been running their air conditioners all day. Normally, the Consolidated Edison central command operators can siphon off power from other lines to compensate for a blown one, but a domino effect of blown power lines and generators ensued, and instead of closing down the affected areas, creating minor blackouts, an operator chose not to "shed load." His error, among other faults in the system, contributed to a "cascading effect" that consumed Westchester Country and the entire city, except for a small sliver of Queens that got its power from another utility company.

The electricity servicing the World Trade Center from a substation under Barclay Street failed. The complex's six-megawatt emergency generator turned on but temporarily blew out before being fixed by a maintenance supervisor who realized that the cooling system was at fault.

The central air system at Windows on the World went off, and it was almost immediately apparent that the temperature was rising in the restaurant. Lewis told Egger and the captains to inform guests that they could take off their jackets. The candles that were being lit throughout the restaurant unfortunately made things warmer. Men began loosening their ties and shirt collars.

People talked nervously about how they'd get home if the trains weren't running. It appeared that even the traffic lights weren't functioning. They began asking for their checks, but the cash registers, which were controlled electronically, didn't open. So waiters worked out what they could by scribbling on check pads and making cash transactions.

By 10:40 P.M., Sweeney told Lewis that one of the elevators was working and was on its way up to bring people down. Some of the staff were eager to get home to their families, but Lewis said that the guests had to leave first. Many of the waiters didn't mind; they were enjoying their cocktails, as were the guests, some of whom had to be asked to leave. "It was a lot of fun," Skurnik says. "It was bedlam and pandemonium, and we made the best of it."

Shifts of twenty to thirty people took the elevator. When they got down to the concourse level, they found themselves in a vast sea of darkness except for Dennis Sweeney's flashlights. He escorted those who wanted to go to the street there first and then took the ones who were parked in the garage to the B2 level. He shuttled back and forth.

By 1:30 A.M., everyone was out, so Lewis let the staff go. They headed out into a city that was preternaturally calm. In Central Services, Lewis and Sweeney, lit by candlelight, were joined by Baum, who somehow appeared out of the darkness. "Let's have a meeting," Baum said. "Let's figure out what we're going to do."

They discussed the backup generators and security, but their biggest concern was spoilage. All the walk-ins and refrigeration units would need to be inspected; meat, milk, and produce would have to be tossed. They'd need the restaurant's health consultant to come in and itemize what steps they had taken to adhere to the city health standards.

Someone asked, "Could there be looting in the World Trade Center?" Unlikely, they decided.

What they didn't know was that the surreal calm that can come from chaos hadn't lulled all parts of the city. Many Windows guests and staff went on magical, unforgettable journeys home, stopping at candlelit bars to share the excitement, enjoying the dissolution of the social order spreading through the boroughs. But the shedding of social norms took different shapes in different parts of the city. On the Upper East Side, it meant sitting with strangers at a restaurant and using the headlights from a car to see, or, in Greenwich Village, an unbridled gay orgy on Weehawken Street. And in many impoverished, underserved sections of the city, people began breaking into stores, taking what they could.

Within a quarter of an hour of the loss of power came reports of looting. The order was given out to the already demoralized and diminished police force to report to their home precincts rather than the ones where they worked, further minimizing the New York Police Department's ability to confront the waves of crime that struck thirty-one neighborhoods. More than one thousand six hundred stores—grocery stores, drugstores, clothing stores, appliance stores, jewelry stores, a car dealership—were looted, targets of criminals, opportunists, and the desperate.

A thousand fires, dozens of them major, were set. In Bushwick, Brooklyn, firefighters trying to douse a burning building turned around to blast water at looters who were breaking into a store across the street. More than 3,700 people were arrested, the biggest wave of arrests in the city's history. Mayor Beame opened up shuttered jails to contain the overflow.

When the sun rose, parts of the city looked like war zones. Some of Windows' staff trekked to the restaurant to see what they could do. Jane Dawkins, Baum's secretary, walked from her apartment in Greenwich Village. "We were glad we were there; we needed to be there," she recalled. There wasn't much to do except help trash spoiled food. Sweeney, who lived in Rye, New York, had slept in his office. They went through the walk-ins in Central Services, Windows on the World, and the Big Kitchen, and unloaded the fish and other temperature-sensitive produce.

The mayor called it a "night of terror." Later estimates put the damage to the city at three hundred million dollars. The newspapers—they had printing presses in New Jersey and Long Island—revealed to many New Yorkers the disturbances of the night before, the masses of people running rampant on Grand Concourse in the Bronx, Flatbush Avenue in Brooklyn, and up Third Avenue in Harlem. Some shop owners vowed to stay in their communities; others rifled through the debris, wept, and said they'd be leaving this godforsaken place. Norman Gallen, who owned a looted clothing store that his grandfather had opened on Myrtle Avenue in Brooklyn, told the *Daily News*, "I will not come back to this neighborhood." As he was being interviewed, he chased lingering miscreants still looking for something to grab.

Twenty-five hours after going out, the city's electricity was fully restored on the night of the fourteenth. For some New Yorkers, it was a moment to take stock of the city they lived in. Many could recall the last major blackout, in 1965, when hours of a city shutdown hadn't led to rampant crime. Sure, maybe that earlier blackout was in the fall, and it didn't last as long, but it certainly suggested a kinder, gentler era.

Four months later, the blackout must have had an impact on the city's turn to Ed Koch, making him the mayor over Cuomo, who was considered weaker on law and order. (Fortunately, the Son of Sam killer, David Berkowitz, had been apprehended in August, thanks to a parking violation that led police to his home in Yonkers, New York.)

Other than the people directly affected—the store owners who had to rebuild their businesses and the thousands harmed by the fires—life could move on. After the World Trade Center's water and ventilation systems were back up and running, Windows on the World reopened on Friday, July 16.

Lost to most was the maddening misfortune that the July 15 edition of the *New York Times*—an edition almost entirely dedicated to the blackout—contained a glowing review of Market Dining Rooms & Bar by Mimi Sheraton. She gave the restaurant a three-star, "excellent," rating, and poured on the superlatives for both it and the Big Kitchen, which she gave two stars.

"A complex of fascinating and stunning restaurants has been developing on the ground floor concourse," she wrote, lauding Milton Glaser's design and praising the Market's "sensational" appetizers: the "properly acidic" sorrel soup, a pistachio-studded pâté en croute with an aspic "that actually has flavor," shrimp with Chinese radish, and "absolutely perfect" fresh calf's liver. Sheraton also heaped praise on the rest of the Big Kitchen, even if it was less ambitious, and called the Grill's hamburgers some of the best in the city.

Slipped in the back of the Weekend section on page C14, after reams of blackout coverage, it probably caught the attention of very few. But Joe Baum wasn't about to let a city-stopping riot eclipse a great review. Over the next months, he used Sheraton's appraisal in a steady stream of full-page newspaper ads that included the entire review and banner copy that read, *When a New York restaurant opens, New Yorkers want to see what Mimi Sheraton has to say about it. Well, we're a New York restaurant, and here's every word Mimi Sheraton had to say about us.*

Sheraton didn't know that management had been fully aware when she was at the restaurant, and although Baum had steered clear, Michael Whiteman oversaw her meals from the kitchen. "We knew her taste foibles," he says, such as her preferences for garlic, salt, and oregano. "When the orders came into the kitchen, we rearranged the flavor profiles."

After the review, Baum wrote Sheraton a note, thanking her and promising that he would never let her down.

CHAPTER 18

AN ITALIAN WEDDING

On December 19, 1978, far below the Twin Towers, a cold wind blew past the cracked sidewalk corner in Clifton, Staten Island, where Bay Street and Norwood Avenue meet on the northern shore. Facing Brooklyn, with the Verrazzano Bridge on your right and the World Trade Center on your left, you could smell New York Harbor. It was a forgettable midway point between the bridge approach and St. George Terminal, where the ferry came in, and no place where outsiders would want to stop. But if you lived in one of the big single-family houses up Norwood or Townsend, or you were on your way to catch the Staten Island commuter train across the street, it was a convenient spot to pick up some booze at the liquor store or something to eat at the corner deli, Food 'n' Things.

On this Tuesday afternoon, it was the usual crowd inside the deli: eight or so people ordering sandwiches and chatting with Gloria, the daughter of the store's owner, Joseph Nebbia. Linda prepared sandwiches on rolls, and eighteen-year-old Scott worked the register.

A Wells Fargo armored truck pulled up outside, and two of the guards, Richard Henrich and Fred Caputo, joined the line, as they often did, to pick up lunch before driving into the city to transfer the morning's pickups to Manhattan banks. They were supposed to vary their route, but they liked the sandwiches at Food 'n' Things.

As Henrich and Caputo shook off the cold, a group of six men wearing ski masks tumbled inside after them. They wore dark, workingmen's clothes except for one, who was in a white lab coat. Or maybe it was a butcher's smock. They had guns.

"Nobody move, this is a stickup," one of them said.

A guy on the sandwich line thought it was a joke. He started to gesture toward the men, but one of the thugs, a fat guy, pistol-whipped him in the head, a heart-stopping burst of violence, a sickening thud of the menacingly hard object hitting flesh, which iced the room. The men herded the customers, the guards, and the three employees into the back kitchen, where they handcuffed them and told them to get on the ground.

"If you want to have a merry Christmas, keep down," one of the men said in an accent that sounded local. They took the guards' keys.

The men went to the front, removed their masks, left the store, and approached the Wells Fargo truck, a Ford relic that looked like a fortified ice cream truck, where guard Thaddeus Gregorek was sitting in the driver's seat. The men got Gregorek's attention by pointing to the front tire and saying it had a bubble and would blow if someone didn't do something about it. As they were speaking, he didn't notice that one of the robbers had placed the key in the passenger side door. Before Gregorek knew it, he was looking down the barrel of a shotgun.

The robbers blindfolded him, taped his mouth, cuffed his hands, and drove away with him in the back. They pulled up around the corner on Greenfield Avenue, where a blue Cadillac with a white top was parked near the bowling alley. The men removed the bulging bags of cash from the truck and put them into the Caddy's trunk. They sped off with $2.25 million in small bills.

If it had been another year or another place, the robbery might have meant much more. But this was happening at the close of another ridiculous year in New York City law enforcement—there were six hundred thirty-two bank robberies in total. And this heist was under one very long shadow: Just eight days earlier, five masked men had stolen five million dollars in cash and another million dollars in jewelry from a Kennedy International Airport cargo vault. Dubbed the "Lufthansa Heist," it was getting the full-throttle treatment from the tabloids that feasted on the details of the largest cash robbery in U.S. history.

The Staten Island Food 'n' Things heist might not have entered city lore quite like the Lufthansa Heist—later immortalized in Martin Scorsese's 1990 film *Goodfellas*—but it would nonetheless earn a unique place in New York criminal lore and add a colorful footnote to Windows on the World's history.

* * *

Five months later, on May 26, 1979, Claudette Fournier, now Windows on the World maître d', and Joe "Pepe" Marino were getting married. This was her second marriage except that it wasn't, because she had never actually married her first "husband," Jimmy Dell, the father of her three children, who were now in their early teens. Dell had been a singer and horn blower for the Goofers, a five-guy variety act that got its start playing for Louis Prima, the Italian-American "King of Swing."

Dell was, at best, five-foot-three, so when he and Fournier were together, people would gawk. Dell had a towering ego, so he'd make cracks to the rubberneckers. He proudly held the arresting, six-foot-tall, statuesque blonde on his arm like a trophy. That made her feel special, but he was also an incorrigible philanderer, and she knew it wouldn't last.

Fournier was originally from Brookline, Massachusetts, the child of a French father, Marcel, a hairstylist, and an English mother, Lillian. From her parents, Fournier developed a refined sensibility. With dinner, they gave the very young Claudette a small sherry glass that held a teaspoon of wine mixed with water. They gradually increased the dose so that by the time she was fourteen, she was drinking a glass of wine with meals with her parents.

Fournier started tap lessons when she was five. She joined the Water Follies, a traveling synchronized swimming act, when she was still in high school. Fournier could dance and was a great looker, so she quickly landed a succession of jobs, first in *The Latin Quarter* on Broadway and then in *Gypsy*, which was touring the States. That brought her to Las Vegas, where she did a series of shows and hooked up with Dell. They had their three children between 1962 and 1966.

They traveled around the world, but by 1970, Fournier had had enough. She left Dell in London and moved with the kids to the city, where she did some modeling and worked as a cocktail waitress until she happened into the Beef East, on Manhattan's East Side, a small bar that served food. "Pepe" Marino owned the place and was a consummate host. Like Dell, he was a hell of an entertainer. He told great, funny stories. Some of his best were about the prison upstate, where he'd been locked up for robbery for ten years.

One thing led to another, and Fournier began dating and working for Marino, managing his books. He ran a couple of after-hours clubs. He lent people money. Fournier once saw him punch a guy, drop him into a laundry basket, and wheel him into an alley. In 1976, she was talking with Marino on the phone, and she heard a racket in the Beef East. When she got there, a stage for dancing girls had been built. Soon after, the club was shut down. That's when Fournier applied for the job at Windows on the World.

After working for a year as a captain in the Windows on the World Club, she'd been promoted to assistant manager at the Market Dining Rooms & Bar downstairs. "She was gorgeous, but not just nice to look at," Dennis Sweeney recalls. "She was a serious manager. She was good at her job."

But Fournier didn't take to it. She liked working with the club members. She quit and left New York until she got a call from Alan Lewis, who asked, "What position do you want at Windows on the World?" Fournier replied, "I'd like to be maître d' during lunchtime for the members." He told her to come by.

Lewis dropped the afternoon maître d' for "Miss Claudette," who couldn't have been happier. And the members loved having her back. Management supported her. Lewis was even setting her up with a six-week, food-consultant training course in Canada to develop her role at the restaurant.

By 1979, Marino was saying that they should get married. Fournier asked herself why he wanted to. But she was thirty-five, and she figured the security would be worth it. And he just wouldn't stop asking. So, over dinner at the froufrou Sign of the Dove restaurant on the Upper East Side—not Marino's kind of place, but he knew what she liked— she agreed.

This second marriage wasn't quite real either, not yet, because Marino was still technically married to his wife, even though they hadn't been together for over a decade. Fournier knew the whole thing was sort of sideways, but she hoped for the best. So, May 26 wasn't really their wedding date, but it was the day of the reception. And it was going to be at Windows on the World.

Fournier didn't want it to be there. Why couldn't they do it in New Jersey or Staten Island? "We're not having an Italian wedding on the 107th floor of the World Trade Center as long as I'm working there," she said. But Marino said it didn't have to be a big pasta and tomato sauce affair. He just wanted it there.

He had been flying high recently, buying a Cadillac Coupe De Ville, a new place in Florida, and a boat. He also had cash. He asked Fournier to deposit about nine thousand dollars into an account. A reception on top of the world seemed about his speed.

The party was going to be in the governor's suite: one hundred twenty guests served cocktails and salmon on black bread, steak tartare, oysters, and lamb kebobs under large potted palm trees while a pianist played. Fournier's children were going to be there, as were her parents, her sister and brother-in-law, and some friends and cousins. But it was mostly his people, dozens of family members and friends driving in over the bridges or through the tunnels.

* * *

This is a good moment to take a step back and acknowledge that Claudette Fournier is the source for much of this chapter and that some of her account diverges from the memory of the FBI agents who had been monitoring her and Marino for weeks. But let's go with her story, which puts her in the dressing room on the 107th floor at about 6:00 P.M., when she hung up her gown, a white-and-gold two-piece she'd asked the Windows on the World seamstress to make. She then took the elevator down to meet Marino before bringing him up to get dressed in his suit.

She saw Marino on the concourse walking across the carpeting toward her. At five-foot-ten and over two hundred pounds, he was a big guy, but he carried it well enough. He was wearing a polo shirt, golf jacket, and checkered slacks. And he was surrounded by ten, twenty, maybe more, men who looked like cops. And his hands were cuffed in front of him.

Marino eyed the guys with a resigned expression. He looked at Fournier, who was frozen in place. Her mouth was open, but she didn't know what to say. There must have been a crowd gathering and watching, but she couldn't take it all in.

Finally, Marino spoke. "I have a wedding present for her," he said to the police officer or FBI agent or whatever he was. "Let me give it to her." It was in his breast pocket, and with his hands cuffed, he couldn't reach it. So the agent helped by putting his hand in Marino's pocket. He pulled out a diamond necklace and handed it to her.

Fournier asked where they were taking him. The Metropolitan Correctional Center just up the street, they said. She watched them walk together in a group. "He was a gentleman. He offered no resistance," police lieutenant Joseph Carroll later told the press. "We hated to do it that way."

Fournier walked back to the elevator bank and threw her hands up on the marble wall and tried to steady herself. The world was spinning, and she could hardly breathe. "Are you all right?" a building security guard asked. "No, I'm not all right," she said. "Can I help you?" he asked. "No, no, I'll be OK," she replied. When the elevator doors opened, she entered and had a minute to figure out what to say to everyone gathering upstairs.

On the 107th floor, her fourteen-year-old daughter, Michelle, and the boys were waiting for her, their eyes big. Several FBI agents were there. The family walked into the dressing room, where there were more agents. "Get out," Fournier said to them, trembling. "Just get out and leave me alone. Please, I don't want to talk to you. Just get out!"

One of them said she'd have to come in on Monday to talk, but the men filed out, leaving Fournier alone with her children. She told the kids that Marino had been arrested. "What are we going to do with all of these people coming?" Fournier said out loud as much to herself as to them. Michelle replied, "Mom, put that gown on," and then she echoed what she'd heard her mother say many times before: "The show must go on."

The guests would be arriving at any minute. Could Fournier get through the next two hours? She had no choice. She decided to tell people that Marino had had an accident on the way over and he was all right but they had taken him to St. Vincent's Hospital for X-rays. It was an obvious lie but plausible enough to maintain a facade.

As guests arrived, groups huddled. They drank champagne and ate hors d'oeuvres while the piano player played Joe Cocker's "You Are So Beautiful." Fournier felt them eyeing her—not unusual for a bride—but here she was the center of a nightmare.

She approached Marino's mother, Grace, who was sitting in a round, open-clam-shaped Papasan chair, wearing black, an unusual color for the mother of a groom. Fournier leaned in close to her and said, "Grace, you must have known something." The Marino matron looked at her with contempt, and Fournier quickly walked away.

"They must have known," she says. "She must have known."

At least, this is how Fournier tells it. According to the arresting FBI agents, Frank Spero and Matthew Tricorico, and the prosecutor of Marino's case, Michael Guadagno, a subpoena had been issued for Fournier before May 26. If so, although she had not yet appeared in court, Fournier would have known about his impending arrest for bank robbery and assault. Fournier denies this. Spero and Tricorico say that they arrested Marino in the B2 garage level of the World Trade Center, where they were waiting for him. They say that NYPD officers and other FBI agents booked Marino while the two of them went up to Windows on the World, where they informed Fournier that they had just arrested her soon-to-be husband. Fournier, they say, sat in her dressing room and slowly rolled a bottle of Dom Perignon in her hands, while saying, as if in a trance, "The show must go on."

Joe Baum stands in the Pool Room during the construction of the Four Seasons, which opened in 1959.

Baum (seated, middle) holds court during a tasting at La Fonda del Sol with chef Albert Stockli (standing), 1960.

Designer William Pahlmann provided the inspiration for the Forum of the Twelve Caesars, which opened in 1957.

The Twin Towers were under construction from 1966 until 1973.

Baum with his culinary muse, James Beard, who wrote in a letter, "If we're going to climb 107 floors, let's tickle the senses from top to bottom."

From left: Hilton International president Curt Strand, Baum, Port Authority executive director A. Gerdes Kuhbach, and World Trade Center director Guy Tozzoli, early 1970s.

Baum, members of his Windows team (from left: Dennis Sweeney, Barbara Kafka, and Elizabeth Siber), and Hilton International's Toni Aigner share the joy of dinnerware for a promotional photo, circa 1975.

From left: Consultant Barbara Kafka, Baum, Windows director Alan Lewis, and Cellar Master Kevin Zraly, in yet another endless meeting, 1976.

Pages from Baum's weekly calendar, 1976.

The 7-foot Big Kitchen letters were designed by Milton Glaser, who collaborated with architect James Lamantia and firm Harper & George to construct the eatery in the World Trade Center concourse.

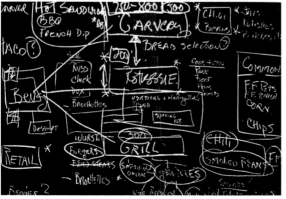

Menu items for a Big Kitchen food station were sketched out on a chalkboard in Baum's office at 111 Eighth Avenue, circa 1972.

The Twin Towers went from being loathed "filing cabinets" to reigning
as the prized signature of the Manhattan skyline, 1973–2001.

Construction crews preparing for the 1976 opening.

From left: Alan Lewis, Windows opening chef André René, and Baum have their cake, 1976.

An early Windows menu, 1976.

DINNER

Terrine of Veal and Pistachios
Prosciutto with Watercress Mousse
Little Neck Clams with Spring Onion Aspic
Iced Curried Fruits
Cheese Profiterolles—Hot

or

Tomato Consommé with Wild Thyme
Cream of Minted Sweet Pea—Cold
Corn and Crab Soup

Braised Striped Bass Wrapped in Lettuce
Roast Prime Sirloin, Mushroom Purée, Sauce Périgourdine
Baked Shrimp with Pernod Imperial, White Rice
Local Duckling Roasted Crisp, Green Beans au Gratin

Three Green Salad

The Golden Lemon Tart   Chocolate Pastry Cake
Mocha Mousse Praliné   Kentucky Julep Parfait
Pineapple Sorbet with Fresh Berries   Ice Creams—Best of Brands

Colombian Coffee   Tea Selection

$13.50

Baum courted friendly media coverage to market his restaurants. He was a darling of the industry press, and mainstream outlets, such as the *New York Times*, featured his restaurants regularly. Clockwise from left: The 1976 *New York* magazine cover that is often credited with ensuring the restaurant's success; on the cover of *Restaurant Hospitality*, with architect Warren Platner, in 1977; and a 1977 *Holiday* cover story written by restaurant critic Craig Claiborne, who lavished praise on Baum's Four Seasons in 1959.

The 65-foot entry "Gallery" transported guests through a kaleidoscopic fantasia of light, geodes, and international imagery.

Although the window seats were most valued by diners, the interior tables provided the best panorama of the city.

Baum asserted that "there wasn't a bad seat in the house" because of its tiered design.

The City Lights Bar, with a "library of liquor" and mirror-paneled ceiling, faced Brooklyn and Queens.

After guests disembarked from the one-minute elevator journey into the sky, they were seduced by Warren Platner's "sensuous modernism."

Kevin Zraly (standing) accommodated confident oenophiles and wine neophytes alike.

Platner's layout gave guests a sense of privacy despite the 350-seat capacity of the restaurant.

A collapsed section of the West Side Highway, near Canal Street, in 1973, when the World Trade Center loomed over a city in decline.

Kevin Zraly in the Cellar in the Sky, circa 1976.

Doorman Karl Feile in the early 1980s at his lectern on the ground floor.

Windows was one of the few fine-dining restaurants in the city in the 1970s that hired women to be captains and maître d's.

From left: Sous chef Siegfried Hohaus, executive chef Hermann Reiner, and executive sous chef Karl Schmid, mid-1980s.

Captain Claudette Fournier (standing), years before her "fiasco," serves Guy Tozzoli and guest, 1976.

Front of house Windows staff (Paul Egger is in the black suit in the middle), circa 1977.

Chef Marc Murphy (far left) with his Cellar in the Sky crew, circa 1996.

Bartenders at the Greatest Bar on Earth, circa 1999; from left: Richard Chew, Frances McDonald (now Delgado), George Delgado, and Angel Santiago.

Chef de cuisine Michael Ammirati with executive chef/director Michael Lomonaco, at the pass, circa 1998.

Architect Hugh Hardy's 1996 reboot of Windows featured bright colors and origami-inspired ceilings.

Baum celebrates his 75th birthday with the Radio City Rockettes at the Rainbow Room, 1995.

Michael Whiteman and Rozanne Gold during the "Cooking Med-Rim in America" dinner honoring Gold and chef Michael Ginor at the redesigned Windows, 1996.

Milton Glaser–designed plates complemented the view of the Brooklyn Bridge, 1996.

"We are bullish on New York," asserted Baum and Michael Whiteman in their renewal proposal.

Luis Alfonso Chimbo emigrated from Ecuador and was working his way up in the Windows receiving department, 2000.

The collapse of the South Tower as seen from Church Street, on which Michael Lomonaco and other Windows employees fled uptown.

Smoke and debris from the destroyed Twin Towers, including a letter addressed to Joe Baum, drifts toward Brooklyn.

The World Trade Center footprint became known as Ground Zero.

On September 11, Frank Mancini was part of the Bronx Builders construction meeting for a new bar on the 107th floor. Terence Manning (above, right) was attending the Risk Waters conference on the 106th floor.

"Missing" posters blanketed the city for weeks after the September 11 attacks.

WINDOWS
ON THE
WORLD

❧

An Interfaith Memorial Service

The Windows on the World community mourns its dear friends and colleagues who lost their lives on September 11, 2001. We grieve with their families. By their dedicated professionalism, respect for guests and colleagues, and the shared belief that every person matters, our colleagues raised the restaurant to world-class levels of excellence and renown. With their spirit of hard work, goodwill, personal dignity, and sense of optimism, they represented the best of our city, our country, our world. They remain our beacon and will never be forgotten.

❧

La comunidad de Windows on the World estamos llorando a los queridos amigos y colegas que perdieron sus vidas el 11 de Septiembre del 2001. Nosotros lamentamos junto a sus familiares. Con su dedicado profesionalismo, el respeto por los clientes y por sus compañeros de trabajo, y la compartida creencia que todas las personas son importantes, nuestros colegas llevaron el restaurante a un nivel mundial de excelencia y renombre. Con su espíritu trabajador, buena voluntad, dignidad personal y sentido de optimismo, ellos representaron lo mejor de nuestra ciudad, nuestro país, nuestro mundo. Ellos siempre serán nuestra luz de inspiración y nunca los olvidaremos.

Stephen Adams	Clara Hinds	Jesus Ovalles
Sophia-Buruwaa Addo	Heather Ho	Manuel Patrocino
Shakhir Ahmed	John Holland	Victor Paz-Gutierrez
Antonio J. Alvarez	Francois Jean-Pierre	Alejo Perez
Idrise Ahsour	Eliseas (Junito) Joahua, Jr.	John F. Puckas
Manuel O. Asitimbay	Howard Kane	Moises N. Rivas
Sandy Ayala	Eugene Kniazev	David B. Rodriguez-Vargas
Veronique (Ronnie) Bowers	Abdoulaye Kone	Gilbert Ruiz
Jonathan Briley	Victor Kwarkye	Juan Salas
Jesus Cabezas	Alan Lafrance	Jacqueline Sayegh
Johan Carpio	Jeffrey LaTouche	Khamladai K. (Khams) Singh
Manuel-Gregorio Chavez	Yang-Der Lee	Roshan (Sean) Singh
Luis Chimbo	Orasri Liangthanasarn	Abdoul Karim Traore
Mohammed S. Chowdhury	Leobardo Lopez	Jupiter Yambem
Jeffrey Coale	Jan Maciejewski	
Jaime Concepcion	Jay Magazine	MAS SECURITY
Annette Dataram	Charles Mauro	Mohammed Jawara
Jose Deprea	Manuel Mejia	
Nancy Diaz	Antonio Melendez	BRONX BUILDERS
Luke Dudek	Nana Minkah	Manuel DuMota
Doris Eng	Martin Morales	Obdulio Ruiz-Diaz
Sadie Ette	Blanca Morocho	Joshua Poptean
Henry Fernandez	Leonel Morocho	
Lucille Virgen Francis	Carlos Munoz	ON BEHALF OF BRONX BUILDERS
Enrique A. Gomez	Jerome Nedd	Frank Mancini
Jose B. Gomez	Juan Nieves, Jr.	Joe Mistrulli
Wilder Gomez	Jose R. Nunez	Thomas F. Hughes
Norberto Hernandez	Christine Olender	
Ysidro Hidalgo-Tejada	Isidro Ottenwalder	

Pages from the program for the October 1, 2001, service at the Cathedral of Saint John the Divine for the 79 victims who were working at Windows on the World on September 11.

Former Windows waiters and captains remain friends. From left: Sol Policar, Albert Lee, Nick Dervishaj, Zahed Hussain, and Magdi Labib joined five others for dinner at their long-time favorite, the High Pearl restaurant, in Elmhurst, Queens, 2017.

Enrique and Jose, two of the four legendary Gomez brothers who worked in the Windows kitchen, died on September 11. Enrique's family paid homage to him on September 11, 2018.

One of the agents said, "We just did you a favor." She stared daggers into them.

Fournier still maintains that she didn't know, but she concedes that she should have. Marino had served those years for robbery long before she knew him. He would sometimes shift furniture around in his home so that he could sit facing the entrance door. He said someone was getting out of the pen, and he had to be on the lookout. She'd found a .38 under a chair pillow. But he had promised her, many times, that he would never do anything that would put him away again.

Dinner was buffet style: tomato consommé with noodles, whole striped bass, roast beef, and vegetables. A four-piece band, arranged by Baum's music director, Tony Cabot, played jazz and show numbers. Fournier danced the first dance with her mother, putting on the best face she could.

"I don't know how she did it," says Gladys Mouton Di Stefano, the banquets manager who oversaw the catering that evening and watched Fournier dance to the bitter end. "I felt for her."

This horrible "fiasco," as Fournier would come to label it, would eventually end. Finally, she cut the four-tier, strawberry kirsch cake with white icing and columns and a beehive of fresh flowers on top, with Marino's sixteen-year-old son. Everyone clapped. They ate, took a last look at those incredible twinkling lights spreading out like a carpet down below, and began to leave.

* * *

"The FBI took the guest list" is nothing a newlywed wants to hear. When Alan Lewis said it to Claudette Fournier quietly in her dressing room, she caught the insinuation. As cataclysmic as it was enduring that evening, a brooding implication hung heavily in a room full of outer-borough Italian-Americans being watched by FBI agents: Organized crime had made it to the 107th floor of the World Trade Center in a very public way.

Although Michael Guadagno, the U.S. attorney for the organized crime task force, was heading the investigation, prosecutors wouldn't confirm to the *Staten Island Advance* that the Mafia was involved in the Food 'n' Things robbery. The paper noted, however, that there were "many men with mob ties" at the reception.

"Beansie" Campanella, a tough guy and associate of the renegade Bonanno crime family, was there. He and his wife had gone to Acapulco with Fournier and Marino. Angelo Ponte, the owner of the Italian restaurant Ponte's on the West Side Highway just north of the World Trade Center and the reputed garbage disposal kingpin for the Genovese crime family, was on the guest list, but he didn't show up. He sent the couple a bottle of Dom Perignon, though. Also invited was Paul Castellano, who had recently taken over control of the Gambino family after the death of its head, Carlo Gambino.

Fournier says Marino wasn't a connected guy. "There was nobody who could say he was involved," she says. She says she would have known. Of course, if he was, and she knew, it would implicate her.

The prosecutor, Michael Guadagno, characterizes Marino's crime as his attempt to be "an earner," an associate who was proving himself to be a valuable asset to the mob. The more scores you get, the closer you are to being "made." The Windows on the World reception, according to Guadagno, was his coming-out party.

But Marino was the only perpetrator who got caught for the six-man heist at Food 'n' Things. His fingerprints were on the Wells Fargo truck's steering wheel. Plus, he bought the house, boat, and car with cash that was still in the original bank wrappers. He got thirty years.

The bank truck money was never recovered. Marino didn't win his appeal, and he also never flipped on his accomplices. Some would say that that was as good a sign as any that Marino's loyalty ran deep.

The story was fodder for the tabloids. After Marino's arraignment at the Brooklyn Federal Court, Fournier appeared on the cover of the *Daily News* dashing from paparazzi, wearing a white blouse and wide-brimmed hat, over the headline, WEDDING ARRAIGNED OUT.

She was never accused of any crime. Or asked to give up any possible ill-gained possessions. Fournier was called before a grand jury and asked to look at photographs and identify possible accomplices to Marino, but she said she didn't recognize anyone. She moved into Marino's house in Boca Raton. The last contact she had with Windows on the World was a court order to pay the wedding bill of $8,877, which she never did.

CHAPTER 19
GLASS HALF FULL

Claudette Fournier's "fiasco" was a particularly colorful moment for the otherwise consistently winning Windows on the World banquets department. It had become the most successful food services operation in the World Trade Center. And it was under orders from the Port Authority to keep things clean and out of the morning tabloids. "They wanted no problems," Gladys Mouton Di Stefano says. "They wanted everything to be on a straight line."

Windows on the World had become the ultimate "special occasion" restaurant, where New Yorkers brought friends and family from out of town and went to celebrate anniversaries, job promotions, birthdays, and graduations. They hosted large events. Its west-facing Hudson River Suites banquet area was where people with the resources—and, increasingly, as the city clawed its way out of financial ruin, more people had more money to spend—had weddings, bar mitzvahs, and sweet sixteens. And for companies downtown, there weren't comparable spaces to be found anywhere.

Each year, Mouton Di Stefano was booking more than a hundred, give or take, hundred-person parties into multiple banquet-sized rooms that could be extended or condensed by a series of movable dividers; additionally, she was booking a good forty or so parties for four hundred people; and there were several parties for eight hundred or more guests. For Inhilco, the margins for churning out buffet-style meals were much higher than à la carte, making the profits significantly larger.

By the 1978 holiday season, the restaurant's success was no longer directly in the hands of Joe Baum. As stipulated in his contract, in September 1978, he had stepped down as the president of Inhilco. Although he and Michael Whiteman retained a consulting contract with the Port Authority, they were no longer supervising the day-to-day operations. Curt Strand said that his old friend had brought the World Trade Center food services into "a profitable phase" and that he was now free to engage in external projects. Alan Lewis remained the Windows on the World director.

Inhilco picked Toni Aigner, a mild-mannered German veteran of the company who, as its director of food and beverage planning and development, had overseen international grosses of two hundred sixty-six million dollars, to replace Baum as president.

Restaurant Hospitality magazine caught up with Baum in a confident mood, reporting that the World Trade Center food services operation was doing twenty-five million dollars in volume and that the sixteen million dollars made by Windows alone made it the largest-grossing restaurant in the world.

"When I signed on to develop food services at the World Trade Center, I anticipated the most single success story in restaurant operations anywhere," Baum said in his elliptical manner. "I really knew what I had to do. I had to take chances and be the aggressor and say, 'I'm going to make this the single best known restaurant in the world in a year.' I didn't anticipate success; I anticipated that we would be successful."

He also offered more pragmatic, possibly temperate, reflections: "If you review our work over the years, you'll find that much of what everybody considers to be new and daring didn't come about because I suddenly had a crazy idea," he says. "They developed because of the way we approached the problems posed by a location or condition."

Left unsaid was what Baum would be working on next. (Major consulting jobs from Kansas City to Hiroshima.) Also undeclared was that both Inhilco and the Port Authority were buoyant about the prospect of being able to assert cost-cutting measures that had been too difficult to enforce under Joe Baum.

Baum left Windows on the World touted as a "wizard," an "impresario," who successfully completed his eight-year mission. The restaurant was a hit. His rude dismissal by Restaurant Associates was a forgotten indignity. The popular sentiment was articulated by the *New York Post* when it said he was "the one person who saves the World Trade Center from being a white elephant." Even hostile judges of the World Trade Center, such as critic Paul Goldberger, conceded that Baum's contributions in the concourse and on the 107th floor were "signs that Manhattan's fabled southern tip may be entering an intriguing new phase of development."

"It was unthinkable to say a good word about the Twin Towers in polite company," Goldberger wrote in the *New York Times*. "But then Joseph Baum, the irrepressible impresario of restaurants, began to show his stuff."

It fell to Baum's replacement, Toni Aigner, to oversee the consolidation of Inhilco's office and storage spaces on the 106th floor to make room for the construction of a huge ballroom area for seven hundred people. Inhilco also began constructing an eight-hundred-twenty-five-room hotel at 3 World Trade Center, the first new major hotel in the area in decades. Hilton International couldn't use its name in the United States, so the company called it the Vista International, which wouldn't open until 1981.

In addition to catering, another reliable financial bulwark was the restaurant's original reason for being: the private club. After a period of capping membership to increase its allure, the Club opened up to more members and went from one thousand five hundred to three thousand, which, along with a rise in dues, translated into more than a million dollars in club membership charges per year.

The Port Authority had a lot at stake in the Club's success as an exclusive entity. The Club remained Guy Tozzoli's way of selling the Twin Towers to the world. He took prospective tenants on tours, taking them out to lunch, showing them the library for quiet reading, the humidor, and the Little Spa, which had a small sauna, whirlpool, exercise room, and "all-over-needle" shower. The Club, as stated in its bylaws, went a long way toward defining the Port Authority's mandate to encourage world trade by bringing internationally minded businessmen together in a social setting in its billion-dollar buildings. The club's director from 1977 to 2001, Jules Roinnel, says it plainly: "The Port Authority was only interested in the Club."

The Club provided several core services: as a meeting place for businesspeople; for an internationally focused businessmen's speaker series, which brought in the likes of Henry Kissinger (a regular, who was paid sixteen thousand dollars for a half-hour speech), Secretary of Defense Donald Rumsfeld, and British TV journalist David Frost; and for its traveling trade and cultural missions.

When Windows on the World opened, there were sixteen World Trade Centers throughout the world, where Club members had shared privileges. (Eventually, there would be more than one hundred.) The Club sponsored a traveling tour series that brought forty or so members in a group to countries such as Russia (in 1978) and China (in 1980), new frontiers at the time. Port Authority brass often attended. Pictures suggest that Guy Tozzoli, wearing a toga and standing in a horse-drawn chariot at a hotel in Rome, enjoyed the benefits of membership.

The Club wasn't to everyone's liking. "Not much of a club, frankly," sniffed the otherwise impressed Gael Greene. "No squash courts. No tennis. No swimming pool or crisping in the sun." But for the Port Authority, and a particular New York professional clientele, it was just right. Club members did not tend to be elite businesspeople, more mid-level executives who enjoyed the benefits, such as organized trips to Broadway shows. Others were looking for a leg up—say, an entrepreneur with a small business in New Jersey who was hoping to get international distribution or a broker who wanted to entertain his investors.

Breakfast was always free for members, but not many took advantage of it. There might be a couple dozen guests on the busiest of mornings. More came for lunch. Roinnel made sure to check in with all members. If he knew that a member's son had just had his bar mitzvah, Roinnel might get the kitchen to treat the proud father with a "blizzard of desserts," an unexpected treat of six desserts for four people.

The Club brought in a steady income, provided a selling point for the Port Authority, and helped manifest the World Trade Center's raison d'être as an international meeting place. It was also a strong complement to Kevin Zraly's successful wine program. Of the restaurant's sixteen-million-dollar annual gross, one million dollars was coming from the wine cellar. Zraly was selling ten thousand bottles per month. One in three guests was ordering wine.

Zraly's wine program was a major draw for Club members who were accustomed to the structures of elite membership in organizations such as the Confrérie des Chevaliers du Tastevin, a decades-old society dedicated to promoting the food and wine of Burgundy through gathering for formal dinners, dressing in silk robes, and bestowing knighthoods. They reserved their own bins, as Ted Kheel had, and held elaborate dinners on the 107th floor under Zraly's direction.

For lunch, club members could, if they wished, maintain their own wine locker bins in the restaurant cellar without charge, and they could buy wine at 25 percent above the restaurant's cost (about 25 percent below retail).

Club member Jules Epstein (bin #7), a Manhattan insurance broker and rabid wine enthusiast, started his own wine society, called Club de Huit, its meetings held in the Cellar in the Sky each year, in which the core eight members invited three guests apiece. The hosts were each responsible for bringing two bottles, so that there were at least sixteen on hand. They brought Burgundies, Bordeaux, and Rhônes, and none was younger than 1961. Some were from the nineteenth century.

Club de Huit had four rules: Business talk was not allowed; black tie was required; no one was allowed to drive himself home; and there were no other rules. For many of those involved, a meeting was the wine event of the year.

Kevin Zraly presided with genial authority. He taught his flock not to drink for vintage or label but to develop one's own taste. Even when he wasn't teaching a class, he spread knowledge of and a passion for wine, because he couldn't stop talking about it. Because Baum originally said Zraly couldn't have any sommeliers or wine stewards assisting him, he trained the captains until they were a fleet of wine experts.

Zraly's good-natured proselytizing was infectious. As Michael Skurnik moved from being a lunch waiter to a dinner waiter, he'd admired how Zraly tore through the restaurant with flair. Zraly would dash from the stockroom to the Cellar in the Sky to the main restaurant and over to the Hudson River Suites, checking that the wines were being chilled, stocked, and poured properly.

Skurnik was eager to learn more about the wine trade; he might have been just a kid from New Jersey playing in bands, but he had a genuine curiosity bred from growing up with parents who kept a heavily stocked cellar in their home. He didn't mind taking a pay cut to work directly with Zraly. Skurnik would be making eleven thousand dollars as an assistant sommelier, much less than as a waiter, but he didn't have to think long when he got the offer. Serving wine to John Wayne and Mick Jagger sure made up for the loss of income, but more important was the professional training. After working in the Windows on the World wine department, Skurnik went on to become one of the largest independent importers and distributors of wine in the country.

Early on, Zraly figured he was spending so much time informally instructing staff between lunch and dinner service, why not formally teach classes to the guests? His degree was in education. In the fall of 1976, Inhilco agreed to let Zraly host a Windows on the World wine class for the club members.

* * *

The heart of Windows on the World's wine culture was in the Cellar in the Sky, the thirty six seat restaurant on the eastern side of the 107th floor, surrounded by wine bottles with dramatic, dappled lighting caused by the sunlight refracting through the bottles or the stained-glass lighting fixtures, which evoked sun rays passing through grapevine foliage.

The restaurant had one set menu, served at 7:30 P.M., which was changed every two weeks. It was featured in the *New York Times* in a weekly ad that touted the seven-dish meal and five complementary wines that were carefully picked by the chef and cellar master. It was telling that the ads didn't detail the food but specified the wines instead. One menu included a Wisdom & Warter Fino Sherry 1908 Solera; a Chassagne-Montrachet, Domaine Sauzet 1978; Cabernet Sauvignon, Silver Oak 1975; Spanna Traversagna, Vallana 1967; Eltviller Langenstück Auslese, Schloss Eltz 1976. The prix fixe meal originally cost fifty dollars.

As musician John Lehmann-Haupt played classical guitar, guests sat on soft, leather-strapped chairs at polished oak tables for the meal, which started with an appetizer (quiche tartlets with bacon and chive; smoked trout fillet in vegetable aspic) and a choice of champagne, Lillet, Kir, or perhaps a white Burgundy. After canapés, the dining experience would last two or more hours. The lobster salad with crayfish went with a Riesling; broiled sweetbreads with a Beringer Fume Blanc; the roast veal loin served with Beaune Clos des Mouches, Drouhin; the cheese board went with Barolo; and the poached pear with hazelnut ice cream was followed by a port.

Zraly's most dedicated oenophile followers ate at the Cellar in the Sky. They were accustomed to the royal treatment, but one group got an especially special lunch thanks to a new wine steward working in the Cellar. The guests were delighted to be getting a one hundred fifty dollar Chambertin for just forty dollars. The steward made a mistake— he thought he was giving them the *Gevrey*-Chambertin. The students ended up ordering five bottles.

As exorbitant as things could get, Windows on the World's wine department was better known for its accessibility than its elitism. One of Zraly's first master wine lists may have contained a $236 Eiswein, which came with a letter of invitation to the vineyard in Germany, but it also had a $3.25 Yugoslavian Cabernet Savignon, which wasn't half bad. Zraly sold half bottles of wine, considered gauche in some circles. And he sold them at prices that defied business convention. Baum's rule of serving twenty dollar bottles for forty-one dollars was already a bargain in a town where the same bottle normally went for fifty dollars, or more, in other restaurants.

The wine culture at Windows had been thriving since day one. And then, despite its success, Kevin Zraly changed everything. In 1976, British wine specialist Steven Spurrier organized a wine competition in Paris, which shocked the establishment when the French judges picked two California wines—a 1973 Chardonnay from Château Montelena and the 1973 Cabernet Sauvignon from Stag's Leap Wine Cellars—over their French competitors.

Zraly, already a champion of American wines, rode the wave caused by the so-called "Judgment of Paris."

"Let's turn our international friends on to the American wines," he recalls telling Baum. From 1976 to 1978, the restaurant's wine list was at least 80 percent French. By 1981, it was 75 percent American. It was also said to be the biggest dollar-volume seller of wines in the world.

In 1980, Zraly turned his six-week wine class for club members into the Windows on the World Wine School, open to the public. He also ran a consulting business, and he handed off the title of cellar master to Ray Wellington, his sommelier who had worked his way up from busboy to waiter to captain. Zraly continued to oversee the wine program as wine director for Hilton International, but he was done with the day-to-day racing through the restaurant. Because of his defection, Alan Lewis didn't talk with Zraly for a year.

CHAPTER 20
GROWING UP IN THE EIGHTIES

Five years after Windows on the World opened, a new downtown restaurant in the shadow of the World Trade Center began drawing the city's nightlife. Just nine blocks up West Broadway, brothers Keith and Brian McNally and Lynn Wagenknecht spent one hundred forty thousand dollars—less than one-fiftieth what it had cost to construct Windows on the World—to open the Odeon, a modern twist on a French bistro.

The McNallys and Wagenknecht, who eventually married and then divorced Keith, had stripped away layers of the old Towers Cafeteria and added their own polish—a curved, 1930s mahogany bar, a sparkling frieze of the city's skyline (pre–World Trade Center), gorgeous waiters—to create a retro, self-aware brasserie that provided a comfortable and cool oasis on a gritty cobblestone street surrounded by urban blight. They hired a European-trained, twenty-four-year-old African-American cook from Brooklyn, Patrick Clark, who cooked up a nouvelle cuisine bistro menu that was as adventurous and lustful as its clientele.

Clark turned out a reliable steak frites as well as leeks over lobster, racks of lamb with whole garlic cloves, snails in parsley cream sauce, and foie gras with endive. The self-consciously sexy menu tickled guests. Comedian John Belushi harped on the unusual sound of "aruuuugala." It was good quality and not too fussy but not cheap either. And the frothy white chocolate mousse being served was the perfect complement to the heady culture emerging there.

The Odeon opened just when the SoHo art scene was exploding, with millions of dollars suddenly being spent on paintings by artists who been holed up in the rickety nearby lofts or rat-infested tenement flats in the East Village. Paula Cooper and Leo Castelli's galleries might have been open for a decade, but new dealers such as Tony Shafrazi and Mary Boone were pouring in, creating a scene with commercial spaces next door to where the artists were living—forcing buyers to come downtown. Such artists as Jean-Michel Basquiat, Julian Schnabel, and Keith Haring made the Odeon their own, as did old-guard artists such as Frank Stella, Roy Lichtenstein, and Andy Warhol.

Quick to follow was a cocaine-and-celebrity cocktail of *Saturday Night Live* regulars Belushi, Dan Aykroyd, and Lorne Michaels, as well as actor Robert De Niro, director Martin Scorsese, and writers such as Tom Wolfe and Jay McInerney, whose 1984 novel, *Bright Lights, Big City*, had on its cover its leather-jacket-clad protagonist facing the alluring, Art Deco neon sign of the Odeon under a dark sky, while the brightly lit World Trade Center looms in the background. The meaning was in 1980s high relief; the World Trade Center could stand in for the "big city," but the action was at Odeon.

There had been life downtown before, but it had been in pockets; the improving economy enabled different elements, including new restaurants such as the no-fuss-but-fantastic Chanterelle, to coalesce into a culture. Between 1976 and 1987, the city added four hundred thousand jobs, four-fifths of which were in the private sector, a significant jump from the last job growth spurt in the 1960s. The city was changing. The service economy, health care, finance, and construction were booming. Although there was a national recession between 1981 and 1982, New York City fared better, thanks to Wall Street. From 1980 to 1987, the financial workforce nearly doubled, gaining seventy-three thousand jobs for a total of one hundred sixty-three thousand by 1987, as the stock market rose by 229 percent from 1982 to 1987.

More money being made meant more going into the city's tax coffers as well as into a white-hot real estate market that led to housing price increases of over 150 percent throughout the city between 1980 and 1989. The new money fueled more comfortable lifestyles for some and untenable rents for others as gentrification swept through the city.

The white working class was fleeing the city. In 1950, 85 percent of the city's 6.8 million people were Caucasian. By the 1980s, the white population had decreased by more than 3 million while the million or so black, Asian, and Hispanic New Yorkers increased to 4 million. As the city was becoming more economically stratified, it was also becoming more racially diverse, welcoming immigrants from Asia, South America, and the West Indies in record numbers.

This diversifying population had voted for Ed Koch to be mayor in 1977, and although his numbers with black and Latino voters diminished in subsequent years, he was reelected in 1981 and 1985, with 75 percent and 78 percent of the total vote. Koch liked to ask New Yorkers, "How am I doing?" By 1985, he answered his own question by declaring the city's financial crisis over.

Earlier, as an up-and-coming Democrat from the Village, Koch had called the World Trade Center "a conspiracy by people who think they know what is best for New York City." And, as mayor, he had his tussles with the Port Authority. In 1980, he began whinging that the agency's ten million dollar annual payments to the city agreed to in the initial deal hashed out between the Port Authority's Austin Tobin and then mayor John Lindsay was just a fraction of the one hundred million dollars in property taxes the city would have been getting if the World Trade Center were owned by a private company.

But as a New Yorker who loved to eat, the mayor was a frequent guest of the complex's restaurants. And by 1985, Koch could also politically stomach the World Trade Center's relationship to the city when the Port Authority signed a twenty-year lease for seven hundred million dollars with Dean Witter Financial Services. The deal finally made the World Trade Center a legitimately successful real estate property. The financial services company was willing to pay thirty-one dollars to fifty-two dollars per square foot over the life of the lease, versus the ten dollars the state had been paying.

Not long after Peter Goldmark Jr. became executive director of the PA in 1977, he gave up on the commitment to have only foreign-trading companies in the World Trade Center. He believed there weren't enough such companies to fill up his buildings. Engineering and finance companies began moving in, and the agency saw its World Trade Center revenue increase from eighty-three million dollars in 1978 to two hundred four million dollars in 1983.

The Dean Witter deal was a win-win for the city and Port Authority. The PA had agreed to transfer the increased income to fund regional development. Additionally, it would pay the city more.

In a ceremony held in July 1985 at the World Trade Center, the mayor referred to "Nelson Rockefeller's folly" as having become "one of our greatest assets." The PA's Goldmark handed a one million dollar check to Mayor Koch as an advance on the payments it would be giving the city. "We would be lesser without them and are greater with them," the mayor said of the Twin Towers.

* * *

By the 1980s, Windows had bid adieu to its original chef, André René, who returned to his position as executive chef at the upscale Pierre hotel on Fifth Avenue. René, who was in his late seventies, was an amicable Alsatian who seemed eager to return to the relative order of the Pierre. He had had good relations with his staff of eighty working at Windows, but he didn't have complete control of his kitchen. Cooks arrived late without reprimand. His food costs—the amount of money the food on the plate costs the restaurant as a percentage of what it was charging its guests for it—were on the high end.

Another Frenchman replaced René: Henri Boubée, who had been the Hilton International chef for the Middle East region. Boubée was another classically trained, respected, old-school chef, but he lacked René's ability to brush off the Sturm und Drang of working under Alan Lewis. René could endure a Lewis rant without seeming to care, but Boubée would turn red and lose his composure.

In 1982, Boubée was replaced by Hermann Reiner, a stout, moustached Austrian with thick glasses who had started at Windows as a sous chef in 1978 and had moved up to be executive chef of the Market Dining Rooms & Bar. Reiner had chafed at times under Boubée, whom he considered to be inefficient.

"There was a lot of waste," says Reiner, who admits to having a "strong personality." He would question Boubée on his choice of ingredients and over scheduling issues. Boubée left to work at a hotel in Dallas during the oil boom, bringing with him a number of Windows' kitchen staff, which allowed Reiner to start with a clean slate and a new set of rules, including no drinking alcohol until the last setting. Reiner says that previous chefs had had a habit of drinking wine during family meal, or staff lunch, which gave license to the cooks to do the same, including one of the older French cooks who would drink red wine with ice throughout service. Reiner put an end to that.

The overall cuisine itself wasn't markedly different. Reiner kept the quasi-continental, fine-dining menu of his predecessors; he kept the James Beard winners, such as the rack of lamb and the chicken hash. But he was willing to follow new trends as well, such as the Coho salmon that everyone wanted to eat, and to deemphasize old ones, like aspic.

When Reiner became executive chef, there was already one particularly promising young chef on staff, Eberhard Müller, who had been one of the many Europeans shipped to Windows on the World to do apprentice work. Müller, who had come from Paris's three-star L'Archestrate, worked for just two weeks in 1981, but he made an impression on Alan Lewis, who said he could have a permanent spot in the kitchen if he wanted it.

He did. Müller was a new breed of European chef, unconvinced by what he calls "nose to the grindstone nouvelle cuisine," some of which was still being served at Windows on the World. "Nouvelle cuisine" had taken hold in the 1960s and 1970s, when French chefs such as Paul Bocuse departed from the complex dishes and heavy sauces of the French cuisine classique. New emphasis on freshness, simplicity, innovative presentation, and a shorter menu took hold.

But Müller resisted the new orthodoxy of nouvelle cuisine. He found a mentor in Lewis, who was open to integrating different ethnic foods and ideas, especially in the Hors d'Oeuvrerie. Müller was part of a cutting-edge food scene just ready to burst in the city. In 1983, Larry Forgione, who, as a chef at the River Café, had developed a food-source novelty called "free-range" chickens with a local farmer, opened his An

American Place, a name suggested by his mentor, James Beard. And in 1984, Jonathan Waxman opened California-influenced Jams uptown; Drew Nieporent and Tony Zazula found a space downtown near Chanterelle, where they created Montrachet with fierce French chef David Bouley firing up postmodern and delicious dishes such as chicken livers with cornmeal madeleines in the kitchen (where other promising chefs, among them David Burke and Rocco DiSpirito, would work); and the Gotham Bar and Grill began its playful spin on haute cuisine. The next year, Danny Meyer put caps on the New American Cuisine with his Union Square Cafe, with Michael Romano in the kitchen. And, in 1986, a young chef with French and Asian food training named Jean-Georges Vongerichten came to the city to work at the new Lafayette.

Müller, twenty-seven and confident, was left alone to run the Cellar in the Sky, according to Reiner, who let him create menus that Reiner would occasionally check on. "I had no problem with Eberhard," Reiner says. "He did a good job." Reiner would take successful dishes from the Cellar and adapt them for the much larger main restaurant. He later promoted Müller to executive sous chef, so that he could help oversee all the restaurants on the 107th floor.

Müller's innovative dishes created a buzz in the city, earning him respect from other young chefs such as Thomas Keller (long before he was a three-star chef-owner of French Laundry). But Müller was frustrated in his attempts to make the Cellar's food lighter and fresher, because he couldn't get access to the necessary good ingredients. He couldn't get fresh sunflowers or a speck of chervil or fresh chives. The parsley was old and wilted. Ramps were unheard of. Maybe sometimes good tomatoes would come from New Jersey in the summer, but that was the exception.

He wanted fresh halibut and scallops. But he couldn't go to the Fulton Fish Market to buy seafood directly; Inhilco went through middlemen. He knew the Four Seasons was serving fresh porcini, so he wanted some too, but the Inhilco food services purchaser told him he'd have to settle for canned.

"Too many hands had to be greased to be able to procure what you really wanted," Müller says.

With time, however, things got better. In the early 1980s, a new distributor, Flying Foods, started bringing an array of fresh ingredients to restaurant chefs. College roommates Andy Arons and Walter Martin had experience working in restaurants where they'd noticed the discrepancy between what ingredients chefs had to work with compared to what they had in France.

They went to the abundant Rungis and Les Halles markets in Paris and began importing fresh Dover sole, haricots verts, chanterelles mushrooms, and mesclun salad to a grateful and discerning clientele, including Le Cirque, La Côte Basque, and catering savant Martha Stewart.

Arons slipped into the World Trade Center and found Reiner, who asked him to work directly with a very willing Müller. Arons supplied Windows on the World with a variety of ingredients, including squab and duck breasts for the dish Magret de Canard. When ducks are force-fed grains and fats to fatten their livers to make foie gras, there's an ancillary fattening effect on the breasts, which Windows on the World served seared, like a steak, with haricots verts. Arons would bring in one hundred sixty pounds' worth of duck breasts twice a week.

Different chefs found different ways to circumvent the Central Services pipeline. Henri Boubée found a Mrs. Fields in New Jersey who grew herbs and made her own vinegar. He had her provide both for the entire restaurant. Hermann Reiner got his chanterelles FedExed from Oregon and fresh venison raised in and shipped from the panhandle of Texas.

The greatest obstacle of all for the Windows kitchen was volume; producing so much food inevitably has an adverse effect on quality. A significant factor was that the physical kitchen itself was simply too small. According to Reiner, it was built for perhaps two hundred fifty covers per night. But the kitchen would serve four times that number.

They achieved that feat through timing. There were only five "burner" areas, with seven cooks on the line. One or two cooks would be for Cellar in the Sky and another for banquets. If the Cellar in the Sky was serving at 7:30, then the banquets chef had to prepare most of his menu before that time. Sometimes the Cellar cooks would just have to wait.

They had two electric broilers, four convection ovens, and the charcoal grill. Each tool had to be used in a timely fashion. Roast beef could be cooked earlier in the day, to the point of being 80 percent done, and then put in storage. When it was ordered during dinner service, a chef would then put it back in the oven to finish it. Steaks would be cooked on the charcoal grill to achieve the proper sear to about 50 percent finished before being placed in the broiler.

There was also a cold kitchen area where prep work and finishing were attended by several cooks. Four butchers cut the steaks and prepared the meats. Scaling and filleting and other types of fish preparation were primarily completed in Central Services, so only one cook was responsible for the seafood on the 107th floor.

Several cooks were responsible for retrieving items from the walk-in boxes, one for fish, one for meat, and the so-called "beer refrigerator," which kept the dairy products. The units varied in dimension from large closets to bedroom-sized containers. They were supposed to be organized perfectly to expedite access, but they never were; racks of appetizers or other prepared foods were constantly being dragged out to make room.

Conducting this enormous orchestra, trying to make each table of guests feel it was being treated to a special, exquisitely prepared meal, was challenging enough, but the Windows kitchen was further handicapped by those damn electric stoves. They were horrible. You never had the exact firepower you needed. They would get so hot that the surfaces would buckle. Pots would warp, so there was no point in using good ones.

Müller resorted to his more reliable convection ovens or the charcoal grill, but you could only rely so much on the broiler cook. He had about twenty square feet of surface area on which he was constantly placing and arranging steaks, hamburgers, and lamb chops.

And it didn't happen often, but when too much oil or water was splashed on the electric range, it would virtually explode, causing a burst that would set off the fire alarm. Much worse than the shocking signal was the ANSUL system, which would release fire suppressant foam everywhere: on cooks, food, pots, pans, and all surfaces. When it did happen with four hundred people waiting for their meals in the dining room, guests were given complimentary champagne while the chefs made do with the Hors d'Oeuvrerie kitchen as backup.

* * *

On Thanksgiving, Easter Sunday, Mother's Day, and Christmas, the most popular days at the restaurant, Reiner would strongly consider following the early exits of the executive chefs who had preceded him, René and Boubée. He would get home and say to himself, "Tomorrow, I go to the old man [Alan Lewis] and I quit."

The stress of managing the kitchen—not the actual cooking—was his and Müller's responsibility. The chef de cuisine is deputized to work the line and oversee the actual, day-to-day cooking. The executives' task was to oversee all of production, from food orders to personnel to writing menus. They came in early in the morning and worked for hours on the orders, with the assistance of a receiving steward. They had to know what was in the walk-ins and Central Services and what needed to be replenished. Future days' menus also had to be anticipated.

After several hours of paperwork and phone calls, Müller, the executive sous chef, would walk through the kitchen and make sure preparations were in order. Reiner would then go through and put his finger in the sauces and taste what he could. Although Reiner concedes he may have yelled at staff at times, he says he believed in proper business management and chain of command. If something was wrong, he would call over the sous chef, inform him, and let him tear into the staff if he needed to.

When lunch service began, the executive chefs would oversee expediting working the pass, the area between the kitchen and the front of the house where the waiters would relay the orders and pick up the food. Reiner was assisted by a steward, who made sure all the flatware and glasses and other essential elements of the service were properly in place. The chief steward and several assistants were always running from the butcher to the dishwashers to the back waiter, providing whatever was needed.

After lunch service was completed, Reiner would have lunch, maybe some leftovers or a steak, with his chefs. And then there'd be a series of meetings covering the various banquets happening that week or handling staffing issues.

With dinner about to start, Reiner would check in on the fish butcher and also make sure essential prep tasks for the next day's banquets, such as trimming the beef tenderloin for one hundred people, had been done. And then back to the pass for dinner service at 5:00. There were generally three seatings per table, and he made sure he was on hand at the beginning, because if the first seating got screwed up, then the rest of the night would be a disaster. As the waiters came to the pass with the order receipts, Reiner would call them out, saying, "Two steaks, both medium rare," through a microphone so that everyone could hear him. No one talked in the kitchen. There was no music. Just the chopping, clanging, boiling sounds of cooking. Everyone had to be heads down, focused on the task assigned to him or her.

If a table ordered steaks and roast beef, Reiner would first call out the steaks, which take five or six minutes to cook. A couple of minutes later, he'd call for the roast beef. When he thought a dish should be done, he'd call out, "Checking on . . ." naming one cook or another, and they would reply with something such as, "Give me two minutes, chef."

When the entrée was plated, it would be placed on the slide, a heated metal surface where the food would line up, overseen by a steward while waiters lingered in the hallway to pick up their orders. Some would chat until the steward barked at them to shut up.

By the second seating, Reiner would be out of the kitchen. He found satisfaction in trying to satisfy Inhilco's drive for profitability and an efficient, full restaurant. He didn't expect to run the best restaurant in the city, but he had his goals. He proudly relays that Henri Boubée's food cost was closer to 32 percent while his was 25 percent. "How can you serve eight hundred, nine hundred dinners and expect three stars?" he asks. "It is not possible."

Müller jumped ship when, in 1986, French restaurateurs Gilbert Le Coze and his sister, Maguy, asked him to be the chef for the American version of their seafood-centric Parisian restaurant, Le Bernardin, also called Le Bernardin. He was soon walking the aisles of the Fulton Fish Market, cash in hand, to regularly purchase the kind of fresh fish he wanted. With Müller in the kitchen, Le Bernardin took the city by storm when it scored a coveted four-star review from the *New York Times* three months after opening.

The food at Windows on the World might have been eclipsed by what the city's finer restaurants had to offer, and it was no longer being lit up by the Joe Baum magic. But long after he'd gone, it remained a destination restaurant that served reasonably good food. And although Windows on the World was developing a reputation as a tourist-heavy restaurant—it determined that about 30 percent of its guests were from out of town—that meant a lot of people eating there were still local.

And the main restaurant and its satellites, the Hors d'Oeuvrerie and Cellar in the Sky, were getting good marks. The *New York Times'* food critic Bryan Miller wrote a review of the restaurant in July 1986, proclaiming, "[Windows on the World] has proved that being a serious restaurant and a sky-high tourist attraction are not mutually exclusive."

Miller praised the "lovely" chilled pea soup with fresh mint and Andy Arons's "rare and lean" roast breasts of duck. He may have correctly divined that the sauces were sometimes overused and produced in mass amounts, but there was still much to recommend, including the "succulent" roasted baby chicken and the rack of lamb.

And he found solace in the "monastic" Cellar in the Sky, where he praised the calf's liver and the lobster out of the shell in a truffle beurre blanc. Miller gave the Cellar in the Sky two stars. And although his otherwise upbeat review of Windows on the World produced only one star, he gave his answer to the question that Mimi Sheraton had thrown down like a gauntlet ten years earlier: "Windows on the World, while not a dazzler, is a solid and conscientious restaurant that would have appeal even if it were on ground level in midtown," Miller wrote.

CHAPTER 21
CHOPPING BLOCK

The high-flying 1980s brought significant changes to America's corporate landscape. Tremendous surges in the stock and housing markets, coupled with decreases in taxes and regulations, helped fuel feverish prospecting throughout the economy. The Airline Deregulation Act of 1978, which had freed interstate flight travel from the burden of artificially high pricing and government inefficiency, let the airline companies loose to become fiercely competitive. Many changed hands. Many went bankrupt.

The parent companies of Pan Am and American Airlines shed their hotel holdings in order to sustain their battling airlines. But the Trans World Corporation, owner of Hilton International and Inhilco, bucked the trend by holding on to its various hotel divisions and food services companies and instead spun off its financially troubled airline, Trans World Airlines, in 1983. In 1985, Trans World grossed $2.1 billion in revenue, of which Hilton International earned close to $700 million.

By 1986, while corporate raider Carl Icahn was tearing into the airline TWA and making a bundle for himself, Trans World Corporation was gleefully rich in cash and profitable businesses. It was looking to acquire more. But when Revlon chairman Ronald O. Perelman began maneuvering a possible takeover, Trans World CEO L. Edwin Smart began selling most of the company's assets. That included Hilton International, which Smart sold in December 1986 to an ambitious CEO, Richard J. Ferris, the chairman of UAL, the parent of United Airlines, who was on a two billion dollars spending spree, acquiring Hertz car rental and Westin hotels with a bold vision of a multifaceted company that could provide one-stop shopping to the weary traveler: flight, hotel, and car rental.

UAL bought Hilton International's ninety hotels around the world and six U.S. Vista hotels for just under one billion dollars, on its way to forecasting nine billion dollars in revenue. In this grand scheme,

Windows on the World and the World Trade Center restaurants were "not a factor," according to Curt Strand. "It was a relatively small part of operations." As the company changed ownership, there wasn't a noticeable effect on management or in the restaurants.

But Ferris's ambitions weren't matched by his popularity on Wall Street or with the powerful United Airlines pilots union. Soon after changing the name of his juggernaut of a company to Allegis—a name he later conceded sounded like "a bad cold"—he was forced to resign. Allegis's new leadership quickly changed the company's name back to UAL and off-loaded Hilton International, in September 1987, to another company, Ladbrokes, a British conglomerate best known for its gambling and bookmaking shops.

When Ladbrokes bought Hilton International for $1.07 billion, the hotel company's second transfer of ownership in just ten months, the transaction with an unusual, foreign buyer had a more palpable effect on the restaurant staff, according to its public relations director, Phil Romeo. "We were thinking, 'What does this bode for us?'" he says. "'What does this mean?'"

The gambling outfit may have owned seventy-five hotels in Europe, but the purchase seemed to be a stretch. "If you mentioned their name, no one would know who they were," Strand says. Rumors spread that Ladbrokes was primarily interested in renaming its hotels Hilton to improve their brand traction with guests. The company was also eager to gain control of the Vista International Hotel, which stood between the two towers, its first beachhead in New York City. But where would that leave Inhilco food services operations in the World Trade Center?

According to Tony Potter, whom Ladbrokes appointed the vice president of Hilton International's North America division, Inhilco was not "of particular strategic consideration in the deal." Ultimately, he adds, "The total profitability of Inhilco was not of any real consequence to Ladbrokes." (Potter emphasizes that his comments are very much his opinion and don't necessarily reflect that of the company.)

Some change appeared to be imminent at the restaurant. And then the city was rocked on Monday, October 19, when the Dow Jones plummeted more than 22 percent in one day. The widespread panic of the so-called Black Monday had been precipitated by five years of gains, tensions in the Persian Gulf, and newly computerized trading that contributed to the gutting of the market.

Still, the damage was limited. Although there were a lot of fraught nerves among brokers working in downtown Manhattan, within three months the losses would be recouped. And the economy would steamroll ahead.

But Windows on the World was derailed. And after the purchase by Ladbrokes, which began bringing in new managers, the restaurant endured yet another seismic shift that October: Alan Lewis announced that he would be leaving to join Joe Baum as general manager of a highly anticipated restaurant in midtown.

"That hurt," says Jules Roinnel, the director of the Windows Club, whose wariness toward Lewis had developed into affection and respect. "Alan was too expensive for Ladbrokes, and he wouldn't stand for the bullshit, them hiring the wrong people."

Lewis gathered the Windows on the World staff and gave a speech, telling them he was leaving them in good hands. But the management was worried. "We were heartbroken," says Romeo. They were also afraid: "There was a sense that Joe was building something formidable uptown, something we'd have to contend with."

* * *

Joe Baum had indeed been busy. Since leaving Windows on the World in 1978, he had had a series of consultancy jobs, such as for the food services for the Hallmark Cards' Crown Center, which involved a reboot of The American Restaurant in Kansas City and a restaurant tie-in with *Sesame Street*. And, for more than two years, he had focused his energy on an intensely personal project. In 1985, he had, for the first time, put down his shield as a consultant and opened up his own restaurant, Aurora, on East Forty-Ninth Street. There was no financial entity or consulting contract that kept him once removed from the product. Aurora was Baum's baby.

Not that it was his money. Financial backing came from his long-time friend and occasional lawyer Arthur Emil, a real estate mogul and investor who had inherited money from his father and was prone to risky ventures. Baum and Emil knew each other because their children had gone to school together.

With Aurora, Baum had taken the plunge, defying his own oft-said belief that one should never put oneself on the line for a restaurant. Perhaps it was Emil's money—it is unclear if Baum himself invested any of his own; he was always asking for money, so that was hard to consider—but it was Baum's neck. Once again, he brought in Milton Glaser to punch out the graphics and work on the interior design with Philip George, who had worked with both men on the Big Kitchen in the World Trade Center concourse. And he tapped architect Hugh Hardy to come up with a sophisticated, elegant, French grill atmosphere that was comfortable but decidedly "a restaurant for grown-ups." To Baum, that meant wood trim and lush leather banquettes and grand, champagne-bubble-inspired lighting fixtures.

French chef Gérard Pangaud's menu was decadent and expensive: tuna tartare with golden caviar; scallops with urchin roe in a curry sauce; and stuffed pheasant breast roasted in caul (stomach lining, that is) fat. And as a gratis bridge between appetizer and entrée, pheasant consommé served in a cup.

Milton Glaser considered Baum an artist and ran with it. For the lighting, he designed fixtures that contained separate white, red, and blue dimmers so that the room could be cast in a diffuse white during lunch and a pink glow during the cocktail hour. "Everything has a potential for meditation," Glaser says. So they talked about what was meant by "toast" or "sitting." It was a way of looking at the world with fresh eyes, "as though these questions had never been answered before," says the designer. At Aurora, all the silverware, including the forks, ended up being set on the right.

Another Baum inspiration was to hire Dale DeGroff, a close friend of Gerry Holland, ad man Ron Holland's little brother. DeGroff and Gerry had moved to New York City and had tagged along with Ron, thrilled to ride on his expense account as he caroused with Baum in the 1970s. But as much as DeGroff enjoyed being in Baum's orbit, he was astonished by his public, bloodthirsty tirades at his staff. *God, I would never work for this asshole,* he thought.

Or, at least, waiting tables at RA's Charley O's in 1973 was as close as he'd want to get. DeGroff turned that stint into a bartending gig in California, where he plied his trade tending bar at the Hotel Bel-Air for six years. And then Ron Holland called him and told him that Baum wanted to see if he was interested in being the head bartender at Aurora.

DeGroff interviewed with the restaurant's general manager, Ray Wellington, who had previously worked his way up to cellar master at Windows on the World. And then he met with Baum, who told DeGroff that he wanted a classic cocktail bar. And he wanted him in his bar "to tell the stories."

"That's why he hired me," DeGroff says. "He wanted me to tell the stories, because I'd heard Ron tell them over and over again. Joe lived on his reputation. He loved the idea we were always telling those stories about him."

For DeGroff, it was a pleasure to tell the one about the consommé not being right or the brothel-anticipation story, but fulfilling Baum's request for a "classic" cocktail menu was a conundrum—which, he knew, was how Baum worked. "He didn't give you enough information. He gave you a problem, and you were supposed to figure it out," DeGroff says.

Baum provided some clues. He told DeGroff to look up a book called *How to Mix Drinks,* by Jerry Thomas. He went to a number of bookstores but couldn't find it. That's because it had been out of print since 1929. DeGroff eventually found a copy and went to work, mixing drinks. DeGroff knew that Baum wasn't looking for fireworks—he just wanted DeGroff to make drinks properly, the pre-Prohibition way, the right sours and the perfect Bloody Mary.

Baum didn't want the bar to use soda guns or the industry-standard, premade mixes. Both were essential time-savers for a busy bar, but Baum wanted to create an authentic Old World environment. For the Bloody Bull, conventionally a Bloody Mary with beef broth, DeGroff was using the kitchen's pheasant consommé, which didn't taste quite right. But Baum wasn't happy with the beef broth either. Finally, DeGroff was inspired by a meal at a Chinese restaurant where Orange Beef was on the menu. He replaced the conventional lemon and lime with orange, and Baum signed off on his Bloody Bull.

Alas, the restaurant business can be unforgiving. About two-thirds of restaurants, no doubt more than that number in New York City, go out of business within the first three years. "Never open a restaurant with your own money. Never. Use other people's money," Baum told Kevin Zraly, who adds, "And he proved that. Except he opened Aurora. They were losing tens of thousands of dollars a month."

Aurora's costs had run into the millions of dollars. Baum's perfectionism got the best of him. He changed the restaurant's awning canopy four times. Or was it five? He ordered heavy, ridiculously expensive silverware.

And although Bryan Miller gave it three stars in the *New York Times* in January 1986, there was something unsettling about the one hundred twenty-five-seat restaurant. Even Miller noted that Baum was "presiding over everything," he wrote. "Looking as edgy as a long-tailed cat in a room full of rocking chairs."

Aurora wasn't filling seats. Gael Greene too noticed that Baum seemed nervous. And, perhaps, defensive. New Yorkers were flocking to the hot new restaurants, like Jonathan Waxman's Jams, to eat his twenty-three dollar grilled chicken and fries, just a little farther uptown. "I no longer understand what everyone means about American cuisine," Baum griped, sounding like he'd missed the bus.

Something about Aurora didn't quite add up for DeGroff. The restaurant's bar didn't warrant his deep dive into cocktail history. It was more of a champagne and wine kind of place. "I was totally confused," says DeGroff, until he shared his concerns with Ray Wellington, who said,

"It's the Rainbow Room thing." "What do you mean?" DeGroff asked. Wellington told him about the two-year restoration of the storied restaurant that Baum had recently signed on for: David Rockefeller was pouring two hundred fifty million dollars into a refurbishment of the entire Rockefeller Center, and he had hired Baum for another crown jewel.

Oh, fuck, DeGroff thought. *I want a piece of that.*

There was a lot to go around. Baum had twenty million dollars (eventually twenty-five million dollars, maybe more) to revive the restaurant he had so admired as a Cornell student, fifty years before. Once again, he brought in the "Baum squad," including Michael Whiteman, Milton Glaser, and architect Hugh Hardy. The idea was to return the restaurant, which encompassed dining rooms and lounges at the top—the 64th and 65th floors—of the RCA Building, to their 1930s Art Deco glamour. Broadway costume designer Carrie Robbins, who had worked on the musical *Grease,* was hired to create the uniforms.

And, in the kitchen, former Windows chef André René put together a menu that would recall 1930s opulence. It was as much an ode to the past as it was to Baum's personal history. He promised to bring back flaming table-side dishes, such as baked Alaska. Also on the menu: steak tartare with caviar, oysters Rockefeller (of course), Black Angus steak with béarnaise sauce, lobster thermidor, and a rack of lamb that would make James Beard quiver.

The bar was decorated with a model of an ocean liner designed by Baum's old boss, Norman Bel Geddes. And, here, rather than at Aurora, Baum and DeGroff's classic cocktail menu could be fully realized. DeGroff wanted to come up with a drinks menu that would recall the heyday of the Stork Club and the Colony, but Baum said he'd done that before. He wanted something different.

So DeGroff went deeper, researching drinks like the sidecar, the Ramos Gin Fizz, and the Sazerac, of the pre- and post-Prohibition periods. Juice would be fresh pressed on the spot for customers at the bar. No trendy "disco drinks." And Baum didn't let him use jiggers, the small measuring cups used by bartenders to get exact liquor measurements, because he wanted everything free-poured, invoking the lavishness of an earlier time.

DeGroff is now largely credited for launching the dawn of the craft cocktail renaissance. Cocktail menus became a thing. And it might not have been the restaurant's best moment, but when Madonna was photographed drinking a Cosmo in the Rainbow Room, a decade's armada of pink drinks set sail.

When the Rainbow Room reopened in December 1987, it was a hit. Baum's overhaul of the restaurant, as much an Old New York icon as Radio City Music Hall or the Chrysler Building, had been an enormous undertaking. And Gael Greene and *New York* magazine were again on hand to announce another Joe Baum triumph with a cover story and the headline OVER THE RAINBOW.

Rainbow's success helped soften the blow of the financial losses at Aurora, which Baum eventually walked away from. He had his hands full at Rockefeller Center; Arthur Emil carried the lease for the Aurora space but eventually turned the restaurant over to a new operator under a new name.

* * *

Alan Lewis appears briefly in Greene's *New York* magazine article looking "as if he's been run over once or twice a day by a truck," to indicate how much work and stress the restaurant's manager had to endure to bring Baum's vision to fruition. But Lewis knew how to spin the media. "I've never had so much fun," he told Greene.

In truth, Baum's top lieutenant was no longer so formidable. He had lost a lot of weight. He had been fighting a number of ailments, including recurring heart trouble. His long-term girlfriend, Verna Hobson, an actor, exercise instructor, and all-around firecracker who had hooked up with him in his hard-partying years in the late 1970s, took care of him, pushing him around in a wheelchair and getting him to go to the doctor, who told him he should stop working.

Eventually, Lewis was moved to a smaller office, where he occasionally put in some time. But he was barely hanging on. Baum would steal glances at him and shake his head while Lewis slept through another meeting. True, Lewis would sometimes seem to be checked out, when he would suddenly call out, "You can't fucking do that. Never going to happen," and he'd be right.

Hobson took him on a cruise, and Lewis continued to go out to weekly dinners with his son, Seth. In late September 1991, he was putting together a Jets and Giants football-team function for the Rockefeller Center Club in the Rainbow Room. He called Windows Club director Jules Roinnel at about five o'clock, leaving a message on his voice mail about the time the players should be picked up and asking whether or not Roinnel would be attending. And, he added, "Fucking Port Authority workers, out the door at five o' clock. Don't you know that the restaurant business doesn't end at five?"

The next day, Lewis was in yet another one of Baum's endless management meetings for the Rainbow Room, and the boss was telling the six or so people in the room the Newarker-three-claw-lobster story again, and Lewis mentioned that he had recently eaten a delicious four- or five-pound lobster. The restaurant's young chef, Andrew Wilkinson, marveled that Lewis could still indulge. As the meeting went on, and on, Lewis appeared to fall asleep again. It was par for the course until he began to slump in his chair, and what might have appeared amusing immediately became alarming: He had slipped out of consciousness. He was put on the floor. Carrie Robbins called her husband, a doctor, and confirmed the rate of compressions while Wilkinson, whom Lewis had taken under his wing for the past year or so, tried to resuscitate him.

Baum appeared horrified and pushed back from his desk, unsure what to do as frenzied calls were made to building security and 911. But the paramedics were unable to save Lewis. He had passed away, with his shoes on, something he used to joke about. He had had a heart attack. Later that night, Joe Baum was heard sobbing in his office.

CHAPTER 22
LOOKING FOR A STAR

When the Rainbow Room reopened, Windows on the World general manager Toni Aigner couldn't ignore Joe Baum's sparkling restaurant uptown, not least because a number of his staff were trickling that way. Management was on edge. The recent stock market crash had put a pinch on the restaurant business across the city, especially the all-important end-of-year bonus-check season, when Windows staff benefited from Wall Street's holiday cheer.

Banquet business was down, despite the construction of the nearby World Financial Center, a massive complex of four office buildings across West Street, with a vast, glass-roofed public space called the Winter Garden, and a marina. American Express, the Dow Jones stock exchange, and Lehman Brothers were gradually occupying those office buildings. But so were in-house catering operations that siphoned money away from Windows' catering business.

With revenues declining, Ladbrokes was looking at the books. "We didn't like that they were too restrictive," says Paul Astbury, the associate director of the Club, who worked directly for the Port Authority. "They wanted to cut, cut, cut." The perception among management was that Ladbrokes didn't know how to run a restaurant.

"The restaurant and Inhilco were losing money," says Jules Roinnel, who also worked directly for the Port Authority. "We're not getting any rent, because it's net profit. Inhilco was responsible for expenses. Windows was starting to go down. Banquets was going down. À la carte going down. Wine going down. And we're getting a lousy reputation for our food. We, the Port Authority, didn't have many hammers. We were very unhappy with Ladbrokes. They were not investing a lot of money. They were just cutting back on everything. The carpets were getting worn, as was the furniture. They were not using fresh flowers."

Ladbrokes was equally frustrated. "Although we had a great respect for our colleagues at the Port Authority, too much time was spent

dealing with that massive juggernaut of administration and bureaucracy," Tony Potter says. "The relationship was good but sometimes
fraught and always frustrating. This situation often wrote the agenda
and distracted management." Potter suspected that the Port Authority's
bureaucratic ineffectiveness "possibly could have even been a ploy" to
avoid costs and responsibility.

PR man Phil Romeo was given a directive by Inhilco to keep the
restaurant relevant and in the news. He got Georges Duboeuf, France's
best-known wine merchant, to hoist bottles of his popular Beaujolais
Nouveau up the side of the North Tower on a window-washing scaf-
fold. Baum and Duboeuf awaited its arrival at the top of the building
and sipped and smiled for the cameras. Pity that the best coverage
went to an earlier image when Monsieur Duboeuf dropped a bottle on
his foot. Another PR event was the Windows on the World's submission to the *Guinness Book of World Records* to host the world's longest
lunch, at ten hours. The restaurant brought in masseusses and an
opera singer to soothe and stimulate the diners. You could consider
it showmanship in the Baum tradition, or perhaps the restaurant was
trying too hard.

Windows on the World director Johannes Tromp calls the leadership under Ladbrokes "rudderless." Aigner didn't have enough authority. Hermann Reiner tried to step up and discipline the staff, but he
had a harsh, implacable approach and further demoralized the people
working under him. He couldn't command their respect. On the stairwell between the 107th and 106th floors, someone scrawled, *Fuck You,
Nazi Bastard.* It was painted over, and a warning was issued that anyone
caught writing on the walls would be fired immediately.

"If you have to run the largest food operation in the country, you
will have some people who don't agree with your management style,"
says Reiner.

Tromp, who during his early training in Holland would literally get
his butt kicked when he didn't put a knife away properly, says Reiner
was in an unfair position. He was under pressure to lower food costs,
and he was old-school. "Hermann had a European sensibility," Tromp

says. "He had a professional approach and work ethic that clashed with the staff, especially the union leaders."

During premeal lineup, where everyone once was quivering in their well-shined shoes, there was now eye-rolling and smirks. The waitstaff, occasionally caught drinking on the job amid other bad behavior, would hide behind the union's arbitration rules. A lack of mutual respect crossed between the kitchen and the front of the house. Managers seemed deflated, unable to stem the negative attitudes.

And then, as if to put a stamp on the restaurant's dissolution, in June 1990, Bryan Miller returned to give the restaurant another review. "For most of its lofty 14 years, Windows on the World has been a tourist restaurant that has not behaved like a tourist restaurant," he wrote in the *New York Times*. "Its disciplined service staff, uncomplicated fare, and innovative wine program made it a spot that even locals could rely on for a pleasant dining experience with a knockout view. Lamentably, that has changed."

He mourned the food that was overdone or "nondescript." He was disappointed by a staff that had become "phlegmatic and indifferent."

Some of the food was good, such as the grilled blue prawns brushed with garlic oil and the duck breast over confit of endive with caramelized apples. But the tomato-and-crab soup with cilantro "could have come from a can," and the glazed scaloppine of chicken breast was "ruined by an insipid tomato sauce." Miller sounded as if he spoke for a let-down city when he wrote, "Considering its celebrated past, it is disheartening to see that Windows on the World is now performing like a run-of-the-mill tourist restaurant."

To make his disappointment clear, Miller took away the one star he'd given the restaurant in 1986. As word of the review spread, a dark cloud descended on the 106th and 107th floors.

"These people worked really hard every day to get guests through the restaurant," Phil Romeo says. "The staff was totally dejected by the tone of the review."

Kevin Zraly and Bryan Miller were friends. They sometimes played in a band together in sound studios around the city. Windows on the

World management had been asking Zraly if he could help get Miller to review the restaurant, but Zraly didn't begrudge the no-star review. "It wasn't like food that Joe Baum would have done," Zraly says. "It was food that Hilton did."

Ladbrokes was aghast, demanding an explanation and putting pressure on Toni Aigner and management to turn things around. Aigner had an all-hands-on-deck meeting with the staff in the main restaurant, where he spoke emotionally, almost tearfully, about how this was a call to arms. The restaurant would have to do better. Maybe they could get Miller back in for a reconsideration.

Management decided to put on a campaign to change the down-trodden atmosphere. They started by cleaning up the locker rooms. They created a T-shirt that read, WE WANT OUR STAR BACK, and distributed it to everyone. They hosted motivational talks that addressed how a positive, more gracious attitude on the floor would translate to more dollars in their pockets.

They came up with new promotions: Sunset Suppers, an early bird special with reduced-price meals for guests who came in before prime time, which began at 7:00 P.M. It was a success. But maybe too much of one. A free-for-all vibe was infesting the floor. Guests were crowding the windows, popping off camera flashes that made the restaurant feel like a circus. Windows was earning its new mantle as a tourist spot.

Hermann Reiner had moved from being executive chef to director of operations in 1989, a more administrative position. German chef Karl Schmid took his place in the kitchen. Schmid was unable to turn the kitchen around, and, in June 1991, Inhilco shook up its management, firing or transferring about a dozen of its senior staff. Jean-Marie Grouard was named general manager of the Vista hotel and Windows on the World, and Johannes Tromp ran the floor as director of Windows on the World, while Willy Blattner was given the role of director of operations. Toni Aigner left, as did Reiner, who went to the Hilton in Shanghai. Inhilco was, in effect, trying to consolidate the hotel with the restaurant, a dubious and possibly desperate prospect, according to Romeo, who saw the restaurant suffering under a hotel mentality.

"The restaurant and hotel businesses are both in the orbit of hospitality," says Romeo, who went on to become the executive director of food and beverage at Wynn Las Vegas. "But they couldn't be from more disparate worlds. They have two totally different heartbeats. In hotels, you are obsessed with forecasting occupancy and rates in the upcoming weeks and months. In the restaurant business, you are wondering how you are going to get through lunch."

In April 1992, Inhilco passed off the lower-floor food services operations—including the Big Kitchen, the Market Dining Rooms & Bar, and the Corner Café—to Restaurant Associates, which would pay rent to the Port Authority, unlike Inhilco. "They were strong concepts and revolutionary in the mid-1970s," Romeo said at the time. "Yet, over the years they have suffered tremendous wear and tear."

The city's lunch trade had also changed. A Japanese takeout spot and the fast-food pizza joint Sbarro opened in the concourse. New players like Hale & Hearty soon moved in. Inhilco let one hundred sixty workers go.

"Those were tough years," Kevin Zraly says. "But, you know, the restaurant wasn't the only one suffering. Everyone was suffering."

* * *

The dramatic one-day collapse of the stock market in October 1987 might have been what economists call a "black swan event," basically an aberration, but that didn't mean there wasn't an underlying weakness in the national economy after years of robust health. A recession that ultimately lasted from July 1990 to March 1991 affected New York City more because the greatest decline was in the financial sector of the economy, which was stumbling well before and long after the rest of the country was hardest hit. And the financial industry contributes more than 20 percent of New York City's cash income.

From 1987 to early 1990, Wall Street lost more than twenty thousand jobs. When investment house Drexel Burnham Lambert was forced into bankruptcy because of Michael Milken and the junk bond market craze, the gaping hole got wider. Merrill Lynch & Co. and Shearson Lehman Hutton announced more layoffs to come.

The downturn had a ripple effect. From 1989 to 1992, Manhattan suffered more than a 25 percent decrease in median home prices; the construction industry came to a virtual halt, and 10 percent of the city's jobs disappeared.

For many New Yorkers, the darkness of the 1970s wasn't feeling like such a distant memory. The relative economic health of the Koch years had at least partly veiled the city's problems. The AIDS epidemic, which had begun in the early 1980s, was terrorizing the city, having claimed more than nineteen thousand New Yorkers by 1989. It was the leading cause of death among men aged twenty-five to forty-four. It was a plague that reached all parts of the city, including Windows. In 1992, Ray Wellington, one of Zraly's protégés, died of AIDS complications at the age of thirty-nine.

At the same time, the city was suffering another epidemic, the scourge of crack cocaine; from 1986 to 1988, according to city officials, the number of New Yorkers regularly using cocaine went from one hundred eighty thousand to six hundred thousand, most of whom were addicted to the cheap drug derivative that could be smoked after it was processed by adding water and baking soda. During the same time period, the number of drug-addicted parents reported to be abusing their children also tripled. The lethal drug had a direct impact on the crime rate; 1990 saw a record two thousand two hundred forty-five murders and ninety-two thousand cases of aggravated assault. The city's demise felt like a top-down affair; Mayor Ed Koch had been crippled by a series of municipal corruption scandals, leading to his loss to David Dinkins in the 1989 Democratic primary.

New Yorkers were once again in a defensive crouch. Criminality was part of the culture. You could barely walk a block without seeing a car with a pathetic NO RADIO or THE LAST GUY GOT EVERYTHING sign. The clamor of car alarms at night was the city's sick spin on chirping crickets.

It was a difficult time to be in the restaurant business. The Odeon's Keith McNally joked that he couldn't afford to use fresh pepper in his pepper mills anymore. With business volume down about 15 percent in 1989, once-hot restaurants were adding cut-rate menus just like Windows on the World's Sunset Supper; the Lafayette featured a three-course lunch special for twenty-five dollars—what it had previously charged for the entrée. "It used to be, if you were working on a billion-dollar deal or sold $50 million of bonds in a day, your employer didn't worry if you spent 200 bucks on an expense-account dinner," Tim Zagat, who started the eponymous restaurant review manual with his wife, Nina, told *New York* magazine. "He wanted you to spend those extra few hours downtown, so you could talk on the phone to the West Coast. That basically has largely stopped." Limited resources meant that everyone was scrambling, heightening conflicts over pieces of a diminishing pie. In 1989, a ten-week workers' strike at Tavern on the Green cut into business by 60 percent. At the Rainbow Room, tense labor situations led to a walkout in May 1992 by more than on hundred fifty waiters, bartenders, and hat checkers who went on strike because contract negotiations with ownership, B. E. Rock Corporation, which was Joe Baum, Michael Whiteman, Dennis Sweeney, and Arthur Emil, had stalled.

The workers had elected to join Local 6 of the Hotel and Restaurant Employees International Union in December 1991 and produced a list of allegations, including that there had been cuts in their health benefits, that their tips had been garnished, and that some of them had been laid off unfairly. Ownership had its side of the story, and one of its lawyers responded to the union's demands by asserting that meeting them would be "like asking Joe Baum to commit economic suicide." By July 1992, the two sides came to an agreement, but relations remained strained.

Partly as a salve to the ailing industry, Zagat and Baum cooked up the concept of Restaurant Week in 1992 during the Democratic National Convention. They were charged with promoting the industry and helping to host the visiting media and convention delegates. They came up with four days of bargain, three-course lunches for $19.92 from ninety-four restaurants, such as Windows on the World, Tavern on the Green, and Tribeca Grill. Most expected the meals to be money-losers, but their popularity with both guests and locals, who knew a good deal when it came along, made it a permanent fixture.

* * *

In the early 1990s, Jules Roinnell and Kevin Zraly were called into closed-door meetings with the Port Authority brass, which was exploring how it could improve its situation on the 106th and 107th floors of the World Trade Center. They wanted to part ways with Hilton International.

According to Hilton International's then VP, Tony Potter, it is "no real surprise to understand the PA were seeking alternatives," he says. "They had never made the deal easy and had not carried out essential refurbishments especially within the [Vista] hotel. To be frank, I think it may have been a question of the grass was greener on the other side of the fence driving the PA. The reality was that, given the age of the product and lack of refurbishment and interference, my view was that Hilton International did a good job. This is a view that was endorsed by other hoteliers and third parties. The PA were clearly seeking to enhance their benefits under the management contract."

Zraly and Roinnel went to the "21" Club, where they met with the restaurant's young American chef, Michael Lomonaco, who had recently helped restore the classic standard to its former glory. The Port Authority asked Zraly and Roinnel to see if they could bring Lomonaco to work at Windows on the World. "He knew what was happening with Ladbrokes, and he didn't want to get involved," Zraly says.

Lomonaco says that the timing wasn't right. The restaurant wasn't in the best shape, and it had long since lost its Joe Baum luster. After making twenty-five million dollars in revenue in 1988, Windows on the World eked out eighteen million dollars in 1992. The Club, which had peaked at close to four thousand members in the early 1980s, had shrunk to two thousand six hundred members.

"The place sucked," Zraly says. "It's terrible to say, but it was probably going to die. It would end because it was losing so much money."

CHAPTER 23
FEBRUARY 26, 1993

On Friday, February 26, 1993, snow was swirling in light flurries between the North and South Towers, but not enough to stick to the ground of the World Trade Center's concrete plaza.

In the lobby, there was no line to get on the express elevators to Windows on the World. You could just walk up to the soft-spoken doorman, Karl Feile, moustached and dark hair side-parted, dressed in a suit. He stood behind a wood and marble podium and welcomed an uneven trickle of guests, some Japanese bankers, and mostly city businessmen heading up to conferences in the banquet rooms.

It was Feile's job to make sure that lunch guests who were not club members were willing to pay the surcharge. And, as always, he had to check that the guys were wearing dress jackets and no one was wearing jeans. After the guests entered the elevator, he'd reach in, press 107, and step out.

Feile, who had come from Long Island to go to NYU's film school, loved his job. He had been at Windows on the World since 1980, and it was his way of being part of a big show, close to the celebrities he admired. He beamed with pride when he heard guests' gasps at the view on a full-moon night. Although he spent plenty of time upstairs, he felt privileged to be stationed in the grandeur of the lobby. He could see the boats, such as the *Queen Elizabeth II* ocean liner, majestically float by on the Hudson. He enjoyed Easter, when the lobby was decorated with white lilies, or the end of the year, when Christmas trees were lit. One holiday, Feile observed John F. Kennedy Jr., hands in pockets, looking at the tree decorations.

That February afternoon, Feile thumbed through a magazine and occasionally looked up to watch the clerks who worked in the airline kiosks that had been set up across from him in the lobby. He began to read a movie review.

Up on the 107th floor, the à la carte lunch traffic might have been slow, but the banquets department was busy. Insurance brokerage company C. A. Shea and law firm Cleary Gottlieb each had conferences, and brokerage firm Dean Witter Reynolds, the largest private tenant of the World Trade Center, was hosting a lunch. The three companies had, collectively, dozens of employees in several conference rooms in the Hudson River Suites as well as the main restaurant, nibbling on rare roast beef with cornichons.

Waiter Albert Lee, a Chinese immigrant from Hong Kong who had followed his sister to America seven years before, was paired up with Shabbir Ahmed, who had immigrated from Bangladesh; they were serving wine to the first guests, a party of ten at a large round table, in the main restaurant.

At 12:18, Lee and Ahmed heard an incredibly loud noise, practically jolting them out of their uniforms. What could that be? Lee thought that the kitchen's industrial dishwasher, a monster of a machine that could reach scorching temperatures, had somehow exploded.

The restaurant's new wine director, Andrea Immer—just two months earlier, Zraly had made her the first woman to run the department—was in an office behind the storage room checking the deliveries of pallets loaded with cases of wine against her order sheets, making sure her stock was ready for the weekend. She had already checked the previous night's sales.

Immer was, like so many before her, a Zraly protégé. In the 1980s, she had been a banker working at Morgan Stanley when she volunteered to be a pourer at his Windows on the World Wine School, a volunteer position for budding oenophiles. When Immer asked Zraly for advice on making the transition to working in wine, he said, "Stick to Wall Street, kiddo. There's no money in wine."

But Immer's heart was stuck on pursuing what she loved, and so he suggested she follow his path and travel the vineyards, which she did. She spent six months in Europe, where she used Zraly's name as a "golden ticket." Not long after she returned, Zraly offered her a job as the wine department secretary. Immer quickly supplemented the position with apprenticeships in the wine cellar, which she turned into a sommelier position until Zraly gave her the top spot.

With the pallets on her mind, Immer plodded through the paperwork, so when the enormous bump shook her, she thought that one of the hydraulic carts carrying a full pallet must have malfunctioned and dropped several cases of Absolut vodka. But, within minutes, the unmistakable whiff of burning gave way to a deluge of smoke pouring from the elevator bank.

On the 106th floor, Phil Romeo was in his office looking over the Hudson River, talking with his mom on the phone, watching the snow fall. When he heard the huge *pow* and felt the building shudder, it was so propulsive that he jumped out of his seat. "What was that?" his mother asked. "I've got to go," he replied.

By the time Romeo was on the 107th floor, there was an eerie stillness in the restaurant. The ventilation system was off. He went into the entrance lobby, and he too saw the smoke gushing—thick, black smoke—from the elevator shafts. He went around the welcome desk and tried the red phone to the Port Authority police command station below, but the line was dead. Most of the management staff weren't on 106 or 107. They were in a training session in the Vista hotel.

Johannes Tromp, the director of the restaurant, called his office phone on 107 from downstairs. Romeo picked it up, and Tromp said, "Something has happened. We're trying to figure out what's going on. Are you OK?"

"Yes," Romeo said. "For now."

Guests and employees were congregating, so Romeo felt he had to do something. Someone said there had been an explosion, and it was probably a transformer; maybe one on the roof had blown. Captains went to the conference rooms and told guests to sit tight, stay where they were, and that they'd provide instructions as soon as possible.

As more guests and employees emerged, Romeo went into a banquet room and nervously spoke to the crowd with a quavering voice raised several octaves: "There has been an emergency event on the ground floor." He was afraid the guests would panic, but they didn't.

Immer had entered the stairwell to assess the situation. The restaurant had had regular fire drills, but this time, there was no announcement over the intercom system. That's how she knew the situation was real. She, Romeo, and a steward discussed what they should do. The elevators, the source of the smoke filling the floor, weren't accessible. There was a pregnant woman in the group, so the idea of walking down 107 floors seemed risky.

Someone suggested going to the roof. But, a little after 12:30, they decided to adhere to their fire drill training and evacuate down the stairs. The staff walked throughout the floor and told everyone to go to the stairwells near the kitchen.

With several dozen people bottlenecking before they went down, a long line formed near the banquet table, which was full of salads, cold cuts, smoked salmon, vegetables, and cheeses. Allan Sperling, a partner at Cleary Gottlieb who was also a club member, eyed the food. He was hungry and considered grabbing something but decided not to. At least he had his coat and briefcase.

A steward grabbed pitchers with water and dunked napkins in them. As the guests entered the stairwell, they were given a wet napkin to cover their mouths and noses to protect them from the smoke. Peter Chen, a captain, had taken a napkin to use in the stairwell. When he saw Albert Lee, the waiter, he ripped it in half and gave him the other piece. Lee did the same for another person in the stairwell.

Movement was slow. The stairwell was packed, hot, and filled with the strong odor of smoke. And then the emergency lights went out. Working their way down, people would stumble. Occasionally someone would shout encouragement. "Don't worry!" "We'll get there." "Stay calm, people!"

Strangely, Allan Sperling saw several sushi chefs, wearing their side-tied coats and carrying knives, climbing the stairway. He wondered if they knew something he didn't know.

Few people spoke, but occasionally a couple would confer about what could have happened. Immer suppressed the thought that they could be walking closer to a fire. Someone actually yelled, "We could be walking into an inferno!" But Immer was firm. "We have to keep going," she said.

"We were in hospitality mode," Immer says. "We had to display a command of the situation."

After they were stumbling for close to an hour, an idea spread to put one's hands on the shoulders of the person in front. It provided immense relief. The human contact was one thing. But, more important, it diminished the fumbling around in the dark.

For some, it took close to two hours to get down to the 20s, where the first firefighters appeared. What a relief. Loaded with gear, the firefighters encouraged people to keep descending as they went up on their left. A few people needed assistance, including several people in wheelchairs who were carried all the way down.

The A and C stairways terminated at the mezzanine level where there was overcrowding and some confusion about how to get to the lower concourse. People were eventually guided through the lobby toward the exits that led to West Street, where Feile, the doorman, was standing, looking for his Windows on the World colleagues.

Feile had been reading when the explosion occurred. The sound and physical reverberation were overwhelming. He saw the enormous sheet of glass of the Vista hotel ground-floor window shatter. The attendants at the airline kiosks scattered in all directions away from the blast, except for one man who had friends in the hotel. He jumped over his desk and ran straight toward the explosion.

Feile stood on the lobby floor and watched as panic ensued around him. He waited. He went to his phone and tried calling upstairs, but the line was dead. As he tried to make sense of the scene, he began to smell the smoke. Even though the ceiling was so high, he noticed the dark cloud filling the space above him. As it lowered, like an upside-down bath filling up, he decided to go outside, passing by a Port Authority guard with blood on his face. Feile waited across the street and watched the tower's office workers break windows, apparently in an attempt to get fresh air, sending more shattered glass to the ground.

Bedraggled, soot-covered World Trade Center workers exited the stairwells. They squinted in the light. Many had rings around their mouths, caused by the handkerchiefs they'd used to protect their breathing. Albert Lee had ripped so many pieces of his napkin off that when he reached the ground he barely had enough cloth to cover his nose.

"I went from Windows on the World," said Yasyuka Shibata to reporter Jim Dwyer after walking down the 106 stories, "to a window on hell." Shibata was a guest who had arrived in New York that same day and had just sat down to eat lunch when the explosion occurred.

When Phil Romeo finally arrived on the ground floor, one of the guys from the restaurant's reservations department who had traveled extensively in Europe said, "This is terrorism." He was familiar with this sort of damage. Romeo was confused. Terrorism? There? In New York City?

Tromp and other Windows staff began to find one another in the crowd, and the word passed around that they should go to the World Financial Center across the highway, where a Red Cross station had been set up to provide water and check people's vitals.

After restoring themselves in the World Financial Center, Windows staff were given subway tokens to get home. Andrea Immer had walked straight to the subway. She had left her purse and coat upstairs, but when the subway token collector saw her covered in soot, he waved her through. In an altered state, she took the train home to Park Slope in Brooklyn, where neighbors helped her into her apartment because she didn't have her keys.

* * *

Some fifty thousand people were evacuated from the towers. The terrible smoke conditions were intensified because so many car tires were smoldering in the garage and the damaged elevator doors created an updraft for smoke to fill the buildings. Fortunately, neither the smoke nor the exodus of all those people caused any fatalities. The greatest complication for the firefighters was securing the ninety-nine elevators that each of the towers contained. Ten people on one elevator passed out after hours of waiting for rescue. Firefighters were able to resuscitate them all. A number of schoolchildren were also caught in the towers, most of them having been on the observation deck in the South Tower. Thirty-three third and fifth graders were stuck for five hours in an elevator that filled with smoke until their teachers were able to pry the door open.

The New York City Fire Department dispatched eighty-four engine companies and sixty truck companies. It was the equivalent of a 16-alarm fire. More than a thousand people were injured. Of those, fifteen had traumatic injuries from the blast; eighty-eight firefighters and thirty-five police officers needed medical attention. One of the firefighters, Kevin Shea, was rushing to assist a survivor on the B1 level when the floor below him crumbled and he fell forty-five feet through the main crater, suffering multiple broken bones, before landing on the B5 level.

When a concrete wall on the B2 level was obliterated, four Port Authority workers were killed instantly. Three of them, mechanical and maintenance supervisors Robert Kirkpatrick, Stephen Knapp, and William Macko, were eating lunch in a break room. And Monica Rodriguez Smith, Macko's secretary, who was seven months pregnant, was in the room next door. A fifth victim, a dental equipment salesman from Valley Stream, New York, John DiGiovanni, died of a heart attack as he was being transported to a hospital after he was found near his parked car.

Two people who worked in the basement were still missing, including Windows on the World purchasing agent, Wilfredo Mercado, a quiet, affable, thirty-seven-year-old immigrant from a small town near Lima, Peru, who also worked as a security guard on weekends at the World Trade Center. He was supporting his wife, Olga, through beauty school. They were raising two daughters, who were ten and three years old. Mercado had been in America for seventeen years, "looking for a better life," according to Olga. He had earned an accounting degree at a community college in the Bronx.

Mercado's office on the B1 level was near the epicenter of the explosion, and it was assumed he couldn't have survived. Within hours, the other missing worker, who had evacuated, was identified. Olga went to several hospitals, hoping she'd find her husband—perhaps he had become incoherent and hadn't been able to identify himself, she thought.

* * *

The fire department also initially believed that a transformer had exploded. But when firefighters descended into the garage, they realized that they had something far more serious on their hands. The damage was extensive, extending six floors deep through the World Trade Center's basement, mangling cars, shredding metal, and decimating concrete. Still, the idea that what had happened could be an act of terrorism seemed so foreign.

But an hour after the explosion, the NYPD began receiving calls from people claiming they'd set off a bomb. By the 6:00 P.M. nightly news, the realization that New York City had been struck by terrorism was a "very educated assumption," according to NBC correspondent John Miller. Four days after the bombing, the *New York Times* received a letter from a group calling itself the Liberation Army Fifth Battalion that asserted, "The American people are responsible for the actions of their government, and they must question all of the crimes that their government is committing against other people." It focused on U.S. intervention in the Middle East, especially the country's support of Israel. "The American people must know that their civilians who got killed are not better than those who are getting killed by the American weapons." The letter was eventually traced to a network of Islamic fundamentalists, largely based in Jersey City, New Jersey, who had come to America to commit acts of terror. Kuwaiti-born Ramzi Yousef had arrived in September 1992. Yousef followed the preachings of Omar Abdel-Rahman, known as "the blind sheikh," who advocated for the destruction of America.

One of the conspirators, Mohammed Salameh, rented an apartment in New Jersey in January 1993, where he helped build the nitro-urea bomb. The intention was to topple the North Tower into the South

Tower and kill tens of thousands of people. On February 23, Salameh rented a Ryder van, which he drove in the early morning of February 26 to the B2 level of the parking garage below the twenty-two-story Vista hotel, which was just across the plaza from Tower One. Yousef ignited a twenty-foot fuse, and four of the terrorists left the garage.

On March 4, Salameh was arrested when he tried to claim the deposit for the van, which he had reported as stolen. The FBI had been led to the van when they found its vehicle identification number in the rubble. After arresting Salameh, they were able to unravel the plot and eventually arrest six of the seven conspirators, as well as the blind cleric, who was convicted for engaging in a "war of urban terrorism."

The Monday after the bombing, as the nation was just facing the reality of foreign terrorists within its borders, the city stumbled back to work. The Port Authority went from predicting the cleanup would take a week to suggesting a month or more. Clearing the debris, the need to secure the crater, and the FBI investigation created a complex balancing act. And casting a painfully sad pall over the site was the fact that Wilfredo Mercado was still missing.

Olga, his wife, was coming from her home in Brooklyn each day to a room in the Vista hotel, where Johannes Tromp and others from Windows on the World sat with her. The other families of the bombing victims buried their loved ones, but Olga continued her vigil. In their native Peru, earthquake survivors had survived after days of being buried under a crumbled building.

Not until March 15—after sixteen awful days of waiting—was Mercado's body found, buried under two thousand tons of rubble. His body, still in his office chair, had fallen three floors to B4, along with all the pots and pans and kitchen equipment from Central Services.

* * *

The city had endured a series of hard knocks since the election of its first African-American mayor, David Dinkins, who barely beat Republican nominee Rudolph Giuliani in 1989. For many New Yorkers, Dinkins provided hope that a more egalitarian city could be a safer one as well. He had an inauspicious start, though—twelve people were murdered on his first day in office, on January 1, 1990.

Before that, in April 1989, a white woman jogging in Central Park had been brutally raped, supposedly by five young black and Latino men who were wilding in the city. The tabloids stirred up acrimony by reveling in the tensions. A *New York Post* headline—A SAVAGE DISEASE CALLED NEW YORK—epitomized the notion that the city was at war with itself. It seemed as if poverty, the crack epidemic, and increased crime were pushing New York City toward a precipice. Another incident, the killing of Yusef Hawkins, a young black man, by a gang of whites in August seemed to confirm those fears.

The mayoralty of Dinkins couldn't magically heal the rifts. Other incidents included the murder of white tourist Brian Watkins, a tennis star from Utah, who was on his way to dinner at Tavern on the Green with his family when they were mugged by a group of young black men in September 1990. In August 1991, the Crown Heights section of Brooklyn, where blacks and orthodox Jews had lived side by side, exploded with race riots after a Guyanese boy, Gavin Cato, was hit by a car in a motorcade transporting the prominent Rebbe Menachem Mendel Schneerson. The child died, and protests and violence resulted in the mob murder of a Jewish man, Yankel Rosenbaum. Dinkins was criticized for mishandling the four days of rioting that ensued, just as he had been for his meek response to the African-American boycott of Korean grocery stores the year before and six days of rioting in Washington Heights, after cops killed a suspected drug dealer, in 1992.

The crime rate peaked in 1990—a *Post* headline read, DAVE, DO SOMETHING!—and continued to be untenable throughout Dinkins's administration. The month before the World Trade Center bombing, the city reached a record 13.4 percent unemployment rate. The week of the bombing, New York State warned that it was about to run out of funds to pay for unemployment benefits. It seemed as if there was a panhandler on every corner, and at every traffic light, a squeegee guy was shaking down drivers.

The city might not have been collapsing the way it was in the mid-1970s, but it was adrift. And Dinkins appeared incapable of leading. He seemed to dither. When the World Trade Center was smoldering, Dinkins was ridiculed for being on an official trip in Japan at the time.

The weekend after the bombing, a crew went to Windows on the World to assess the impact and begin the cleanup. The damage was primarily soot and smoke stains. Place settings and full glasses of wine remained on tables, giving the restaurant a spooky vibe. The wine cellar coolers were off for twenty-four hours, but Zraly said the forty thousand bottles wouldn't be adversely affected. The Windows employees removed over ten thousand pounds of fruit, produce, and other foods and donated them to City Harvest, a nonprofit that feeds the needy.

The cleanup team noticed dozens of bottes of beer and liquor opened in the bar. Someone had taken five or so bottles, including a rare Remy Martin Louis XIII cognac, which retailed for two hundred dollars. A note read, *Thank you for your hospitality.* It was signed, *FDNY.*

The *New York Post* ran a story about the apparent theft with the headline, WHO GOT BOMBED HIGH IN THE SKY? The paper suggested that perhaps a member of the NYPD had lifted the bottles and written the note as a prank. The restaurant itself didn't care who took them; Romeo says that they were grateful to both departments.

On March 4, the day Salameh was arrested, Phil Romeo told the press that Windows on the World would be reopening at the end of the month. But privately that same day, Inhilco sent out letters from its temporary offices in the American Express building informing staff that the company was being forced to "close its operations in the World Trade Center until such time as we have been able to assess the full extent of the damage" and that it had to "regrettably, implement a temporary layoff of our employees."

Staff would be paid through March 6, giving them eight days' pay. Inhilco encouraged employees to file for unemployment. The letter, signed by Franz Zeller, the general manager of the Vista hotel, and Tromp, indicated that the company didn't know how long the shutdown would take.

More than a thousand Inhilco workers were let go. Dozens of weddings, corporate parties, and other events had to be rescheduled. A skeleton staff of a dozen or so, including Kevin Zraly, were retained. When Zraly went to the 107th floor, he recalls, "It was a very depressing place."

By late March, the North and South Towers of the World Trade Center began allowing office workers back in, with most of the complex back to normal by mid-April. The Port Authority called the quick bounce back a triumph for the agency. But Windows on the World remained closed.

CHAPTER 24

DANGER AND OPPORTUNITY

In the weeks after the bombing, Bob DiChiara, the assistant director of the World Trade department of the Port Authority, worked at a bank of computers that he'd set up as a command center in a corner of the Big Kitchen. His computers spewed out maps and diagrams that laid out the next necessary steps in the massive World Trade Center repair project. DiChiara ran the complex job using the "critical path method," the same algorithm to schedule interdependent project activities that was used during the Manhattan Project and also for the construction of the World Trade Center.

When DiChiara thought about what needed to be done for the restaurant gathering dust at the top of the North Tower, he considered a pearl of wisdom he'd once read about managing stress. If you take apart the Chinese character for "crisis," it said, you would be left with the words "danger" and "opportunity."

His Chinese-language insight, popularized by President John F. Kennedy in a speech he gave in 1959, when the United States was contending with Soviet technological advances, might not be an entirely accurate translation of the characters, but the wisdom drawn from it was nonetheless relevant. The Port Authority and Inhilco, under Ladbrokes, had had a tough five or so years. No one was happy with how things had been going. And here, everyone had a moment to stop and evaluate the situation.

In the 1973 deal, the major parties' interests overlapped in such a way that everyone was satisfied. Joe Baum was being well compensated, and he had a superlative canvas to work with; Guy Tozzoli was getting for the Port Authority what he thought it needed to make the World Trade Center a success; and Hilton International was running a marquee food services operation plus the option to build a hotel in the greatest tourist city in the world.

But the original deal gave the Port Authority 85 percent of the net profits instead of rent, and it had been getting little to no remuneration. "The worst deal you can make is when you have a net unless you can put down on paper everything that goes into making that net," DiChiara says. "If you don't, they'll load it with salaries and bonuses, and at the end of the day you don't have much. Probably nothing. They used up the net."

"It was a high-risk venture," he says of the deal. "No one was knocking on our door at the time to build a restaurant downtown. And when you do a high-risk venture, you have to bend over a little bit."

When the Twin Towers opened, they were practically giving the building away to tenants who were paying below-market rates. By 1993, however, the building was at least 78 percent occupied, and Lower Manhattan's financial real estate sector was no longer a wasteland. The Port Authority's Board of Directors pressed for an internal review to assess if the top of the North Tower would be better off without a restaurant at all. It estimated it could get fifty dollars per square foot to lease the 106th and 107th floors, meaning four million dollars in rent.

But Charlie Maikish, the director of the World Trade Center, now sitting in Guy Tozzoli's chair, retained his predecessor's belief that a restaurant was an integral part of the life of the towers. He just thought that the Port Authority needed a better deal to make it worthwhile.

First, he needed to end, or dramatically change, the arrangement with Ladbrokes, whose operating lease agreement was due to end in December 1994 but with an option to renew. With the board's approval, Maikish went to London to meet with Ladbrokes' chairman, Cyril Stein, the intrepid and proud businessman who had turned around the failing company in the 1960s. He had seen Ladbrokes through hard times, and despite the travails of Inhilco in the World Trade Center, the Hilton International deal had put him back on top. In just four years, Stein's nearly one billion dollar acquisition of the worldwide hotel chain had quadrupled in value. "It's not just the best deal I've made," Stein said. "It's the best deal anyone has ever made."

Maikish, a career Port Authority man who had worked as an engineer on the construction of the World Trade Center, had the termination contract in his breast pocket when he met with Stein, who was
reluctant to tear up the old deal. Stein wanted the Port Authority to
make investments that could help him turn the hotel into a business
conference space. He asked Maikish what the Port Authority wanted
to do. When Maikish pulled out the paperwork and told Stein that
they wanted him to bow out entirely, Stein replied, "We are British.
We never surrender."

But eventually, after haggling over the price of a buyout—Maikish
says that Stein wanted well north of twenty million dollars, but he settled for five million dollars—Ladbrokes released the Port Authority to
look for a new operator of the restaurant and hotel.

Major changes were afoot for the World Trade Center. For years,
DiChiara had tried to push through an eight hundred million dollar renovation plan to bring the complex up to date. The air-conditioning system could use an overhaul. There was asbestos throughout the buildings
that needed abating. And the Twin Towers were built for four watts of
electrical use per square foot. That might have been acceptable twenty
years prior, but the standard had become ten watts per square foot.

But the board and the states didn't want to put up the money.
DiChiara had begun to break up the projects into smaller ones and had
finally had the electrical project approved before the bombing. But the
impact of the attack turned the Port Authority board on its head. Studies revealed that the one-month economic impact of the closed World
Trade Center was felt throughout both states—even dry cleaners in New
Jersey felt a drop in business. The board wanted to act.

"It was no longer a political football," says DiChiara, who saw all of
his stalled projects approved. "There was an emotional response. People realized the importance of the World Trade Center."

Charlie Maikish assured the Port Authority board that there was
an intangible value in having an attractive restaurant on the top of the
tower. "Don't look at the eighty thousand square feet," he told them.

"Look at the ten million square feet [of] office space that we have. What does the restaurant add to the base rent? If you say it's a dollar or two dollars, then you're looking at ten to twenty million dollars. So why would you sacrifice this great amenity?"

While the Port Authority planned to help renovate the hotel and sell it to a new company, it issued a request-for-proposal (RFP) for a new operator of the restaurant in September 1993. Central Services, which had been destroyed in the bombing, was converted into retail space, and the rest of the original Inhilco food services in the World Trade Center were broken up, to be run by different, individual companies.

The Port Authority asked restaurateurs Barry Wine, formerly of the Quilted Giraffe, and Tom Margittai, of the Four Seasons, to consult on the RFP, which suggested a main three hundred fifty-seat international restaurant, a club, and a small Japanese restaurant that would take the place of the Cellar in the Sky. The agency expressed its desire to continue Kevin Zraly's wine school and acknowledged a new obstacle: Public parking would no longer be allowed in the basement, where the terrorists had left the bomb-carrying rental truck.

* * *

Who could restore Windows on the World to its former glory? The city was a very different place in 1993 than it had been in the 1970s. Downtown was becoming a residential area, where pioneers and financial types who wanted to walk to work were snapping up apartments in recently converted high-rises. Nearly seven million square feet of nearby office space had been developed since 1976.

From 1992 to 1993, the recession may have been hurting the metropolitan area, which was shedding jobs, but financial-sector salaries went up by 45 percent, to an average of one hundred sixty-four thousand dollars. Some New Yorkers were spending money again. Broadway ticket sales went up by 22 percent. Hotel occupancy was up. Stores had a record Christmas season. And by 1994, real estate was on the first step toward unprecedented highs.

The dining culture in the city was thriving; it was less fussy, more forward, and more fun. Olive oil was replacing butter on tables. Sushi restaurants went from being an oddity to being on practically every other corner. And Tribeca was now a thing. Drew Nieporent, who had opened Montrachet in 1985, teamed with actor Robert De Niro to launch Tribeca Grill in 1990, and it had become the cool place to be, with movie-star glamour in an exposed-brick setting complemented by such reliable American fare as perfectly grilled salmon. The restaurant's fans were eagerly awaiting Nieporent and De Niro's upcoming Tribeca collaboration with chef Nobu Matsuhisa, who had blended Peruvian and Japanese cuisine for a rabid following in Los Angeles. Chef David Bouley had opened his own restaurant, Bouley, also in the neighborhood, where he was serving exquisite, four-star French country dishes—for instance, roasted Muscovy duck with Brussels sprouts—which were leading an emerging movement: organic *and* local.

When the Port Authority issued its RFP, it invited some of these up-and-coming players, the likes of Nieporent, Bouley, and Larry Forgione (An American Place), to consider working on the 107th floor, as well as Alan Stillman, who had founded T.G.I. Friday's and was running his popular steak house, Smith & Wollensky, and Warner LeRoy, the showman restaurateur who had renovated Tavern on the Green in Central Park.

But the deck was stacked in favor of one restaurateur who had a magical reputation for creating great restaurants in the city and who was a good fit for an agency unaccustomed to thinking outside the box: Joe Baum.

At seventy-three years old, Baum might not have been a fresh pick—in fact, Leon Lianides, who was only three years older than he, was in the process of shutting down his beloved Coach House restaurant—but he had done a remarkable job with the restoration of the Rainbow Room, another New York City landmark, just six years prior.

But Baum was hesitant. "He may have felt that he could not repeat it," says David Emil, the son of Baum's financial partner and friend

Arthur. "Or he may have felt, which I feel now, like you can't be in your early seventies and be able to capture the smoky sense of the world that you have to have to know the restaurant business in New York. He may have been afraid of it."

According to Whiteman, "Joe didn't want to compete in the process," he recalls. "I can't say for sure why he didn't want to compete. He was afraid of losing. He very rarely competed with anyone. He was usually number one in a field of one."

When Baum hesitated, Whiteman told him he would do it without him, and so, according to Whiteman, Baum "came along." In late 1993, Whiteman put together the proposal.

"You never hear about Whiteman," Kevin Zraly says. "But he was the guy. Smart. I don't think Joe wanted to do it, but Michael Whiteman wanted the challenge."

And Whiteman had Rozanne Gold, his wife, in his corner. Gold had had a successful culinary career, starting in 1977 at the age of twenty-three as the private chef for Mayor Ed Koch. She had worked for Lord & Taylor's restaurant line and had joined Baum and Whiteman's company in the mid-1980s as a menu consultant. Baum didn't look kindly on his partner becoming romantically involved with their employee, but he tolerated it, and in 1987, Gold and Whiteman married.

Gold worked on the Rainbow Room menus and was a primary force in the development of the menu for the Hudson River Club, which opened in 1991 at 4 World Financial Center across the street from the World Trade Center. At the Hudson River Club, chef Waldy Malouf took the concept of Hudson River cuisine—there really wasn't such a thing, other than some Native American and German settler–inspired meals—and served such dishes as braised rabbit pot pie and pheasant in a pear and cider sauce.

Whiteman credits Gold for developing the menu for the new Windows on the World proposal. His directive, Gold recalls, was to create "showstoppers that would hold their own against Windows' great views, but they also had to stand up gastronomically."

The master plan proposal by Baum and Whiteman was simply titled "The Renewal." The consultants hired architect Hugh Hardy, with whom they had had such creative success at Aurora and the Rainbow Room. Hardy had a core group of about eight people working on the plan, which cast the evolution of the old Windows to the new Windows as a move from a contemporary aesthetic to a modern one.

According to Hardy's project manager, Pam Loeffelman, the original Windows lacked the steel, glass, and crisp edges that Philip Johnson, the champion of modernist architecture, embodied. Warren Platner had developed sensual, "of the moment" curves and "trays of space."

Hardy's new architectural vision was "to create larger spaces, which were as much about the view as the people experiencing them," Loeffelman says. Also, where Platner had created an aesthetic that smacked of ocean-liner opulence, Hardy kept some of the maritime formality but injected it with color—brilliant blues, yellows, purples, and reds.

In February 1994, after months of preparation, Baum, Whiteman, and Hardy submitted their proposal to the Port Authority with a fair amount of swagger. "We aren't a weak-sister restaurant division of an off-shore hotel company that's owned by a chain of London gambling parlors. We aren't at all like the company that sat helplessly by while Windows was shamefully run into the ground," it read, in a clear shot at Ladbrokes.

Other competitors didn't get off lightly either. "We aren't a chop-house company with no experience in promoting and servicing big banquet business" addressed Alan Stillman. "We haven't opened two large-scale, hyper-glitzy restaurants, each bigger than Windows' main dining room, that perished with great publicity. Because they were hated by local residents" was a shot at Warner LeRoy.

Focusing on the need to magnify the restaurant's banquet and catering business, the plan projected a thirty million dollar revenue, because, it said, "We are bullish on New York. We are bullish on the Port Authority's master plan for the World Trade Center."

The plan proposed converting a significant part of the Inhilco office space on the 106th floor to banquet rooms. In addition to the smaller administrative area on that floor, there would be the employee cafeteria, locker rooms, and various storage spaces.

The plan also reorganized the 107th floor: While the main restaurant remained on the northeast corner of the building, the most notable change was the shift of the Cellar in the Sky from the east interior to the southern perimeter, where it would have a wall of windows. There was also to be a vast space opened up on the southeast corner, where the boldly titled Greatest Bar on Earth would be, replete with bandstand and dance floor.

Ceilings would be multileveled and cantilevered. New, dynamic lighting would be installed. And "everything about its design," the proposal read, "must enhance and celebrate the view." Sloping floors and wide aisles would be constructed to keep up with the new Americans with Disabilities Act legislation, passed in 1990, for wheelchair accessibility.

In the main restaurant kitchen, the emphasis would be on "the world's most spectacular dishes . . . wherever they come from. Chinese Beggar's Chicken baked in clay. A whole fish roasted in sea salt, from Barcelona . . ." It would not be "fusion cooking" or "New American cuisine" but a representation of the best food from around the world.

The Baum and Whiteman proposal retained the smaller restaurant with the faith that it could extend Windows on the World's impeccable reputation for wine. By giving it window views, they hoped to make it a destination restaurant and also a brand ambassador. The Cellar also allowed the 107th floor to offer a more expensive dining option.

Significant changes would be in the Hors d'Oeuvrerie's replacement, the Greatest Bar on Earth, which would continue its predecessor's small-plate, ethnically diverse menu, but it would be more fully integrated into a full-on entertainment and dancing venue. Food stations at the bars would serve sushi and grilled chicken skewers. It was Baum and Whiteman's answer to the more casual dining and drinking culture that had emerged in the last ten years.

Curiously, the proposal broke convention by not including one executive chef to oversee the many moving parts—the main restaurant, banquets, Greatest Bar on Earth, and Cellar in the Sky—of Windows on the World. Baum and Whiteman said that they would have a chef de cuisine running the main restaurant, another chef running banquets, a third overseeing the Greatest Bar on Earth, and an executive sous chef running the Cellar in the Sky. Each would report to a different general manager instead of to one executive chef. It was their way of handling the multiple eateries under one umbrella name, Windows on the World.

The Port Authority had indicated that its decision would be made on candidates' technical competence as well as financial capacity and ability to make the adequate capital investment. In its proposal, Baum and Whiteman projected a baseline construction cost of $12.6 million, which didn't include the build-out, which would likely double its budget. Their financial partner was Arthur Emil, who had lost his shirt with Aurora but was reaping returns with the Rainbow Room.

On March 3, the team went to the Port Authority conference room on the 63rd floor of the North Tower to make its presentation. Hardy had created models and amassed a number of wood and fabric samples evoking the feel of the new restaurant. In fact, the presentation materials were so many and unwieldy that Hardy's crew couldn't bring them in a cab, so, after working until 4:00 A.M., they managed to requisition a Dietz & Watson cheese delivery truck to transport the proposal parts in a driving snowstorm.

Baum impressed World Trade Center director Charlie Maikish with his introduction: "What I originally did with Windows on the World was indeed spectacular," he said. "And I'm also the only one who knows what went wrong, so I'm the only one who can fix the problems."

There were just three serious rivals to the Baum-Whiteman team: Alan Stillman, David Bouley, and Warner LeRoy. And of those, only LeRoy seemed to really want it, according to Kevin Zraly. But LeRoy's proposal, which incorporated flames coming out of a cauldron, glass blimps floating from the ceiling, and a "Devil in the Sky" bar, was "over the top," according to Zraly, who was advising the panel. "It was more Vegas than New York City," he says. After the presentation, someone asked "Warner, are you going to be serving food at this restaurant?"

"Whiteman and Baum had the best plan," Zraly says.

Still, the Port Authority approached Baum and Whiteman with reservations. One Port Authority executive summed it up best; "We love Joe, but he's the only guy who can outspend an unlimited budget."

CHAPTER 25
KING LEAR'S KITCHEN

In May 1994, the Port Authority announced its decision to hire the Joseph Baum & Michael Whiteman Company to run the restaurants on the top of the North Tower. This time, the Port Authority would be collecting rent, which started at $1.3 million, as well as 7 percent of the gross if the income was at least $18 million, and a higher percentage at different ascending levels.

But Baum and Whiteman's partnership was unwinding. Conflicting memories from the people involved shroud the original contract signed between Baum and the Port Authority, but Whiteman and Baum were clearly not on the same page. Whiteman felt that he was not being adequately compensated in the agreement to run Windows on the World. Arthur Emil made an offer to Whiteman that he considered insulting. But Baum signed a fifteen-year agreement with the Port Authority, without Whiteman's consent, anyway.

"Arthur was being an asshole and a shit," Whiteman says. "And they had an invalid lease." Whiteman then turned to the Port Authority and reminded them that they had awarded the contract to the Joseph Baum *and* Michael Whiteman company. Maikish says he considered the squabble to be between Whiteman and his partners and that Baum had had the authority to sign the agreement.

Baum apparently recused himself. "He was off in a corner," says Whiteman, who filed a lawsuit against Emil and Baum, disputing the legitimacy of the agreement they had made with the Port Authority.

The restaurant couldn't move forward, much to the consternation of Maikish, who called a meeting with Whiteman, Baum, and Arthur Emil. Over lunch at the Vista hotel, Maikish said, "If you can't work out your differences, I'll drown the puppy."

A resolution emerged. Whiteman backed down when he and Dennis Sweeney were able to win a six-figure consulting fee in addition to a fixed annual payment of 1 percent of the annual gross of the restaurants, bar, and banquets on the 106th and 107th floors. Despite the acrimony between the parties, design and construction of the new Windows began. Hugh Hardy's team kept their noses to their drafting boards.

The nature and details of the tensions among Baum, Whiteman, and the Emil family are difficult to glean, tainted by fading memory and prejudice. To those who were aware of the strife, it seemed like a battle of egos, a clash of personalities, or the typical strain between financial partners in the complicated restaurant business where contributions, costs, and financial rewards are fluid.

One vested perspective on the turmoil comes from David Emil, who says that around this time, Baum and he had rekindled a relationship that dated back to when Arthur's and Joe's children were students at Fieldston High School. Joe's wife, Ruth, had become good friends with Arthur's wife, Jane. The two couples socialized, and after Jane passed away in 1973 and Arthur remarried, he and Joe remained professional acquaintances and friends. And Arthur got into business with Baum at Aurora and the Rainbow Room.

David had always looked up to Baum as a "supreme appreciator and lover of life," he says. The two hadn't had much contact until Baum expressed an interest in what David had been doing as the president of the Battery Park City Authority, where he was overseeing the construction of the parks, residential and commercial areas, and the building of Stuyvesant High School's new facility, which was completed in 1992.

After the RFP had been won, David says that Baum approached him and asked him if he would run the business side of Windows on the World. A lawyer by training, Emil concedes he knew "nothing" about the restaurant business, although he was coming from having overseen hundreds of millions of dollars in construction.

The budget for construction and to open the restaurant was twenty-five million dollars, of which the Port Authority was willing to contribute nineteen million dollars. David had to raise the rest, money neither he nor his father had. Although the Rainbow Room was making as much as thirty-two million dollars a year, Arthur was on the hook for millions of dollars in loans for his much-touted conversion of the downtown police headquarters building into a luxury co-op, which he had personally guaranteed. When the banks called the loans before the real estate boom had kicked in, Arthur was left scrambling.

Arthur didn't have a mind for day-to-day operations, according to his son, who was left with coming up with approximately six million dollars to rebuild Windows on the World. David says his father loved the thrill of backing a variety of ventures, so much so that he had lost most of the wealth accrued by David's grandfather—a self-made man, lawyer, and entrepreneur.

It was David's responsibility to oversee the finances, design, construction, and hiring for Windows, as well as raise the millions of dollars to complement the Port Authority's investment. David secured the money with a loan from Chase, using his and his father's names as guarantees.

To many of the people who worked with both men during this time, the arrangement between David and Joe was unsettling. "It's like getting a Little League manager to tell Joe Torre how to manage the Yankees," Jules Roinnel says. "David is very bright, but he's not a restaurant man."

In a 2002 *New York* magazine article, David Emil cast the relationships of those closest to Joe Baum, including his son Charlie and his partner Michael Whiteman, in Shakespearean terms, "Everyone perceived that Joe would choose Charles or Michael to run the company. This was a King Lear situation," he said. "It was a father-son succession battle, but the true fathers and sons—Charles and my father, Arthur—were pushed to the sidelines. It's hard for them because they didn't get the cathartic experience of love and expression."

Emil says that, in general, the article was accurate, but Whiteman denies there was any conflict between himself and Charlie. And he adds that he didn't want to run the operating company anyway. Charlie, Baum's older son, declines to respond to Emil's King Lear quote; "Some comments are better left unsaid," he says.

Of Baum's three children, Charlie, who loved herring so much that his parents induced his first baby steps by using the fish as bait, had perhaps the most torturous relationship with him. Charles had grown up with a childhood of vicarious restaurant thrills, but he had been reluctant to examine whether he wanted to enter his father's line of work. Instead, he worked different jobs and developed a passion for photography.

Edward, his younger brother, had steered clear of the business, other than early stints as a waiter, and found a career in marketing and communications for big banks. Baum's eldest child, Hilary, a mother of two who had worked for the precursor to the Central Park Conservancy, had always been interested in the back-of-the-house domain of food sourcing, particularly making it more sustainable, and had heeded her father's admonition that his children shouldn't work in his restaurants because it would disrupt staff morale.

In the early 1980s, Charles was helping his mother and sister's business, Sansel, which produced a salt-free condiment called Lifespice, when he had an epiphany. He was married, with a daughter, living in New York City, slicing a tomato—seemingly a benchmark food of the Baum lineage—for dinner, when he realized how much satisfaction he received in its preparation. He wanted to honor that, but he had resisted following in his father's footsteps.

Soon after, Charles confronted his father with the idea that he get into the business. "Are you serious?" Joe asked before retreating into an evasiveness on the matter that lasted years. The issue simmered until Charles had another sit-down with his father as the Rainbow Room was nearing completion, when he thought he would finally get his father's approval to work with him. Instead, Joe said, "You know, I don't think it's such a good idea."

"It was a head banger," Charles says. "What the fuck. I'd traveled all this way, all this risk, all this vulnerability, all this finally to get my life together to do the thing I always wanted to do."

Despite the discouragement, Charles went ahead and took classes at culinary school, and when the Rainbow Room opened, he volunteered to "hang out" at the restaurant and to serve in any capacity that he could. His father might not have been able to say yes to that, but he couldn't say no. Alan Lewis hired Charles, who ran with the middle managers for months. Eventually, he was given a job as a manager for the business lunch club.

After Lewis died, the restaurant went through a few general managers until Charles's number came up. He became the general manager and went on to manage Aurora before returning to the Rainbow Room.

Charles wanted to be a part of the second iteration of Windows, but his father kept him at bay. "Joe very much wanted me to 'hold down the fort' at Rainbow's," Charles says.

* * *

Joe Baum was slowing down. He had been diagnosed with prostate cancer in the early 1990s, and by 1995 he was coping with health problems. Emil ran meetings at the World Trade Center and at the Rainbow Room, where Baum had his office and could attend more frequently.

But Baum, even at half sail, still had a powerful presence. He contributed to meetings with his signature long talks about dining as "almost a mystical experience," Emil recalls, whether it was the way to influence a guest's emotional state as he or she walked through liminal spaces or how the taste of a dish would change during the time it took a guest to eat it, from first bite to last.

Although his presence in the room had changed from quixotic, lethal leader to that of genius-in-residence, his mark could still be seen throughout the restaurant. An enormous rug was handwoven with a Manhattan street grid that included the intermittent streetlights under a night sky. The chairs were in different hues of orange to complement different rooms. He had costume designer Carrie Robbins stitch and tailor thirty-six different types of uniform, because Baum wanted to make sure guests would be visually aware of the distinctions among captains, waiters, busboys, concierges, and parking valets.

Baum remained obsessive about details. He asked Irena Chalmers, who wrote Baum's speeches, among other consigliere duties, to loiter in the Cantor Fitzgerald elevator banks to study the fabric of the clothes that the financial services workers wore to determine the dimensions and material that should be used on the barstools in the Greatest Bar on Earth.

The restaurant motifs were to represent the brilliance of the sky, with blues, pinks, and oranges. There were countless conversations about colors and palettes and how to visually greet guests when they got off the elevator. Baum again turned to Milton Glaser to come up with the graphic designs that would define the look of the restaurant, from the logo to the flatware to the first thing guests would see upon arriving on the 107th floor. Glaser loved to work with Baum because his impulses were poetic and he was open-minded.

For the entrance, Glaser devised a stunning, multilayered wall that would simulate the colors, lights, clouds, and movement of the sky. The wall would be painted with rich blues, yellows, and reds, but the coup de grâce was a nine-foot-by-thirty-eight-foot curtain made of two hundred sixty-three thousand yellow-and-blue beads. And not just that; the sewn beads would achieve greater luminosity from a series of small dangling lights.

Glaser had had experience creating an illuminated wall for the Minton-Capehart Federal Building in Indianapolis. And he was inspired by Monet's Giverny garden paintings for the color palette. Glaser based the curtain's function on the scrims used in the theater; depending on the lighting, they could be used to create different effects and moods, as he had done for Baum at Aurora. The strings of lights would be on both sides of the curtain, creating a dynamic, colorful, sparkling effect.

Overall, Hugh Hardy's design was one of color and whimsy, a tribute to the sky above and the city below, in a style that was difficult to define—a negative to some observers, but not so for architecture critic Paul Goldberger, who later called the origami-shaped ceiling and multiple brilliant colors "architectural jazz, full of syncopation."

The main restaurant was somewhat more manageable at two hundred forty seats, down from three hundred fifty, another indication that primacy was being given to the more profitable banquet rooms. An internal, construction-phase memo made the directive crystal clear: "The most important thing to keep in mind is, every action must enhance the Banquet Department."

Baum was particularly concerned with gueridons, the movable carts on which waiters would be presenting dishes to guests. He could talk about them for hours. He spoke about their dimensions, how to stock them, how to push them, and where they should be in relation to the table. Chalmers wrote a recollection of a meeting that happened in October 1995 at Hugh Hardy's offices on Broadway and Eighteenth Street. The meeting was supposed to be a general review of the Windows on the World design and construction progress so far, but Baum hijacked it for more than four hours to talk about gueridons. After his seemingly interminable monologue finally ended, Baum sat down with Chalmers and put together a to-do list for the opening that was a mere eighteen weeks away. It read as follows:

1. Finish building The New Windows on the World—from scratch.
2. Make sure the tables, chairs, china, glass, and knives, forks and spoons, salts and peppers get to the restaurant on time.
3. Order 550 pairs of pants, shirts, dresses, jackets, and other articles of clothing for the waitstaff and the uniforms for the 52 cooks.
4. Find a chef—actually 4 chefs.
5. Buy some silver polish and vacuum cleaners.
6. Get some coat hangers.
7. Fix the crooked origami tile on the northwest corner of the ceiling in the restaurant.
8. Order 2,000 bottles of beer and 700 bottles of wine and some champagne and coffee.
9. Decide if 6 ($10\frac{7}{8}$") plates, 6 bread and butter plates, 12 forks, 12 knives, 6 glasses, salt and pepper and flowers will fit on a 27" table—bearing in mind orders, with hefty nonreturnable deposits, have already been made for the china that was being manufactured in the north of England.
10. Make an invitation list for the opening night party.
11. Hire the dishwashers. Hire a purchasing person to buy 20,000 pounds of prime beef to be delivered each week. Also 7,000 pounds of bread, pastry and cake flour, 4,000 pounds of fish, 2,250 dozen eggs, 3,000 pounds of poultry, 3,200 pounds of salad greens.

12. Hire 6 florists to arrange 3,000 flowers purchased every week.
13. Reassure guests there are no mad bombers within 500 square miles.

* * *

With construction underway, David Emil and Hugh Hardy weren't seeing eye to eye. Exacerbating the creative and personality differences was the shortage of resources. It was particularly wearying for Charles Maikish when Hardy tried to convince him that a large structural beam was going to be left visible on the floor because it was an aesthetic choice. Hardy told Maikish that it was there to remind guests of where they were, on top of this massive building. "You're full of shit," Maikish said.

In addition to the nineteen million dollars that the Port Authority was investing, it spent three million dollars to abate the asbestos on the two floors during the initial demolition in 1994, which it committed to doing whenever any of the buildings' offices went through significant renovations. These were huge sums of money the agency was committing, and here Maikish thought Baum and Emil were being tight. Emil concedes that they "had no money," he says. "It was totally done on spit and tissue paper." Twenty-five million dollars goes quickly, it seems, when you are rebuilding Versailles in the sky.

While Whiteman was at odds with his old partner and the Emils, a cumbersome division of labor developed among the principals. Michael Whiteman helped with design elements such as flatware and cutlery. Dennis Sweeney was responsible for the kitchens. David Emil handled construction. Whiteman and Emil avoided each other as much as they could. Things were tense. People like Kevin Zraly were caught in the middle. "I don't know what side I was on. I wasn't on anyone's side," Zraly says. "I was just, like, 'I'm the wine guy.' But I like Michael. And I like David."

The development of the menu was ostensibly in Baum's hands, but for practical purposes, Rozanne Gold was the primary with Whiteman. David and his sister Jennie, who had gone to culinary school and worked at the Rainbow Room and was taking over Windows' catering department, were removed from the development of the food.

The culinary leadership plan was to flout the old adage of too-many-cooks-in-the-kitchen. Georges Masraff, an Egyptian-born chef who had worked at many of Paris's top restaurants and had run the kitchen at Tavern on the Green for six years, was chosen to be the sort-of top chef with the cumbersome working title of "back-of-the-house general manager."

"I didn't know what that was," recalls Masraff.

When he was hired, Masraff was wary of the mandate to provide an eclectic taste of Korea, Japan, Greece, and all over. "I don't call it fusion," he says. "I call it confusion." But, at the time, Masraff assured a journalist that his kitchen would avoid a "mishmash" effect. "You won't find rabbit bastilla with guacamole inside," he said. "Everything may not be 100 percent authentic, but it will have an integrity that respects the original."

Still, Masraff was honored to be working for Joe Baum, and he looked forward to the challenge of the reboot of such a famous restaurant. The chef was a good talker and a passionate, classically trained European cook, and so he and Baum developed a bond.

But when the chef got into a room with any combination of Baum, Emil, Gold, or Whiteman, it didn't feel right. "From the beginning, I felt there was too bad a feeling," Masraff says. "Too many people were talking, and always the last person to talk was right."

Not until April was Windows on the World able to announce its team of chefs. With Masraff as the director of culinary operations, there would be four chefs with equal responsibility: Running the Windows on the World kitchen would be Philippe Feret, who had been chef at Café Centro in the MetLife Building; Frederic Kieffer, from the American Museum of Natural History, was running the kitchen for banquets, which was to be expanded by a third in size; Patrick Woodside, from Manoir aux Quat'Saisons in England, was the pastry chef; and Masraff had his eyes on Marc Murphy, who was a twenty-six-year-old sous chef at the very hot Layla, a Drew Nieporent restaurant, to run the Cellar in the Sky and the food for the Greatest Bar on Earth. Masraff had been a consultant for Layla, and he had seen what Murphy could do in the kitchen. He was impressed by Murphy's balls-to-the-wall swagger, which reminded him of himself in his earlier, hardscrabble days when he worked crazy hours, sleeping in his restaurants in Paris.

But when Masraff asked Murphy to visit him on the 107th floor, while the kitchen was still under construction, and offered him the job, Murphy turned him down. Murphy had just recently been a line cook and occasional saucier six months earlier at the tony Le Cirque, but to be a chef was too much, too soon, he thought.

"I was just a fucking beast of an animal of a cook," Murphy recalls. "I assumed I would be a sous chef for the next ten years and then maybe I'll be chef. Because that is how it was back then; you didn't go from line cook to sous chef to chef just like that. Back then, you busted your hump."

But the kid could cook, and, because his father was a diplomat, he had lived all over the world and was fluent in Italian and French. Masraff liked that they could speak French together. He had a sensibility that Masraff wanted in his kitchen. "Food is not just manufacturing," Masraff says. "It's culture."

Masraff asked him again, and this time he wrote a number on a piece of paper and gave it to Murphy. The number, about sixty thousand dollars, was twice what he was making at Layla. He accepted the offer.

When Murphy gave notice to Nieporent, the owner slammed his fists on the table. "That motherfucking Masraff, stealing my people," he said. ("I like you already," Joe Baum said to Murphy when they first met. "You've pissed off Drew.")

Feret was hired by Michael Whiteman in late March. He says he was initially told that he was responsible for putting together the menu, so he felt blindsided when Gold and Whiteman presented him with the dishes they wanted him to make. "There were too many chiefs and not enough Indians," Feret recalls. Whiteman says that Feret was hired to execute the menu that he and Gold had created.

Feret couldn't make sense of the eclectic set of dishes, because they didn't complement one another. He was flummoxed by how each main dish would have to be served with three different side dishes, an astronomical amount of food and complexity that could barely fit on a table. And he struggled with the equipment, which hadn't been updated since long before the bombing. All the refurbishment money had been spent on the front of the house, and Feret was left to work with subpar equipment that had been sitting, unused, for three years.

There wasn't any organizational structure either, according to Feret, who called for regular meetings and tastings to develop the eclectic array of dishes that Gold and Whiteman had proposed. The dining room wasn't finished yet, so Baum, Whiteman, Gold, and a few others would sit at a table in the kitchen and taste Feret's cooking.

The chef made a crisp duck that he was particularly enthusiastic about. He put the duck in a boiling hot marinade of wine, orange juice, oranges, and lemons infused with Asian seasonings for forty-eight hours. He then placed the ducks on trays to dry and then roast them. He was also fond of a freshwater pike dish, served with pineapple and shiitake mushrooms in a coconut cream sauce. He had to fight to get both entrées on the menu.

Rozanne Gold was equally frustrated and blames the "tug of war" between Emil and both Baum and her husband for her estrangement from the kitchen. It was "impossible to get the menu translated properly," she says.

Feret wasn't fond of Gold's veal shank, which was served inside parchment with Mexican spices. The dish was too onerous to make, needing ten hours to cook in the oven, and too difficult to handle. The shank and the duck, like the rack of lamb and other dishes, were to be served on copper plates, presented to the guest, and then brought to a central cooking station in the middle of the floor where a chef would carve the meats. Feret thought front-of-the-house pomp was a good idea, but with hundreds of covers being served at once, wouldn't there be a traffic jam?

During Feret's tastings, Baum took a passive role, commenting only vaguely about a dish. The friction among Feret and Whiteman and Gold got worse when Gold would come through the kitchen with her tasting fork. Feret was worried his staff was about to walk out. He was coming in at 9:00 A.M. and leaving at 10:00 P.M., "banging my head against a wall," he says.

According to Martin Doyle, Feret's executive sous chef, they were doomed from the start because they were not given enough autonomy. Murphy was in a better position. The Cellar in the Sky, which was opening later in the year, was an exclusive small room with a set menu that would change every two weeks. Murphy was given "total control," he says, with the freedom to get whatever ingredients he wanted. Murphy was allowed to go "crazy," he says.

Murphy's tastings were held in the bar. Every meal was paired with six wines, so Kevin Zraly, Andrea Immer, and Ralph Hersom, the cellar master, were critical; Whiteman, Emil, Baum, Gold, and Dennis Sweeney were also there. They set up a long table and gave comments to Murphy.

In Whiteman's notes for himself, he wrote that a July tasting was "distressing," and, "chef, it appears to me, was given no instruction about what to cook, how to present food, what objectives were." He mentions that he had to "lecture all about what Cellar in the Sky is all about," because Baum simply made "nonspecific comments."

Marc Murphy found the process ridiculous. He knew he could wow them with a rouget, or red mullet, stuffed with anchovies and bread crumbs. He didn't need their notes.

Murphy bridled at the notion that he was "cooking by committee," he says, but Masraff told him, "Could you shut the fuck up? Just do it. They're all going to go away when they have other things to do."

* * *

In the front of the house, restaurant director Patrick Faup was in charge of training the staff with his iron grip and sharp accent. He was of the old school, which was why Joe Baum took a shine to his fastidious ways. Faup leaned heavily on his own training as a captain in the French Special Forces. To many of the waiters, his two-month regimen felt like military training, which made him feared, loathed, and, by some, respected.

"I realized I didn't know shit about restaurants," says Luis Feglia, who immigrated from Uruguay in 1974 and had worked his way up from busboy to waiter at the Plaza, the Russian Tea Room, and Le Cirque, among other restaurants. "It was such a good training."

Feglia encouraged his peers to not quit. It would be worth it, he told them. There were intensive food education classes. And Faup drilled his staff on how to walk properly in a dining room, how to handle different plates, and how to talk to guests. He punished errant behavior with tirades, cursing, and by cutting shifts or demanding that underperformers redo the training course.

For Shamim Hassan, who was training to be a captain, Faup's approach was demoralizing. The Bangladeshi immigrant had felt like, there he was, working at one of the greatest restaurants in the world, but he was being yelled at as if he were a child. The mistreatment deflated his loyalty.

"Of course, Georges and I weren't well liked," Faup concedes. "I had a lot of friends and a lot of enemies."

Faup's idea of having fun with his team was to have his waiters carry an egg on a tray to make sure they could keep it level. He bristled under too much corporate oversight, something that bonded him further with Baum. When Faup was too tough on his staff, he was asked to report to Human Resources. Complaints became so common that he began starting his day by checking in with HR to find out his latest offense.

Baum and Faup would sit at a table, and Faup would glare around the room, looking for improperly folded napkins or a straw on the ground, and bark at the staff, not unlike Baum or Alan Lewis once did. Despite a no-smoking rule, Faup and Masraff would smoke, as Baum did, on the 106th floor. It was the European thing to do, after all.

CHAPTER 26
REBIRTH

In the spring of 1996, twenty years after the first Windows on the World opened, the second iteration of the restaurant launched with a menu that was eclectic, flashy, and all over the place. It hosted several private parties, sparks that Joe Baum and company hoped would revive its original glow.

The first event was an evening celebration for the publication of the book *Recipes 1–2–3,* by Rozanne Gold, on May 14. Close to four hundred people attended, including Baum's family, as well as chefs Bobby Flay, Michael Lomonaco, and others from the food world. Although the party was held in the refurbished banquets area on the 106th floor, many were eager to see what they could of the new Windows on the World upstairs.

There was a "1–2–3" orchestra and four-foot-tall "1," "2," "3" ice sculptures that adorned the food tables, an unintentional tribute to the chill coming from the kitchen. Although Feret put on his chef whites and entered the room with a smile, he had refused to cook for the event—he thought it was ridiculous to put on an event promoting Gold's book when they were trying to open the restaurant—and handed off the duties to his sous chef, Martin Doyle, who had to follow the conceit of Gold's book to simplify cooking by creating dishes that had only three ingredients (in addition to water, salt, and pepper).

Doyle and his team produced dishes such as cod beignets, seared scallops on sweet-pea puree, and crispy salmon with pancetta and sage for the party, but the kitchen had become so tense when Gold came in to direct the staff that David Emil had stepped in and banned her from entering the room.

In the buildup to the official opening in late June, the press was encouraging if tentative. In the *Times,* Paul Goldberger said some nice things, calling Hardy's main dining room "grand and surprisingly sensuous" and closing with the accolade, "The great joy of this new restaurant is not just to look outside, but to turn back inside and take pleasure in the comfort of what has been designed within."

Appearances can be misleading, even to the trained eye. Glaser's beaded curtain didn't really work. It didn't illuminate as intended. Glaser had been forced to compromise on the cost by cutting back on the number of lights. *New York* magazine's Gael Greene ravaged it, saying the curtain looked like a "backdrop in a Queens banquet hall for the wedding-party portrait."

"I wasn't as happy with it as I thought I would be," Glaser says. "The curtain never quite delivered. It was an idea, but it hadn't been quite realized. It needed more density, more light control. It was okay, but it wasn't 'Wow!'"

New York magazine wasn't playing kingmaker again, neglecting even to give its story on the restaurant a cover line. Its article on the opening also included some cynical jabs, like a caption that went with Glaser's bright yellow and blue plates adorned with lamb-and-merguez-sausage kebabs and Gulf shrimp; "Playing it safe for the Sioux City folks," it read.

And if you read between the lines of the article, you could see another story. Michael Whiteman fretted that his contribution to the new Windows on the World would be "written out of history."

Whiteman was butting heads with Georges Masraff, who resented being asked to present the specials menu several weeks ahead of time. To illustrate his indignation, he told management, "I don't tell my wife that I am going to make love to her in two weeks."

With hundreds of covers a night, the kitchen staff were just trying to get through service. Chefs were working seventy-five-hour weeks. Philippe Feret had to have his staff doing finishing work in the hallway outside the kitchen because there wasn't enough room within. The menu was too ambitious, an encyclopedia of cacophonous dishes that was too hard for the kitchen to keep up with.

And the electric stoves were infuriating; as they had been with previous generations of cooks, they were popping and virtually exploding when too much liquid hit the surface. Even when they worked well, they buckled so that a pot or pan would have only a third of its surface on direct heat. It was impossible. Some nights, three of the sous chefs would be working on one stove because the others had blown.

Alex Gormant was the grill man who oversaw the three-by-five-foot wood grill that had been fueled by charcoal in the first Windows on the World. The grill was essential to getting the right char on the meat and fish, and it was often relied on for giant pots and pans of vegetables because it was the one reliable source of heat.

One Friday night, with three hundred fifty guests expected, Gormant fed the wood into the grill perhaps a little too aggressively and barked at his commis—what one calls the assistant to a station chief in the French system—to get perfect diamond-cut grill marks on the Chilean sea bass they were grilling. As Gormant left the station, he heard a loud spark and sudden *whoosh,* and he turned around to see a flash of flame and the ANSUL system kick in, releasing a deluge of chemical foam.

Gormant instinctively grabbed a pot of water and tossed it onto the grill, which sent ash and foam in every direction. Feret yelled to the saucier, "Save the sauces!"

It was a disaster. Everything ground to a halt. The staff threw up their hands. "Fuck this," someone said. Several walked out, but as the fire department arrived, enough of the staff remained to salvage what they could from the kitchen for the disappointed guests, who were moved to the 106th floor, where they ate an improvised meal from the banquet kitchen.

Mortified by what he had done, Gormant went straight to the Raccoon Lodge with some of the crew and got hammered. He felt terrible. The next day, he came in ready to be fired and apologized to Feret, who shrugged and said, "Pfft. What do you mean?"

But the wood grill was shut down by order of the fire inspector. Feret knew he was screwed. The replacement, an electric grill, "a fucking joke" piece of equipment, according to the chef, performed as unevenly as the other electric equipment.

It was another part of the everyday "shit show," as Gormant calls it, that bound the kitchen staff ever closer. Things were so messed up, and everyone was working so hard. The cooks mirrored the insanity with their own. Heavy, late-night drinking binges followed ten-hour days. Curried kumquats became ammunition projectiles thrown twenty yards, at high speed, across the kitchen. Gormant couldn't go without returning fire: He once hurled a twelve-ounce steak, missing his assailant and nearly hitting a sous chef who threatened to fire the next guy to throw food.

A gallows humor permeated the crew, some of whom regretted that guests weren't getting the quality of food they could have been. "There were so many talented people in that kitchen," Martin Doyle recalls, but they were overwhelmed by the size and complexity of the menu and the lack of direction. "It was shambolic. If someone said our execution wasn't very good, I'd agree with that."

"It wasn't the opening of a fine-dining restaurant," he adds. "It was the opening of a tourist trap."

* * *

Despite the chaos in the kitchen and in the back rooms, guests were returning to Windows on the World, starting their meals with a "world-view of seafood," including oysters on ice, chilled lobster meat and periwinkles ($35 for two), beluga caviar ($32.50 for two), or foie gras served with pears and potatoes ($45 for three). The dishes were designed to delight and entertain in the classic Baum style; the rack of lamb "Statue of Liberty" was roasted as a tied crown to emulate the famous statue within view; Feret's dreaded veal shank was cooked in parchment that could be snipped at the table so that the smells were released before the meat was brought to the carving station.

If they didn't want to pay top dollar or wear the jacket required in the dining room, people—a large proportion of whom were local—were going to the Greatest Bar on Earth to eat shabu-shabu, an Asian hot-pot dish; sushi; seared quail in grape leaves; or less exotic fare, such as gourmet pizza and nachos, and to listen to live rhythm and blues.

But the banquets department was struggling to book weddings and corporate functions; according to the division's director, Greg Hein, it felt like a "ghost town." People were afraid to return to the Twin Towers, although they were getting some business from nearby companies such as accounting firm Deloitte & Touche, investment banking company Goldman Sachs, and financial services firm Cantor Fitzgerald.

There was also the Club, with new annual dues of four hundred fifty dollars for World Trade Center tenants, five hundred dollars for anyone south of Canal Street, two hundred fifty dollars for people in the metropolitan area, and on hundred fifty dollars for out-of-towners. Members could again have breakfast for free, lunch in the bar or in the restaurant, guaranteed reservations, and window seating for dinner. There would also be another, more pared-down, slate of guest speakers and events.

Baum always tried to meet his audience where he thought they wanted to go. But he also knew to hedge his bets. That's why there were three price points (the bar, main restaurant, and Cellar in the Sky) on the 107th floor. Baum said at the time that the new clientele was "more casual and lighthearted, yet more sophisticated." On the lower end was the bar, where there was no dress code. In the restaurant, the code had been relaxed a little: Male diners no longer had to wear a tie, and the overall enforcement was looser.

According to Michael Whiteman, Joe Baum didn't hold a magical key to making a restaurant successful. Success or failure, Whiteman says, "is an absolute mystery. That's why Joe would throw every possible idea at a restaurant in order to mitigate the chances of failure. That didn't always work. And it was costly."

The restaurant did have the good fortune of reopening during lush times. Despite a relatively high (yet declining) unemployment rate of 9.1 percent, the city was undergoing an unprecedented boom in important parts of the economy—finance, an emerging technology sector, and real estate—and the average square foot for office building sales was on its way to doubling within a year.

Republican mayor Rudy Giuliani, the former district attorney for New York, had benefited from taking office in 1993, when the economy had already reached a nadir in the recession and the violent crime rate had been declining for three years. Giuliani had narrowly defeated Dinkins on an anti-crime, clean-up-the-streets platform that he implemented with police commissioner William Bratton. Their "broken windows" approach meant cleaning up the city by addressing petty crimes such as panhandling, graffiti, and minor drug possession. The policy dovetailed with an improving economy that put Giuliani at the helm of a new, more comfortable New York, with amenities more commonly associated with the suburbs.

Chelsea Piers, the vast one hundred million dollar sports and entertainment complex jutting out into the Hudson, opened in 1995, offering open fields of play. Times Square, the one-time seedy center of the city, had undergone what detractors called a "Disneyfication," the gutting of the city's grit or soul, depending on one's perspective, for new development. Indeed, Disney had literally led the way, in 1991, investing eight million dollars to renovate the New Amsterdam Theater on the grounds that the city and state would help clean up the area and attract other forms of family entertainment. With city and state loans and tax breaks, the area radically changed in just five years.

Downtown, Wall Street traders were on their way to earning twelve billion dollars in 1997, more than double what they had earned during the best of times in the 1980s. Year-end bonuses were unprecedented. Giant mergers of financial companies such as Morgan Stanley and Dean Witter were reaping huge paydays. Wall Street tycoons were multiplying: In 1982, there were thirteen American billionaires; in 1997, there were one hundred seventy—many with residences in Manhattan.

Vanity Fair's Michael Shnayerson called it "a new golden era: confident, powerful, exuberant and flush with cash. Manhattan," he wrote, "[is] in full, giddy swing."

The excess cash created a culture of excess, a boon for the hotel and restaurant industries. Champagne bars and caviar were sweeping the nightlife scene. Cigars were suddenly everywhere, including Windows on the World, which had its own humidor and sponsored stogie-themed dinners. City restaurants were grossing five thousand dollars a day in cigars alone.

By the fall of 1996, Windows management knew the all-important *New York Times* review was due to appear. They even knew, at least for one of her many visits, when critic Ruth Reichl was eating in the restaurant. When Feret heard she was there, he dashed out to her table, where she was sitting with several other diners, and exchanged pleasantries as he often did with guests. Not that he let on that he knew who she was. All the food was already on the table, so it was too late to assure the quality and presentation. Feret hoped for the best.

Reichl's review ran in early November just before the essential holiday season. She admitted that, given the restaurant's back-from-the-ashes story line, her waiters' warm and enthusiastic service, and her admiration for Joe Baum (her mother had worshipped his early restaurants), it would be "churlish" to quibble about the food. But she had a job to do.

She wrote that the restaurant was serving "an international menu that was little more than retooled Continental cuisine." Her dishes were "watery," "dreary," "timid," or "gluey," and, all in all, a "disappointment." She liked the mahi-mahi with seaweed salad, the seafood in ginger broth, and the rack of lamb, but Reichl decided that Windows on the World warranted only a one-star rating. The best she could say about the desserts was that she liked a giant plate of raspberries. Reichl suggested that readers go to the Cellar in the Sky or to the bar to eat instead.

* * *

As frustrating as it was for Philippe Feret and his team to get Ruth Reichl's negative review, the criticism articulated the truth: The menu wasn't working. Feret believed he was going to be given greater independence to improve it, but in January, he became a victim of the need for change. He was told that the only way for the restaurant to get the *New York Times* to come back to give it another chance would be if they removed the chef. Otherwise, they could be stuck with the one-star rating for years. Feret was asked to leave. He received a generous severance, and Georges Masraff stepped into the void.

But Masraff, according to Kevin Zraly, was "a disaster from day one. He went over Joe and created his own menus. Joe went with the flow. He wasn't like the superstar that he was like when he was younger," he says. "And we were still getting complaints about the food."

The kitchen's implosion was further punctuated by the accolades raining on the Rainbow Room, where the transfer of chef Waldy Malouf from the Hudson River Club had Reichl swooning for a menu that included a vegetarian plate and, for a real throwback, a lobster thermidor with tender flesh in a thick, rich sauce. She gave the Rainbow Room three stars.

Marc Murphy wasn't happy to see Feret go, but he didn't have time to pause while he was tearing things up in the Cellar in the Sky, which was serving a set menu to one seating of guests at 7:00 P.M. The floor was a lush marble, the lower ceilings mahogany, and the chairs upholstered and very comfortable. And this time, the room had a marvelous view looking southward. It was luxurious with food to match; Veuve Clicquot complemented a starter of scrambled eggs with caviar (served in a half eggshell that rested on a surface of rock salt bound by egg whites); fettucine with lobster, shellfish, and fava beans; a Mediterranean turbot on the bone with three perfect porcini mushroom caps that had been braised in a porcini, sherry, and veal reduction. Murphy kept the best for his kitchen and gave his discards, among them the porcini stems, to the Windows on the World kitchen.

As Masraff had predicted, the "committee" tastings stopped after several weeks, and Murphy was left to run his kitchen. He'd brought with him a hardworking, hard-drinking kitchen crew that matched his professional and recreational inclinations. After service, they drank a case of beer, talking and sitting in the walk-in refrigerator on upside-down ten-gallon containers. Sometimes, if the crew got the meal's prep work done well before service, Murphy let them go to a nearby gentlemen's club. In their minds—hey, beers cost three bucks at the Raccoon Lodge, but they were just two dollars at New York Dolls—it only made financial sense to drink where women were undressing. They'd run back to the World Trade Center just before service, to make amuse-bouches.

The Cellar in the Sky dining area was structurally raised from the rest of the 107th floor, so there was a storage crawl space about six feet high underneath it. Murphy made it his second home. He put in a desk and a phone and would hold wine tastings with cellar master Ralph Hersom, who would show up after service with a precious bottle that he said had accidentally been damaged.

At the time, Murphy's first marriage was falling apart. He began sleeping on a makeshift bed of stacked tablecloths that he carefully kept in the middle of the room because mice would scurry around the perimeter walls. He used one of the oversized lockers in the locker room as his closet.

Murphy cut a hole in the wall between his space and the service bar so that he could have cold Heinekens delivered to him expeditiously and surreptitiously, out of sight of manager Joe Amico. When he wasn't holed up, he was going out late at night, returning from clubs the next day, arriving in different states of mind or with his fingernails painted, God only knew by whom.

Murphy relished his role of pirate captain, and he was proud of his over-the-top restaurant. He would tell his staff to steal flowers from the 78th-floor sky lobby so that they could use them for the Cellar's arrangements. He came up with a dish of grilled brioche with seared foie gras and a beurre blanc sauce with warm, peeled grapes from which his staff had to extract the seeds with toothpicks. The dish was served with Château d'Yquem, an expensive wine from the Sauternes region of Bordeaux, but, one time, the labels fell off four of the bottles, so they couldn't be served to guests. Murphy was told to use those bottles to make the beurre blanc, but, instead, he used the usual cooking wine for the sauce and kept the good stuff for himself and his crew.

"I was having a great time," he says. "I was cooking food. I was enjoying the work. Me and my boys were having a blast. I was getting laid, and I was doing press, getting on the front page of the *New York Times* 'Living Section.'"

Murphy was also constantly getting into trouble with HR, for his own indiscretions or for his flouting of union rules, including how many consecutive hours his cooks would work. "I was a kid. I was like, 'You want to quit? Put on your big-boy pants or get the fuck out of my kitchen,'" says Murphy, who was reprimanded for threatening to throw one of his staff down the stairs for insubordination.

Georges Masraff, who could be a mercurial and harsh overseer, supported his young chef. So did Joe Baum. Murphy was his type. He was, as Baum liked to say, "a good drinker." He praised Murphy's cooking and told him, "Keep doing what you're doing." And Murphy appreciated Baum's irascible manner, such as when Baum complained about the expensive menus that were standard for holidays like New Year's and Valentine's Day. "Why is it that we feel it's important to fuck our customers on holidays?" Baum asked in a meeting. "Maybe we should be *buying* them dinner."

Baum had a grandfatherly dynamic with Murphy, who would sit next to him in those meetings. When Murphy noticed that Baum had placed the wrong end of a cigarette in his mouth, he gently pulled the cigarette out and put it back in correctly. "You help a guy out, you know what I mean?" Murphy says. "You don't let the old man look like a fool."

* * *

On May 2, another important review hit newsstands. This one was for the Cellar in the Sky. Marc Murphy and David Emil went to the *New York Times* building on Forty-Third Street off Times Square to pick up an early edition of the paper. It was a cool, partly cloudy morning, and although Ruth Reichl had praised the Cellar in the Sky's doting service, the "lovely" atmosphere, and the sense of exclusivity, she was daunted by the one hundred twenty-five dollars per person (one hundred ninety dollars today, adjusted for inflation) cost, for which, she wrote, you demand "perfection." Reichl was overwhelmed by Murphy's over-the-top dishes, such as the grilled swordfish, with an onion ring on top, which was in a ginger sake sauce and a bed of pea shoots, surrounded by mushrooms and poached cucumbers. She preferred the cheese course, the wines, and the simpler desserts. The restaurant, she deemed, was only worthy of two stars.

Murphy was crushed, according to David Emil. Although the actual income of the restaurant was a fraction of the rest of the restaurant's—eighty-nine thousand dollars, compared to the rest of Windows on the World's revenue of $2.5 million that May—Emil was also disappointed.

"It's what I got," Murphy says. "They wanted three stars. I felt like a salmon swimming upstream. They gave me this jewel box of a restaurant, but it's at the top of the most touristy building in the world."

If their best couldn't even be put in the win column, Emil knew that the culinary side of his restaurant was failing. Masraff hadn't improved things since Feret's departure. In fact, he was more unpleasant to work with than the Frenchman had been.

That spring, Zraly called Emil and told him, "You and I need to talk about what's going on. The situation is falling apart." They agreed to discuss it further in person.

Emil drove up the New York State Thruway to New Paltz, in the middle of the Hudson River valley, where Zraly lived and ran the Windows on the World Wine School from his house. They met at the Plaza Diner, a classic, Greek-Italian joint with red booths and spanakopita, burgers, and eggplant on the menu.

"Kevin, what do you think I should do?" Emil asked.

"It's obvious," Zraly said. "You have to fire everybody in the kitchen. You need a new culinary program." But Emil reminded Zraly that the food was Baum's responsibility, and Joe would resent Emil stepping on his toes. "If anyone can fix this, you can," Zraly said. "You are going to get support if you do this. It's the right thing to do." They discussed replacing Masraff with Michael Lomonaco, who was no longer at "21." The time might be right to get him.

Emil returned to the city and told Baum that he wanted to fire Masraff and bring in a new team. Baum spoke around the problem until

Emil pinned him down. "I'm firing Masraff and hiring Michael Lomonaco," Emil said.

Baum exploded. "No, you're not! I'm responsible for that, " he yelled.

"Yes, I am," Emil yelled back. The men cursed at each other, called each other names, and Baum began throwing whatever he could get his hands on in his office onto the ground.

"It was a true, knock-down fight," Emil recalls.

"You're going to ruin us," he said to Baum. "Both our families are going to lose money. I am not going to let you do this just because you have some attachment to this guy."

Baum stormed out of his office and went to the elevator, with Emil trailing behind him. Emil entered the elevator with him. As they descended, Baum screamed, "You are going to ruin this place! You can fuck yourself. You are a fucking idiot. I should never have brought you in." He slammed his fist against the wall of the elevator to accentuate his every word.

When the door opened, Joe walked out, heaving, steaming, and said, "Goodbye. And fuck you!" Emil, his face flushed, breathing heavily, replied with a similar sentiment and remained in the elevator.

And as the doors closed, Emil knew what he was going to do.

CHAPTER 27
REBIRTH REBOOT

In September 1982, the radio dispatch called out a new ride. "Pick up the chef at the Odeon." It was past midnight, and other drivers working for the gypsy car service were closer to 145 West Broadway, but Michael Lomonaco wanted it. He knew who the customer was: Patrick Clark. Lomonaco had read about the star chef, a new kind of New York celebrity. Clark was getting write-ups in newspapers and magazines for his creative application of French techniques to American foods at Odeon.

Lomonaco wanted a change. He had driven a yellow cab, but that was a pain because you never knew the kind of car you'd be getting. Working for a gypsy car service was more reliable. Certainly better than being a stagehand, stage manager, theater electrician, bartender, or any one of the many other day jobs that the Brooklyn-born twenty-seven-year-old was doing to support his acting career.

Young Italian guys from Brooklyn were in high demand, at least as extras in movies like *Dog Day Afternoon,* which he worked on for a couple of days, but Lomonaco wasn't breaking through. So, as a guy who loved to cook, he thought that by picking up Clark, there was some door he might be able to open.

Fortunately, Clark was generous. He answered Lomonaco's numerous questions about how he got started and what it was like to work in a professional kitchen. Clark suggested that Lomonaco follow his path and go to City Tech, the New York City College of Technology, which had a hospitality program. Clark was big on formal training. His father was a chef who had worked at Forum of the Twelve Caesars and the Four Seasons.

Lomonaco had been dreading the prospect of turning thirty-five, still driving a cab, and struggling to get acting gigs. So he decided to go to school to become a chef. "It seemed like a way to be creatively in control of my life," he says.

After graduating from City Tech, Lomonaco worked several jobs before getting an interview at Le Cirque. The three-star restaurant had opened in 1974 and had one of the best reputations in the city, thanks in part, no doubt, to its charming founder, owner, and the man who greeted patrons at the door, Sirio Maccioni, as well as for its French haute cuisine. But, most of all, its popularity rested on its being a gathering place for A-listers and other city titans, who were regularly being documented on Page Six of the *New York Post*.

Lomonaco had grown up with one of Maccioni's relatives, but he'd had to earn his spot. From there, Lomonaco's star rose until he spent seven years at "21," where he started as a morning saucier and eventually became the executive chef. He left "21" to do a Food Network show, *Michael's Place,* in the then-budding food-television industry, and to start his own restaurant, but that wasn't working out.

So Lomonaco was far more available in 1997 than he had been when Zraly had first approached him. This time, David Emil had Waldy Malouf, his chef at the Rainbow Room, whom Lomonaco respected greatly, speak with him about working at Windows on the World. Lomonaco was interested. After negotiating his salary, Lomonaco agreed to the job that had an air of poetic inevitability. Years before meeting Patrick Clark in the shadow of the World Trade Center, Lomonaco had relished the weekly ads for the Cellar in the Sky in the *New York Times*. He loved reading about the prix fixe meal, the dishes paired with wines, and the promise of candlelit, Spanish-guitar ambiance. Not that he could afford it. "I was a broke actor. It was literally a dream in the sky," Lomonaco says. "Windows on the World was a mythical place for me."

Michael Lomonaco was Windows on the World's first American executive chef, who may have worked at Le Cirque but was best known for "21," where country club fare like hefty hamburgers, steak, Caesar salad, and chicken hash trumped its French offerings.

New American cuisine had already swept through the city in several waves. The city was now knee-deep in restaurants serving different kinds of exciting regional food, from all-American chefs and restaurateurs such as Tom Colicchio and Danny Meyer (Gramercy Tavern),

Bobby Flay (Mesa Grill), and married couple David Page and Barbara Shinn (Home).

And yet, Baum initially resisted the changes proposed by Emil. "Joe was in charge [of the food.] He wanted to keep it French," Zraly recalls. "He said, 'I don't know what you are talking about. I don't even know what "American" means.' Something to that effect. It became a standing joke. 'Joe, you ever hear about Union Square Café? Gotham Bar and Grill?'"

Baum's most significant culinary muse, James Beard, was American. So were advisors Barbara Kafka, Mimi Sheraton, and Rozanne Gold. The American Restaurant, which he opened in 1974 in Kansas City, was the definition of midwestern fine dining for decades. More than any other restaurateur, Baum had unshackled fine dining from French clutches, but he clearly still had attachments to the Continent. Baum's greatest contribution to American cuisine, the Four Seasons, had developed its own distinct, American-style menu, but it was with a kitchen run by Swiss-born Albert Stockli. There certainly wasn't a market of suitably trained, American-born chefs at the time, but that was the era Baum came from.

All of Windows on the World's executive chefs had been Europeans. "When you look back, you never knew what kind of cuisine Windows was," Jules Roinnel says. "Joe used to say it was continental. What the hell is continental? Is that European?"

Lomonaco's first day was, fittingly, Bastille Day, July 14, the annual celebration of the turning point in the struggle against the French monarchy. Lomonaco says he sat down with as many of the staff as he could to get to know them. "That was my first day of school," he says. "I listened. And I tried to reassure everyone that I wasn't there to drop the hammer on anybody."

Lomonaco had been introduced to Baum several times when Baum came to eat at "21." Their relationship at Windows was, at first, tentative. Lomonaco says that Baum was protective of the menu that he had overseen but that their conversations about the restaurant's food began to evolve.

"I thought what we had to do was get back to his original vision," Lomonaco says. "To spotlight American cooking, ingredients that were American, grown and raised and caught here, local meats and vegetables. What they now call 'locavore.'"

The previous menu "wasn't a strong enough story," he says. "A menu should have a life of its own. So we talked about American cooking. Joe, David, and I, we talked about American cooking for three months."

Lomonaco suggests that Baum's tendency toward a Talmudic rehashing of ideas wasn't necessarily resistance. "Once we started to talk about American food, he wanted to really know what that meant," Lomonaco says. "You know, 'What are we really talking about?'"

They spoke about making the connection between what was on the table with the Hudson River valley, where the farms that were practically in view from the restaurant were producing vegetables and fruit, wines and meats that could be served at Windows. "Michael identified what the food should be," Roinnel says. "He convinced Joe it was to be the best regional American cuisine. Lobster pot pie from New England and red snapper from Florida. He said, 'That's what I do best.' Braised short ribs. I hate to call it comfort food, because that's a term that's been overused, but it wasn't going to be a place where you said, 'What the hell is this?'"

Baum suggested they grow an herb garden on the roof of the North Tower. And why not a vegetable garden? Lomonaco recalls Baum making inquiries about whether or not that would be possible but being denied by the Port Authority, which said that the doors from the roof had to remain locked. But it appears that Baum was embracing the idea of local food and what he began calling "sustainable cooking."

Baum's enthusiasm turned to demands to see Lomonaco's new menu, but the chef needed time. He enlisted David Emil, who, Lomonaco says, was his "buffer." He said to Emil, "What we need to do now is get the kitchen in order."

Lomonaco had experience as a fixer, having done similar duty cleaning up "21," which he had taken over after its initially unsuccessful reboot in 1987. But Windows on the World was much larger, and he was inheriting the onerous, multi-chef management structure that had been installed in 1996. He needed to get everyone committed to one program.

Lomonaco combed through the menus for the main dining room, the bar, the Cellar in the Sky, and banquets and kept them as they were, while progressively making tweaks to adapt them to his taste. But the first, most important change he wanted to make was to construct a proper receiving area for the tons of food that were being delivered to the 106th floor each day. There was no longer the Central Services commissary in the basement to sort things out. In the second iteration of Windows on the World, all the restaurant and food divisions were getting what they needed delivered on 106 and then taking it to their kitchens. It was chaos. Chefs couldn't get a handle on what food items were on the premises. Ingredients were getting lost.

Lomonaco wanted to unify the system and to bring the food costs down. He began with the creation of new organizational systems and the construction of a twenty-by-twenty-five-foot receiving walk-in box on the 106th floor. The walk-in was an essential beachhead to organizing the kitchen.

* * *

When Marc Murphy first heard that Michael Lomonaco was replacing Georges Masraff, he figured his time was up. With a new sheriff coming to town, Murphy says he set up a meeting with Masraff and general manager Bradley Reynolds and told them he was ready to step down and that he could help with a transition team. But, according to Murphy, they insisted that Lomonaco was taking over the main restaurant and banquets and that he would continue to run the Cellar in the Sky and the bar.

So Murphy went back to his kitchen and continued to write his menus as he had been, until later that summer, he says, when he saw Lomonaco in the Cellar in the Sky, or, as Murphy thought, "in my dining room," talking with a journalist. Murphy didn't like that. "I was a young whippersnapper," says Murphy, who recalls thinking of Lomonaco, "Who the fuck is this guy?"

Soon after that, Murphy recalls an article being published announcing Michael Lomonaco's new food coming to Cellar in the Sky. He went apoplectic. He walked into his kitchen and told his guys, "Don't fucking pick up a knife. Don't do a thing." He went downstairs to David Emil's office. Emil wasn't there, so he waited until Emil's worried assistant gathered Lomonaco, Emil, and Bradley Reynolds.

Murphy yelled, "You guys don't have the courtesy or the balls to tell me? I was ready to walk out of here and keep things amicable. You guys are the biggest motherfucking assholes." He lit into them. "I don't even know if this motherfucker knows how to cook," he said. Among other things.

Emil thought Murphy was doing a good job but, still, that he had to work under Lomonaco, which Murphy considered a betrayal. " 'You are reneging on our deal,' " Emil recalls Murphy saying. " 'You have fucked me, and you did the wrong thing. You should have honored the deal that this would be my place.' "

"Maybe," Emil said. "But that's not what I am going to do."

Emil asked Murphy to leave. He stormed back to his kitchen and told his crew, "Guys, I'm out. Do whatever the fuck you want. We can all find work elsewhere." He then went to the locker room and filled several garbage bags with the clothes he'd been storing there for months. His crew helped him bring the bags to the elevator.

Murphy was out of a job. He was divorced. His latest girlfriend had broken up with him. He had also recently crashed his motorcycle. But as he took the elevator down, he was still cocky. He thought, *I can go anywhere in the world, and I can do whatever the fuck I want.*

Murphy says that Baum called him soon after. "I'm so sorry about my partners," Baum said. "They are a bunch of assholes."

"We needed to be able to work together, and sometimes people give ultimatums and say, 'If this doesn't happen, I'm going to leave,' " Lomonaco says. "I think Marc didn't want to be managed. And I looked like I was coming in to manage him. What I was coming in to do was bring the whole restaurant together, the whole ninety thousand square feet and four hundred people. And to create a fresh start so that we could make it a viable business.'"

* * *

By the end of September 1997, Lomonaco had thrown out a number of menu items that required long lead times so that the kitchen could commit itself to à la minute cooking: actual cooking of dishes when they were ordered rather than mere reheating. Sauté pans were hitting the electric heat, and the grills were being used to the best of their ability.

Lomonaco's first hire had been his second-in-command in the kitchen, chef de cuisine Michael Ammirati, who had cooked for him at "21." He was a workhorse of a chef, a big guy too, who ran a disciplined team. Ammirati oversaw more than a dozen cooks who worked on the hot line while another five worked in the cold area. He adapted to the electric kitchen by having his cooks heat up stacks of pans in the ovens, which was the only way to get them really, uniformly hot, and then they would pull a pan out to sauté dishes on the flattop. When the pan cooled down, they pulled out another pan that was heating in the oven. It might have been ass-backward, but it worked.

Behind the cooks who faced the flattops was what previously had been a giant steam table; vegetables that had already been cooked would sit there, waiting to be plated. Lomonaco and Ammirati filled those steam tables with ice and put their raw vegetables there before they cooked them fresh.

In October, the restaurant announced Michael Lomonaco's new menu, which it trumpeted as "an alluring roadmap to the best American cooking around." The menu featured Chatham cod pan-roasted with butter beans and bacon and North Carolina quail with black-truffle risotto and mushroom stew. Lomonaco had blocked Baum from enacting his torturous, preliminary tasting sessions. "I said, 'You will taste the food in the restaurant,'" Lomonaco recalls. And so, when the kitchen was already serving the public, Baum and Emil sat down to taste each dish. Lomonaco took notes and discussed modifications with Baum, but he asserted his authority over the kitchen.

New York Times critic Ruth Reichl came to sample Lomonaco's menu just weeks after it debuted. She couldn't give a review so early, but she tipped her hand in a "Diner's Journal" article in which she wrote that there was a "vast improvement" and that "the food, at last, was competition for the view."

On the last day of the year, Reichl published a proper review that questioned the décor—Milton Glaser's curtain had been eclipsed by a "bizarre" still life of a stuffed deer standing in snow amid pine trees—but she pronounced that Michael Lomonaco had indeed "fixed the food." Her favorite dish was the beer-braised short ribs, with meat so soft you could spread it on toast. Topped with American blue cheese, it was an "American version of a gutsy pâté."

There were misfires, like some of the seafood, but she recommended the oysters, lobster salad, and venison with whiskey-and-pecan-laced yams. Reichl gave Windows two stars, a triumph for the main restaurant, which couldn't be held to the same standard as the Cellar in the Sky. The two stars for the 240-cover restaurant was the highest rating it had ever received.

CHAPTER 28
THE SHOW GOES ON

Windows on the World kicked off 1998 with a New Year's Day inauguration breakfast for Mayor Rudy Giuliani, who had a parade of commissioners and his eighty-eight-year-old mother, Helen ("Someday I will see him sworn in as president," the proud mama crowed), in tow. He was just beginning a three-day, multi-event celebration of both his second term as mayor and the hundredth anniversary of the city's unification of its five boroughs. Four years earlier, for his first mayoral inauguration in 1994, Giuliani had had just one event at the Borough of Manhattan Community College.

With the crime rate having dropped to the lowest levels since 1967, Giuliani had won 59 percent of the vote in November, barely breaking a sweat to defeat Democratic Borough President Ruth Messinger. Now it was Giuliani's time to shine. Windows seemed like a good place for him to start, before taking the party to nearby City Hall.

As former *Spy* and *New York* magazine editor Kurt Andersen later editorialized, the 1990s were an uplifting decade for much of the nation. The U.S. economy grew by an average of 4 percent per year between 1992 and 1999. And over the decade, the median American household income grew by 10 percent. Beyond the country's borders, the demise of the Soviet Union might have created instability, but it also brought hope, as did the dismantling of apartheid in South Africa.

New York City was also undergoing significant changes. While manufacturing continued to decline, technology, finance, and health services were booming, as were tourism-related industries, which had undergone more than 25 percent growth in employment from 1977 to 1994, six times more than the rest of the city.

The foreign-born population of the city was returning to turn-of-the-century proportions, but instead of Europeans, these new New Yorkers were mostly from Latin America, Asia, and the Caribbean. The 1990s saw the largest increase of foreign-born New Yorkers since 1900.

By the end of the decade, 36 percent of the city, or 2.8 million out of a population of 8 million, was from beyond its borders. And these immigrants from countries such as the Dominican Republic, Guyana, and Bangladesh were finding work, outpacing native-born New Yorkers in joining the labor force.

New York City felt different. It was the dawn of the Internet. Although there may have always been New Yorkers who babbled incoherently to themselves on street corners, now they were doing it with 2G technology cradled in their shoulders. It would have been lunacy in any previous decade to have a television sitcom set in the city as anodyne as *Friends*; even the twisted cast of *Seinfeld*, which also then ruled prime-time viewing, cast a warm glow over Gotham, enough to make college kids like *Felicity* feel safe going to the Big Apple. And, in the summer of 1998, *Sex and the City* did the same for all the single ladies.

Wall Street bonuses had risen more than 20 percent between 1996 and 1997, and Windows' beverage director Andrea Immer could see the effect on the floor. As soon as bonuses were distributed in early December, the magnums, double magnums, and imperials (equivalent to eight standard 750-ml bottles) of wine were being ordered à la carte, and not just for private banquets. Immer was selling big, pricey California Cabernets, like Opus One—wines that went for two hundred fifty to three hundred dollars.

The city's enthusiasm for the approaching millennium was further fueled by the bull market and the launch of a thousand start-ups. Dubbed "Silicon Alley," which approximately extended from Manhattan's Flatiron district to Dumbo in Brooklyn, here was a part of the city where the right idea and the right pitch could open up venture capital like a bag of chips. Companies such as DoubleClick, which pioneered advertising on the Internet, and Razorfish, which didn't have as clear a profile but had something to do with web consulting, turned their founders into zillionaires overnight.

The city was changing in ways comforting for some, unsettling for others. The first Starbucks arrived in 1994 and was met with devotees and haters alike, the latter of whom distributed stickers that rebranded the logo with a vulgar message suggesting the city was better off without it.

Similarly, Barnes & Noble superstores were bringing the promise of reduced-price books along with Shaker-style furniture and free gift wrapping in what was perceived as a direct threat to the city's authentic-if-ornery bookstores like Shakespeare & Co. and the Strand, where the aisles were narrower and the lighting less easy on the eyes.

The comfortable life seemed to be more within reach for New Yorkers, especially with Martha Stewart there to tell them how to arrange the canapés, as well as consolidate one's assets into one omniscient media company, which she did in 1997.

* * *

By 1998, Windows on the World had turned a corner. Michael Lomonaco had established order in the kitchens, and a new, experienced general manager, Glenn Vogt, who previously worked at Patroon and Montrachet, was running the restaurant with a firm grip but without the tyranny of Alan Lewis.

Vogt was willing to delegate responsibilities. His regular meetings with forty-plus managers weren't filled with invective. As a kid from New Jersey, he had dressed up and gone to Windows on the World. Now he felt as if he'd been called up to play center field for the Yankees.

David Emil was finding his footing, and the restaurant was making money, thanks largely to the development of the banquet business, run by his sister Jennie, which had made changes such as lowering the per-head costs for weddings from more than three hundred dollars to two hundred twenty-five dollars, developing the conference business, and incentivizing the sales team by tying bonuses to their ability to book events.

"The Emils loved it. The PA loved it," Jules Roinnel says. "For the first time in years, it was a win-win situation in every respect. And Michael [Lomonaco] had a lot to do with that."

Vogt agrees that Lomonaco was more than just a great chef. "As a person, he's a real motivator," he says. "He's great in front of people. He created an incredible energy." Because of his television appearances, Lomonaco had a public persona that was big with out-of-town diners. Assistant general manager Michael Desiderio joked with Lomonaco that if he had a dollar for every photograph that guests took with him, he could retire early.

Lomonaco reintroduced Sunset Suppers, a three-course meal for $29.99, making the restaurant more accessible. From five o' clock to six thirty, a hundred people were filling up the restaurant. The hope was that they'd have a cocktail or two and wine with dinner, and the per-person check would be more than sixty dollars.

There was an ebb and flow of guests throughout the restaurant's day, from morning to late night. About thirty regulars would be at the club for breakfast—people who didn't have to order their coffee, because the waiters knew how they took it. The guests acknowledged one another, if not by name, then at least with a welcome nod and morning salutation. Roger Ross and Robert Guida, who ran Guidance Corporation, a global staffing firm, were there almost every morning. It was a great place to bring clients. They befriended Michael Nestor, inspector general of the Port Authority, a hard-nosed amateur boxer who rooted out corruption related to the agency and who liked his eggs poached and his coffee black. Nestor was often there with one of his investigators, Richard Tierney, who would come up after doing laps in the pool at the Marriott hotel in the plaza. When Lucio Caputo was the Italian trade commissioner in 1970, he was wooed by Guy Tozzoli to move his offices to the World Trade Center. Now, working as the head of the Italian Wine and Food Institute on the 89th floor of the North Tower, he came to breakfast almost every morning to drink his coffee (black with three sugars), read an Italian newspaper, and make a list of the day's to-dos.

Sometimes, the 106th and 107th floors became too *much* a part of the building's everyday life. The Windows on the World employee cafeteria on the 106th floor was one of the great perks of the job; most of the staff came in a half hour before their shift and ate the regular fare of burgers and sandwiches, but they were also often treated to leftovers from catering events, so desserts, steaks, shrimp, and prime ribs weren't complete rarities.

But Michael Lomonaco began to notice that there were more meals being eaten in a day in the cafeteria than there were Windows workers. Managers determined that other World Trade Center employees— security, elevator operators, cleaning people—were eating their food.

Glenn Vogt had a memo distributed throughout the building that reminded everyone that the cafeteria was for Windows employees only. Two days later, a security manager told Vogt that they had a new problem—the elevators were no longer being made available when the restaurant needed to dispose of its garbage.

Vogt figured out that there must be a connection to the cafeteria memo he had sent out. He spoke to the building manager, who told him, "I'm going to send you the guy you need to know."

It didn't take long for a dapper man, dressed in a suit, a perfect Windsor tie knot, and jewelry to match, to approach Vogt and say, "Mr. Vogt, I'm Joe Amatuccio, the director of vertical transportation for the building. I can fix your problem."

Amatuccio informed Vogt that if he gave him ten of his business cards, signed, so that security would know that the people holding those cards could eat in the cafeteria, the elevator problems would go away. Vogt knew not to question Amatuccio's authority, gave him what he wanted, and the restaurant's access to the elevators was restored. The two men became friends from then on.

In the beginning of the reboot of Windows, the Greatest Bar on Earth was drawing a regular World Trade Center crowd that would come to the bar for a drink after work but would vanish after 8:00 P.M. Bartenders and waiters were standing around with nothing to do. It was up to the bar's manager, Brooklyn-born Joe Amico, to find a way to fill the floor. In April 1997, Amico hired a Lebanese-born DJ named Lucien Samaha, who spun a lounge-sound mix of sixties and seventies LPs he'd collected from around the world when he was a TWA flight attendant. Samaha picked Wednesday nights—because not much was going on then—to play an eclectic mix of James Bond soundtracks, James Last tunes, and Hindi pop.

It slowly began drawing a hipster, international crowd. And then downtown journalist Michael Musto wrote a rave about the scene in July in the *Village Voice*, decreeing, "Let me document the weekly moment that proves the cocktail nation is alive and well and sitting on life's big swizzle stick. It's the fab Strato-Lounge party Wednesdays at the Windows on the World's Greatest Bar on Earth, a kitsch 107th-floor mix of lounge lizards, mambo kings, self-styled geeks, leftover tourists, and Kate Moss," he wrote. "After two drinks, you also forget that you're at the place where your parents brunch." Record labels began sponsoring guest lists, and downtown glitterati like musician Moby started dropping by.

Amico added more theme-night dance parties that turned the top of the North Tower into a local nightspot for different subsections of the city. Brooklyn-born DJ Nino Torre went from mixing club music and Top 40 material to running Glitter Parties on Friday nights. Mondays were dedicated to funk; Tuesday nights were an R & B live set; Wednesday night was Samaha's Strato-Lounge; Saturday nights were for swing dancing, which had become a crossover craze. And the most popular night was Thursday, when Torre DJ'd the Mambo Baby Latin nights, and the city's top salsa acts, like El Gran Combo, played with bands with as many as twelve musicians, making the windows vibrate. The crowd changed from night to night, but it was typically diverse: corporate types, tourists, the bridge-and-tunnel crowd, club kids, and other New Yorkers curious about partying in the stars. Celebrities like Armand Assante, Katie Couric, or Wesley Snipes were usually tucked in the crowd.

The cover charge was five dollars to twenty dollars. Coronas cost $5.50, so you could have a special night out for a song. Of course, the waiters had to hope that, for every cheapskate, there was a trader with an expense account running up a tab.

The bar began raking in money. With three actual bars in the space, each with two bartenders in constant motion, the drinks were flowing: martinis, Manhattans, sidecars, daiquiris. Five hundred people could be packed in there at a time. More than a thousand could make it through before closing time at 2:00 A.M. Bartenders were making one thousand one hundred to one thousand eight hundred dollars a week in tips.

The Greatest Bar on Earth was making more than three hundred thousand dollars a month, serving a broad menu of burgers, vodka pizza, and chicken fingers as well as sushi, Beluga caviar, and cheesecake. The shabu-shabu option, which was vegetables, seafood, and thinly sliced meats boiled in a hot broth over an individual burner on one of the three island bars, had to be nixed because the boiling hot pots were a constant headache for bartenders who had to explain the process too many times a night and then contend with spills. (The P. T. Barnum grandiosity of the bar's name wasn't lost on the Ringling Brothers and Barnum & Bailey Circus, which took Baum and Emil to court for infringing on its trademark "The Greatest Show on Earth." Apparently the circus couldn't win its case and ended up providing a large annual allotment of circus tickets to B. E. Windows Corporation.)

One of the bartenders, George Delgado, who had been working at a bar in Hoboken, New Jersey, and survived six interviews to land the job in the tower, felt he had reached the pinnacle of his profession. He liked getting hazed by Joe Baum, who wasn't drilling his bartenders as he used to but was still testing them, making them prepare drinks that he wouldn't finish, making different bartenders prepare the same drink or the same bartender make the same drink on different days, to make sure they were being consistent.

"I felt like I was working for the master," says Delgado, who heard the why-didn't-you-make-it-that-way-the-first-time Bloody Mary story from Dale DeGroff and listened closely to Baum's ruminations on the aesthetics of how a drink should appear in a glass.

"Go make me a little money and make yourself a lot of money," Baum told Delgado. And he did. Wall Street types were coming to the bar celebrating multimillion-dollar deals with bottles of Cristal champagne, tallying up two thousand dollar bills, and dropping two hundred fifty dollar tips. Bartenders didn't have time to take breaks during service. "I loved being in the weeds," Delgado says. "It was thrilling."

Delgado was a team player who wanted to contribute to the bar's success. In addition to being the shop steward for the union, he became head bartender in 1998. He devised new drinks for the Greatest Bar on Earth, like the Lady Libertini, a martini made with Grey Goose vodka and kiwi syrup to give it the greenish-copper hue of the Statue of Liberty, who stood in view below.

Delgado noticed that the ten-ounce martini glasses they were using were too large for the five-ounce drinks. Martinis are pure alcohol, and the liquor cost—similar to the food cost; the percentage of a drink's liquor cost to the bar as a fraction of the retail price of the drink—was running around an untenable 32 percent. (So a $9 martini was costing the bar about $2.88 in liquor cost.) Bartenders, who had to free-pour, as directed by Baum, were overpouring to better fill the big glasses.

Delgado convinced management to absorb the cost of changing to seven-ounce glasses, and restaurant comptroller Howard Kane soon sidled up to Delgado one evening and told him he'd crunched the numbers: The bar's liquor cost had been reduced to 19 percent.

The Greatest Bar on Earth was a huge leap forward from the original bar and Hors d'Oeuvrerie arrangement, and Baum didn't stop tinkering. He asked his public relations woman, Kathy Duffy, to come up and sit with him in the comfortable chairs close to the window. Duffy thought Joe was going to give her new ideas to carry out, but he just sat there. She looked at him expectantly. Eventually, he said, "Just sit," which they did, for what felt like an hour, after which Baum began talking about new furniture arrangements. He had been studying the movements of the guests as they approached the windows and wanted to optimize their seating options.

Regulars from the building came up several nights a week, having a drink to blow off steam or to avoid the peak rush hour crowds on the commute home. Delgado knew more than two hundred regulars by name, many of whom were traders from Cantor Fitzgerald, the company that had immense success servicing the Treasury security market and had close to a thousand employees working in its headquarter offices on the 101st to the 105th floors in the North Tower. Some of the younger guys ran up the stairs after the closing bell, passed by the kitchen, and made a beeline to the Greatest Bar.

The bar was a "monster" to manage, according to Glenn Vogt: so much space, so many patrons, and so much booze. Joe Amico, affable and well-liked, shouldered most of the logistical burdens and oversaw ten staff bartenders, six of whom would be working at a time. "You are dealing in thousands," Delgado says. "Thousands of people, thousands of bottles, thousands of dollars." So busy was the venue that some of the more jaded bartenders would hide the cocktail menus because they didn't want to slow down to fix more complicated drinks.

And, despite the altitude, the Greatest Bar was still a bar in New York; incidents happened. Fights broke out. Often between guys hitting on women. Sometimes between women. One of the reasons the venue didn't host a regular hip-hop night was that during one such evening early on, a fracas occurred between rival crews, prompting the staff's mad dash to secure the safe exit of P. Diddy's mother.

Another night, Amico asked two well-dressed women to not smoke, which was still legal indoors at the time but not permitted in the entranceway. Amico's request prompted the ladies' friend, an English bruiser, to jump the manager, grab him by his tie, and swing him around like a doll until Windows staff intervened. On another night a particularly aggressive guest was hassling women at the bar, so Amico told the bartender to stop serving him drinks. The man, heavily intoxicated, became irate. He was escorted into an auxiliary lobby, where he threw one of his shoes at the security guard. He then proceeded to throw everything he was wearing at the guard. Port Authority police arrived and handcuffed the man. Amico helped by giving the cops a giant tablecloth to cloak the naked man, who asked the police where they were taking him. "Where everyone else is wearing white," one of the cops said.

With so many people coming through, there were bound to be what Vogt calls "colorful characters causing issues." Scammers would hover near a group that had a bar tab and claim to be on the same tab. Both sides of the bar had to be kept in check. Vogt regularly hired spotters to infiltrate the crowd and observe his own bartenders, to make sure all of the cash changing hands was going into the register. "There's a proverbial backdoor in every restaurant," Vogt says.

* * *

But as Windows on the World emerged from its messy relaunch, the restaurant's leading light was flickering. Seventy-seven-year-old Joe Baum wasn't well. The prostate cancer was taking its toll, and he was coming to his office on the 106th floor less often. His illness compounded his feeling that he was being shunted aside.

"It was a very sad time for Joe," Jules Roinnel says. "I used to call it the 'Call of the Wild.' Remember that book? When the lead dog goes down, the other dogs pounce on him. I used to call it 'Call of the Wild syndrome.' Joe was a tough son of a bitch. You wouldn't fuck with Joe. But once they saw a weakness, they started ganging up on him."

Baum wasn't able to make the decisions anymore. And despite the positive momentum at Windows on the World, B.E. Rock Corporation was in a heated fight to retain control of the Rainbow Room. Real estate company Tishman Speyer had taken over Rockefeller Center and was reportedly asking for an annual lease of more than four million dollars. David Emil wasn't able to negotiate an agreement, so the team was walking away from its other crown jewel. It was a crushing blow for Baum, who had poured so much of himself into its renovation.

Baum said to David Emil, "I feel like a tarnished silver cup."

Emil asked, "What do you mean?" Baum said, "I feel unloved, but if I were more loved and appreciated and cared for, so much more could be there." Emil was moved by the image of the silver cup, and he felt that their past fights were just Baum's way of doing business, so he reassured him, "There is still another dance, Joe. You don't have to feel that way. We can still work together."

Emil thought, even after their big fight in the elevator, that Baum still believed in making their business relationship work. If not, he could have tried to dissolve the partnership, but he didn't. In fact, they were working on another project in England.

Still, Baum was ailing, and he was no longer the ringleader he'd been. Plus, his wife, Ruth, was also ill. She had been diagnosed with lung cancer many years before, and, after a remarkable recovery, her health too was failing. By the summer of 1998, Baum was spending more and more time going to the doctor or at New York Hospital on the Upper East Side.

His family became his gatekeepers. Some of Baum's professional acquaintances were told they wouldn't be able to see him, including Dennis Sweeney, who couldn't understand what had become of his long, close relationship with his boss. His having been aligned with Michael Whiteman during the lawsuit against Baum and Emil may have had something to do with it.

"I always assumed that when Joe would retire, Michael and I would take over," says Sweeney. "We had worked together since 1971. I couldn't figure it out. I still can't figure it out."

By September 1998, Baum was put in hospice care at his home on Sutton Place, near the East River. On October 4, when Tony Cabot, Baum's music supervisor and close friend for more than forty years, visited him, Baum asked him how things were going at Windows. The next day, Baum died.

On December 21, a mild Monday, a memorial was organized at the one thousand five hundred seat Town Hall performance space. The stage was set up as if it were the Rainbow Room, with tables for two from which speakers walked to the lectern and retold the great Baum stories that everyone had heard before but wanted to hear again. A booklet entitled "The Book of Joe: Stories and Glories" was distributed; it opened with a picture of Baum, smiling and holding a sparkler, and closed with the simple quote, "Smile."

Former mayor Ed Koch spoke, as did many who had known Joe best, including Ron Holland, Milton Glaser, and Mimi Sheraton, the last of whom recalled one of her Baum standards, about the purveyor who was getting morel mushrooms for the Four Seasons. Baum, Sheraton recalled, told the poor guy, "If I print them on this menu, you'd better find them, even if you have to grow them in your armpits." Eighty-three-year-old David Rockefeller, who had pushed the first domino that had led to the construction of the World Trade Center and Windows on the World, closed the service with words of his own. Rockefeller had long since retired from running Chase but had been remained active in politics, world finance, and philanthropy, as well as the selling of Rockefeller Center. Rockefeller invited the massive gathering for an after-party at the Rainbow Room, where a buffet and drinks would be served. The gathering also, fittingly, functioned as the closing-night party for the Rainbow Room.

Joe Baum is buried in a cemetery in Westchester. His children had his gravestone fabricated from the same green granite that he'd chosen for his kitchen countertops. On it, they inscribed, *No more changes . . . Yet.*

CHAPTER 29
THE HIGHEST-GROSSING RESTAURANT IN THE WORLD

"Smile. It's showtime." That's what someone had written in a back room close to the kitchen, where there were mirrors for the waitstaff to check their appearance before they went on the floor. They stood and gazed at their reflections, examined their brightly colored uniforms for threads, stains, or other aberrations, redid their eyeliner or pushed back their hair just so, and walked to the front of the house.

"It was right out of *A Chorus Line*," Michael Lomonaco says. "That was what we were doing there. We were entertaining people."

Many a waiter who had passed through the multiple interviews and application gauntlet to beat out thousands of others, and who had survived Patrick Faup's "Foreign Legion" (as some called it) training, considered his or her job to be a golden ticket. It paid well. It was in an exhilarating environment. It was secure, and it offered great benefits.

"What else do you ask for?" asks Albert Lee, the waiter who had made it to the ground floor with just a shred of napkin after the 1993 bombing. He had immigrated from Hong Kong when he was thirty-one in 1986 and had worked at a Chinese restaurant and in room service at the Waldorf Astoria before getting the job at Windows on the World in 1991, a job he hoped to keep until he retired. "We are all immigrants. Back in our country, we don't make that kind of money. Life was good," he says.

For the front-of-the-house waiters, the high pay was contingent upon the total of the day's tips, which wasn't necessarily a constant. Like many of his peers, Sol Policar, an Egyptian Jew, the only one of his siblings born in Brooklyn, had a nightly target goal of covers. If the restaurant was expecting four hundred reservations for the night, and there were eight or nine stations open, each comprising about five to eight tables, he hoped to get his team (captain, two waiters, and two busboys) through fifty covers by 10:00 P.M. so that he wouldn't be lingering past 11:00.

Overall, guests tipped well, especially during the holidays. But European tourists were notoriously tight. Many—the Brits and Spaniards, in particular—are used to not paying a tip, either because they assume it's included in the bill, it's not their tradition, or, let's just say, they are not inclined to.

One waiter would directly confront guests and say, "This is unacceptable," if the tip was particularly low. He could have gotten fired for the practice, but he got away with it. He liked to say that he was helping to educate his "European friends." Some waiters—few and very rarely—added the tip to the bill themselves. If the guest noticed and the waiter got called on it, he or she was fired.

To encourage tourists to pay up, the union got management to include a card with the bill that reminded guests that the tip was not included and that a gratuity would be appreciated. Another push was provided by the checks having two tip lines, one for the captain and one for the waiters. Although those numbers were combined at the end of the night, the two lines could compel customers to give more than if there was just one line. Most guests got the hint and would put down 10 percent of the bill for each line, totaling 20 percent. But sometimes out-of-towners would get confused and end up leaving 40 percent. The waiters didn't complain.

"A lot of people didn't like going to work," Sol Policar says. "We liked going to work."

Each night, a cashier processed the checks and divvied up the teams' tips, the highest percentage going to the captain and then the front waiters, followed by the busboys, runners, and a portion to the bartenders. Payouts were in cash. A mediocre night would be one hundred fifty to two hundred dollars. A good night was over three hundred dollars. Great nights—and they happened—were well over five hundred dollars.

Policar and a number of the staff funneled some of their earnings into day trading. "Everybody had a penny stock," says restaurant director Melissa Trumbull, who recalls a waiter saying to her, "What kind of world is this that we're taking stock tips from busboys?" But it didn't matter if they schlepped trays of discarded food for a living; if some-one's stock pick just doubled in a day, you paid attention.

For Luis Feglia, the Uruguayan captain everyone called "Papi," the rewards were more than financial. He shared Joe Baum's high stan-dards and accepted Patrick Faup's domineering style because he felt it imbued the work with honor. Feglia studied the different strains of couscous and sake, the origins of chocolate, and the distinctive qualities of Dominican cigars, and he particularly appreciated the wine-school class he took as part of being a captain who could recommend wines to guests.

"We wanted guests to leave happy. We always tried to exceed expectations," Feglia says. "[Training manager] Ron Blanchard said we should have 'legendary service,' and we did." Blanchard was as much of a life coach as he was a floor manager. He taught staff how to properly care for their shoes, and he recommended books such as *Who Moved My Cheese?*, Spencer Johnson's bestseller about coping with changes in one's life, and Stephen Covey's *The 7 Habits of Highly Effective People*, which many of the waiters read and discussed.

Glenn Vogt often emphasized the importance of teamwork and the idea that if everyone contributed to making Windows a more success-ful restaurant, everyone would see a financial return. But even though management and the unionized staff shared certain interests, ten-sions remained.

For some at Windows on the World, a strain between management and staff was set by a bloodbath of layoffs at the end of 1996. As part of the agreement with Local 100, management was able to fire workers before the year's end without going through an arbitration process that would be enforced once the union protection rules went into effect in 1997. It was ugly. Management said it had overstaffed for the open-ing, so the cuts were necessary; some workers believed that perceived troublemakers were let go. Either way, it heightened an us-versus-them relationship.

Fekkak Mamdouh, a waiter and shop steward for the union, says he was constantly butting heads with Vogt, who agrees that one of his greatest challenges was dealing with the union. They fought over personnel issues, shifts, vacation time, pay, and breaks. Mamdouh also protested when, he says, Michael Lomonaco would yell at a waiter. "I would stop him and say, 'You cannot talk to people like that,'" he says. "A lot of people were scared of him—a tough guy from Brooklyn."

It probably didn't help relations between Vogt and Mamdouh when, early on, one particularly indulgent staffer took a giant bottle of wine and helped himself to its contents in a back room. Vogt says he doesn't remember the incident, but Mamdouh recalls that the general manager confronted him about the indiscretion. At the time, Mamdouh explained, with a straight face, that the offending waiter had had a bad reaction to medication. Vogt couldn't prove otherwise, so he asked Mamdouh to make sure that his coworker no longer took the medication at work.

"We were a band of brothers when we needed to stick together," former waiter John Bernieri says. Waiters covered for one another. They traded shifts. Some would have hiding stashes where they put discarded food to eat later. They respected each other's spots. If you stumbled upon some sushi behind the water pitchers, you knew whose it was.

The camaraderie usually remained within sections, such as the bar, the kitchens, or the main restaurant of Windows. The bar staff was known to party the hardest, drinking out late, hooking up, and going on occasional jags like the trip to Atlantic City where someone brought a car trunk full of liquor. It was mostly a group of Chinese waiters and busboys who went to Hop Lee in Chinatown for bowls of noodles at around three o'clock, between lunch and dinner service. A more diverse group would go out together at eleven after work for steaks and red wine in the meatpacking district or for Japanese food at Sapporo East in the East Village. Sapporo's kitchen was open until midnight, so the Windows workers would rush there, order their sushi, gyoza, and sashimi, pile it on tables that they pushed together, and eat until one in the morning.

But as convivial as it could be, it was also a place of work where the most intrepid made the most money. It was hard to prove, but sometimes a busser would notice that a captain or waiter was handed some cash by a guest and that that cash didn't make it to the collective tip pool. "As much as we were a family," Melissa Trumbull says, "everybody was out for the money."

* * *

Over eighteen months, Michael Lomonaco and David Emil made many changes to the front and back of the house, but January 1999 was special. After being closed for months for renovations, the Cellar in the Sky reopened as Wild Blue, what Lomonaco described as almost a chophouse, more because of its rustic American roots than its being a straight-up steak house. "Cellar wasn't really working," Lomonaco says. "It was very pricey. At one time, it may have been special, but it wasn't keeping up."

Wild Blue's emphasis was on organic produce, meats, and fish, the taste of char—few guests knew it came from an electric source—and the subtle interplay between the fruitiness of a Cabernet Sauvignon and the satisfying sensation of teeth sinking into tender flesh. Prime beef, squab, quail, and venison steaks were served family style, with side dishes that guests could share.

Lomonaco did away with the formal, one-serving meal of the Cellar in the Sky, replacing opulence with comfort but keeping its emphasis on wine, with fifty different varieties served by the glass.

Unfortunately, in June, *New York Times* critic William Grimes, who had started a few months before, was unimpressed by the restaurant's "hypertrained," enthusiastic waiters and simple menu that verged on austere. The eight appetizers, nine entrées, and one daily special were, he wrote, "pleasant but not terribly interesting."

Upon arrival at the *Times,* Grimes had been adamant about correcting the paper's star system; he believed Ruth Reichl had rated restaurants on a curve and that the one-star rating had become unfairly positioned as a negative review. His adjustment, he admits, was "shock therapy" for chefs and restaurant owners. Grimes looked at it this way:

A one-star meant that, say, if you went out to dinner after a movie, you might enjoy the food while you talked about the film. A two-star meant you talked about the food while also talking about the movie. A three-star rating meant you stopped talking about the movie entirely and talked only about the food. And if you were at a four-star restaurant, you dropped to your knees and gratefully ate a meal that you would never forget. By this standard, he thought, one star wasn't a negative review. He gave Wild Blue one star.

In his review, Grimes mentions the tourists there, but he says he never considered Windows a "tourist trap," a designation that he would apply to Tavern on the Green or Mamma Leone's, because he actually felt bad for the poor rubes dining there, eating awful food at ridiculous prices. Windows was something different, Grimes says, a "special occasion restaurant," which served food that was, at least, reasonably good and with an exceptional wine list.

And yet, the tourist-clientele reputation had dogged the restaurant ever since Joe Baum assured the *Times* in 1970 that his restaurant wasn't just for out-of-towners. But when you're seating hundred-person groups from Japan, it's hard to deny their importance.

"The annoyance of going to a place and feeling like 'I'm a New Yorker and this place should be for me, but it's full of tourists' is a knee jerk reaction that every New Yorker has felt," says David Rockwell, the prolific designer responsible for Nobu, Jean-Georges Vongerichten's Vong, and various Planet Hollywoods, among many other restaurants, including some redesign work for David Emil at Windows on the World. "But imagine when all of those tourists who are annoying you leave. The businesses you want to go to no longer exist. There is a double-edged sword to that conversation. Over the long haul the audience for a restaurant morphs and changes just like for a Broadway show. The ideal scenario is that a restaurant is a place that feels like home for lots of different kinds of people."

The great advantage of being a popular "special occasion" restaurant in New York City is that there are a lot of special occasions spread out among the millions of people who live there and the millions more who visit. And Windows was never just one thing. When husband-and-wife and *Wall Street Journal* wine columnists John Brecher and Dorothy J. Gaiter came up with "Open That Bottle Night" in 2000, an event at which people opened a special bottle of wine they'd been hoarding for a special occasion, David Emil thought of an "Open the Bottle Week," when guests were invited to bring in their special bottle to Windows, which waived the usual corkage fee and provided experts to discuss the wine's attributes.

"It was so successful. It was a genius idea," Glenn Vogt says. "These weren't tourists coming in. These were New Yorkers who were saying, 'We thought this was a tourist place. We never thought of just coming here to eat.' "

Between the main restaurant, Wild Blue, the Greatest Bar on Earth, and banquets, Windows on the World was drawing a diverse clientele. The restaurant was entering the most successful phase of its life, enough so that, in 1999, David Emil was emboldened by the restaurant's increasing revenue and his own understanding of what it took to make it successful. He approached the Port Authority and said, "I now understand this business in a way that I didn't when I came here," he recalls. "Here's what we have to do to make it really hum." He wanted to invest in refurbishments, what he considered improvements to Joe Baum and Hugh Hardy's design flaws. And he wanted to upgrade the entranceway and build a new, smaller bar and a walk-in wine cellar on the 107th floor. But if he did so, he needed an extension of his lease. The Port Authority liked Emil's proposal and agreed to a fifteen-year lease agreement to January 3, 2023.

Soon after, Windows hosted a New Year's Eve party like no other on the eve of the millennium: Priceline founder Jay Walker, who started his name-your-price web company in 1997 and was already a billionaire because of it, took the Liberty, Hudson, and Pinnacle suites, spending well north of a million dollars for dinner for over three hundred people who were entertained by models with scrims on their faces on which projections of historical figures such as Marie Antoinette appeared. They also faked a Y2K meltdown during the ball-drop countdown.

* * *

The Port Authority's dealings with David Emil and the new Windows were a small part of the sea change that the agency and its World Trade Center complex were undergoing. New York State governor George Pataki and New Jersey governor Christine Todd Whitman had been looking for a private buyer for the center for three years, until, in April 2001, the agency signed a ninety-nine-year lease agreement with real estate developer Larry Silverstein and Westfield America, which owned malls, for $3.2 billion. It was the largest real estate deal in the city's history.

The Port Authority had had a tumultuous relationship with the Trade Center from the beginning. And although it had claimed its first profit in 1981, when Guy Tozzoli said, "For all practical purposes, we are full," ten years later, occupancy was at 78 percent. After the 1993 bombing, the agency had made investments that dovetailed with the burgeoning of the area, enough so that it was in a place to reap a return. In 2001, the Port Authority was ready to realign itself with its original mission, transportation. It trumpeted the agreement as a windfall for the agency, which could dedicate the funds to projects such as the Second Avenue subway line and the extension of the Long Island Rail Road to Grand Central Station. For the city, the Silverstein group would pay much-needed taxes, which the Giuliani administration estimated would come to one hundred million dollars a year, a sizable jump from the twenty-six million dollars that the Port Authority had been paying.

Silverstein, a Brooklyn-born dealmaker whose first major venture was the construction of the forty-seven-story 7 World Trade Center, which he built with the Port Authority, had leveraged his way to the top of a real estate empire. He already owned more than five million square feet of office space downtown. The developer was counting on World Trade Center operating income projections of two hundred million dollars annually.

And yet, in 2001, an economic downturn had befallen the city. Although the housing boom continued unabated since 1996, most businesses were feeling a pinch. The hotel occupancy rate was at 73 percent in the first quarter of the year, down from 79 percent the year before. Restaurants were reporting a 30 percent decrease in business. Commercial vacancy rates in Manhattan were on their way to more than doubling from the second quarter of 2000 to the second quarter of 2001, with rental rates slipping several dollars per square foot. During that same period, revenues from financial trading were down by 7 percent. Finance companies were shedding thousands of jobs after the dot-com bubble had burst the year before and as the national economy, in a recession since March 2000, contracted. Few felt the rug go out from under them more than Priceline's Jay Walker, who went from wealth of about ten billion dollars, on paper, to a mere three hundred thirty-three million dollars in a near instant.

Mayor Giuliani didn't show up at the Port Authority–Silverstein signing ceremony at the World Trade Center in July; the mayor hadn't been getting along with the agency, which he regularly carped was giving short shrift to the city. In fact, a cloud had been darkening over the mayoralty since Giuliani had publicly humiliated his wife, Donna Hanover, when he announced at a press conference in May 2000, unbeknownst to her, that they were separating. (The mayor often dined at Windows on the World, including, allegedly, when he was having an affair with Judith Nathan, whom he later married.)

The mayor's marital issues had contributed to what was described as "Giuliani fatigue"; the mayor, who was also battling prostate cancer, even said himself, "I don't really care about politics right now." At least, not local politics. He was preparing to try the national stage, with a run for senator. Even he seemed relieved that his second term as mayor was ending soon.

But despite the unease infecting parts of the city, Windows on the World was doing better than ever. It was blowing past its initial projections of thirty million dollars in a year. David Emil bought out Joe Baum's children in December 2000, so the restaurant was now fully owned by his and his father's Night Sky Holdings. In 2000, the gross revenues of all food and beverage, room rentals, audiovisual rentals, club dues, guest fees, souvenir sales, and other income amounted to

$38.8 million. The banquets department was making eighteen million dollars. Windows on the World was the highest-grossing restaurant in the world.

July 24, 2001, was the first day of the ninety-day transition period, in which the Port Authority, which would still own the property, passed control of the vast complex to Silverstein and Westfield. The Silverstein deal didn't have an impact on the operations of Windows on the World. Of greater significance was that David Emil was getting a handle on the business, and the restaurant was becoming increasingly profitable.

With summer ending, the restaurant was looking forward to another successful fall and holiday season. September, an in-between month for the restaurant and most of the city, when kids were heading back to school, was the beginning of the buildup to the busiest time of the year, when banquets could sometimes gross a million dollars in a week. And October was going to be special: The restaurant was going to celebrate its twenty-fifth anniversary with a big event. Kevin Zraly ordered five hundred cases of Veuve Clicquot, specially bottled for the restaurant with its own label with Milton Glaser's blue-sky-and-gold logo and the words, WINDOWS ON THE WORLD, 1976–2001.

CHAPTER 30
THE LAST MEAL

Monday, September 10, was looking to be a miserable day, with torrential rain and wind. The day before, Australian tennis upstart Lleyton Hewitt had aced American Pete Sampras, and, on Saturday, Venus Williams had beaten her sister Serena in the finals of the U.S. Open. But the city was looking forward, waking up to the first full week of school and the next day's mayoral primary election, in which Public Advocate Mark Green was in a heated race with Bronx Borough President Freddy Ferrer for the Democratic ticket, and the few Republicans in the city were entertaining the prospect of financial services billionaire and political newbie Michael Bloomberg as mayor of New York.

Green, Ferrer, and Bloomberg raced around the city, shaking hands and slapping high fives with New Yorkers while their staffers and volunteers filled crowds, waved signs, and shouted slogans. About twenty thousand people were getting excited to see the second Michael Jackson show at Madison Square Garden that night; the king of pop was mounting a comeback, and the show was rumored to include a galaxy of special guests after his Friday-night concert, in which Marlon Brando, Whitney Houston, Britney Spears, and Elizabeth Taylor, among others, performed or spoke.

A different sort of congregation gathered at the morning rededication of fire station Engine 73, Ladder 42 in the Bronx, where Mayor Giuliani cut a ribbon and said a few words. Before the mayor spoke, Father Mychal Judge, a fire department chaplain, gave a homily.

"Good days. And bad days. Up days. Down days. Sad days. Happy days. But never a boring day on this job," Judge said, moving gently in a white frock among the firefighters and their families. Most just knew him as Father Mychal, but Judge was pretty unusual, a gay recovering alcoholic who had lovingly administered to a more diverse set of New Yorkers than perhaps anyone else wearing the cloth. He was typically affective that morning. "You get on the rig and you go out and you do the job, which is a mystery. And a surprise. You have no idea when you get on that rig. No matter how big the call. No matter how small. You have no idea what God is calling you to." In the World Trade Center plaza, dancers were doing a run-through of the performance they'd be giving the next day on the Evening Stars stage that had been set up at the foot of the North Tower, facing the *Sphere,* the twenty-five-foot-tall golden globe sculpture that had anchored the plaza since it was opened in 1971. The performance was the end to the World Trade Center's free summer outdoor entertainment schedule, which had featured acts including Celtic dancing, Odetta, and Herman's Hermits. But the dance rehearsal was called off when the sky unloaded buckets of rain.

Downtown, at Windows, a new beverage manager, Steve Adams, had just been promoted and was working his first day while the beverage director, Inez Holderness, was home in North Carolina for her sister's wedding. Adams was a devotee of English ritualistic Morris dancing and came from a small wine store in Vermont and had finally, at fifty-one years old, found a foothold on a career path he was proud of. He had always been the guy who was passed over. Now, here he was, entrusted to run the stocking and distribution of the wines and other beverages for the top-grossing restaurant in the world.

Managers were expecting a light night because it was a Monday and it had been raining buckets throughout the day. Lunch service was pretty quiet: several dozen guests. Captain and sommelier Paulo Villela broke down the buffet table—the same one that Joe Baum had Warren Platner design in 1976—with his supervisor Doris Eng. The two placed the trays of salads and shrimp and breads on enormous Queen Marys, the stainless steel, multi-shelved banquet carts that roll on wheels. A lot of the food was thrown out, but staff made plates of the good stuff for themselves to eat later.

Villela had been a manager at a restaurant on the Upper East Side, but he applied for a captain position at Windows in 1996. There wasn't one available, so he came back several times until he was offered a newly created position, a cross between a busser and runner. Villela took it.

He quickly moved up to being a captain and had been spending his time off working in the cellar and taking wine courses until he became a sommelier. He was making one hundred thirty thousand dollars a year. And Villela's nineteen-year-old son, Bernardo, joined him at Windows as an assistant cellar master.

As Villela and Eng, with a couple of busboys, moved the food to the Queen Marys, they joked about her role as a manager and how he used to be one. Eng said that, to Chinese people, being a server was the highest place one could rise to before going to heaven. The conversation continued into her office.

General manager Glenn Vogt had been in a two-hour meeting with David Emil, restaurant comptroller Howard Kane, and a few others to discuss Windows' New Year's Eve party. It was the first meeting, so it wasn't stressful, more exciting to be brainstorming what they hoped to do that year.

After the meeting, Vogt went to the office he shared with assistant general manager Christine Olender to review what had been said. Michael Lomonaco wandered by and mentioned that he needed his glasses fixed but that his opthamologist was out of town. Lomonaco was going on a trip to Italy soon. Chefs can be obsessive list-makers. He wanted to get the glasses checked off his list, so he made an appointment at the LensCrafters in the concourse downstairs for noon the next day.

Lomonaco had just returned from shooting *Epicurious* for the Travel Channel the week before. He was getting up to speed for the busy autumn season of events and weddings, drawing up the new fall menus, and hiring people, one of the most important being a replacement for his executive pastry chef, Heather Ho, who had given her notice in August. Ho had just started in June, but she didn't like working at Windows. On that Monday, Ho talked on the phone with her best friend from high school. "I don't know when I am going to get out of here," she said. "I have to wait. I can't burn any bridges."

Vogt had a meeting with Paulo Villela, because the manager wasn't happy with the number of hours Villela had been clocking. Ninety-four hours in the last week was way too much overtime. But Inez Holderness was away, and she'd asked Villela to help. Villela had come in early that morning, he was going to work late that night, and he planned to come in the next morning to help Steve Adams, the new beverage manager, in the wine cellar.

"If you don't want me to work so many hours, I won't work tonight," Villela said angrily before storming out of Vogt's office. He told Bernardo that he should not come to work the next morning either. It was, after all, Villela's younger son, Felipe's, eleventh birthday; they could see him before he went to school and then go to work in the evening.

The office day was wrapping up, and Olender headed over to the cubicle of Doris Eng, the Club manager; they were both single women living in the big city and were equally devoted to their parents. Eng lived with her mother in Flushing, Queens. And Olender was on the phone practically every day with her parents back in Chicago. The two had gone on vacations together and had recently celebrated Eng's thirtieth birthday.

Both women were tough, even if Olender was a girly-girl who wore fancy, impractical shoes. She was Vogt's gatekeeper, so if you needed him to sign off on something, she was your best friend. But when Vogt wasn't around, Olender was in charge, and the staff respected her.

Eng wore a jade-pig necklace—she was born in the year of the pig—and practical shoes, because she stood all day and her feet often hurt. Eng had a wry sense of humor, would joke about "the Asian way," and would sometimes laugh about the most inappropriate things. That day, she was looking online at shoes to buy. Olender ribbed her about the shoes she had selected. Both women came to work early and left at around five in the evening. Eng could often be at her desk as early as 6:00 A.M., getting ready for the opening of the club breakfast.

Because of the construction on the new wine cellar and bar, breakfast was being served in Wild Blue. Everything was a little out of sync, so Eng asked Villela if he could help her with breakfast, but he was leaving the building in a huff and said he couldn't. Olender offered to help Eng with the morning setup before Olender had a meeting with Vogt at nine.

Jules Roinnel surprised them with the news that he wasn't going to be coming in for pre-meal. You could count on two hands the number of times in the past two decades that he had worked dinner, but he had been upstairs on 107, where restaurant director Melissa Trumbull had asked him to work with her during Tuesday evening's service. "I have no one on the floor with me," she said. "Come on, why don't you work it? You can have the floor or the door. And we can have dinner together. I'll even let you pick out the wine."

Trumbull often teased Roinnel about his wine choices. He accepted her offer and said he'd take the door—an easier gig—and looked forward to the next day. With only 240 reservations registered for the night, it should be manageable.

"I'll see you at three-thirty," Roinnel said to Eng and Olender, leaving at 5:00 P.M.

Dinner service began at the usual 5:00. Despite it being a Monday and there being limited visibility, more people than expected were coming for dinner. The waiters were feeling good; for some reason, almost every table was ordering wine or champagne, some of it on the higher price end, so the money would be good.

In the Greatest Bar, in the SkyBox lounge, George Delgado was hosting, with Dale DeGroff, a Spirits in the Sky cocktail seminar, a monthly event in which the two spoke and demonstrated for a gathering of about a dozen people who dropped $35 each for the educational merriment of mixing cocktails and drinking. Tequila was the focus that night. DeGroff was doing the gig to fulfill a contract obligation to Emil, for whom he worked at the Rainbow Room.

Delgado's day had started badly; his car battery had died that morning after he'd driven through the torrential rain, so he had to drop fifty bucks to take a taxi to work, all the way from Hackensack, New Jersey. The class began at 6:00 P.M., but Delgado came in about three hours before to set up each student's station at long, classroom-style tables, where he carefully placed the shaker kit, garnishes, juices, salt, ice buckets, and a selection of tequilas that each student would get to taste.

Delgado and DeGroff took turns demonstrating their mixology skills and telling stories, with DeGroff leading the classic margarita instruction and Delgado teaching the class how to make two of his own Greatest Bar tequila specialties, La Rumba and the spicy Bendito Loco.

Also at the Greatest Bar that night, the new head of World Trade Center security, John O'Neill, was having a drink before heading to his favorite watering hole, Elaine's, where writers and cops mingled with celebrities. O'Neill had recently retired from the FBI, where he had been the Bureau's counterterrorism chief in Washington, D.C., and was instrumental in the capture of the 1993 World Trade Center bomber Ramzi Yousef.

O'Neill had had his FBI retirement party at Windows. He was just a few weeks into the much-better-paying job. That night, he told a friend that a terrorist attack was coming soon. "We're due," he said. "And we're due for something big."

By 9:00 P.M., the sky had cleared, leaving the city wet-slicked and vivid. Closer to midnight, a few parties were unwilling to let the night end. A couple of tables for two lingered, savoring the views

Waiter Carlos Medina was taking care of two Italian newlyweds at table number 64, facing due north. When it was time to pay the check, their credit card was denied, which wasn't unusual for international cards. Medina offered to escort the new husband, who had invited him to visit his cheese factory back home, to the Citibank ATM in the concourse. They went all the way down and back up. "What a beautiful building," the Italian said. But when he laid out the cash, he realized he didn't have enough dollars for the tip. He gave Medina and his coworkers one hundred fifty thousand lira (seventy dollars) instead.

Captain Luis Feglia tried to adhere to the "legendary service" code that Ron Blanchard preached, so he let his guests linger. As captain, "Papi" had the discretion to tell the front and back waiters in his team to go home, so it was just he and one busboy, Telmo Alvear, who remained. Twenty-five-year-old Alvear, who had a one-year-old son and whose wife was studying computerized accounting, often heard from Feglia how he should pick up as many shifts as possible to make more money. As a teen, he had immigrated from Ecuador, and just that summer he had quit a midtown waiting job to work at Windows, where the tips were better.

Alvear had added a shift for the next morning, taking another staffer's spot. After the guests finally called for the check, Feglia and Alvear changed in the locker room and went down to take the E train to Queens. As shop steward, Feglia was coming in the next day for a 10:00 A.M. meeting, and Alvear would have to sleep quickly; he was expected back in six hours.

After they left, the night still wasn't over on the 107th floor. In the bar, in the booths outside the SkyBox, DeGroff and Delgado were entertaining their students with some extra credit after the class had ended at 7:30. One of the women students was enthralled by the music DJ Penelope Tuesdae was playing, and so they decided to stay for dinner. They had ordered small dishes, and DeGroff had ordered bottle after bottle of Veuve Clicquot for the group, tickled to be sticking Emil with the bill.

After one o'clock, Delgado suddenly remembered he didn't have his car. It would have cost a small fortune to take another taxi back home, so he called his wife, Fran, a fellow bartender he had met working at the Greatest Bar but who no longer worked there, and asked her to put their eleven-month-old baby, Genevieve, into the car seat and to take the hour-long drive to get him.

About eight people were still in their party until DeGroff asked for the check. He signed off on what was probably the last bill of the night, well north of a thousand dollars.

When Fran arrived in her Volkswagen Beetle, Delgado headed out. He saw the cleaning crews arriving and gave the security guard, Mo, short for Mohammed, a half-handshake, half-backslap on his way out before taking the elevator down to meet his family on West Street. The baby was awake, so he took her out of the car and held her in his arms and raised her slightly so that she faced the World Trade Center buildings.

"Look, Genevieve," Delgado said, gazing at the reflection of light in her big brown eyes. "That's where Daddy works, way up there."

CHAPTER 31
THE MORNING OF SEPTEMBER 11

"Every story about 9/11 will start with what a beautiful day it was," Michael Lomonaco says. The humidity from the day before had lifted, and a hint of fall was in the air. In the morning, the temperature would reach the upper sixties with clear, blue skies.

While an overnight crew of about a dozen workers was still cleaning the restaurant, Howard Kane, restaurant comptroller, was getting ready for work. He woke up at 4:30 in the morning and drank a cup of coffee on the train from his home in Hazlet, New Jersey, where his wife and son still slept.

He normally got in by seven to get ahead of the desk work. His shoulder bag was always filled with papers. Kane, balding, slightly slumped, a Mets fan, was the very image of the nebbishy New Yorker. He would wearily rifle through his bag and pull out a check for whoever had been haranguing him for a payment. He worked more hours than even his boss wanted him to. His wife, Lori, called him a "workaholic."

By the time Kane was at his desk, the prep team was already working in the 106th-floor banquet kitchen. Meat was being cut, shrimp cleaned, and salad washed. The night before, banquet chef Barry D'Onofrio had doubled the morning shift. A Tuesday event had been canceled, so he told the P.M. prep crew to come in with the A.M. crew so that they could all be done by the afternoon.

The banquet kitchen was more spacious than upstairs, so a fair amount of the prep work for all of the Windows kitchens was done there. And the engine running that machine was the four Gomez brothers—Enrique, Jose, Miguel, and Ramone—who were legendary in the industry. They could peel, devein, and clean three hundred pounds of shrimp or prep four hundred oysters with alarming speed. D'Onofrio and Lomonaco's chef de cuisine, Michael Ammirati, would give them lists the night before, and they'd have it all done by 2:00 P.M. the next day, wrapped and ready on the rack.

The Gomez brothers were intense, heads down, each pushing the other to keep pace. That morning, Enrique, forty-two, and Jose, forty-four, the older of the brothers, were at work. Miguel and Ramon were coming in later.

There were about six prep cooks in the kitchen, peeling cases of Yukon potatoes for the mashed potatoes, peeling bags of onions, sweating over the enormous eighty-gallon and sixty-gallon pots with chicken and lobster stock, or prepping vegetables, blanching them, and then shocking them with ice water just before they were tender.

Overseeing the banquet kitchen was sous chef Leonel Morocho, a thirty-six-year-old Ecuadorean who had declined a better-paying job at another restaurant because he was undocumented and was using his position at Windows to gain legal status. He had just taken two weeks off to work in Queens at the U.S. Open, because he was saving money to bring his older daughters, who were twelve and fourteen, to live with him, his wife, and their three younger daughters in Brooklyn. Morocho's sister, Blanca, whom he helped get a job at Windows as a salad prep worker, was also at work.

The two-week gig at the U.S. Open had meant brutal hours, so Morocho asked D'Onofrio if he could have a couple of days off, but D'Onofrio needed him. He promised Morocho he'd take care of him on the back end.

The kitchens on 106 and 107 were coming to life. Jose Nunez was supposed to be manning "La Machina," the superpowerful dishwasher that worked on a conveyor system. To keep the area cool, there were two industrial fans running that could blow your shirt off. Nunez was called "El Forte"; he was built like a football player and was often asked to do any heavy lifting.

Also at seven that morning, Windows on the World hostess Beatriz Susana Genoves was at her post on the 78th floor, because the express elevators were out of service. Genoves was there to greet guests, especially the hundred or so people expected at the Risk Waters conference on the 106th floor, and to escort them to the next set of elevators that would take them up.

Risk Waters Group, a London-based financial information company, was hosting a three-day conference. The day's activities were to begin at 8:30 A.M., but attendees were trickling in before to visit booths run by companies such as Bloomberg L.P. and DataSynapse.

* * *

That morning on the Upper East Side, Michael Lomonaco and his wife, Diane, cast their votes in the New York primary, and then he drove their Toyota 4Runner to her office on Hudson Street. Lomonaco dropped her off and parked in his lot on Washington Street, which was a short walk to the World Trade Center.

Others driving in included Glenn Vogt, who first dropped his kids off at school. He had the top down on his Saab convertible as he drove from his home in Croton-on-Hudson. Vogt was listening to Howard Stern joke with his "mooks" about who had the best chance of bedding model-actress Pamela Anderson. Longtime club breakfast guest Lucio Caputo had arrived earlier in his silver Mercedes E320. Caputo parked his car and took the elevator to 78 and transferred to 107, where he went to have breakfast.

The club breakfast was normally held in the main restaurant, but Bronx Builders, a construction crew of six men, was working on the new bar and wine cellar, so guests were redirected to Wild Blue, where Doris Eng cheerfully welcomed most of them by name. Caputo sat at a table in the back, away from the windows, while Mike Nestor, the Port Authority deputy inspector general, ate poached eggs and toast with one of his inspectors, Richard Tierney, who had smoked salmon with capers on an English muffin.

Jan Maciejewski, one of a tight group of Polish waiters, was serving them. He loved tennis and had taken time off to go to the U.S. Open. He was filling in for another waiter, serving coffee and taking the order of Liz Thompson, the executive director of the Lower Manhattan Cultural Council, who was having breakfast with Geoffrey Wharton, who worked for Silverstein Properties. At another table were six stockbrokers, and at another, Neil Levin, who had become executive director of the Port Authority in March, was sitting alone reading a newspaper by a window.

Outside Wild Blue, Bronx Builders and Larry Bogdanow's design firm were having a kickoff meeting to discuss the new cellar and small bar they were building. The meeting began at eight, but the millwork foreman, Manuel DaMota, was late, as he often was. Bogdanow partner Thomas Schweitzer, the architect project manager on the job, joined Bronx Builders' site foreman Josh Poptean and three subcontractors, who discussed the work that needed to be done and checked out the space for the new cellar. But Schweitzer couldn't wait for DaMota, so he began to leave after 8:40.

When Schweitzer's elevator arrived on 107, DaMota and one of his draftsmen, Obdulio Ruiz-Diaz, were on it. But the architect was already late for a 9:00 A.M. meeting, so he told DaMota to take photographs and that they'd discuss it later. DaMota apologized, and Schweitzer went down.

Sipping his coffee in Wild Blue, the Port Authority's Mike Nestor was thinking about a criminal case he was working on. Some PA workers were allegedly cashing phony checks at a credit union. A PA detective was coming in with videotape evidence, and Nestor was eager to see it, so he suggested to Tierney that they cut their breakfast short. They got up to leave, but not without greeting Neil Levin, their new boss, before heading down the hallway. Nestor heard someone following them, so he held the elevator, and Thompson and Wharton entered. Nestor pressed the button for the 78th floor, and the elevator doors closed at 8:44 A.M.

* * *

At the same time, Howard Kane got a call in his cubicle on the 106th floor, where he faced a pile of papers and a picture of his son, Jason, in a frame the eleven-year-old had made from doctors' tongue depressors. The call was Kane's wife, Lori, who told him she was planning to take Jason to the doctor because he wasn't feeling well. She told him he had to be home early, because she had a parent-teacher meeting to go to. "I'll be there for you and Jason," Howard said.

And then, abruptly, he started repeatedly screaming her name, "Lori!" She thought he was having a heart attack. He dropped the phone. And then someone else got on and told Lori that there was a fire and that Howard was helping with the situation. Lori heard a woman scream in the background, "Oh, my God. We're trapped!"

It was 8:46 A.M. Lucio Caputo was in a temporary office on the 78th floor. His real office was on 89, but the asbestos abatement there had moved him down eleven floors. He was rising from his seat to walk to the fax machine when he heard an enormous explosion and felt a shaking that caused a large mirror on the wall to slide one yard one way and then another yard the other way. A large cloud of plaster dust slowly snowed down from the ceiling. The lights went out. His computer went dead. His phone wasn't working.

One floor below him, Mike Nestor and Richard Tierney were walking through the inspector general offices when the explosion shook Tierney enough that he grabbed on to a cubicle wall for support. The sway was so immense, he thought the top of the building was tipping over. But then it steadied itself. And although there was debris falling outside their windows, it didn't exactly seem life-threatening. Maybe because there were no alarms or sirens. Tierney thought that a Piper plane must have hit the building. Still, Nestor made sure everyone in his office headed toward the stairs.

Caputo knew how fragile the buildings were. Decades before, when they were under construction, Guy Tozzoli had crowed to him about how there would be no obstructions in Windows' public spaces because the pillars were all in the interior. Caputo was still trying to figure out what had happened when his phone started to ring. On the line was an Italian journalist who said he was watching CNN and told him that a plane had hit the building. "Run, run," he told Caputo, who bolted for the door.

Nestor and Tierney joined a stream of people heading into the three darkened stairwells. Caputo must have entered the stairs earlier, because there were so few people that he was able to run down about thirty flights before a throng of people slowed him down. He saw a woman who had terrible burns on her body. Tierney, who had a bad hip and could get asthmatic, stopped at 52 to get some water.

Among the throng was Beatriz Genoves, the Windows on the World greeter from the 78th-floor sky lobby. She heard the voice of a man on 106 asking for help on her walkie-talkie as she descended the crowded stairs.

CHAPTER 32
THAT TERRIBLE DAY

"I don't mean to break in on the fun, but this is a serious news story," Howard Stern said on the radio. "A plane has crashed into the World Trade Center." Glenn Vogt was listening as he drove down the West Side Highway. He couldn't believe it. At around Fifty-Seventh Street, fire engines began speeding past him with their sirens shrieking.

A police officer stopped Vogt, but he showed her his business card, and she told him he should drive down the northbound lane. Vogt's was the only car on the road; proceeding downtown with the convertible top down, he must have been quite a sight. Two guys yelled, "Hey, asshole!" as he drove past. Vogt drove until he couldn't drive anymore because of the fire trucks and hoses everywhere. Unaware of the gravity of the situation, he parked and checked himself in the rearview mirror as he put on his tie. He walked toward the North Tower lobby, and glass crunched under his feet. He thought, *It's going to be months before we can clean up this mess.* He, like most people, assumed a small plane had hit the building.

Firefighters were standing around, seemingly awaiting orders. Vogt was under an overhang when a body fell onto it. Vogt went numb. He was overwhelmed by sensory overload. There was so much noise, so much happening, that there seemed to be a quiet descending on him. A firefighter said, "You have to get away from the building." He did.

Greg Hein, the restaurant's director of catering, had stayed up late the night before drinking one dollar Michelob Lights at a local bar watching the New York Giants play the Denver Broncos on *Monday Night Football*, so he slept in. He took the 7:43 train from Massapequa, Long Island, instead of the 7:11, to Penn Station. He was on the E train when the first plane hit. Aboveground, at Vesey and Church, he heard the tremendous grinding sound of the second plane overhead. When it exploded, he saw a fireball and debris as big as cars flying in all directions. A young woman landed in front of him outside the Stage Door Deli, her legs terribly mangled, and died right there.

Hein tried to shield some people who were cowering from falling debris. He put on his Walkman to listen to 1010 WINS, the news station, to find out what was going on. When he looked up at the towers, he was worried about the people standing near him who were also looking up. He told a firefighter that the building was going to fall, and the firefighter asked him to help move the crowd away. He tried to assist others, but when people started falling from the sky, Hein decided to move north.

Glenn Vogt was still by the North Tower when the second plane hit. The sound was overwhelming. He walked over to Liberty Street, where three senior police sergeants in their white uniform shirts were standing. One of them received a call. He told the others that there was a third plane in the air, and it might be coming their way.

Vogt wanted to get a better view of what was happening at the top of the North Tower, so he walked toward West Street. He passed a firefighter, suited up in full uniform, sobbing. He eventually got a clearer view and could see people waving large sheets—what must have been Windows tablecloths, he thought. And then more people were falling. They were falling in succession, some holding hands. Vogt felt helpless. He walked back to his car and drove home, where his wife and neighbors ran out of their houses to greet him when he pulled up.

Michael Lomonaco was among the thousands of people moving uptown, not far from Vogt and Hein. When the second plane exploded, a maintenance worker from a nearby office building had grabbed Lomonaco in the street. He was shepherding people into a service elevator. He said to Lomonaco, "Come with us. We're going downstairs."

But Lomonaco didn't want any part of that. He remained in the street with hundreds of people, everyone in different degrees of shock, some weeping, some hysterical. People were pouring out of office buildings. Emergency crews were rushing in all directions. Lomonaco's impulse was to get out of the way of the first responders. He also wanted to see what was happening to his restaurant. He walked uptown to Chambers and Church, where he was able to see the gaping hole in the North Tower, the windows his friends and colleagues had broken, and the people waving tablecloths. His tablecloths. His people.

He thought of his staff up there and the building workers who had become friends, like "director of vertical transportation" Joe Amatuccio. Unbeknownst to Lomonaco, Amatuccio had also been on the street and had reportedly run into the building when others were streaming out.

Lomonaco cried quietly. He felt it was impossible not to look. And then the South Tower collapsed. If there were different phases of impact for those outside the towers—the first plane hitting, the second plane hitting—then the implosion of Building Two was the one that crossed the line and turned the mass of observers into potential victims. The collapse was a fatal threat, with deadly debris and immense dust clouds pouring everywhere. The people who had come to Chambers Street to see what was happening, including Lomonaco, ran in the other direction. Thousands ran uptown or east toward the Brooklyn Bridge. Lomonaco ran the mile to his wife's office, where they met in the street.

From there, he and Diane walked the five miles to their home on the Upper East Side. Along the way, they heard people relaying news of what was happening downtown: that the North Tower had collapsed, that hospitals were accepting blood donations. Fire engines from outside the city sped by as they walked north. Two F-15 fighter jets flew overhead. Lomonaco charted a path home to avoid the city's other landmarks, like the Empire State Building and Grand Central Terminal, in case they were also attacked. He wanted to protect Diane, and he didn't know where and when the terror would strike next.

* * *

The conditions at the top of the North Tower will forever remain shrouded. But they were so unendurable that scores of people jumped

to their deaths rather than remain inside the inferno that was engulf-
ing them. It's been estimated that two hundred people jumped, but it's
unclear how many intentionally chose that path and how many were
propelled by fire, explosions, broken windows, or falling debris.

There are rumors about who from Windows jumped, information
partly deduced by how early or intact their bodies were found. Public
conjecture focused on the Falling Man, the victim who became one of
the most iconic images of the day. One convincing theory holds that,
because he wore a white tunic much like what many of the Windows
staff wore, and because of other physical similarities, the restaurant's
sound engineer, Jonathan Briley, who died that day, is Falling Man.

The fires were reportedly burning at more than one thousand
degrees, and the air was so saturated with suffocating, toxic smoke that
it was unbreathable. Within two or three minutes of impact, people were
seen falling from the building. The little that is known is mostly gleaned
from the calls and e-mails that came from the people trapped inside.

Many of the attendees at the Risk Waters conference made calls—
pleas for help and desperate requests for information—as did Windows
on the World employees. Club manager Doris Eng called the fire command center in the lobby, asking, "What do we do?"

Assistant general manager Christine Olender made repeated calls
over the course of twelve minutes, starting at around 9:00 A.M. She
spoke with Port Authority police officers Steve Maggett and Ray Murray. The conversations were fraught, and it appears Olender knew that
the stairwells were impassable. She asked for directions about where on
the floor she could direct her guests to get away from the smoke. The
officers' guidance and assurances were futile.

Her last call to the police was answered by Officer Murray. "Hi, this
is Christine again, from Windows on the World on the 106th floor. The
situation on 106 is rapidly getting worse," she said.

Murray spoke to the people he was with. "I got a fourth call from
Windows on the World; it's getting rapidly worse up there," he said.
"We," Olender said, "we have . . . the fresh air is going down fast! I'm
not exaggerating."

"Uh, ma'am, I know you're not exaggerating," Murray said. "We're getting a lot of these calls. We are sending the fire department up as soon as possible. I have you, Christine, four calls, seventy-five to one hundred people, Windows on the World, 106th floor."

Olender asked, "What are we going to do for air?" And, "Can we break a window?"

"You can do whatever you have to . . . to get to, uh, the air," Murray said. "All right," Olender replied.

She made calls to Glenn Vogt's home, where she spoke with Vogt's wife. "The ceilings are falling," she said. "The floors are buckling."

Ivhan Luis Carpio Bautista, a Windows cook from Peru who was turning twenty-four that day, left a message on his cousin's answering machine, saying, "I can't go anywhere, because they told us not to move. I have to wait for the firefighters." Moises Rivas managed to get a call out as well. He called home to speak with his wife, Elizabeth, but she was in the laundry. He left a message that he loved her—"no matter what," he said.

Josh Poptean and Manuel DaMota, from Bronx Builders, were with a number of other people when Poptean called their boss, Mark Goldberg, from a room that was filling up with smoke. Goldberg told Poptean to follow the PA protocols they'd recently learned and to call the emergency phone numbers they'd been given. "You're going to be OK," Goldberg said. Poptean uttered a sound that could have been a chuckle. "Maybe not," he said.

* * *

"We are under attack," Howard Stern said as he watched the planes crashing into the two buildings over and over again on a television screen in his studio. "We have to bomb the hell out of them. This is more upsetting to me than not getting Pam Anderson."

It is estimated that two billion people eventually saw the images of 9/11. The reactions to the unprecedented events rippled through a third of the planet's population. Former Windows captain Claudette Fournier was all the way in Antarctica—she had followed her younger son there after a divorce and had an administration job six months out of the year—where her roommate woke her up. She watched the disaster on TV and was asked later by her boss to say some words. Her audience wept as she gave her colleagues a verbal tour through the grandness that was once the 107th floor.

Donald Trump, who was then a real estate tycoon still two years from being a national celebrity on NBC's *The Apprentice,* was interviewed that day on local channel 9, and he reflected on the seventy-one-floor downtown building he owned. "Forty Wall Street actually was the second-tallest building in downtown Manhattan," he said. "And it was actually, before the World Trade Center, the tallest—and then, when they built the World Trade Center, it became known as the second-tallest. And now it's the tallest."

As president of the World Trade Centers Association, Guy Tozzoli was on his way from New Jersey to his office in the towers that morning. As he approached the Holland Tunnel, he saw the North Tower on fire. He was stuck in bumper-to-bumper traffic, so he got out of his Mercedes and joined others outside their cars. "It's going to take us a long time to fix that," he said, before the second plane hit the South Tower.

Chef de cuisine Michael Ammirati's trainer turned to him in his gym in Garden City, Long Island, and said, "Isn't that your building?" as the images flickered on the big screens. In Queens, Luis Feglia had driven his son to school and then come back home, where he had nodded off. He was woken up by a phone call from another captain. "Papi, Papi, turn on the TV," he said. Feglia did, and he watched the second plane hit.

The calls between staff members spread throughout the city. Waiter Awal Ahmed, who was scheduled to work that night, was asleep when his wife woke him up. Ahmed knew that his friend Shabbir Ahmed, with whom he'd experienced the 1993 bombing, was working that morning. He called captain Shamim Hassan, and they were talking while watching their televisions. When the South Tower collapsed, Ahmed put the phone down without saying anything. He didn't know how to react.

Word of the disaster spread through different networks, even reaching children at school. "There's no way your dad is alive" is what the kids were saying to one of Greg Hein's grade-school daughters, who didn't find out until her mother came to school to tell her otherwise.

David Emil had spent part of the morning reviewing issue papers for his friend Andrew Cuomo, who was running for governor. He had driven his son to school and was back home in his apartment putting his tie on when he received a call from his sister Jennie who told him what had happened. Jennie was normally in the office by eight, but she had gone to a doctor's appointment, where she'd heard the news. She'd also received a desperate call from Christine Olender.

Charles Baum was in his apartment in the city, unaware of what was happening downtown. A relative called and told him to turn on his television. Baum says that his father's reaction would have been horror and grief for the people who suffered and died. "We were relieved that our father wasn't alive," he says. "The emotional impact would have been so overwhelming."

"And the impact of the restaurant on Lower Manhattan was part of his restaurant dream life—to make dining experiences meaningful in very broad ways," Charlie adds. "He would have felt [that] an enormous part of him had been erased."

* * *

When the first plane, American Airlines Flight 11, hit the north face of the North Tower at 8:46 A.M., there were an estimated fifty-eight thousand people in the World Trade Center area, at their desks, heading to work, or grabbing breakfast, exiting the PATH train, or walking in the plaza. That number included approximately sixteen thousand people in the two towers, of whom there were seventy-three Windows on the

World employees, the six men working on the renovation job on the 107th floor, and ninety-one guests, most of whom were on the 106th floor for the Risk Waters conference.

The burning jet fuel of the plane scheduled to fly from Boston to Los Angeles launched fireballs down at least one elevator shaft that exploded on the 77th and 22nd floors, the lobby level, and in the B4 basement. A tremendous amount of dense black smoke immediately engulfed the upper floors. Parts of the plane went right through Building One; landing gear was found more than five blocks south on Rector Street.

Minoru Yamasaki's steel tube exterior had been split open like a soda can. Survivors of the impact clustered on certain floors, like 92 and 103. It is believed that Christine Olender had the Risk Waters conference attendees and others gathered in a hallway on the 106th floor near an impassable stairwell and a phone for calling the fire command center.

The building's emergency intercom phone system was damaged, and the 911 operators were overwhelmed with the number of calls; many people received an "all circuits busy" message. Those who did get through were often advised to stay where they were—standard operating procedure for high-rise fires—by dispatch operators, although the fire chiefs in the North Tower lobby were telling the police to evacuate the buildings.

Most of the Building One tenants in the floors below 91 immediately began to evacuate, although many people listened to directions to remain where they were. When Mike Nestor and Richard Tierney were approaching the bottom floors, they were struck by an overwhelming shudder and sound: *Boom! Boom! Boom!* Tierney thought that the building was collapsing down on them. He instinctively put one hand above his head and placed the other on the person in front of him, perhaps for stability but also, he thinks, to touch another human being as he was dying. But the sound was the South Tower collapsing at 9:59 A.M. They continued to descend.

When they reached the ground floor, they couldn't believe the devastation, the debris, the mangled metal and broken glass, the fire and smoke. A giant mound of wreckage was blocking Tierney's path toward Vesey Street, and so he stopped to assess the situation. His bum hip wasn't going to get him over the pile. Suddenly a hand reached down to grab his, and he was pulled up the mound. He never saw the face of the person who helped him. He just kept moving.

Flight 11 had crashed into a space that spanned the 93rd to 99th floors of the North Tower, killing scores of people instantly and wreaking enough destruction in the core of the building to make the three stairwells impassable above the 91st floor, allowing no escape for the one thousand three hundred fourty-four people trapped on the top 19 floors. The doors to the roof were locked, and, anyway, the NYPD decided conditions were too dangerous, with the heat, smoke, and other obstructions, for a helicopter to perform a rescue.

About 95 percent of the people who died in the World Trade Center were at the impact zones or above them. Most of those who were below the impact sites were able to get out. It appears that greeter Beatriz Genoves was the only Windows on the World employee to clock in for work who survived, because she was on the 78th floor, and she could access a stairwell.

According to *The 9/11 Commission Report,* the FDNY began its response to the catastrophe five seconds after impact. One engine and one ladder company from the fire department began ascending the North Tower stairs at 8:57 A.M. The fire department almost immediately recognized that theirs was a rescue operation, not a firefighting one.

When the South Tower collapsed, many firefighters who were in the North Tower were not aware of what had happened. They felt the tremendous shudder, but some thought a bomb had gone off and others that part of the North Tower had collapsed. Radio communication was maddeningly impaired. One fire chief grabbed a bullhorn and went to the stairwells and yelled, "All FDNY, get the fuck out!" Many heeded the call and rushed down.

The North Tower collapsed at 10:28. Somehow, a dozen firefighters, a cop, and three civilians who were still in one of the stairwells were able to get out while the building crumbled.

* * *

Mayor Rudolph Giuliani was having breakfast in a midtown hotel talking about the primary when he was told that a plane had hit the North Tower. He jumped into a van and headed down Fifth Avenue and got out two blocks away from the World Trade Center. When the second plane hit the South Tower, he realized, "We were into something different than anything we had ever prepared for or any of us thought we would ever live through," he said soon after. "I realized I was in some kind of a horrible, awful, horrific human experience."

Giuliani walked through the debris-covered streets with composure and authority. He was visibly moved, covering his mouth, shaking his head at the horror before him. He watched people falling. As the towers collapsed, the mayor ran down streets and called out to New Yorkers, "Walk north." He told people to put on masks to protect themselves from the suffocating clouds of dust, while he held his in his hand. News crews ran along with him, documenting the city's mayor in the crisis.

After establishing a base on Barclay Street, the mayor, the police and fire commissioners, and the Office of Emergency Management director moved to the Police Academy on East Twentieth Street. Giuliani and Governor George Pataki went in front of the press just before 3:00 P.M., and the mayor was spare but strong. "Today is obviously one of the most difficult days in the history of the city," he said. "The tragedy that we are undergoing right now is something that we've had nightmares about. My heart goes out to all the innocent victims of this horrible and vicious act of terrorism. And our focus now has to be to save as many lives as possible."

When asked how many lives had been lost, he declined to speculate. "The number of casualties," he said, "will be more than any of us can bear."

He appeared several more times that evening to inform the press of any developments, and he spoke of some of those who had died whom he had known personally, including Father Mychal Judge. He referred to the terrorists who had committed the attacks as "barbarians," but he focused on inspiring New Yorkers. "We are going to need strength," he said. "And the people of New York will be an example to the rest of the country and the world that terrorism can't stop us."

CHAPTER 33
AFTER

The day after, fires blazed from the remains of the World Trade Center. Plumes of smoke drifted upward where the Twin Towers had been. You could smell the devastation throughout the city. The streets were disturbingly still as the staff of Windows on the World traveled to locations in midtown Manhattan not far from one another. One was the elegant, two-story Beacon restaurant, which David Emil owned with former Rainbow Room executive chef Waldy Malouf. The other was the Local 100 Union headquarters—offices with wall-to-wall carpeting, cubicles, conference rooms, and worker demonstration photos on the wall—on West Forty-Fourth Street.

On Tuesday, David Emil and Glenn Vogt agreed on the phone that they needed a head count. With a staff of approximately four hundred fifty people, and with everyone on different schedules and multiple workers regularly switching shifts, it was impossible to immediately know who was in the towers that morning. Vogt and bar manager Joe Amico called their colleagues and spread the word that everyone should go to Beacon.

At the same time, Local 100 recording secretary Bill Granfield and his union organizers were calling the shop stewards and Windows workers who were in the union's executive committee and telling them to come to the headquarters to figure out what they should do.

There were a hundred or so people—staff, families, friends, and colleagues—at Beacon. A visibly shaken Emil rose up and gave an emotional, heartfelt speech to the gathering. He spoke of how difficult this was for everyone and how it was certainly the hardest thing he had ever encountered in his life. He also assured everyone that he would assist them in any way that he could.

Without a physical restaurant or its paperwork, Emil's managers had to start from scratch. They started taking down Social Security numbers. Manager Ron Blanchard meticulously updated lists of employees as well as the missing in an attempt to achieve order.

Twelve blocks downtown, Bill Granfield spoke to another gathering: union members and the families of the missing. They were too many for the reception area and conference rooms, so everyone moved to nearby Local 6. Granfield told them that he knew that if they faced the situation together, they would get through it.

He and his union stewards divided up the work. At first, they sent members to hospitals to see if they could find the missing. When that seemed increasingly unlikely, they shifted to caring for the families. Human resources director Elizabeth Ortiz also went to hospitals, where she combed over lists of survivors. Ortiz stumbled upon a poster of dishwasher Jose Nunez pasted to a mailbox on the street, with the words MISSING . . . MISSING . . . MISSING.

By the end of the week, Bill Granfield decided they needed more information, so he went over to Beacon, but it turned out that management had even less. Granfield invited Emil to set up an office in the union, where they worked together for several weeks. "There was no more company and union," Local 100 union organizer Juan Galan says. "We were working as one."

The union headquarters and the team from Beacon attended to the immediate needs—such as child care and groceries—of the families of the missing Windows workers and connected them with agencies to figure out how to handle bigger, looming concerns, such as rent, car and mortgage payments, and health insurance.

At Beacon, Michael Lomonaco's cooks and other friends from different restaurants helped in Waldy Malouf's kitchen, producing a huge, continuous family meal for those who came to the restaurant. Food was being donated by various sources. The restaurant's meat supplier rolled up one morning and simply said to Malouf, "What do you need?"

Emil, Malouf, and Lomonaco were being inundated with calls from everyone they knew in the restaurant industry. "Everyone was so desperate to do something," Malouf says. "And people needed help." Emil owned another restaurant, Ouest, with chef Tom Valenti, who, with Darlene Dwyer, a food industry publicist, helped bring together about thirty other chefs and restaurateurs who went to Beacon to discuss what they could do. They decided to start a fund for the families of the people who had died. They quickly landed on a name, Windows of Hope. Valenti drew the logo on a napkin. And they also picked a date—October 11—when they would sponsor a "Dine Out" night in which all participating restaurants would be invited to contribute 10 percent or more of their income from that night to the fund.

* * *

Some Windows staff went to observe the destruction. Michael Ammirati was tormented by thoughts of pastry chef Norberto Hernandez, a father of three daughters, dying, when he, with no kids, was alive. He made a pilgrimage to what was being called "Ground Zero." Ammirati walked onto the platform that had been built so that visitors could look down on the devastation, which just seemed weird to him. To Vogt, the site looked like a vision of hell. Waiter Sol Policar slipped into the cleanup crews and worked the pile for several days.

By the end of the next week, workers and relatives were able to pick up the final paychecks. Emil announced to one of the gatherings of workers at Beacon that there would be another Windows on the World. Not soon but maybe in five years. The staff cheered and applauded.

"In no way to diminish the suffering of everybody else," Emil said to a reporter, "the people in the food services industry were probably least financially prepared to deal with this tragedy."

Many Windows workers spent much of the next month at Pier 94, where the city had gathered the 9/11 relief organizations, from the Red Cross to the Tzu Chi Buddhist charity, in a giant warehouse. The Federal Emergency Management Agency was helping defray mortgage and rent costs for up to eighteen months. Workers' compensation death benefits were available, as was money from the state's crime victims board to cover burial expenses or psychotherapy. The survivors could also apply for unemployment insurance and get food stamps.

For those with deceased family members or who had themselves been injured by the attacks, there was also the promise of an unprecedented federal compensation program. On September 22, the U.S. Congress passed a financial aid package called the Air Transportation Safety and System Stabilization Act to save the airline industry from imploding due to the massive liability exposure caused by the hijackings. As part of the package, which promised fifteen billion dollars of support for the airlines, there was a plan to create a fund for the families of the victims of the attacks. The amount of the fund was yet to be determined by a "special master"; those who agreed to receive the government money would forgo the right to sue the airlines.

During this painful grieving period, friends and colleagues mourned at scores of funerals. Human resources head Elizabeth Ortiz, often accompanied by Glenn Vogt, went to more than forty. The procession of services—Jewish, Buddhist, Hindu, Muslim, and, mostly, Catholic—became a final reminder to Ortiz of the United Nations–like diversity of the staff. Local 100 leader Bill Granfield was grateful that the ceremonies, however painful, restored some sense of normalcy. "This is a little bit of what the end of a person's life should be like," he recalls thinking.

On Monday, October 1, hundreds of mourners gathered at the Cathedral of Saint John the Divine, on 112th Street near Harlem, to memorialize the Windows on the World workers. Amid the families and former employees were Mayor Giuliani and New York senators Hillary Clinton and Charles Schumer, the latter of whom spoke of the many personal, cherished events, including his wedding in 1980, that had happened at the restaurant. Clinton said Windows on the World had been "halfway to heaven."

Finally, on October 11, came a reason to celebrate. Over three hundred New York City restaurants, stores, wine shops, and many more businesses from almost every state and many countries took part in the "Dine Out" event for Windows of Hope. The night raised more than six million dollars for the fund, which, ultimately, reached more than twenty-two million dollars.

It was more than Michael Lomonaco and the other founders had expected. Windows of Hope quickly gave a round of ten thousand dollars to each family of a 9/11 food services victim. It abided by a lenient definition of family, allowing gay couples and domestic partners and other legitimate dependents to receive the money. More rounds of cash grants followed.

Restaurateur Danny Meyer believes "Dine Out" and the promotional restaurant week that followed was a turning point for a city, which was unsure if it could thrive again. "People were afraid to go out and laugh and have drinks," Meyer says. "They were afraid to be seen dancing on the graves of the people who had died. It allowed them to live again."

* * *

At a service at St. Patrick's Cathedral at the end of September for the three hundred fifty-eight Marsh & McLennan victims, Mayor Giuliani confided that he had wept earlier that day. "The tears have to make you stronger," he said. "America will prevail."

Giuliani, who had been transformed from scandal-plagued grump into "America's mayor," was leading the city, and the country, by example. He supported the grieving families by showing up at a reported two hundred funerals. In his shadow, mayoral candidates vied to become his replacement. After the primaries were delayed, Democrat Mark Green defeated Freddy Ferrer in a runoff before losing to Michael Bloomberg in the general election in November.

Bloomberg, a billionaire businessman with an outsider's can-do approach, was the surprising new mayor of a city looking for a way forward. At his inauguration, Mayor Bloomberg declared the city "safe, strong, open for business, and ready to lead the world in the twenty-first century." Of course, for a proud New Yorker to have to even say that suggested there were doubts.

The city had indeed been reeling since 9/11. The economy had already been cooling, but six weeks after the attacks, the city was facing a $1.2 billion deficit. The mayor called for cuts to the budget of a depleted city, which was losing one hundred forty-three thousand jobs a month and had suffered thirty billion dollars' worth of damage; the gross city product fell by forty to fifty billion dollars.

Windows staff were looking to rebound while the city's restaurants were suffering a massive decline of nearly 50 percent in revenue compared with the previous year. Fifteen thousand restaurant employees were laid off following the attacks.

In this fraught climate, there was inevitable anticipation for the June 2002 opening of David Emil's new Times Square restaurant, Noche. The restaurant was originally a David Copperfield–themed entertainment extravaganza, but after a contentious falling-out, Emil turned the space into a Latin nightclub and restaurant patterned on Mambo Baby nights at the Greatest Bar on Earth. There were going to be DJs, live bands, empanadas, and margaritas on four floors.

Michael Lomonaco helped open the kitchen and planned his next move with Emil while consulting on Noche's menu. But in addition to all the typical difficulties of opening a new restaurant, Emil had the expectations of Local 100 to contend with. One hundred ten former Windows on the World workers applied for jobs at Noche, and Emil offered jobs to fifty-five of them, thirty-one of whom were union members (sixteen of them accepted the offers).

Local 100 leadership said that that wasn't enough. The union had created an activist group, the Restaurant Opportunities Center of New York, which picketed a preopening party at Noche. Emil's former Windows employees carried signs that read, DAVID EMIL, WE WANT OUR JOBS BACK.

Emil insisted he simply didn't have enough jobs for the union. ROC countered that Emil was resisting hiring more of its members for fear of them turning Noche into a union restaurant.

"I'm very upset by all this," Emil said at the time. "There are only so many problems that one person can solve."

Just before the restaurant's opening, a compromise was reached: Emil committed to hiring thirty-three unionized former Windows workers; ROC and the workers agreed not to picket.

ROC turned its attention to uniting rank-and-file workers behind a new restaurant of its own that could emulate the success and fine-dining experience of Windows and also provide the working conditions that they considered their right. In 2003, they were hoping to open a restaurant called Windows on Tribeca, which would have been in the former North Tower's shadow and would have served partly as a memorial to the previous restaurant. But they couldn't get the financing.

Finally, in January of 2006, ROC and about forty former Windows workers opened COLORS on Lafayette Street, still downtown but almost two miles north of the World Trade Center. They had failed to get traditional funding but had cobbled together financing from a consortium of about twenty different, offbeat lenders. They also got support from themselves: Each worker contributed one hundred hours of sweat equity.

ROC had discarded the concept of connecting the restaurant to 9/11 and focused instead on workers' rights. COLORS was a cooperative restaurant; all the workers were part owners. No one was paid less than $13.50 an hour. And tips would be pooled. An ergonomics expert was hired to reduce injuries.

About a dozen of the staff, including the chef and general manager, hadn't worked at Windows. The menu was American with a global twist—each of the workers, who came from more than two dozen countries, contributed a recipe from their homeland. Entrée prices (twenty to twenty-five dollars) put the one hundred twenty-seat tablecloth restaurant in the pricier range.

It was a business but also a model for a new way to run a restaurant. ROC, which wasn't a union but a nonprofit, wanted to provide training and English classes, organize protests, and propose legislation to support workers. It was ambitious and a little messy. There was confusion about whether or not a cooperative should be a union. Some of the former Windows workers, who knew they wouldn't be making the money they had at Windows, left before it opened. A year or so later, only a handful remained.

CHAPTER 34

ENDURING CHANGE

"My first fifty years of life were magical," Kevin Zraly says. "And then September 11 happened."

In the months after, Zraly developed shingles, and then in early 2002, he lost his sense of smell, an essential ability for a wine expert. "I survived," says Zraly, who had been in New Paltz on September 11 to celebrate his son's birthday the next day. "But emotionally, I didn't survive." Despite the emotional burden, Zraly kept hosting his eight-week Windows on the World Wine School courses, relocated to a Marriott hotel in midtown. And after several years, he got his smell back.

After closing Noche in 2004, David Emil worked on several restaurants with Michael Lomonaco, who was doing his television show *Epicurious* on the Travel Channel when chef Thomas Keller invited him to open a restaurant next to his Per Se in the new Time Warner Center on Columbus Circle. Lomonaco's Porter House New York opened in 2006, making him the upstairs neighbor of Landmarc, the restaurant owned by Marc Murphy, who had traded in his precious Cellar in the Sky menus for successful Italian and French bistro fare. The two chefs put the past behind them.

Their ability to move forward far outstripped the city's painfully slow rebuild of the World Trade Center, which became mired in a process marred by politics, ego, money, and vying self-interests over land that was both vital to the life of the city and sacred ground.

Real estate developer Larry Silverstein, who had leased the World Trade Center and had lost four employees in the attacks, felt it was his "right and obligation" to rebuild all sixteen acres of the site. The native New Yorker, who wanted to restore the area to its full, commercial glory, locked horns with public agencies and officials, including Mayor Bloomberg and Governor Pataki.

After tussling with the Port Authority, Silverstein agreed in 2006 to give up control of One World Trade Center to the agency in exchange for securing public debt financing for the other World Trade Center buildings he was developing. That same year, his 7 World Trade Center, at fifty-two floors, opened.

In 2007, New York governor Eliot Spitzer appointed Emil president of the Lower Manhattan Development Corporation. Spitzer wanted the city-state authority to help him facilitate the stalled redevelopment of the area. Emil saw it as his chance to be a part of the reconstruction.

Eventually, fueled by $30 billion in government and private investment, the various entities began to fill the gaping construction hole. Silverstein had taken out a $3.5 billion insurance policy on the WTC, but his lawyers contended that the attacks were two separate events, so he was due twice that amount. He ultimately was awarded $4.6 billion in 2004. He also received an allocation of $3 billion in tax-exempt Liberty Bonds from the government.

Silverstein gave half of the sixteen acres to the National September 11 Memorial & Museum, which, on September 12, 2011, opened the memorial space with its two magnificent waterfalls and reflecting pools surrounded by bronze panels inscribed with the names of the 9/11 victims as well as those who died in the 1993 bombing. The names of the Windows workers were arranged on the uptown side of the north pool, pretty much directly below where the main restaurant once was.

Silverstein's seventy-two-story 4 World Trade Center opened in 2013. In 2014, the Durst Organization, which had taken over for Silverstein, finally opened One World Trade Center, the flagship of the complex. And then the transportation and retail hub known as the Oculus, costing an astounding four billion dollars, opened in 2016. The cool, white public space, an enormous atrium on the inside and a skeletal eyelash-like edifice from the outside, houses top retailers, such as Apple and Kate Spade, and connects to 4 World Trade Center, where a new Eataly, the upscale Italian food court, feeds visitors and maybe some locals too. In 2018, Silverstein opened 3 World Trade Center, an eighty-story building. (An arts center is projected to open in 2020 or 2021, and the fate of 2 World Trade Center is still in question.)

By 2018, 80 percent of One World Trade Center was occupied. And although 4 World Trade had achieved 100 percent occupancy, the area was underperforming office leasing expectations. Still, Lower Manhattan's private-sector employees, two hundred forty-two thousand workers, finally rose above pre-9/11 numbers. Seventeen years after the attacks, Lower Manhattan's population had tripled. And Mayor Bill de Blasio's office could tout the seven hundred two thousand jobs added between 2009 and 2017 as the largest and longest expansion in the city since World War II. You could see the rebound in the skyline. Fifteen of Manhattan's twenty tallest skyscrapers were built after 9/11.

All this despite some major setbacks, particularly the Great Recession of 2008 and 2012's Hurricane Sandy, which devastated large parts of the city, killing forty-three people, flooding the subway system, and ultimately causing nineteen billion dollars in destruction.

The World Trade Center site, although not fully realized, is coming closer to being the thriving city center that Guy Tozzoli and Joe Baum had hoped for, one that has helped foster an economy that could support the construction of more than twenty new hotels in Lower Manhattan, quadrupling what was there before 9/11.

But the restoration of the area didn't include a new Windows on the World. In 2003, David Emil said, "When the time is right, we would love to talk with Larry Silverstein about leasing the space. We'd love to work on creating a great new restaurant there, though we couldn't re-create the original."

But after the Durst Organization took over the building and the Port Authority issued a "request for expressions of interest" from restaurateurs in 2008, the agency shifted to developing the top space into a concession-style tourist amenity. Port Authority Executive Director Chris Ward told the *New York Post* in 2011, "New York City already has plenty of great restaurants." And he more pointedly said to the *Daily News*, "We don't build vanity projects at the top of tall buildings."

Despite the shift, in 2012, there were two bona fide New York City restaurateurs still in the running: Danny Meyer and Marc Murphy. Each had partnered with foreign corporate investors in competing proposals.

A third contender was Legends, which ran the concessions for the Dallas Cowboys and the New York Yankees. Emil chose not to pursue it, because he did not want to relive the "horror," he says.

In 2013, Legends won the bid with an economic plan that would make Inhilco blush. It was poised to generate eight hundred seventy-five million dollars in fixed and variable rent over the course of its fifteen-year lease. Legends was to pay the Port Authority $14.6 million in rent and about 40 percent of its gross receipts for the observation deck and the food offerings, which include One Dine (the restaurant), One Mix (the bar), One Café (a quick-service area with pizzas, hot dogs, and salads), and Aspire (the banquet space on 102).

With the entire observatory operation grossing seventy million dollars a year and the food services pulling in just 10 percent of that amount, it is no wonder that Legends is more oriented toward the overall experience that the 2.5 million visitors each year expect from a visit to the top of the tallest building in the Western Hemisphere. From the start, by requiring a thirty-two dollar observation deck ticket and a long wait on line with the other visitors, Legends positioned the culinary offerings as secondary to the view. When One Dine opened, it was pilloried by the press. And then it seemed to recede from New Yorkers' view.

But the food is better than you would expect. And seventy-five workers in the kitchen and waitstaff, including former Windows on the World back waiter Mohammad Quddus, are making a living there. There's a required 18 percent tip added to every bill, so no one is getting stiffed. And with the minimum wage hitting fifteen dollars an hour in 2019, the kitchen workers are poised to make well more than their predecessors.

The views are impressive if not magical. The restaurant is mostly set back on the 101st floor, so you see out of four-foot-plus-wide windows, but you are effectively in an atrium looking over the heads of tourists who crowd the windows on the 100th floor. There's nothing intimate or luxurious about the place, but it gets the job done. There are no tablecloths.

Knowing that just 15 percent of visitors to the observatory come from the tristate area, One World Observatory general manager Delfin

Ortiz is looking to make the space more attractive to locals. "This building needs more life," he says. "Even people who work here aren't aware we're here. I want them to come up and make it their place to go for a drink after work or Sunday brunch." He's considering a prix fixe meal that would include the observatory ticket and a dedicated elevator for diners so they don't have to enter with the masses.

Ortiz is aware of how special Windows on the World was to many people. He reads about it in the occasional comparisons posted on OpenTable. He's a New Yorker who got his start in the business working the front desk of the Vista hotel right between the North and South Towers in the 1980s. Back then, he brought his girlfriend, now wife, to Windows for her twenty-first birthday, and when they were seated in the back, he greased the palm of the maître d', who subsequently found them a window table.

Ortiz says he doesn't want to compete with the memory of Windows. He doesn't see a place at One Dine for a plaque or something similar honoring the restaurant. He thinks the National September 11 Memorial & Museum does that well enough.

It is probably a better tribute to the restaurant to look for its spirit of conviviality and spectacle, as well as its diverse tapestry of employees, in different New York City restaurants that carry on those traditions.

A good place to start is Porter House, where Michael Lomonaco and Michael Ammirati, according to *New York* magazine, put out the best steak in the city, with their "gold standard for the postmillennial, chef-driven, fat-cat New York steak house."

Another place is Danny Meyer's Manhatta, which opened in 2018 with stellar views of the city that elicited comparison to the panorama that Windows once offered. It is on the sixtieth floor of 28 Liberty Street, the building formerly known as One Chase Manhattan Plaza that David Rockefeller constructed, kicking off the downtown development juggernaut that helped launch the World Trade Center. But Meyer, the creator of Union Square Café, Gramercy Tavern, Eleven Madison Park, and Shake Shack, among others, is less interested in spectacle and more in what he calls "enduring restaurants with soul."

"Every high-altitude restaurant I have been to, whether it's at the ninety-fifth floor of the Hancock Building in Chicago, in the Eiffel Tower in Paris, or Windows on the World, there is an attempt to create a capital 'S,' capital 'O,' special occasion restaurant," he says. "Manhatta is different. We want the restaurant to be the same as if it would have been on the ground floor."

Still, Manhatta's heightened, downtown atmosphere is pretty exciting. And the views are dazzling.

Meyer is relieved that 28 Liberty is far from the top of the list of the tallest buildings in the city, making it a less likely target, betraying a wariness that the city hasn't quite expunged. Maybe it never will. He confides an "eerie" feeling when he thinks about One World Trade Center, which he hasn't entered since it opened.

Neither has Michael Lomonaco, who is working on another restaurant in the city's next improbable, mammoth renewal project, the Hudson Yards, more than eighteen million square feet of mixed-use development, with about two dozen restaurants and "food concepts" on the far West Side of Manhattan. Lomonaco's Hudson Yards Grill will be on the fourth floor. London-based hospitality company Rhubarb, under the guidance of culinary director Warren Geraghty, is overseeing, and this should be stated tentatively, a Windows on the World heir apparent; a 101st-floor restaurant, at 30 Hudson Yards, which promises One World Trade Center views with a swank, Manhatta-like atmosphere.

Lomonaco's alliances may have shifted to midtown, but the chef did leave something behind. When the spire was installed on One World Trade Center, bringing it to its one thousand seven hundred seventy-six foot height, Michael Lomonaco, with some other 9/11 survivors from the Twin Towers, were invited to visit. They went to the roof and breathed the same air where Joe Baum had once brought his drawings, his consultants, and his visions of creating something spectacular.

Lomonaco and the others were given indelible markers and asked if they wanted to inscribe something on the spire. The chef approached it, overcome by emotion, the city, small, whirring below. He wrote, *The WOW family.*

EPILOGUE: ANA'S STORY

Nothing could fully salve the pain of 9/11, but there is some solace in recognizing how the country pulled itself together, not in its anger but with compassion for the victims and for the city. This sympathy took its most material form in the Victims Compensation Fund, which was distributed in 2004. Special Master Ken Feinberg determined that more than seven billion dollars was appropriate for the five thousand five hundred sixty people who applied as injured or dependents of the deceased. The average payout for the latter was more than two million dollars. By supporting the families of the 9/11 victims in such an unprecedented fashion, Congress and, by extension, the American people showed an unparalleled degree of empathy.

Feinberg developed a formula of payment partly based on "economic loss": how much income a person would have made over his or her lifetime, an assessment that is tied to one's interpretation of some fundamental American principles. For instance, if one is to believe that pot washers and grill cooks are fated to never rise above their near-minimum wages, what does that say about their right to the pursuit of happiness?

David Emil and Michael Lomonaco testified to Feinberg that their employees indeed had the potential to rise. And they provided ample evidence. For one, Luis Alfonso Chimbo, the son of a taxi driver and himself an undocumented immigrant from Ecuador, had moved from being a stock boy to a manager in the receiving department.

"The structure of the restaurant reflected the American Dream, which I don't use as a cliché but as an actual possibility," says lawyer Debra Steinberg, who represented Chimbo's widow, Ana Soria, and chaired a consortium of New York law firms that represented, pro bono, the families of thirty-seven Windows workers. "When you drill down into the stories of the immigrants who worked at Windows on the

World, most of them said that it was the dream job. They walked with pride in their step. It was an astonishing place."

Feinberg says that the Windows victims had a "tremendous impact" on his thinking about the distribution of the fund, not just because some of them were among the lowest-paid workers killed but because about a dozen of them, such as Chimbo, were undocumented. He says he used his "discretion to bring up the lower end worker and reduce the stockbrokers and hedge fund managers." And, based on his reading of the congressional statute, it was clear to Feinberg that the fund was meant for all victims of the attacks, without question of nationality or citizenship.

"Only in America would you have such a generous compensation program," Feinberg says, pointing out that people from sixty-five foreign countries were ultimately compensated.

Soria was also in the United States illegally. During the first days after 9/11, she was reluctant to ask for support for herself and her twelve-year-old son. "I didn't want to take advantage," she says. "And I was scared. I was thinking that maybe I did not deserve it because this was not my country."

But her son's need for asthma medication propelled her into Manhattan from their home in Queens. Her husband had just returned to work that terrible Tuesday because he had taken time off to care for her after she suffered a miscarriage in late August. It was all a terrifying, confusing blur for Soria, but the help she received, she says, "was so beautiful."

In June 2018, Soria took the train from Queens to the north reflecting pool, which stands inside the footprint of the long-gone North Tower. Soria likes to go on September 11, but she felt like going for her husband's birthday. She brought a flower and a birthday card, on which she wrote, *To the love of my life, happy birthday to you. Surprise, you didn't know I was coming.*

She arrived around lunchtime and placed the card and flower on his name cut in bronze. And then she stepped back a little and stood amid the flow of tourists. Chimbo, who is among the more than one thousand victims whose remains were never found, had once told her that if he died first, he wanted her to scatter his ashes in the ocean. Soria believes his wish came true when the building imploded and her husband disappeared into the air above the Atlantic.

She watched people open the card and read it. Some were moved to the point of tears. Some put their hands on their hearts. They didn't need to talk. Soria quietly watched for hours. *You see, Al,* Soria thought, *all these people came to your birthday.*

Soria had known Luis since she was a child. Their families made pork fried rice and sold it together on the street during holidays. He had gone to live in New York for a couple of years before coming back to Ecuador to bring her to America. After he got the job at Windows, she planned to go to school so that they could open their own restaurant.

In 2007, she took a baking class, financed by Windows of Hope, at the Institute of Culinary Education, partly to follow through with her and Luis's dream and partly to show her son that they could get help if they needed it and to show him "that there is life after what happened."

In 2016, Soria finally received her green card. She now makes dulce de leche, cheesecake, and other desserts for her friends and family, including her son, who became a photographer and graphic designer. Despite what she taught her son, Soria remains terribly conflicted about the money she received, which she calls "blood money." She is tormented by how the achievement of her and husband's hopes for a better life came at the cost of his own.

As evening approached at the World Trade Center memorial, Soria was looking for a moment when she could be alone with her husband, so she could sing him "Happy Birthday," but people just kept coming, until four American women, college-age, tall out-of-towners with long, blond hair, read the card and began to sing, "Happy Birthday."

Soria walked up to them and said, "Thank you so much. Thank you." They asked her how she was related to the memorial, and she told them, "He was my husband. I was going to sing to him."

The young women asked Soria if they could sing with her, and she liked the idea. They sang and cried together. "I felt peace in my heart," she says.

Nearly a generation had grown up since 9/11. And Soria had never even stepped onto the 107th floor. But Windows on the World was still bringing people together to share a New York moment that they would never forget.

NOTES

I was not in the city on 9/11. I was in Toronto, reporting on the international film festival that takes place there every September. I was watching the movie *Monsoon Wedding* when the planes hit the Twin Towers. I came out of the dark theater to a different world, dumbfounded by the images of horror playing on a television screen that was mounted above a popcorn machine.

I was gutted, horrified by the tragedy and despondent with the feeling that I had left my post, not being there when my city—and, especially, my wife, Sandee, who was at our home in Brooklyn—needed me most. It's a void that I will always carry.

Early on, I thought about Windows on the World because it was the place in the World Trade Center that I knew best. Not that I knew it well. But it was a part of my internal cityscape. I was born and raised in New York City, and I went to Windows a few times over the years as a boy brought there by my parents for special occasions in the 1970s and, later, when I was in my twenties, when I joined friends to drink and dance on top of the world.

You didn't have to be a regular at Windows to feel its presence. First, literally, it was a fixture looming from on high at the end of the island. But it was also a part of so many intersecting lives. It seemed like everyone went there. It was a mainstay for graduations, birthdays, anniversaries, and always a consideration when friends or relatives came in from out of town. Windows on the World was always there for us. And then it wasn't.

I am a New Yorker fixated on the past. And when the ninth 9/11 anniversary approached, I was thinking about how Windows—its full, remarkable story—had never been properly eulogized. So I wrote an oral history for my editors James Heidenry and Richard Martin at *Manhattan* magazine, in which I wove together the quotes of a dozen sources, including Michael Lomonaco, Michael Whiteman, Kevin Zraly, and Mayors Ed Koch and David Dinkins.

It was a meaningful story for me, but I knew that I was just scratching the surface. And then I moved on to other work, including a few years writing for Martin after he moved to *Food Republic,* an experience that solidified my interest in writing about food as culture.

Five years after the *Manhattan* magazine story was published, my friend Glen Freyer, a television producer who was then working for Bobby Flay's production company, Rock Shrimp Productions, and I began talking about turning my story and the history of Windows into a documentary. Glen shot some footage but the project didn't get off the ground (yet!), and although I thought that it could still make a good documentary, I realized it was also a great subject for a book.

My agent, Marly Rusoff, agreed, and away I went. I wrote and reported *Spectacular* over two and a half years, doing most of the work between the summer of 2017 and the summer of 2018.

Every week, it felt as if I was receiving gifts. They usually came in the form of a source's generosity, and also in the discovery of a menu or an unplanned connection that helped convince me that I was on the right path. I had to practically go to the South Pole to find Claudette Fournier, but when I found her, she graciously told the story of her "fiasco" for the public for the first time. I marveled at her path and other turns of fate, such as Marc Murphy and Michael Lomonaco's restaurants ending up stacked on top of each other at the Time Warner Center.

And so, as challenging as it was to write this book, it was deeply gratifying from start to finish. Breaking bread with Lomonaco at his Porter House Bar and Grill, eating Rozanne Gold's delicious Venetian Wine Cake in her and Whiteman's Brooklyn town house and drinking homemade wine and eating shrimp-stuffed tofu with former Windows waiters at the Pearl restaurant in Elmhurst, Queens, were cherished opportunities to experience the sort of hospitality and conviviality that were the embodiment of Joe Baum and the restaurants he created.

I spent two 9/11s with former Windows staff at the Colors restaurant in the Lower East Side, thanks to Luis Feglia and Fekkak Mamdouh.

It was important for me to see that legacy continue. And attending two of Kevin Zraly's uproarious wine classes was a delight; if you ever get a chance, I recommend going, first for the wine, and then to be entertained by a master showman.

Those experiences sustained me. They also influenced me. There's a powerful effect when you're in a room with someone. You see their side of things. So, yes, perhaps to the consternation of some, I left a few knives in the drawer. Throughout, I aspired to give people the benefit of the doubt without compromising the truth.

I primarily reported this book by interviewing more than one hundred twenty-five different subjects who worked, managed, cooked, designed, and ate at Windows on the World.

Zraly was an indispensable resource not just for the hours of conversation we had over more than a half-dozen interviews but also because he provided me with his own personal archives. The most precious of his many boxes of papers and materials were the ones that contained responses he'd received for the book he planned to write about Windows but couldn't because the material was too emotionally painful. In 2002, Zraly received almost two hundred memorials from people close to the restaurant. He was so generous to pass these testimonials to me. I used them as background and, where I use them in the book, I endeavored to corroborate the relevant information.

The most essential archive I had at my disposal was the Joe Baum Papers collection at the Brooke Russell Astor Reading Room for Rare Books and Manuscripts in the New York Public Library: one hundred fifty-eight boxes of materials that include menus, correspondences, notes, reports, personal reflections, speeches and photographs. This is where I came upon James Beard's delicious five thousand-plus-word letter to Baum, heralding his vision of the food to be served on the 107th floor. It was here that I was also able to comb through internal memos, financial reports and contractual agreements for Windows, Inhilco, and the Port Authority.

This history wouldn't be possible without the previously published material of other journalists and authors. First, a shout-out to James Glanz and Eric Lipton, for their exhaustive and essential *City in the Sky: The Rise and Fall of the World Trade Center* (Times Books). Other definitive, go-to books I've relied heavily upon have been *102 Minutes: The Untold Story of the Fight to Survive inside the Twin Towers* (Times Books) by Jim Dwyer and Kevin Flynn; *Appetite City: A Culinary History of New York* (North Point Press) by William Grimes; *Ten Restaurants That Changed America* (Liveright) by Paul Freedman; *Divided We Stand: A Biography of the World Trade Center* (Basic Books) by Eric Darton; and *Ladies and Gentlemen, The Bronx is Burning* (Farrar, Straus and Giroux) by Jonathan Mahler.

Other helpful books include *The Apprentice: My Life in the Kitchen* (Jacques Pépin; Rux Martin/Houghton Mifflin Harcourt), *The Colossus of New York* (Colson Whitehead; Anchor), *The Craft of the Cocktail* (Dale DeGroff; Clarkson Potter), *Ed Koch and the Rebuilding of New York City* (Jonathan Soffer; Columbia University Press), *Garlic and Sapphires: The Secret Life of a Critic in Disguise* (Ruth Reichl; Penguin Press), *George, Be Careful* (George Lois; Saturday Review Press), *The Last Days of Haute Cuisine* (Patric Kuh; Penguin), *Notes on a Banana* (David Leite; Dey Street), *Our Precarious Habitat* (Melvin A. Benarde; W. W. Norton & Company), *A Proper Drink* (Robert Simonson; Ten Speed Press), *Recovering 9/11 in New York* (Robert Fanuzzi, Michael Wolfe; Cambridge Scholars), *Savoring Gotham: A Food Lover's Companion to New York City* (Andrew F. Smith; Oxford University Press), *Season with Authority: Confident Home Cooking* (Marc Murphy, Olga Massov; Houghton Mifflin Harcourt), *Setting the Table* (Danny Meyer; Harper Perennial), *What Is Life Worth?: The Unprecedented Effort to Compensate the Victims of 9/11* (Kenneth R. Feinberg; Public Affairs), *Windows on the World: Complete Wine Course* (Kevin Zraly; Sterling), *Windows on the World Wine and Food Book* (Kevin Zraly, Hermann Reiner; Sterling Publishing).

In many ways, the writers I owe most to are Gael Greene and Mimi Sheraton, whose brilliant food writing sliced new trails for the rest of us. Sheraton's *Eating My Words* is an inspiration and Greene's stories about Joe Baum and Windows on the World for *New York* magazine have been as useful as they are entertaining. Greene's most helpful articles were:

• "Restaurant Associates: Twilight of the Gods," *New York* magazine, November 2, 1970.
• "The Most Spectacular Restaurant in the World," *New York* magazine, May 31, 1976.
• "Over the Rainbow," *New York* magazine, February 8, 1988.

And the *New York Times'* food reporters and critics provide the most dependable depository of information about the city's food culture; the paper's searchable online archives may be the most potent research tool freelance journalists have. The pre-9/11 *New York Times* stories I relied on most were:

• "Its Ambiance Will Go from Snack to Posh," Fred Ferretti. *New York Times*, October 28, 1970.
• "Stylish Menu Is Full of Promise That Isn't Yet Full Realized," Mimi Sheraton, *New York Times*, June 24, 1976.
• "Showman for Food," Terry Robards, *New York Times*, December 19, 1976.
• "Joe Baum's Food Machine," Raymond A. Sokolov, *New York Times*, March 6, 1977.
• "Love Theme Restaurants? Here's the Man to Thank," Florence Fabricant, *New York Times*, September 13, 1995.
• "New Windows on a New World," Florence Fabricant and Paul Goldberger, *New York Times*, June 19, 1996.

These articles from other outlets were also particularly helpful:

• "Directed to the Product," Geoffrey Hellman, *The New Yorker*, October 17, 1964.
• "Changemaker: The World Trade Center," Steve Weiss. *Institutions*, October 15, 1976.
• "Joe's in His Heaven—His Window's on the World," Craig Claiborne, *Holiday*, Summer 1977.
• "Inhilco: High Polish on the Big Apple," Peter Wulff, *Restaurant Business*, September 15, 1978.

- "Joe Baum: First Person Singular," Stephen Michaelides, *Restaurant Hospitality*, May 1979.
- "Comfort Food," Meryl Gordon, *New York* magazine, June 3, 2002.
- "The Legacy of Joe Baum," Nancy Matsumoto, *Edible Manhattan*, July 14, 2010.
- "Windows on the World—New York's Sky-High Restaurant," Greg Morabito, Eater.com, September 11, 2013.

The starred World Trade Center restaurant reviews by the *New York Times* are:
- Windows—★; Hors D'Oeuvrerie—★★, Mimi Sheraton, January 28, 1977.
- Market Dining Rooms & Bar—★★★, Mimi Sheraton, July 15, 1977.
- Windows—★; Cellar in the Sky—★★, Bryan Miller, July 4, 1986.
- Windows—"satisfactory," Bryan Miller, June 1, 1990.
- Windows—★, Ruth Reichl, November 8, 1996.
- Cellar in the Sky—★★, Ruth Reichl, May 2, 1997.
- Windows—★★, Ruth Reichl, December 31, 1997.
- Wild Blue—★, William Grimes, June 9, 1999.

Additional newspapers and periodicals that I used as sources include *Architectural Record*, *The Atlantic*, *August* magazine, *Billboard*, *Christian Science Monitor*, *Crain's New York*, *Dwell*, *The Economist*, *Fortune*, *Gastronomica: The Journal of Critical Food Studies*, *GrubStreet*, the *Guardian*, *Interior Design Magazine*, *Life* magazine, *The Nation*, *National Geographic*, *The New York Daily News*, *The New York Post*, *The New Yorker*, *Rolling Stone*, *Salon*, *Signature* magazine, *Slate*, *Smithsonian* magazine, *Sports Illustrated*, *Staten Island Advance*, *TechCrunch*, *Texas Monthly*, *Time* magazine, *USA Today*, *Vanity Fair*, the *Village Voice*, the *Wall Street Journal*, the *Washington Post*, *Wired*.

Broadcast outlets, such as CNN, PBS, WNYC, BBC, and NPR provided additional information.

The following documentaries were also helpful: *9/10: The Final Hours*, *Blackout: American Experience*, *In Memoriam: New York City*,

9/11/01, James Beard: America's First Foodie, Man on Wire, and *NY77: The Coolest Year in Hell.*

The 9/11 Commission Report was another significant resource, as were numerous reports published by federal, New York State and New York City agencies. I also relied on records kept by the National September 11 Memorial & Museum.

All original quotes used in the book come from at least one first-hand source. In the cases where a conversation occurred and a quoted participant is deceased or unreachable, I tried to corroborate the veracity with additional sources.

Joe Baum's pre-Windows years are largely based on my interviews with his three children, Hilary, Charles, and Edward, as well as Curt Strand, Ron Holland, George Lois, and others, and clips, most notably Geoffrey Hellman's "Directed to the Product," in *The New Yorker*, and Baum's many interviews that are archived in the Joe Baum Papers collection at the NYPL.

New York City's economic, demographic and crime statistics come primarily from the *New York Times*. I also used *New York* magazine, *Forbes*, the *Daily News*, the *New York Post*, and reports issued by city and state agencies.

What follows are notes for material that I thought might be of particular interest:

Chapter 1

There wasn't a source in the room with Joe Baum and Alan Lewis when Lewis spoke with Dennis Sweeney on the phone about the dead trout. The setting has been deduced through interviews with Sweeney and Michael Whiteman.

Chapter 6

The changing and ultimate width of the windows at Windows on the World has been gleaned from sometimes conflicting information found in the *New York Times*, *Architectural Record*, *Interior Design* magazine, *City in the Sky*, and from the National September

11 Memorial & Museum and interviews with Dennis Sweeney and Michael Whiteman.

The naming of Windows on the World comes from Gael Greene's "The Most Spectacular Restaurant in the World" in *New York* magazine and from interviews with Curt Strand, Sweeney and Whiteman.

Chapter 8
That the gas leak explosion at 305 East Forty-Fifth Street on April 22, 1974, prompted the Port Authority to nix gas at Windows is based on interviews with Dennis Sweeney. Additional interviews with the PA's Charlie Maikish and Bob DiChiara and other sources who worked on constructing Windows did not disprove this notion.

Chapter 9
Ron Holland told me about Joe Baum watching Philippe Petit's stunt. Baum's daughter, Hilary, didn't recall her father being there but said it was possible.

Chapter 11
The layout and design of Windows comes from documents in the Joe Baum archive at the NYPL, *Architectural Record, Interior Design Magazine*, interviews with Baum's team and from notes written by Warren Platner to Kevin Zraly.

Chapter 12
The background on putting together the article "The Most Spectacular Restaurant in the World" comes from my interviews with Gael Greene, Milton Glaser, and Michael Whiteman.

Chapter 14
My portrait of Alan Lewis comes from more than a dozen interviews with those who worked with and for him, including John Bernieri, John Desanto, Al Ferraro, Claudette Fournier, Jules Roinnel, Dennis

Sweeney, Walter Szumski, Michael Whiteman, and Kevin Zraly. Lewis's son, Seth, and his partner, Verna Hobson, were also invaluable resources.

Chapter 15

Celebrity sightings and interactions at the restaurant are according to Windows staff. Waiter John Bernieri has a doozy of a story about chasing John Lennon into an elevator, which didn't make it into the book. Ask me (or him) about it sometime.

Chapter 17

I primarily used the *New York Times*, the *Daily News*, and the PBS documentary *Blackout: American Experience*, to write about the 1977 blackout. I interviewed Bob DiChiara, John Downey, Michael Skurnik, Dennis Sweeney, and Kevin Zraly, among others, to describe the experience at Windows.

Chapter 18

As noted in the text, the primary source for Claudette Fournier's "fiasco" was Fournier herself. I was able to corroborate some information with clips from the *New York Times*, the *Daily News*, the *New York Post*, and the *Staten Island Advance*. A couple sources from Windows were able to confirm a few of the details. I also reviewed Joe "Pepe" Marino's United States criminal docket, and I interviewed FBI agents Frank Spero and Matthew Tricorico and former prosecutor Michael Guadagno in Guadagno's New Jersey home.

Chapter 19

Much of the information about the Club came from Windows promotional material and interviews with Club director Jules Roinnel. Karl Feile provided me with photos and detailed information about the Little Spa.

Chapter 20

I used Frank DiGiacomo's "Live, From Tribeca!" article in the November 2005 issue of *Vanity Fair* for many of the juicy bits about Odeon.

Chapter 21

My understanding of the relationship between Ladbrokes and Inhilco has been heavily informed by the people who worked at the restaurant, Inhilco, or for the Port Authority. I also used clips from the *New York Times*, the *Guardian*, and other outlets. I sought balance by querying Tony Potter, who was Ladbrokes' vice president of Hilton International's North America division, but whose quotes are his personal opinions.

Regarding Alan Lewis's death, I spoke with Sue Klein, Carrie Robbins and Andrew Wilkinson, who were present at the meeting.

Chapter 22

I was told about the graffiti between the 106th and 107th floors by two sources and Hermann Reiner corroborated the story in general terms.

Chapter 23

The *New York Times* and other local papers provided most of the background for the history of the 1993 bombing, as did the National September 11 Memorial & Museum and reports by the Port Authority and the FBI. The Department of Homeland Security/United States Fire Administration's *The World Trade Center Bombing: Report and Analysis* was also very useful. Firsthand accounts were provided by Karl Feile, Albert Lee, Andrea Robinson, Phil Romeo, Allan Sperling, and Johannes Tromp.

Chapter 24

My understanding of the Chinese character for "crisis" comes from the writing of Workplace Psychology's Dr. Steve Nguyen.

Charlie Maikish provided me with the story about his interaction with Cyril Stein.

The transition and early preopening details about Windows II come primarily from clips, including those in the *New York Times, New*

York magazine's "Windows '96," by Corby Kummer, July 15, 1996, and interviews with Rozanne Gold, Pam Loeffelman, Charlie Maikish, Jules Roinnel, Dennis Sweeney, Michael Whiteman, and Kevin Zraly.

Chapter 25

Joe Baum is not alive to provide his perspective on his dealings with Michael Whiteman and David Emil. There are some who have helped me by trying to speak for him, but they can complete only so much of the picture. Readers should keep this in mind, especially in this and the next chapter. Additionally, I would have benefited from talking with Arthur Emil, who is also deceased.

The writing of Irena Chalmers was a great help to me. In particular, her "Joe Baum: An Exaltation of Larks," which appeared in *Gastronomica: The Journal of Critical Food Studies* (Winter 2003) and her "Final Windows on the World Meeting," which she posted on her website, and which includes the To-do list that she kindly permitted me to use here.

Chapter 26

It's worth noting that women such as Rozanne Gold were rare forces in the top restaurant kitchens in the late 1990s and that they and their contributions were subject to prejudices that are hopefully untenable today.

Michael Shnayerson's description of the city's "new golden age" comes from his article "The Champagne City" in *Vanity Fair*'s December 1997 issue.

David Emil is my source for the details of his argument with Joe Baum about replacing Georges Masraff. My characterization of the decision and transition to Michael Lomonaco in this and the next chapter is largely based on conversations with Emil, Lomonaco, Masraff, Jules Roinnel, and Kevin Zraly, among others.

Chapter 27

The details of the falling out between Marc Murphy and Michael Lomonaco come largely from Murphy; with the general veracity confirmed by several others who worked in the kitchen or in management, including Lomonaco. The article that enraged Murphy was in New Jersey's *Asbury Park Press* on October 8, 1997. It refers to "next month, the cuisine of Michael Lomonaco . . . will be featured at Cellar in the Sky."

Chapter 28

Kurt Andersen on the 1990s comes from "The Best Decade Ever? The 1990's, Obviously." The *New York Times*, February 6, 2015.

The story about the Barnum and Bailey Circus disagreement with B.E. Windows was told to me by several sources; there was a *New York Times* story and a legal filing that helped substantiate the case, but I rely on legend for the details of the resolution agreement.

That Tony Cabot, now deceased, visited Joe Baum the day before he passed away comes from a note that Cabot wrote to Kevin Zraly in 2002.

Chapter 29

I was told about Rudy Giuliani dining with Judith Nathan at Windows by waiters who said they served them; other waiters corroborated the story.

The 2000 gross numbers come from former Night Sky Holdings CFO Sue Klein; that Windows was the highest-grossing restaurant comes from *Restaurants & Institutions* magazine.

Chapter 30

I transcribed the words from Father Mychal Judge's last homily from the National Geographic documentary *9/10: The Final Hours*. Anyone interested in Father Judge should read "The Firemen's Friar," by Jennifer Senior, in *New York* magazine, November 12, 2001.

The September 10th stories come from interviews with Windows staff who were present, including George Delgado, Michael Lomonaco, Jules Roinnel, Melissa Trumbull, Bernardo and Paulo Villela, Glenn Vog,t and others. The documentary *9/10: The Final Hours* and interviews with Malia Boyd, Dale DeGroff and Inez Holderness also helped me describe some of the events of that day.

The John O'Neill material comes primarily from "O'Neill Versus Osama," by Robert Kolker, in *New York* magazine, December 17, 2001 and "The Counter-Terrorist," by Lawrence Wright, in *The New Yorker*, January 14, 2002.

Chapters 31 and 32

Among others, the following interviewees helped me reconstruct details of 9/11: Michael Ammirati, Lucio Caputo, Barry D'Onofrio, Mark Goldberg, Mario Grillo, Greg Hein, Lori Kane, Sue Klein, Michael Lomonaco, Mike Nestor, Thomas Schweitzer, Sekou Siby, Ana Soria, Richard Tierney, and Glenn Vogt.

My understanding of what happened in the Twin Towers on 9/11 is grounded in the extensive reporting of Jim Dwyer and Kevin Flynn, whose *New York Times* articles lay the foundation for their book, *102 Minutes: The Untold Story of the Fight to Survive inside the Twin Towers*. I couldn't have written this chapter without it. Christine Olender's phone call transcript was reprinted by the *New York Times*.

The *9/11 Commission Report* was another essential resource for 9/11 reporting, as was the National September 11 Memorial & Museum .

I relied on other outlets, including NPR and CNN: the *Wall Street Journal*'s "How Five Lives Became One Horror When Terror Struck the Twin Towers," printed on October 11, 2001, and Diana Scholl's "A Second Chance at . . . Life," in *Westchester* magazine, from December 8, 2015.

The *New York Times*' "Portraits of Grief" series, which documented the lives of the 9/11 victims, was another essential source.

Tom Junod's "The Falling Man," in *Esquire*'s September 2003 issue, is the definitive source on the subject.

Donald Trump's reaction on 9/11 was recalled in "What Trump and Clinton Did on 9/11," in *Politico*, September 10, 2016.

The description and quotes from Mayor Rudy Giuliani on that day come primarily from the HBO documentary *In Memoriam: New York City, 9/11/01*.

ACKNOWLEDGMENTS

I am most indebted to my hundred and twenty-five-plus sources who generously shared their stories and memories of Windows on the World and Joe Baum. First, thanks to Baum's children, Charles, Hilary, and Edward who live with the legacy of a larger-than-life father. Joe Baum was a vital, creative force in how people ate in New York City in the twentieth century. I hope this book goes some way toward solidifying his proper place in the pantheon of cultural and food history. Not that that is assured. When I spoke with Mimi Sheraton about why no one had written a biography of Baum, she said, "Nobody knows who he is and nobody cares. You can't sell that kind of book to the public now. Anyone who is interested in knowing should get a free copy." I am glad Sheraton hasn't lost her affinity for salt. I just hope, this one time, she is wrong.

I owe much gratitude to Irena Chalmers, David Emil, Luis Feglia, Rozanne Gold, Michael Lomonaco, Fekkak Mamdouh, Hermann Reiner, Jules Roinnel, Michael Whiteman, and Kevin Zraly for giving me so much of themselves. Lomonaco and Zraly, two gentlemen cut from a finer cloth, were particularly generous. And I thank Claudette Fournier, a book in herself, for sharing her incredible story with me.

Ana Soria's and Lori Kane's willingness to talk with me about their experiences was particularly meaningful. I hope I've done them and the memories of their husbands justice.

There were many acts of support that allowed me to put the pieces together. I call out Jennifer Baum, Sue Klein, and Debra Steinberg for their help. The National September 11 Memorial & Museum's Ian Kerrigan and the staff of the New York Public Library's Brooke Russell Astor Reading Room were also wonderful accomplices in my research.

Thanks to Richard Martin, James Heidenry, and Glen Freyer for getting me to the starting gate; to Matt Zoller Seitz and Katherine Pence for their aid along the way; and to Connie Ress, Rachel Clarke, and Manny Howard for keeping me afloat.

My friends Tom French, Scott Fredrick, and David Nanasi provided more than just legal, libation, and tech support, respectively; they kept me aloft with their friendship. And going way beyond the call of a poker buddy, Neil Pergament, the most literate swing dancer ever to grace the 107th floor, was also the best first reader that a writer could dream of. Thanks, Neil E. Baby.

I have dedicated this book to my parents, but there are two other people I'd like to acknowledge who were there with me from the beginning. My brother, Richard, who may have left the city but whose tags remain. And Alex Grannis, a living embodiment of literary New York, who gave me my first subscription to *The New York Review of Books*.

My family, of course, bore the greatest brunt of the toil and time I spent on the book. They were also the ones who truly kept me going. Thank you, Sandee, for your constant support and for showing me New York through your eyes. And Natalie and Maxine, for letting me hold your hands when we crossed the city's streets.

And then there are those who worked on the book itself. A toast to designer Evan Gaffney, who came up with the spectacular cover. And I would have been lost without my agent, Marly Rusoff, my editor, Jamison Stoltz, and assists from Abrams editorial savant Alicia Tan. Marly always had my back. And Jamison was the one who believed in me and this story, which will always mean so much to me. His elegant and savvy direction helped me turn this book from being a heap in the kitchen to what you now see on your plate.

Salud!
Tom

INDEX

Abdel-Rahman, Omar, 208
Abzug, Bella, 143
Adams, Steve, 279, 281
Adler, Pearl "Polly," 19
advertising
    Cellar in the Sky, 169, 249
    Lois and, 37–38, 40–41, 46, 56
    New York City, 90, 106–7, 114, 141–42
    WTC, 37, 40–41, 56
Afrika Bambaataa, 144
Ahmed, Awal, 117, 297–98
Ahmed, Shabbir, 202, 297
AIDS epidemic, 198
Aigner, Toni
    at Inhilco, 117, 165–66, 193–94, 196
    lack of authority of, 194
Airline Deregulation Act of 1978, 184
Air Transportation Safety and System
        Stabilization Act, 306
Alan's Place, 121
Aldrich, Winthrop W., 48–50
Algonquin Round Table, 19
Ali, Muhammad, 140
Allegis, 185
Allman, Gregg, 130
Alvear, Telmo, 284
Amatuccio, Joe, 260, 294
American Airlines, 184, 298–300
An American Place, 176–77, 217
American Restaurant, 99, 186, 250
American Revolution Bicentennial, 111–14,
        140
Americans with Disabilities Act, 220
Amico, Joe, 244, 260–61, 264, 303
Ammirati, Michael, 254, 286, 297, 305, 314
Ancorp National Services, 73
Andersen, Kurt, 12–14, 256
ANSUL system, 180, 238
Anticipation Story, 21
Armed Forces of Puerto Rican National
        Liberation, 82
Arons, Andy, 178, 182
art scene, 172–73
asbestos abatement, 215, 230, 290

ashtrays, 44, 92, 131–32
Assante, Armand, 261
Astbury, Paul, 117, 124, 142, 193
Aurora, 186–91, 221, 224, 228
austerity measures, 89, 142
Aykroyd, Dan, 173

Balducci's, 146
Ball, Lucille, 129
banquet catering, 118, 161, 164, 202
    burner area, 179
    downturn in, 193
    renovation, 219–20, 228, 231, 239–40
    revenue, 277
    on September 11, 286
Basquiat, Jean-Michel, 173
Bastille Day, 250
Battery Park City Authority, 224
Baum, Anna, 19
Baum, Charles
    childhood of, 20, 41–42, 70
    mugging of, 77–78
    in restaurant business, 225–27
    on September 11, 298
Baum, Edward, 41, 70, 226
Baum, Hilary, 41, 226
Baum, Joe
    Anticipation Story of, 21
    Aurora and, 186–91, 221, 224, 228
    Beard and, 34, 65–68, 80, 83–85, 92,
        96, 108, 250
    B. E. Rock Corporation and, 199, 265
    during blackout, 150
    death of, 266–67
    eating elevated by, 37–46
    Emil, D., fighting with, 247, 265–66
    Forum of the Twelve Caesars and,
        32–33, 35, 39, 44, 46, 120
    Four Seasons and, 33–35, 39–41, 44,
        46, 58, 67, 92, 106, 111,
        120, 136, 250, 267
    health of, 45, 227, 265–66
    Inhilco and, 75, 79, 132–33, 164–65
    of Joseph Baum Associates, Inc., 57

336

Joseph Baum & Michael Whiteman
    Company of, 223
lawsuit against, 223, 266
Lewis, A., and, 15–16, 33, 39, 94–96,
    105, 116, 118–22, 132,
    186, 191–92
Lomonaco and, 250–51, 254–55
marriage of, 22, 30, 40–42, 45, 70,
    224, 266
modus operandi of, 57, 97
Murphy and, 245
New Yorker profile of, 43–44
Pépin and, 86–88
presence of, 15–16, 38, 129, 227
at RA, 15, 30–46, 57, 59, 65, 67, 94,
    104, 120, 165
Rainbow Room and, 22, 190–93,
    217–18, 224, 226–27,
    265, 267
renovations by, 217–36, 240, 242–43,
    246–47, 265
in Saratoga Springs, 18–21
September 11 and, 298, 312
stepping down by, 164–66, 182
Strand and, 21–23, 30, 74–75, 132,
    164, 185
Sweeney and, 15–17, 58, 64–65,
    69–70, 72–74, 92, 104, 266
Tozzoli and, 11–12, 47–48, 59–61, 64,
    71, 73, 79, 86, 92
Truite au bleu and, 17–18, 92, 96–97
Whiteman and, 57–60, 65, 69–70,
    72–73, 83, 86, 96, 104,
    132–33, 153, 164, 190,
    218, 223–25, 230–31,
    233–34, 240, 266
Windows on the World created by,
    12–13, 15–23, 57–75,
    78–88, 96–97, 101, 103–6,
    108–11, 114, 116, 118–22,
    131–34, 137–41, 150–53,
    164–66, 182, 194, 213,
    279, 315
Windows on the World renovated
    by, 217–36, 240, 242–43,
    246–47, 250, 253–55,
    262–63, 265–67
Baum, Louis, 19–20
Baum, Ruth Courtman
    health of, 266

marriage of, 22, 30, 40–42, 45, 70,
    224, 266
Baum Squad, 65, 190
Bautista, Ivhan Luis Carpio, 296
Beacon restaurant, 303–5
Beame, Abe
    failure of, 143
    as mayor, 82–83, 90–91, 115, 141,
        143, 151
Beard, James
    Baum, J., and, 34, 65–68, 80, 83–85,
        92, 96, 108, 250
    The Cooks' Catalogue, 68
    Forgione and, 177
    Four Seasons and, 34, 67
    Hors d'Oeuvre and Canapés, 67
    rack of lamb, 136, 176, 190
    on *Truite au bleu*, 92
Beebe, Lucius, 24–25
Beef East, 156–57
Belushi, John, 172–73
Benihana, 137
Berkowitz, David, 152
Le Bernardin, 182
Bernieri, John, 93, 116–17, 271
Berns, Jerry, 102
B. E. Rock Corporation, 199, 265
Bicentennial, American Revolution,
    111–14, 140
"Big Apple" campaign, 141
the Big Kitchen
    dance floor, 140
    design, 187
    food stations, 63, 138
    RA and, 197
    review, 152
Black Monday, 185–86
blackout of 1977, 146–52
Blanchard, Ron, 270, 283, 303
Blattner, Willy, 196
Bloody Bull, 189
Bloomberg, Michael, 10, 278, 307, 310
blue trout (*Truite au bleu*), 17–18, 92, 96–97
Bobin restaurant, 119
Bocuse, Paul, 176
Bogdanow, Larry, 289
bombing. *See* 1993 bombing, of WTC
Boone, Mary, 172
Bordeaux wines, 134
Boubée, Henri, 175–76, 178, 182

Bouley, David, 177, 217, 221
Bouley restaurant, 217
Brando, Marlon, 278
Brasserie, 36, 95
Bratton, William, 241
Brecher, John, 274
Brenner, David, 130
Breslin, Jimmy, 107, 145
Bridges, Jeff, 140
Bright Lights, Big City (McInerney), 173
Briley, Jonathan, 295
Brody, Jerome, 30, 32–33, 36
"broken windows" approach, to crime, 241
Bronfman, Samuel, 33
Bronx, 28, 77, 119, 142, 144
Bronx Builders, 288–89, 296
Brooklyn, 151, 210
Buchwald, Art, 117
Burke, David, 177
burner areas, 178–79
Bushwick, 151

Cabot, Tony, 161, 266
cafeteria, employee, 259–60
Cage, John, 34
Callaway, James, 56
Campanella, "Beansie," 162
Cantor Fitzgerald, 240, 263–64
captains, 94, 103, 105, 129, 168
Caputo, Fred, 154
Caputo, Lucio, 259, 288, 290
Carey, Hugh, 82–83, 114, 143
Carroll, Joseph, 159
Carter, Jimmy, 114–15
Cascade Linen and Uniform Service, 38–39
C. A. Shea conference, 202
Castellano, Paul, 162
Castelli, Leo, 172
Cato, Gavin, 210
the Cattleman, 120
celebrity guests, 129–30
Cellar in the Sky
    advertising, 169, 249
    burner area, 179
    Club de Huit at, 168
    income, 246
    menu, 169, 177, 243
    Murphy at, 231–32, 234, 243–45,
        252–53
    in New York Times, 169, 249

renovation, 220–21, 231–32, 234, 240,
    242–45, 272
reviews, 182, 245–46
Wild Blue replacing, 272
wine and, 62, 100, 134, 147, 168–71
Central Services
    Bicentennial celebrations and, 113
    during blackout, 150
    circumvention of, 178
    1993 bombing destroying, 209, 216,
        252
    role of, 63–64, 86–88, 178–79
    supply chain of ingredients from, 139
    Sweeney at, 15–17, 58, 64–65, 69–70,
        72–74, 92, 96–97, 104,
        113, 148–51, 157
Chalmers, Irena, 227, 229
Chanterelle, 173
charcoal grill, 80, 238
Charley O's, 67, 95, 188
Charlie Brown's Ale & Chop House, 36,
    47, 67
Chase National Bank, 48, 50–51, 225
Chelsea Piers, 241
Chen, Peter, 204
Cher, 130
Chimbo, Luis Alfonso, 8, 317–19
A Chorus Line, 110
Christ Cella, 137
cigars, 241
Cini, John, 58, 69, 72–73, 79
Le Cirque, 178, 232, 249
City Harvest, 211
City Lights Bar, 62, 92, 94
City University of New York, 89
Claiborne, Craig, 30, 34, 95
Clark, Patrick, 172, 248–49
Cleary Gottlieb conference, 202, 204
Clinton, Hillary, 306
the Club
    membership decline at, 200
    PA and, 166–67
    profitability of, 166–67
    renovation, 240
    surcharge, 201
    Windows on the World and, 98, 103–6,
        110, 123, 128, 166–68,
        186, 192, 200–201
Club de Huit, 168
cocaine epidemic, 198

cocktails, 188–91, 263
Coffee Exchange, 138
Colicchio, Tom, 249
COLORS, 309
Committee for a Reasonable World Trade
    Center, 53
Committee on Public Authorities, 90
Commuters Cafe, 130
Confrérie des Chevaliers du Tastevin, 168
Consolidated Edison, 149
The Cooks' Catalogue (Beard), 68
Cooper, Paula, 172
cooperative restaurants, 309
Cornelia Street Café, 146
Cornell University hotel school, 21, 119
the Corner, 63, 138, 197
Cosmo, 191
Couric, Katie, 261
Covey, Stephen, 270
crack cocaine epidemic, 198
craft cocktail renaissance, 191
crime
    during blackout, 151–52
    "broken windows" approach to, 241
    Food 'n' Things heist, 154–55, 162
    Fournier and, 156–63
    Lufthansa Heist, 155
    organized, 161–63
    rate, 77, 82, 142–45, 151–52, 198, 210,
        241, 256
    Son of Sam, 142, 145, 152
critical path method, 213
Crown Center, 186
Cullman, Howard, 49
Cuomo, Mario, 143–44, 152

DaMota, Manuel, 289, 296
dance parties
    at the Big Kitchen, 140
    at Greatest Bar on Earth, 260–62
Dawkins, Jane, 140, 151
day trading, by Windows staff, 269–70
Dean & DeLuca, 146
Dean Witter Financial Services, 174–75,
    202, 241
Death Wish, 90
de Blasio, Bill, 312
DeGroff, Dale, 188–91, 262, 282–84
De Laurentiis, Dino, 140
Delgado, George, 262–63, 282–85

Dell, Jimmy, 156–57
Delmonico's, 25–26, 43
Deloitte & Touche, 240
Democratic National Convention, 111–12,
    114–15, 199
De Niro, Robert, 173, 217
Desanto, John, 118–19, 127, 129
Desiderio, Michael, 259
Dewey, Thomas, 49
DiChiara, Bob, 75, 121, 213–15
DiGiovanni, John, 207
Dinkins, David, 117, 198, 209–11, 241
disco, 140, 145
Disney, 241
DiSpirito, Rocco, 177
D'Onofrio, Barry, 286–87
Downey, John, 139
Downtown West Businessmen's
    Association, 53
Doyle, Martin, 234, 236, 239
Doyle, William S., 141–42
dress code, 98
Drexel Burnham Lambert, 197
Duboeuf, Georges, 194
duck breast, 178
Duffy, Kathy, 263
Durst Organization, 311–12
Dwyer, Darlene, 304
Dwyer, Jim, 206

Eames, Charles, 34, 37
Eat & Drink, 64–65
Eaton, Bill, 72–73, 79
Egger, Paul
    during blackout, 148–49
    charm of, 126
    at Forum of the Twelve Caesars, 102
    at Windows on the World, 93, 100,
        102, 126–28, 130, 148–49
    Zraly and, 127–28
electric grill, 238
electric stoves, 78–80, 179–80, 237–38
Elizabeth (queen), 113
Ellman, Larry, 120
Emergency Financial Control Board, 83
Emery Roth & Sons, 52
Emil, Arthur
    B. E. Rock Corporation and, 199
    financial backing from, 187, 191, 199,
        218, 221, 223–25, 230,
        266, 276

renovations and, 221, 223–25
Whiteman and, 223–24, 230
Emil, David
at Battery Park City Authority, 224
Baum, J., fighting with, 247, 265–66
Beacon restaurant of, 303–5
Hardy and, 230
Lomonaco and, 246–47, 249, 251,
254–55, 258, 310
at Lower Manhattan Development
Corporation, 311
Murphy and, 245–46, 253
Noche of, 308, 310
"Open the Bottle Week" by, 274
renovations and, 217–18, 224–25, 227,
230–31, 272
September 11 and, 298, 303–5,
310–13, 317
at Windows on the World, 217–18,
224–25, 227, 230–31,
233–34, 236, 246–47, 249,
251, 254–55, 258, 262,
272–77, 280, 284, 312
Emil, Jane, 224
Emil, Jennie, 230–31, 258, 298
Empire State Building, 53–54, 58, 138
employee cafeteria, 259–60
employment rate, 93, 173, 210, 240
Eng, Doris, 279–82, 288, 295
Engine 73, Ladder 42, 278–79
Epicurious, 280
Epstein, Jules, 168
Escoffier, Auguste, 26

the Falling Man, 295
Fanger, Arnold, 139
Faup, Patrick, 234–35, 268, 270
Feder, Phyllis, 105
Federal Science Pavilion, 52
Feglia, Luis "Papi," 235, 270, 283–84, 297
Feile, Karl, 201, 205
Feinberg, Ken, 317–18
Felker, Clay, 106–8
Feret, Philippe, 231–34, 236–39, 242, 246
Ferraro, Al, 38, 108, 120, 122
Ferrer, Freddy, 278, 307
Ferris, Richard J., 184–85
financial industry, 197–98, 216, 227, 241

firefighters
of Engine 73, Ladder 42, 278–79
layoffs of, 89
at 1993 bombing, 205–8, 211
on September 11, 10, 292–94, 300–301
fireplace, 71–72
fish, death of, 15–17
Fisher, M. F. K., 92
Flay, Bobby, 236, 250
Flying Foods, 178
La Fonda del Sol, 35, 41, 45, 95, 132
food courts, 59, 63
Food 'n' Things heist, 154–55, 162
Forbes ratings, 137
Ford, Gerald, 82, 89, 113
Forgione, Larry, 176–77, 217
Fort Benning Officers Club, 21–22
.44 Caliber Killer, 142
Forum of the Twelve Caesars
Baum, J., and, 32–33, 35, 39, 44, 46,
120
Clark and, 248
Egger at, 102
theft from, 132
Fountain Café, 36
4 World Trade Center, 311–12
Fournier, Claudette
Lewis, A., and, 94, 121, 123, 157, 161
as maître d', 156–57
on September 11, 297
wedding of, 156–63
at Windows on the World, 94, 121,
123, 131, 142, 156–64, 297
Four Seasons
Baum, J., and, 33–35, 39–41, 44, 46,
58, 67, 92, 106, 111, 120,
136, 250, 267
Beard and, 34, 67
Clark and, 248
class action lawsuit against, 94
Müller and, 177
reviews, 137
Francis, Lucille, 9
Franey, Pierre, 87
Fraunces Tavern, 25, 82
Freeman, Melvin, 113–14
Frost, David, 167

Gaiter, Dorothy J., 274
Galan, Juan, 304

Gallen, Norman, 151
Gambino, Carlo, 162
gangs, 144
the Garage, 124
gay subculture, 130, 144
Geddes, Norman Bel, 30, 190
Genoves, Beatriz Susana, 287, 291, 300
gentrification, 173
George, Philip, 187
Geraghty, Warren, 315
Girard, Alexander "Sandro," 35
Giuliani, Helen, 256
Giuliani, Rudolph "Rudy"
    inauguration breakfast, 256
    as mayor, 209, 240–41, 256, 275–76,
        278, 301–2, 306–7
    September 11 and, 301–2, 306–7
Glaser, Milton
    designs by, 65, 104, 106–8, 138,
        141–42, 152, 187, 190,
        228, 237, 255, 267, 277
    "I Love New York" campaign and,
        141–42
Godfrey, Arthur, 32
Gold, Rozanne, 218, 230–34, 236, 250
Goldberg, Mark, 296
Goldberger, Paul, 99, 165–66, 228, 236
Golden, Pearl "Pepper," 20
Goldman Sachs, 240
Goldmark, Peter, Jr., 174–75
Goldstein, Al, 144
Gomez brothers, 9, 286–87
Goodfellas, 155
Gormant, Alex, 237–39
Gotham Bar and Grill, 177
governor's suite, 158
Grace (princess), 113–14
graffiti, 144–45
Grande Taverne de Londres, 25
Granfield, Bill, 303–4, 306
Greatest Bar on Earth
    clientele, 274
    Delgado at, 262–63, 282–85
    fights in, 264
    Hors d'Oeuvrerie replaced by, 220, 263
    income, 262–63
    nightlife at, 260–65
    renovation and, 220–21, 232, 239,
        260–61

trademark infringement lawsuit
        against, 262
Great Recession of 2008, 312
Green, Mark, 278, 307
Greene, Gael
    Kheel as guest of, 106, 109
    "The Most Spectacular Restaurant in
        the World," 107–10
    at New York magazine, 35, 45–46, 60,
        106–10, 167, 189, 191, 237
    "Twilight of the Gods," 45–46
Gregorek, Thaddeus, 155
grills, 80, 238
Grimes, William, 272–73
Gross and Baum Hotel, 19–21
Grouard, Jean-Marie, 196
Ground Zero, 14, 305
Guadagno, Michael, 160, 162
gueridons, 229
Guida, Robert, 259
Guidance Corporation, 259
Guinness Book of World Records, 194
Gullett, Don, 147

Hale & Hearty, 197
Hamill, Pete, 143
Hanover, Donna, 276
Hardy, Hugh
    designs by, 187, 190, 219, 221, 228–30,
        236, 274
    Emil, D., and, 230
Haring, Keith, 173
Harper+George, 138
Harris, Kerr, Forster, 30, 59, 74–75
Hart, Gary, 115
Harty, Lee, 33
Hassan, Shamim, 235, 297
Hawaiian Room, 31–32, 38, 120
Hawkins, Yusef, 210
Heimer, Edwin, 119, 132–33
Hein, Greg, 239, 292–93, 298
Hellman, Geoffrey, 43–44
Helmsley, Harry, 53
Hemingway, Ernest, 92
Henrich, Richard, 154
herb garden, on North Tower, 251
Hernandez, Norberto, 305
Hersom, Ralph, 234, 244
Hewitt, Lleyton, 278
Hilton International, 184–85, 200, 213–14

hip-hop, 144
Ho, Heather, 8–9, 280
Hobson, Verna, 191–92
Hoffman, Dustin, 129–30
Holderness, Inez, 279, 281
Holiday magazine, 34
Holland, Gerry, 188
Holland, Ron, 37, 40, 56, 188, 267
Hop Lee, 271
Hors d'Oeuvre and Canapés (Beard), 67
Hors d'Oeuvrerie, 62, 83, 100, 180
    celebrity guests of, 129
    Greatest Bar on Earth replacing, 220,
        263
    line for, 110, 115
    menu, 112, 176
    reviews, 112, 136–37, 182
Houston, Whitney, 278
How to Mix Drinks (Thomas), 188
Hudson River Club, 218, 243
Hudson River Suites, 62, 110, 164, 168, 202
Hudson River valley, 18, 251
Hudson Yards Grill, 315
Hughes, Howard, 30
Hurricane Sandy, 312
Huxtable, Ada Louise, 34, 54–55
Huxtable, Garth, 34

Icahn, Carl, 184
"I Love New York" campaign, 141–42
Immer, Andrea, 202–6, 234, 257
immigration
    to New York City, 174, 256–57
    by staff members, 7–9, 13–14, 117,
        207, 235, 268, 284, 287,
        317–18
    undocumented, 8, 287, 317–18
Inhilco
    Aigner at, 117, 165–66, 193–94, 196
    Baum, J., and, 75, 79, 132–33, 164–65
    food services purchaser, 177
    Heimer at, 132–33
    money lost by, 193–94, 196–97
    1993 bombing and, 211–13
    ownership transfer of, 184–86
    Strand at, 75, 132, 164, 185
    Trans World Corporation owning, 184
insurance policy, WTC, 311
International Naval Review, 112–13
Internet, dawn of, 257

Italian Wine and Food Institute, 259

Jackson, Michael, 278
Jams, 177, 189
Johnson, Bill, 110
Johnson, Howard, 87
Johnson, Lyndon B., 42, 106
Johnson, Philip, 32, 34, 219
Johnson, Spencer, 270
Johnson, William, 18
Joseph Baum Associates, Inc., 57
Joseph Baum & Michael Whiteman
    Company, 223
Juan Carlos I (king), 133–34
Judge, Mychal, 278–79, 302
Judgment of Paris, 170–71
Jue-Let, 66
junk bonds, 197–98

Kafka, Barbara, 68, 95–96, 105, 108, 118,
    250
Kane, Howard, 263, 280, 286, 289–90
Keller, Thomas, 177, 310
Kennedy, John F., 41, 213
Kennedy, John F., Jr., 77, 201
Kennedy, Joseph, 26
Khashoggi, Adnan, 72
Kheel, Ted, 55, 106, 109, 168
Kieffer, Frederic, 231
King Kong remake, 140
Kirkpatrick, Robert, 207
KISS, 130
Kissinger, Henry, 114, 167
Knapp, Stephen, 207
Koch, Ed
    corruption scandals of, 198
    as mayor, 143–44, 152, 174–75, 198,
        218, 267
    WTC and, 174–75
Koenig, Julian, 37
Koppell, G. Oliver, 88
Kraus, Ruth, 86, 114
Kriendler, Peter, 102
Kumin, Albert, 34, 87, 108, 137
Ladbrokes, 185–86
    conflict with, 193–94, 196, 200,
        213–15, 219
    PA and, 193–94, 213–15
Lady Libertini, 263
Lafayette, 177, 199

La Guardia, Fiorello, 28
LaGuardia Airport, 90–91
Lakewood High School, 21
Lamantia, James, 138
Lambert, Phyllis, 33
Landmarc, 310
Lange, Jessica, 140
Layla, 231–32
Lee, Albert, 202, 204, 206, 268
Legends, 313
Lehmann-Haupt, John, 170
Leichter, Franz S., 88
Lenape people, 18
LeRoy, Warner, 137, 217, 219, 221–22
Levenson, Larry, 144
Levin, Neil, 289
Lewis, Alan
    Baum, J. and, 15–16, 33, 39, 94–96,
        105, 116, 118–22, 132,
        186, 191–92
    during blackout, 148–50
    childhood of, 119
    death of, 191–92, 227
    Fournier and, 94, 121, 123, 157, 161
    hiring by, 94–96, 102, 176, 226
    stepping down by, 186
    at Windows on the World, 94–96, 102,
        105, 108, 110, 116–27,
        129, 131–33, 148–50, 157,
        161, 165, 171, 176, 180,
        186, 258
    Zraly and, 116–18, 122, 124
Lewis, Seth, 116, 118, 120, 124, 192
Lianides, Leon, 217
Liberation Army Fifth Battalion, 208
Libertad, 112
Lichtenstein, Roy, 173
Life magazine, 27, 33
Lifespice, 226
Lindsay, John, 54, 174
Lindsey, USS, 22
liquor license, 103–4
Loading Zone, 64–65
lobster, three-claw, 31, 192
Local 6 Union, 199, 304
Local 100 Union, 303–4, 306, 308
Loeffelman, Pam, 219
Lois, George, 37–38, 40–41, 46, 56
Lomonaco, Michael
    Baum, J., and, 250–51, 254–55

Emil, D., and, 246–47, 249, 251,
    254–55, 258, 310
    eyeglasses of, 10, 280
    Hudson Yards Grill of, 315
    menus by, 250–55
    Noche and, 308
    Porter House of, 310, 314
    at *Recipes 1–2–3* party, 236
    September 11 and, 9–11, 286, 288,
        293–94, 306, 315, 317
    as taxi driver, 248
    at "21" Club, 46, 200, 249–51
    Wild Blue and, 272
    at Windows on the World, 9–11, 200,
        246–55, 258–60, 268,
        271, 280
Longchamps, 120
looting, during blackout, 150–51
Lower East Side, 145
Lower Manhattan Development
    Corporation, 311
Lufthansa Heist, 155

MAC. *See* Municipal Assistance
    Corporation
Maccioni, Sirio, 249
Maciejewski, Jan, 288
Macko, William, 207
Madonna, 191
Le Madrigal, 47
Mafia, 162
Maggett, Steve, 295
Maikish, Charlie, 214–16, 221, 223, 230
Malouf, Waldy, 218, 243, 249, 303–4
Mamdouh, Fekkak, 270–71
Mamma Leone's, 35, 273
Manhatta restaurant, 314–15
Margittai, Tom, 216
Marino, Grace, 160
Marino, Joe "Pepe," 156–63
Market Dining Rooms & Bar, 63, 70,
    138–39, 152, 157, 197
Market Square, 63, 70, 138–39
Marsh & McLennan, 307
Martin, Roger, 65, 104
Martin, Walter, 178
Masraff, Georges
    as chef, 242–43, 246
    firing of, 246–47
    at Windows on the World, 231–32,

234–35, 237, 242–43,
245–47
Matsuhisa, Nobu, 217
mayoral races, 143–44, 152, 278, 307
McInerney, Jay, 173
McNally, Brian, 172
McNally, Keith, 172, 198–99
Medina, Carlos, 283
Memorial Plaza, 14
memorial service, for staff members, 306
menu
Cellar in the Sky, 169, 177, 243
cocktail, 188–91, 263
development, 96–97, 105, 176, 230–33
Hors d'Oeuvrerie, 112, 176
by Lomonaco, 250–55
renovation, 218, 220, 230–33, 237, 239,
242–43
Mercado, Olga, 207–9
Mercado, Wilfredo, 207–9
Merrill Lynch & Co., 198
Messinger, Ruth, 256
Meyer, Danny, 177, 249, 307, 312, 314–15
Meyner, Robert, 51
Michaels, Lorne, 173
Michael's Place, 249
Michelin stars, 27, 33
Midnight Blue, 144
Milken, Michael, 197
Miller, Bryan, 182–83, 189, 195–96
Miller, John, 208
Minton-Capehart Federal Building, 228
Mohican people, 18
Le Monde, 71
Monroe, Marilyn, 41
Monte Carlo, 30
Montrachet, 177, 217, 258
Morgan Stanley, 241
Morocho, Blanca, 287
Morocho, Leonel, 287
Moses, Robert, 28–29, 42, 47, 50, 52
"The Most Spectacular Restaurant in the
World" (Greene), 107–10
Mouton Di Stefano, Gladys, 118, 161, 164
muggings, 77–78, 210
Müller, Eberhard, 176–80, 182
Mumford, Lewis, 54
Municipal Assistance Corporation (MAC),
83
Murdoch, Rupert, 143–44

Murphy, Marc
at Cellar in the Sky, 231–32, 234,
243–45, 252–53
Emil, D., and, 245–46, 253
Landmarc of, 310
after September 11, 312
Murray, Ray, 295–96
Muskie, Edmund, 115
Musto, Michael, 261

Nadel, Oscar, 52–53
Nathan, Judith, 276
National September 11 Memorial &
Museum, 14, 311, 314, 318–19
Nebbia, Joseph, 154
Nestor, Michael, 259, 288–90, 299
New American cuisine, 177, 249–50
New Amsterdam Theater, 241
Newarker, 31, 33, 41, 120, 192
new wave music, 145
New Year's Eve party, 274
New York, New York, 147
New York City. *See specific topics*
New York Convention and Visitors Bureau,
90, 141
New York Daily News, 89, 141, 143, 145,
151, 312
New Yorker, 43–44
New York magazine
Felker as editor of, 106–8
Greene writing for, 35, 45–46, 60,
106–10, 167, 189, 191, 237
Murdoch taking over, 143
on restaurants, 35, 45–46, 60, 104–10,
199, 225
New York Post, 165, 210–11, 312
Murdoch buying, 143–44
Page Six, 145, 249
New York Times
Cellar in the Sky advertising in, 169,
249
Cuomo endorsed by, 143
Goldberger at, 166
Grimes at, 272–73
Miller, B., at, 182–83, 189, 195–96
1993 bombing and, 208
Reichl at, 242–43, 245–46, 255, 272
on restaurants, 24, 29, 34, 58–59,
111–12, 114, 136–38,
152–53, 166, 182, 242,

245–46, 255
Sheraton and, 111–14, 136–38, 146,
        152–53, 183
    on WTC, 53, 55, 166
Nieporent, Drew, 177, 217, 231–32
Night Sky Holdings, 276
9/11. *See* September 11, 2001
The 9/11 Commission Report, 300
1993 bombing, of WTC
    Central Services destroyed by, 209,
        216, 252
    cleanup, 211
    evacuation following, 10, 204–7
    firefighters at, 205–8, 211
    Inhilco and, 211–13
    National September 11 Memorial &
        Museum and, 311
    New York Times and, 208
    North Tower, 201, 208, 212–14
    repair following, 212–34
    by Salameh, 208–9
    South Tower, 201, 207–9, 212
    Windows on the World and, 9–10,
        201–34
    by Yousef, 208–9, 283
Nixon, Richard, 102, 111
Noche, 308, 310
North Tower
    construction of, 57
    herb garden, 251
    lobby, 98
    in 1993 bombing, 201, 208, 212–14
    office in, 15
    on September 11, 8–10, 292–95,
        298–302, 318
    wine hoisted up side of, 194
nouvelle cuisine, 176
Nunez, Jose, 287, 304

Oak Room, 96
observation deck, South Tower, 57, 63, 81,
        91, 207, 313
Observation Deck Snack Bar, 63
Odeon, 172–73, 198–99, 248
O'Dwyer, Bill, 28
O'Hagan, John, 78
O'Keeffe, Michael "Buzzy," 145
Olender, Christine, 280–82, 295–96,
        298–99
One Chase Plaza, 50–51, 314

One Dine, 13–14, 313–14
O'Neill, John, 283
One World Observatory, 313–14
One World Trade Center
    National September 11 Memorial &
        Museum and, 14, 311,
        314, 318–19
    opening of, 311
    PA and, 310
    spire, 315
    tourism at, 312–13, 318–19
    WTC replaced by, 13–14, 310–13, 315
opening day, of Windows on the World, 105
"Open the Bottle Week," 274
organized crime, 161–63
Ortiz, Delfin, 313–14
Ortiz, Elizabeth, 304, 306
Ouest, 304

PA. *See* Port Authority
Page, David, 250
Page Six, 145, 249
Pahlmann, William, 32
Pan Am, 184
Pan Am Building, 36–37, 146
Pangaud, Gérard, 187
Papert, Koenig, Lois, 41
Parisian restaurants, 25
Pataki, George, 275, 301, 310
PATH (Port Authority Trans-Hudson), 51
Patrolmen's Benevolent Association (PBA),
        90
Paul Revere's Tavern and Chop House, 36
Le Pavillon, 26–27, 86–87, 106
PBA. *See* Patrolmen's Benevolent
        Association
Pépin, Jacques, 86–88, 108, 139
Perelman, Ronald O., 184
person extraordinaire (PX), 116, 126
Petit, Philippe, 81, 86, 140–41
Pierre Hotel, 26, 175
plane crashes, analysis of, 54
Platner, Warren
    design by, 71–72, 99–101, 108, 219,
        279
    Yamasaki and, 71
Plato's Retreat, 144
Playboy magazine, 135
Policar, Sol, 268–69, 305
police

layoffs, 89–90
PA, 132, 141, 203, 264, 295
on September 11, 292–93, 295,
    299–301
Ponte, Angelo, 162
Poptean, Josh, 289, 296
Port Authority (PA)
    Club and, 166–67
    formation of, 49–50
    Goldmark at, 174–75
    Hilton International and, 200
    Ladbrokes and, 193–94, 213–15
    Nestor at, 259, 288–90, 299
    One World Trade Center and, 310
    police, 132, 141, 203, 264, 295
    rent to, 197, 214, 216, 223, 313
    Roinnel at, 193, 200
    7 World Trade Center and, 275, 311
    Silverstein and Westfield leasing from,
        275–77
    Tobin at, 49, 51–54, 61, 75, 109, 174
    Ward at, 312
    World Trade Center and, 47–55, 58–
        59, 61, 64, 73–76, 78–79,
        81, 88, 90, 106, 109–11,
        121, 130, 133, 164–67,
        174–75, 192–94, 197, 200,
        207, 209, 212–17, 219,
        221–25, 230, 251, 259,
        274–77, 310–13
Port Authority Trans-Hudson. See PATH
Porter House, 310, 314
postwar New York City, 24–29
La Potagerie, 87
Potter, Tony, 185, 194, 200
press strategy, 104
Priceline, 274, 276
Prohibition, 26
punk music, 145
PX. See person extraordinaire

Quddus, Mohammad, 13–14, 313
Quinn, Owen, 85–86, 140
Quo Vadis, 46, 137

RA. See Restaurant Associates
Raccoon Lodge, 130–31, 243
rack of lamb, James Beard, 136, 176, 190
Radio Row, 52–53, 130
Rainbow Room

Baum, J., and, 22, 190–93, 217–18,
    224, 226–27, 265, 267
renovation, 190–91, 217–18, 221, 224
reviews, 243
salmon dinner, 24–25
Rainier (prince), 113–14
Rao's, 146
rap, 144
real estate market, 173, 214, 216
recessions
    Great Recession of 2008, 312
    New York City influenced by, 121, 173,
        197–98, 216, 275, 312
Recipes 1–2–3 (Gold), 236
Reichl, Ruth, 242–43, 245–46, 255, 272
Reiner, Hermann
    European sensibility of, 194–95
    at Windows on the World, 175–78,
        180–81, 194–96
René, André
    at Rainbow Room, 190
    at Windows on the World, 96, 104–5,
        121, 175, 190
renovation, Rainbow Room, 190–91,
    217–18, 221, 224
renovation, Windows on the World
    banquet catering, 219–20, 228, 231,
        239–40
    by Baum, J., 217–36, 240, 242–43,
        246–47, 250, 253–55,
        262–63, 265–67
    Cellar in the Sky, 220–21, 231–32, 234,
        240, 242–45, 272
    the Club, 240
    conflict during, 223–25, 230, 237
    Emil, A., and, 221, 223–25
    Emil, D., and, 217–18, 224–25, 227,
        230–31, 272
    Greatest Bar on Earth, 220–21, 232,
        239, 260–61
    menu, 218, 220, 230–33, 237, 239,
        242–43
    reopening following, 236–47
    Sweeney and, 223, 230, 234
    by Whiteman, M., 218–25, 230–34,
        237
    Zraly and, 230, 234, 243, 246–47
rent
    artificially low, 37, 76
    gentrification increasing, 173

to PA, 197, 214, 216, 223, 313
reservations, 110, 127, 137
Restaurant Associates (RA)
Baum, J., at, 15, 30–46, 57, 59, 65, 67,
94, 104, 120, 165
the Big Kitchen and, 197
hierarchy, 39
hires from, 94–95
lower-floor food services operations
passed to, 197
of Wechsler, 30–31, 33, 36, 45
Le Restaurant Français, 26, 48
Restaurant Hospitality, 165
Restaurant Opportunities Center (ROC),
308–9
Restaurant Week, 199–200
restrooms, 101
reviews
the Big Kitchen, 152
Cellar in the Sky, 182, 245–46
Four Seasons, 137
by Greene, 35, 45–46, 60, 106–10, 167,
189, 191, 237
by Grimes, 272–73
Hors d'Oeuvrerie, 112, 136–37, 182
by Miller, B., 182–83, 189, 195–96
New York magazine, 35, 45–46, 60,
104–10, 199, 225
New York Times, 24, 29, 34, 58–59,
111–12, 114, 136–38,
152–53, 166, 182, 242,
245–46, 255
Rainbow Room, 243
by Reichl, 242–43, 245–46, 255, 272
"21" Club, 109, 137
Wild Blue, 272–73
Windows on the World, 60, 106–12,
136–39, 152–53, 182–83,
189, 195–96, 236–37,
242, 255
by Zagat, 199
Reynolds, Bradley, 252–53
Risk Waters conference, 287–88, 295, 299
Rivas, Moises, 8, 296
River Café, 145, 176
Rizzuto, Phil, 117
Robbins, Carrie, 190, 192, 227
ROC. *See* Restaurant Opportunities Center
Rockefeller, David, 28, 50–51, 190, 267, 314
Rockefeller, John D., Jr., 48, 50

Rockefeller, Nelson, 51, 76
Rockefeller Center, 32, 35, 50, 265
Rockefeller family, 32, 37–38, 42, 52
Rockwell, David, 273
Rohatyn, Felix, 143
Roinnel, Jules
at PA, 193, 200
at Windows on the World, 110,
121–23, 166–67, 186, 192,
225, 250–51, 258, 265, 282
Romano, Michael, 177
Romeo, Phil
during 1993 bombing, 203–4, 206, 211
Windows on the World and, 185–86,
194–97, 203–4
Roosevelt, Franklin Delano, 28
Rosenbaum, Yankel, 210
Ross, Roger, 259
Roth, Michael, 105–6
Rubell, Steve, 145
Rumsfeld, Donald, 167

Salameh, Mohammed, 208–9
Samaha, Lucien, 260–61
Sampras, Pete, 278
sanitation, 89
Sansel, 226
Sapporo East, 271
Saratoga Springs, 18–21
Saturday Night Live, 173
Sbarro, 197
Schine hotel chain, 30, 119
Schlesinger, Arthur, 114
Schmid, Karl, 196
Schnabel, Julian, 173
Schneerson, Rebbe Menachem Mendel,
210
Scholtz, David, 49
Schrager, Ian, 145
Schumer, Charles, 306
Schweitzer, Thomas, 289
Scorsese, Martin, 147, 155, 173
Seagram Building, 32–33, 41
September 11, 2001
aftermath of, 303–15, 317–20
banquet catering on, 286
Baum, C., on, 298
Baum, J., and, 298, 312
casualties of, 11, 13, 300–302, 317–20
cleanup, 305

compensation following, 305–7,
317–18
day before, 278–85
debris, 12–14
Emil, D., and, 298, 303–5, 310–13, 317
firefighters on, 10, 292–94, 300–301
Fournier on, 297
Giuliani, R., and, 301–2, 306–7
impact of, 14
Lomonaco and, 9–11, 286, 288,
293–94, 306, 315, 317
morning of, 8–13, 286–91
National September 11 Memorial &
Museum honoring, 14,
311, 314, 318–19
The 9/11 Commission Report on, 300
North Tower on, 8–10, 292–95,
298–302, 318
plane crash analysis and, 54
police on, 292–93, 295, 299–301
South Tower on, 10–11, 294, 297–301
staff members on, 8–11, 13, 286–302
Tozzoli on, 297
Vogt and, 288, 292–93, 296, 303, 305–6
Wild Blue on, 288
Windows of Hope and, 305–7, 319
Windows on the World and, 8–13,
286–310, 312, 317–20
Zraly and, 310
7 World Trade Center, 275, 311
The 7 Habits of Highly Effective People
(Covey), 270
Shafrazi, Tony, 172
Shanker, Al, 89
Shea, Kevin, 207
Shearson Lehman Hutton, 198
Sheraton, Mimi
as advisor, 250, 267
at *New York Times*, 111–14, 136–38,
146, 152–53, 183
Shibata, Yasyuka, 206
shibui (simple beauty), 34
Shinn, Barbara, 250
Shnayerson, Michael, 241
Silicon Alley, 257
Silverstein, Larry, 275–77, 310–12
simple beauty (*shibui*), 34
Simpson, Harold, 57–58
sixpenny houses, 25
Skurnik, Michael, 121, 130–31, 147, 168–69

SkyBox, 282, 284
Skydive, 85–86, 114
SLA. *See* State Liquor Authority
Smart, Edwin, 184
Smith, Monica Rodriguez, 207
Smith & Wollensky, 146, 217
Smorgasbord, 94, 123
Snipes, Wesley, 261
Sofia (queen), 133–34
soft opening, of Windows on the World,
92–93, 104
SoHo, 146, 172
Son of Sam, 142, 145, 152
Soria, Ana, 317–20
Soulé, Henri, 26–27, 43, 48, 87
South Tower
construction of, 57, 61
in 1993 bombing, 201, 207–9, 212
observation deck, 57, 63, 81, 91, 207,
313
on September 11, 10–11, 294, 297–301
Willig climbing, 140–41
Spears, Britney, 278
special occasion restaurants, 164, 273–74,
315
Sperling, Allan, 204
Spero, Frank, 160
Sphere, 279
Spitzer, Eliot, 311
Spurrier, Steven, 170
staff members, of Windows on the World.
See also individual staff members
during blackout, 147–50
cafeteria for, 259–60
camaraderie among, 271
chaos among, 102–4, 126, 238–39
day trading by, 269–70
diversity of, 108, 202
hiring of, 93–96, 102, 268

immigrant, 7–9, 13–14, 117, 207, 235,
268, 284, 287, 317–18
interview process, 268
management strain with, 270–71
memorial service, 306
opportunities for, 126–35
payment and benefits, 8, 127–29, 231,
268–69, 272
respect of, 194–95
running jokes of, 7

on September 10, 278–85
after September 11, 303–15, 317–20
on September 11, 8–11, 13, 286–302
teams of, 103
tips, 127–29, 231, 268–69, 272
training, 102, 234–35, 268
Starbucks, 257–58
State Liquor Authority (SLA), 103–6
Statue of Liberty Lounge, 62, 99
Stein, Cyril, 214–15
Steinberg, Debra, 317
Stella, Frank, 173
Stern, Howard, 288, 292, 296
Stewart, Martha, 178, 258
Stillman, Alan, 146, 217, 219, 221
Stockli, Albert, 31, 34–35, 70, 92, 250
Stork Club, 24–25, 190
Stouffer's Restaurant and Inn Corporation,
    73
Strand, Curt
    Baum, J., and, 21–23, 30, 74–75, 132,
        164, 185
    at Inhilco, 75, 132, 164, 185
Studio 54, 145
summer outdoor entertainment, WTC, 279
Sunset Suppers, 196, 199, 259
Survivor Tree, 14
Sweeney, Dennis
    Baum, J., and, 15–17, 58, 64–65,
        69–70, 72–74, 92, 104, 266
    B. E. Rock Corporation and, 199
    during blackout, 148–51
    at Central Services, 15–17, 58, 64–65,
        69–70, 72–74, 92, 96–97,
        104, 113, 148–51, 157
    renovation and, 223, 230, 234
Szumski, Walter, 130

table settings, 104
table-side service, 129
Tall Ships procession, 111–13
Tavern on the Green, 137, 199, 210, 217,
    231, 273
Taxi Driver, 147
Taylor, Elizabeth, 278
teachers' union, 89
terrorist attacks. *See also* 1993 bombing, of
        WTC; September 11, 2001
    Fraunces Tavern, 82
    LaGuardia Airport, 90–91

O'Neill and, 283
T.G.I. Friday's, 217
theme restaurants, 32, 35–36
thievery, 131–32
Thomas, Jerry, 188
Thompson, Liz, 288–89
3 World Trade Center, 311
three-claw lobster, 31, 192
Tierney, Richard, 259, 288–91, 299–300
Time & Life Building, 35, 37, 44
Times Square, 82, 241, 308
Time Warner Center, 310
tips, 127–29, 231, 268–69, 272
Tishman Speyer, 265
Tobin, Austin, 49, 51–54, 61, 75, 109, 174
"To Eat, Drink and Be Mentioned," 24
Top of the Fair, 43
"Tops" restaurants, 73
Torre, Nino, 261
tourism
    at National September 11 Memorial &
        Museum, 318–19
    at One World Trade Center, 312–13,
        318–19
    tips and, 269
    at Windows on the World, 195–96,
        239, 269, 273
Tower Suite, 35, 44, 46
Tozzoli, Guy
    Baum, J., and, 11–12, 47–48, 59–61,
        64, 71, 73, 79, 86, 92
    Petit and, 81
    Roinnel and, 122
    on September 11, 297
    WTC and, 11–12, 47–48, 52–53,
        58–61, 64, 73–76, 79, 81,
        86, 88, 90–91, 104, 122,
        141, 166–67, 213–14, 259,
        275, 290, 297, 312
Trans World Corporation, 184
Trattoria, 36, 38
Tribeca, 131, 217
Tribeca Grill, 199, 217
Tricorico, Matthew, 160
Tromp, Johannes, 194–96, 203, 206, 209,
    211
Troy, William, 39
Truite au bleu (blue trout), 17–18, 92, 96–97
Trumbull, Melissa, 269, 272, 282
Trump, Donald, 297

"21" Club, 24–25, 102
    class action lawsuit against, 94
    Lomonaco at, 46, 200, 249–51
    review, 109, 137
28 Liberty, 314–15
twenty-fifth anniversary, of Windows on the
    World, 9, 277
"Twilight of the Gods" (Greene), 45–46
2 World Trade Center, 311

UAL, 184
undocumented immigrants, 8, 287, 317–18
unemployment rate, 93, 173, 210, 240
uniforms, 227
unions
    conflict with, 27, 195, 199, 245, 270–71
    Local 6, 199, 304
    Local 100, 303–4, 306, 308
    teacher, 89
Union Square Cafe, 177
United Airlines, 184–85
U.S. Open, 278, 287–88

Valenti, Tom, 304–5
van der Rohe, Mies, 32, 34
Vanity Fair, 241
Veuve Clicquot anniversary bottles, 277
Victims Compensation Fund, 317
Village Voice, 261
Villela, Bernardo, 280–81
Villela, Paulo, 8, 279–82
Vista hotels, 166, 184–85, 196, 200, 205
Vogt, Glenn
    September 11 and, 288, 292–93, 296,
        303, 305–6
    teamwork emphasized by, 270
    Windows on the World and, 258–60,
        264–65, 270–71, 274,
        280–82, 288, 292–93, 296,
        303, 305–6
Vongerichten, Jean-Georges, 177, 273

Wagenknecht, Lynn, 172
Wagner, Robert F., Jr., 54
Walker, Jay, 274, 276
Wall Street
    bonuses, 193, 241, 257
    influence of, 54, 91, 173, 193, 197,
        241, 257
Wall Street Journal, 274

Ward, Chris, 312
Warhol, Andy, 41, 129, 173
Washington Market, 139
Watkins, Brian, 210
Waxman, Jonathan, 177, 189
Wechsler, Abraham, 30–31, 33, 36, 45
Weisberg, Barry, 113, 122
Wellington, Ray, 171, 189–90, 198
Westfield America, 275–77
West Side Highway, collapse of, 77
Wharton, Geoffrey, 288–89
white flight, 42, 173
Whiteman, Michael
    Baum, J., and, 57–60, 65, 69–70,
        72–73, 83, 86, 96, 104,
        132–33, 153, 164, 190,
        218, 223–25, 230–31,
        233–34, 240, 266
    B. E. Rock Corporation and, 199
    electric stoves and, 79
    Emil, A., and, 223–24, 230
    Joseph Baum & Michael Whiteman
        Company of, 223
    lawsuit filed by, 223, 266
    renovation by, 218–25, 230–34, 237
    as rudder, 72–73
    Zraly and, 218
Whitman, Christine Todd, 275
Who Moved My Cheese? (Johnson, S.), 270
Wien, Lawrence, 53–54
Wild Blue
    Cellar in the Sky replaced by, 272
    clientele, 274
    review, 272–73
    on September 11, 288
Wilkinson, Andrew, 192
Williams, Chuck, 84
Williams, Serena, 278
Williams, Venus, 278
Willig, George, 140–41
Winchell, Walter, 24
windows, WTC, 60–61
window seats, 126–27
Windows of Hope, 305–7, 319
Windows on the World. See also specific
        topics
    aesthetic of, 99–101, 227–29
    clientele, 274
    construction of, 62–63, 70–76, 81
    finances, 73–75, 88, 90, 101, 132–33,

164–67, 200, 223–24,
276–77
last meal at, 278–85
naming of, 59, 61–62
opposition to, 88, 90, 103
ownership transfer and, 184–85
price points, 240
success of, 110–15, 268–77
uniqueness of, 314
volume of, 178–79
wine
Cellar in the Sky and, 62, 100, 134,
147, 168–71
Duboeuf and, 194
Immer and, 202–3
in Judgment of Paris, 170–71
"Open the Bottle Week," 274
school, 169, 171, 202, 216, 310
Wall Street bonuses and, 257
at Windows on the World, 95–96,
103–5, 127–28, 133–35,
167–71, 194–95, 202–3,
216, 257, 274, 277, 310
Wine, Barry, 216
Wolf, Burt, 68
Wolfe, Tom, 107, 173
wood grill, 238
Woodside, Patrick, 231
World Financial Center, 193, 206
World's Fair, 26, 42–43, 47, 52
World Trade Center (WTC). See also specific
topics
acceptance of, 11–12, 81–82
as attraction, 140–41
development of, 47–65, 70–77
importance of, 215
occupants, finding, 76, 214
opposition to, 11–12, 52–55, 61,
81–82, 88–89, 93, 106
revenue, 174–75, 275
windows of, 60–61
World Trade Centers Association, 297
World War I, 49
World War II, 26, 49
Worthington, Skilling, Helle & Jackson, 54
WTC. See World Trade Center

Yamasaki, Minoru
Platner and, 71
WTC designed by, 52–54, 60–61, 71,

98, 138, 299
Yankees, 110, 147
Yousef, Ramzi, 208–9, 283

Zagat reviews, 199
Zazula, Tony, 38, 177
Zeckendorf, William, 28, 30, 50
Zelayeta, Elena, 35
Zeller, Franz, 211
Zraly, Kevin
on Aurora, 189
during blackout, 147–48
Egger and, 127–28
Lewis, A., and, 116–18, 122, 124
Miller, B., and, 195–96
in Playboy, 135
renovation and, 230, 234, 243, 246–47
September 11 and, 310
Whiteman and, 218
at Windows on the World, 95–96,
101, 103, 105, 110, 122,
127–28, 133–35, 147–48,
167–71, 195–97, 200, 202,
211–12, 216, 222, 250,
277, 310
Zum Zum, 36, 41, 45–46